Gender and Kinship

Contributors

Maurice Bloch
Jane Fishburne Collier
John L. Comaroff
Shirley Lindenbaum
Vanessa Maher
Rayna Rapp
Judith Shapiro
Raymond T. Smith
Marilyn Strathern
Harriet Whitehead
Sylvia Junko Yanagisako

Gender and Kinship

Essays Toward a Unified Analysis

EDITED BY

Jane Fishburne Collier and
Sylvia Junko Yanagisako

STANFORD UNIVERSITY PRESS

Stanford, California

Stanford University Press, Stanford, California
© 1987 by the Board of Trustees of the Leland Stanford Junior University
Printed in the United States of America
Original printing 1987
Last figure below indicates year of this printing:
99   98   97   96   95   94   93   92

CIP data appear at the end of the book

TO THE MEMORY OF
MICHELLE ZIMBALIST ROSALDO

Preface

THE ESSAYS in this volume, with the exception of Yanagisako and Collier's theoretical overview, "Toward a Unified Analysis of Gender and Kinship," were first presented at an international conference on feminism and kinship theory convened in August 1982 at the Bellagio Conference Center in Bellagio, Italy. Funding was provided by the Wenner-Gren Foundation for Anthropological Research, the National Science Foundation, and the Rockefeller Foundation. The conference was organized by Jane Collier, Sylvia Yanagisako, and the late Michelle Rosaldo, all of the Department of Anthropology, Stanford University. Nineteen anthropologists attended: Maurice Bloch, James Boon (Cornell University), Jane Collier, John Comaroff, Daryl Feil (University of Queensland), Jack Goody (Cambridge University), Carolyn Ifeka (Australian National University), Shirley Lindenbaum, Vanessa Maher, Fred Myers (New York University), Rayna Rapp, Judith Shapiro, Raymond T. Smith, Verena Stolcke (Universidad Autonoma de Barcelona), Marilyn Strathern, Anna Tsing (Stanford University), Annette Weiner (New York University), Harriet Whitehead, and Sylvia Yanagisako.

The aim of the conference was to assess and further the impact of feminist scholarship on kinship theory in anthropology. By the end of the 1970's, feminist analyses had called into question such fundamental premises of kinship theory as the distinction between domestic and politico-jural domains, the naturalness of the mother-child bond, and the basis and practice of male authority. Conference participants were thus invited to rethink kinship theory by challenging conceptual categories that have long structured anthropological analyses of kinship and social structure.

Not all conference participants presented papers, and not every conference paper is included in this volume. All participants, however, prepared comments on particular sets of papers and contributed to general discussions. All the papers published here were revised after the conference and so benefited from those comments and discussions.

We dedicate this volume to the late Michelle Zimbalist Rosaldo, the friend and colleague with whom we organized the conference and whose contribution to gender studies played an important role in setting the stage for this volume. The idea for the conference emerged from our discussions with Shelly, and together we planned its central themes and format. In October 1981, shortly after we had received word of funding for the conference, Shelly died in an accident while conducting fieldwork in the Philippines.

In spite of her absence at the conference, Michelle Zimbalist Rosaldo's intellectual legacy is apparent throughout this volume. Several of the essays speak to her theoretical overview in *Woman, Culture, and Society* (1974), which throughout the 1970's provided feminist scholars in anthropology and related disciplines with a comparative framework for analyzing the position of women. In the same period during which her conceptual scheme was being widely diffused in gender studies, Shelly continued to reassess its usefulness and to refine it. By 1980 she was less concerned with discovering cross-cultural universals of gender hierarchy than with understanding the ways in which particular systems of gender are socially constructed along with the particular resources, characters, and activities of individuals. All the essays in this volume reflect Shelly's view that "the individuals who create social relationships and bonds are themselves social creations" (1980: 416). Together they display a range of analytical tacks for pursuing a question that became central to Shelly's work, namely, how social totalities constitute individuals.

We are grateful to the Center for Research on Women at Stanford University for its administrative support and, in particular, to Estella Estrada-Freeman for helping with the conference arrangements. We would also like to thank Anna Lowenhaupt Tsing for her work as the conference rapporteur and for the many insights that emerged from discussions with her after the conference. Finally, we thank our editor Clare Novak for her patient and prudent editing.

J. F. C.
S. J. Y.

Contents

Contributors

MAURICE BLOCH is Professor of Anthropology at the London School of Economics. His main field research has been in Madagascar. Most of his work has been concerned with the study of ideology and religion. His most recent book is *From Blessing to Violence*, published by Cambridge University Press.

JANE F. COLLIER received her Ph.D. from Tulane University and is Associate Professor of Anthropology at Stanford University. She has done field research on conflict management in Chiapas, Mexico, and on family change in southern Spain. She has just completed a book on models for understanding the organization of social inequality in classless societies.

JOHN L. COMAROFF is Associate Professor of Anthropology and Sociology at the University of Chicago. He studied anthropology at the University of Cape Town and the London School of Economics, where he received his Ph.D. He has done research in South Africa and Botswana on various aspects of economy and society, politics and law, and has taught at the University of Wales and the University of Manchester.

SHIRLEY LINDENBAUM studied anthropology at the University of Sydney, and is an Associate Professor of Anthropology at the New School for Social Research, New York. She has conducted fieldwork in Papua New Guinea and Bangladesh, and her research interests include the study of ideology, ritual, and the political economy of gender.

VANESSA MAHER is Associate Professor of Cultural Anthropology at the University of Turin, Italy. She studied social anthropology at

Cambridge University and has conducted research in Morocco and Italy on various aspects of women's experience and its symbolic construction. Her interest in the lives of dressmakers began with research on home-work in North London and was further stimulated when she lived in Milan in 1974 through a friendship with a neighbor who had been a dressmaker most of her life. She has since done research into a variety of aspects of Italian social history as they have affected the lives of seamstresses and dressmakers.

RAYNA RAPP received her graduate degress at the University of Michigan and teaches in the Anthropology Department, Graduate Faculty, New School for Social Research. She edited *Toward an Anthropology of Women*, has contributed articles on gender, kinship, and American family life to women's studies and anthropology journals, and is a member of the editorial boards of *Feminist Studies* and *SIGNS*. Her current research focuses on the social impact and cultural meaning of prenatal diagnosis in American life.

JUDITH SHAPIRO is Professor of Anthropology and Academic Deputy to the President at Bryn Mawr College. From 1970 to 1975, she was a member of the Anthropology Department at the University of Chicago. She received her Ph.D. from Columbia University in 1972, and has done research among the Tapirapé and Yanomamo of Brazil, among the Northern Paiute of Nevada, and, most recently, with an international Catholic missionary congregation.

RAYMOND T. SMITH is Professor of Anthropology at the University of Chicago. He has carried out extensive research on kinship, class, and race in the Caribbean and the United States, and is at present a co-investigator on the multidisciplinary Urban Family Life Project at the University of Chicago. He received his Ph.D. from Cambridge University and has taught in Jamaica, Ghana, and Canada as well as in the United States. During 1985–86, he was Director of the Consortium Graduate School in the Social Sciences located in Jamaica.

MARILYN STRATHERN is Professor of Social Anthropology, Manchester University, England. She was formerly a Research Fellow with the New Guinea Research Unit of The Australian National University; a Fellow of Girton College, Cambridge, where she obtained her M.A. and Ph. D., and then a Fellow of Trinity College. Her publications on the Papua New Guinea highlands include New

Guinea Research Bulletins on legal change (1972) and migration (1975), *Women in Between* (1972), and the co-authored *Self-Decoration in Mount Hagen* (1971). She also co-edited *Nature, Culture, and Gender* (1980). She has recently edited a collection of essays by members of the 1983–84 Gender Research Group at the Australian National University (*Dealing with Inequality*, in press), and is preparing a general critique of Melanesian anthropology under the title of *The Gender of the Gift*.

HARRIET WHITEHEAD received her Ph.D. in Anthropology from the University of Chicago in 1975. Her research has centered on religious conversion and on the cross-cultural understanding of gender. She has taught at Stanford University, Haverford College, and Johns Hopkins University, and has held a research affiliation at the Pembroke Center for Teaching and Research on Women at Brown University.

SYLVIA J. YANAGISAKO is Associate Professor of Anthropology at Stanford University. She received her Ph.D. from the University of Washington in 1975, and has done research on kinship and gender among Japanese Americans and family firms in northern Italy. Her book, *Transforming the Past: Kinship and Tradition Among Japanese Americans*, was recently published by Stanford University Press.

Gender and Kinship

Introduction

*Jane Fishburne Collier and
Sylvia Junko Yanagisako*

THE DUAL FOCUS of this volume is informed by a unitary intention. Our goal is at once to revitalize the study of kinship and to situate the study of gender at the theoretical core of anthropology by calling into question the boundary between these two fields. In challenging the view that kinship and gender are distinct, albeit closely linked, domains of analysis, we hope to renew the intellectual promise of these two fields while reconstituting them as a whole.

As a collective attempt to demonstrate the creative power of ignoring the distinction between two well-established analytical domains, the papers in this volume aim to steer a course that diverges from a recent theoretical trend in anthropology. During the past two decades, kinship has declined from its position as the central focus of ethnographies and as the privileged site for theoretical debate about the character of social structure. Recent reviews and commentaries on theory in anthropology (for example, Ortner 1984; Yengoyan 1986; Hannerz 1986; Appadurai 1986) render it obvious that kinship studies no longer generate either the controversy or the conceptual innovation they did during the first half of the century. Certainly neither the ethnographies nor the comparative studies that currently excite the anthropological imagination concentrate on what were once considered the basic building blocks of kinship—descent rules, marriage prescriptions or preferences, and terminology systems.

In retrospect, it seems apparent that the waning theoretical importance of kinship studies in anthropology was heralded in the 1960's and 1970's by various attempts to rethink its core concepts and methods (Leach 1961; Schneider 1964; Schneider 1972; Needham 1971). These efforts were themselves symptomatic of a general erosion of faith in the structural-functional model of society, whose rise to hegemony in anthropology had coincided with kinship's increase in importance. Whereas this trend was most apparent in British social anthropology and, after the Second World War, in an American anthropology that was shifting its focus from culture to social structure, its emergence was also evident in French anthropology. For, although Lévi-Strauss's structural analysis of myth and consciousness (1966, 1967, 1970) offered an alternative to structural-functionalism, his analysis of marriage systems (1969) was firmly grounded in it (Boon and Schneider 1974).

The postwar critique of the structural-functional paradigm eventually undermined confidence in the notion that kinship everywhere constituted a domain of relationships readily accessible to any ethnographer armed with a genealogical chart. Direct challenges to kinship as a discrete domain of analysis (Schneider 1976; Schneider 1984) capped off a period of increasing skepticism about the institutional model of society that structural-functionalism had provided. Given their commitment to attributing the final cause of social forms to social functions, structural-functionalist kinship theorists (Radcliffe-Brown 1952; Fortes 1949; Fortes 1953; Fortes 1958; Fortes 1969; Goodenough 1970) depicted society as universally made up of a number of domains that resembled in function, although not necessarily in form, the institutions of our society. Once the explanatory limitations of the search for synchronic, functionalist causes became apparent, so did the limitations of assuming the existence of functionally differentiated domains. Just as we realized we could no longer assume the existence in every society of a sphere of politics that provides authority and the orderly exercise of power and coercion, or a sphere of religion that provides cognitive resolution of universal dilemmas concerning the meaning of human existence, so we realized we could not assume a sphere of kinship that provides a system of rights and duties for the orderly reproduction of human life. By taking for granted the existence of these domains, structural-functionalism sacrificed the analytical power of asking how such domains come to be constituted in particular ways in specific societies and with what social consequences.

Recent analyses of kinship that have retained a conceptual vitality and have made innovative contributions to theoretical discussion in anthropology have not focused on kinship per se, but on kinship as an aspect of political economy (Meillassoux 1981; Terray 1972; Friedman 1974) or on kinship as an aspect of broader systems of inequality in which gender is a key dimension (Collier and Rosaldo 1981; Ortner and Whitehead 1981). In short, their call for the dissolution of conventional analytical boundaries has offered these kinship studies the greatest theoretical promise.

The above holds as much for kinship in so-called complex societies as in so-called simple societies. According to the evolutionary scheme implicit in structural-functional models (for example, Parsons and Bales 1955), kinship groups in complex modern, industrial societies are stripped of their former wide-ranging functions, which are performed by other institutions—in particular, the workplace and the state. Consequently, kinship is reduced to its primary function of reproduction and to the primary reproductive unit, the nuclear family. By taking for granted what it should explain—namely, how reproductive functions come to be cast as the enduring core of the family—such a perspective fails to understand how modern families are as much shaped by the political economy of our society as are lineages in lineage-based societies. It confuses a reduction in the functions attributed to the family by our society with a reduction in the range of relationships and practices that our analysis of the family should include. So, for example, it overlooks how families in our society both reproduce and recast forms of gender inequality along with forms of class inequality at the same time that they nurture children.

Rather than observing without question conventional analytical boundaries, all the papers in this collection ask what new understanding can be gained by ignoring the line between gender and kinship. This question itself has developed out of the questioning of kinship studies by feminist scholars during the second wave of Western feminism.

With the revival of the women's movement in the 1960's, feminist anthropologists turned to kinship studies for tools to understand women's place and possibilities. Not only was ethnographic information on women and their lives found primarily in chapters on kinship, marriage, and the family, but Fortes's distinction between the domestic and politico-jural domains (1958, 1969) suggested a reason why women's association with the "domestic" might make them and their activities seem universally less valued than the activities and attributes of "public" men (Rosaldo 1974).

The relationship between kinship and gender studies, however, was soon reversed in the 1970's by the development of feminist anthropology. As feminist scholars shifted their concern from understanding the position of women (for example, Rosaldo 1974; Ortner 1974; Friedl 1975; Schlegel 1977), to charting variations in women's roles and experiences, and then to understanding the construction of gender in specific social systems (for example, MacCormack and Strathern 1980; Ortner and Whitehead 1981), they began to call into question the central assumptions of kinship theory.

The Feminist Challenge to Kinship Theory

At the heart of kinship theory lies an analytic dichotomy between "domestic" and "political-jural" domains. This dichotomy, used implicitly by kinship theorists since Morgan and elaborated by Fortes (1949, 1958, 1969, 1978), remains influential in anthropology and related disciplines. Fortes developed the concept in order to challenge Western assumptions about the biological basis of kinship by claiming that kinship has a jural, political dimension. But, ironically, in carving out a politico-jural domain of kinship based on legal rules, Fortes left intact the assumption of a invariant domestic domain built upon the affective ties and moral sanctions of the mother-child bond. The domestic/politico-jural dichotomy thus assumes a "domestic" sphere dedicated to sexuality and childrearing, associated primarily with women, and a "public" sphere of legal rules and legitimate authority, associated primarily with men (Yanagisako 1979). This assumption of two domains—one fulfilling the biological requirements of sexuality and care of helpless infants, the other responsive to historical changes in economic, political and ideological systems—has been very durable. It pervades descent theory, alliance theory, and studies of marriage transactions.

For example, descent theory—as elaborated by Fortes (1949, 1953, 1969), Schneider and Gough (1961), Fox (1967), and Bohannan (1963), among others—rests on the notion of an invariant mother-child bond. While descent theorists have provided many insights into social structure by charting differences in the ways mother-child dyads are linked to larger organizational structures by authority-bearing males, they assume that the mother-child bond is everywhere constrained by affective and moral convictions generated by the universal experience of "mothering" necessary for the biological survival of helpless infants (Fortes 1969; Fox 1967; Goodenough 1970).

Similarly, while it provides many insights into social structure by exploring how exchanges of women between men structure relations between social groups, alliance theory (Lévi-Strauss 1969; Leach 1954; Needham 1962; Maybury-Lewis 1974) also rests on an implicit distinction between domestic and public spheres. Lévi-Strauss, for example, writes of the form, but not the content, of marital exchanges because he is content to assume that women everywhere, as the providers of sexual and domestic services, are of equal and inherent value and that men enjoy the legitimate authority to exchange women. In taking for granted the characters, functions, and social domains of men and women and seeing variation only in their structural arrangement, Lévi-Strauss fails to investigate the dialectical construction of gender categories and structural arrangements.

Finally, studies of marriage transactions have tended to focus on marriage rather than on transactions. Since the term "bridewealth" replaced "brideprice" with its connotations of market exchange, anthropologists have stressed the role of property exchanges at marriage in validating sexual access and legitimating children. They have thus implicitly affirmed a distinction between historically variable economic and political relations, which can affect the amount and nature of property exchanges at marriage, and a universally invariant requirement for granting public recognition to the sexual and parental bonds defining the domestic spheres in which children are born and reared.

Feminist anthropologists who first turned to kinship theory for analytical tools soon began to question the assumption of a domestic sphere organized by the affective and moral constraints of the mother-child bond, to which other functions—economic, political, and ideological—might be added without changing its primary "natural" role of human reproduction. Because of their concern with variations in gender conceptions, women's strategies, and women's powers, feminists began to relate observed differences in women's experiences to different forms of economic, political, and cultural organization, thus questioning the apparent naturalness of mother-child dyads and the relationship between supposed male "authority" and the actual dynamics of power and privilege in particular social systems.

In focusing on women's strategies, feminist scholars did not simply record that women, like men, have goals and work toward them. Rather, they demonstrated that it is impossible to understand interaction within "domestic spheres" without simultaneously understanding the organization of political and economic arenas that provide goals and resources for both sexes. Similarly, feminists focusing on gender conceptions demonstrated that symbolic conceptions of femininity can never be understood apart from a cultural order, because biological facts achieve significance only within wider systems of meaning (Ardener 1975; Ardener 1978).

Feminists have not been alone in questioning the central assumptions of kinship theory. Goody's theory of the evolution of the domestic domain (1973, 1976) challenged the view of kinship as an autonomous system by showing how productive processes and the transmission of property shape domestic groups. Bourdieu (1977), in rejecting Lévi-Strauss's formalistic "rules of marriage," analyzed the "marriage strategies" through which people in particular societies reproduce relations of production and social inequality. Together, Goody and Bourdieu, through their concern for the reproduction of social and productive systems, reveal the limitations of structuralists' emphasis on the communicative and exchange aspects of marriage. At the same time, Schneider's cultural analysis of kinship (1968, 1972) provided a tool for understanding the interrelationship between kinship and other domains. He and others have argued that kinship is not a discrete, isolable domain of meaning, but rather that the meanings attributed to the relations and actions of kin are drawn from a range of cultural domains, including religion, nationality, gender, ethnicity, social class, and the concept of "person" (Alexander 1978; Chock 1974; Schneider and Smith 1973; Strathern 1981; Yanagisako 1978; Yanagisako 1985).

Rethinking Kinship and Gender

In light of the feminist challenge to kinship theory, it now seems the time for kinship theorists to turn to gender studies for tools to reconsider their analyses of descent, alliance, and marriage transactions. As feminists have shown, it is no longer adequate to view women as bringing to kinship primarily a capacity for bearing children, while men bring primarily a capacity for participation in public life. Consequently, an analysis of gender in, for example, traditional Chinese and Nuer societies may well reveal that labelling both as characterized by "patrilineal descent" obscures more than it illuminates. Along similar lines, an analysis of gender may provide a rather different understanding of the kinds of "alliances" men may form through exchanging women. It might, furthermore, demonstrate the impracticality of separating marriage transactions from other property transactions.

The contributors to this volume have disavowed merely using gender studies to understand the traditional concerns of kinship theorists. Instead, their essays implicitly argue, as we do explicitly in our theoretical overview in this volume, that gender and kinship are mutually constructed. Neither can be treated as analytically prior to the other, because they are realized together in particular cultural, economic, and political systems. In short, volume contributors agree that analyses of gender must begin with social wholes, rather than with individuals or with functional domains such as kinship or gender.

Our opening essay in this volume orients the reader to the others that follow by assessing and further developing the theoretical contribution of feminist scholarship to an understanding of gender and kinship. In it, we argue that the next phase in the feminist reanalysis of gender and kinship should be to question the assumption that "male" and "female" are two natural categories of human beings whose relations are everywhere structured by their biological difference. Our critical review of the analytical dichotomies informing gender studies leads us to conclude that they, like the concepts informing kinship studies, assume the biological difference in male and female roles in sexual reproduction to be at the core of men's and women's relationships everywhere. We argue that, as a consequence, what have been conceptualized as two discrete fields of study constitute a single field defined by our folk conception of the same thing, namely, the biological facts of sexual reproduction. To free ourselves from continually reinventing analytical dichotomies rooted in notions about natural differences between people, we propose a specific program for analyzing social wholes. Our three-faceted approach involves the explication of cultural meanings, the construction of models of the dialectical relationship between practice and ideas in the constitution of social inequalities, and the historical analysis of continuity and change.

Our theoretical overview was written after the 1982 conference and, consequently, it has benefited from our reading of the other essays. We have incorporated the insights of our contributors, all of whose analyses are situated within social wholes, even though each emphasizes different aspects of the analytical program we propose. Some focus on cultural systems of meaning, some on systems of inequality, and some on historical transformations. Not all the volume contributors necessarily agree in full with our theoretical stance, in particular with our argument for dissolving the boundaries between gender and kinship and with our specific program for doing so.

We have grouped the papers that follow to show the new modes of analysis that emerge from old topics when conventional analytical boundaries are challenged. We begin with the articles by Comaroff, Yanagisako, Rapp, and Maher because they confront the distinction between domestic and politico-jural domains that lies at the heart of traditional kinship studies. Instead of assuming the invariance of a domestic domain built upon the affective mother-child bond, these authors ask why the peoples they studied recognize a domestic domain associated with women and differentiated from a public domain. To answer this question, each author examines the wider social and historical processes that give rise to an apparent domestic/public opposition.

John Comaroff begins his article by reviewing feminist critiques of the domestic/public dichotomy, contrasting three alternative suggestions for rethinking this distinction. A "comparative" solution would investigate empirical variations in the content and interpenetration of the two domains. A "transactional" solution would examine the chains of individual transactions that give rise to the appearance of a differentiation between domestic and public domains. And a "systemic" solution, favored by Comaroff, would focus not on individual actors but on the total political economy whose logic generates particular structures. Comaroff uses data from the Tshidi Barolong, a South African Tswana people, to illustrate the power of the dialectical approach he proposes. He examines the contradictions lying at the heart of Tshidi organizational principles and political economy to reveal how intentional action yielded a variety of empirical forms, ranging from hierarchical chiefdoms with highly developed public—and thus, domestic—spheres to decentralized, egalitarian systems lacking a clear division between domains. His analysis of the contradictions inherent in Tshidi social structure informs his analysis of the historical transformation of Tshidi society, as capitalist penetration fostered the emergence of a small bourgeois elite within an increasingly proletarianized population.

Sylvia Yanagisako also argues that analyses of cultural domains must be situated in an historical study of transforming social wholes. She compares anthropological and folk concepts of gender and kinship domains to evaluate the heuristic utility of the former, while at the same time seeking to understand the changing social meaning of the latter. She contrasts kinship theorists' use of a domestic/politico-jural dichotomy and feminists' use of a domestic/public distinction with the conceptions of gender and kinship domains among two generations of Japanese Americans. Her analysis of Japanese Americans' movement from a socio-spatial dichotomy of inside/outside to a functional dichotomy of family/work illustrates her point that concepts of gender are mutually constituted with concepts of politically organized space. She argues that both feminists and kinship theorists must tease apart the "mixed metaphors" in their analytical dichotomies in order to understand the historical transformation of folk models of gender, kinship, and polity.

Rayna Rapp's paper explores the blind spots that arise when anthropologists and their European and American informants share the same assumptions about family life. She recounts how neither she nor her French informants coded as "change" a shift in young mothers' reliance on their own mothers to reliance on their mothers-in-law. All saw only the continuity of male-headed nuclear families whose ties with nonresident kin were organized through women. Rapp's observation of the way change was perceived as continuity leads her to explore the ways in which Westerners have appropriated key cultural relations for new ends. She argues that, despite the apparent continuity of male-headed nuclear families in Western societies since at least the seventeenth century, there have been wide variations in family form and content, shaped by different economic and political systems.

Vanessa Maher examines relations between men and women

within the context of the inequalities of a class society. Her study of working-class seamstresses in Turin's high-fashion industry between the wars reveals how evolving relations between the bourgeois and working classes created ambiguities in the ideological definition of domestic and public spheres that seamstresses could exploit. Industrialists' efforts to evade labor laws by characterizing their factories as "domestic" gave young working-class women freedom from parental supervision, while at the same time seamstresses' knowledge of how wealthy women dressed permitted flirtations across class lines with male university students. Similarly, married seamstresses sewing in their homes could satisfy husbands' desire that they "stay inside"; simultaneously, their use of the family home to receive bourgeois clients violated their working-class husbands' desires for privacy, comfort, and monopoly over wifely services.

The next four essays in the volume argue that marriage must be understood as part of a wider system of sexual and political relations, both heterosexual and homosexual, which are the outcome of historically specific social processes. Raymond Smith proposes that "marriage" and "irregular unions" in West Indian creole society are alternate forms of union based on the interaction of race with class and gender inequalities in a class-stratified society. Smith rejects the argument that "Negro lower-class" women and men establish "irregular unions" because they are economically unable to sustain "normal" and "valued" monogamous marriages. Instead, he shows how the ideology of the nuclear family played a different role in the history of West Indian creole society than it did in the class systems of Europe and North America. Through historical documents and modern ethnographies, he is able to trace changing notions of domesticity and of what men and women offered one another and their children. In demonstrating that "irregular unions" are not merely failures to realize the monogamous, nuclear family, he reveals that West Indian marriage, too, is historically constituted and variable.

Jane Collier also examines the wider system of social inequality to discover the nature and meaning of marriage in a particular society, the nineteenth-century Kiowa of the Great Plains. She analyzes what was at stake in Kiowa marriage transactions by drawing on ethnographic accounts of how men acquired wives. She suggests that among the Kiowa, as among the "gumsa" Kachin of

Highland Burma (Leach 1954), the system of inequality was organized through marriage exchanges in which brideprice appeared to be adjusted to the ranking of the bride, even as the amount a groom gave established his rank. In particular, Collier analyzes how marriage exchanges constituted rank by organizing labor obligations, thus giving rise to differences in access to others' labor. These differences, in turn, generated differences in the apparent value of particular brides and grooms.

Shirley Lindenbaum explores both the meaning of marriage and the changing constitution of gendered spheres of social life accompanying historical transformations in a noncapitalist society. She charts variations in kin relations across several New Guinea societies, focusing in particular on two sets of ideas and their related marriage practices. The first set celebrates gifts of semen occurring in societies in which men exchange sisters in marriage, and the second celebrates exchanges of valuables, such as shells, feathers, and pigs, occurring in societies in which men obtain wives through payments of bridewealth. In the former, women and men contribute more evenly to subsistence and to the making of trade items than they do in the latter. Lindenbaum goes on to analyze the complex interweaving of these contrasting systems in "transitional" societies. She suggests ways of tracing how the introduction of pigs and the intensification of women's labor foster both the dramatization of a male sphere of public exchange and the concealment of women's expanded contribution to production, which is placed within an obscured domestic sphere.

Also using data from New Guinea, Harriet Whitehead argues that male control of violence, not men's exchange of women in marriage, explains male dominance in stateless (tribal) societies. In New Guinea, as in the "simple" societies analyzed by Collier and Rosaldo (1981), ideology portrays men as more fertile than women and male fertility is linked with men's capacity for violence. But this celebration of men's capacity to create life cannot derive from a particular type of marriage, as Collier and Rosaldo suggest, because New Guinea marriage forms are complex and various. Whitehead thus advances a more general theory to explain the cultural celebration of male fertility and violence. When Sahlins proposed reciprocal gift exchange as the mechanism preventing Hobbesian "warre" in stateless societies, he posited a continuum of reciprocity from positive gift giving to negative exchanges of accusations and blows (1972). Whitehead thus suggests that those in a position to command both extremes of the exchange continuum—blows as well as gifts—may take charge of the exchanges that, in stateless societies, define social relationships. Men receive credit for creating life because their control of violence allows them to create social bonds.

The final three articles by Strathern, Shapiro, and Bloch illustrate the richness of understanding offered by analyses that attend to the connections between concepts of personhood, gender, and descent. By ignoring conventional interpretations of what might be considered "patrilineal descent systems," these authors demonstrate clearly how different systems of descent are constructed along with different systems of gender and personhood.

Marilyn Strathern undertakes another comparison of two New Guinea societies to examine the structure of ideas underlying concepts of personhood and their relation to conceptions of kinship. Among the people of Mount Hagen, kinship can be "disconnected" from the person, thus providing an ideational context for people to acquire other people and things. Women, for example, can be detached from their own clans and added to those of their husbands, just as objects can be detached from their makers and added to the wealth of those who acquire them. These ideas of disconnection generate the conceptual premises allowing for the accumulation of wives, wealth objects, and prestige, and, therefore, for the building of personal careers by Big Men. Among the Wiru, in contrast, kinship ties are inherently part of the person. Wiru women who marry are not detached from their natal groups. Rather, their marriages create connections between affines. And just as exchanges of women create lasting ties, so exchanges of things similarly dramatize group relationships, not individual prestige. Strathern's analysis of concepts of the person and, consequently, of gender among the Hagen and Wiru reveals the very different kinds of cultural and political dynamics that constitute these two societies that appear to share an ideology of patrilineal descent.

Like Strathern, who shows how cultural conceptions of the person give rise to an appearance of "patrilineal descent" in two New Guinea societies, Judith Shapiro shows how "patrilineal descent" in lowland South America results not from the tracing of genealogical connections, but from the cultural construction of masculinity.

She suggests that Amazonians have "patriliny" not because they form corporate groups based on descent through males, but because they use the idiom of agnatic ties in a politics and religion organized around sexual differentiation. Shapiro examines several Amazonian societies to trace similarities and differences in the ways that male solidarity and political factionalism are linked to marriage exchanges, marital politics, and ritual expressions of gender opposition.

Maurice Bloch also examines broader cultural concepts to explain gender conceptions. He explores sources of contradiction in representations of women among the Merina of Madagascar. He argues that it would be futile for an anthropologist to search for *the* conception of women among the "patrilineal" Merina because the Merina have three contradictory views that cannot be entirely reconciled. One view grants women equal honor with men; accordingly, the Merina use different greetings and terms of address for people of different social ranks, but not for men and women of the same rank. A second view portrays gender as irrelevant; accordingly, Merina ancestors in the tomb are not differentiated by gender. From a third view, however, women are associated with the transitory "house," in contrast to the eternal, and more highly valued, tomb of the ancestors. These three conceptions of women are linked to different social contexts. Bloch's analysis of the Merina circumcision ceremony, for example, displays the processes underlying the association of women with biological decay and death and of men with the integrity and continuity of the descent group.

In challenging the traditional boundaries of "descent systems" to arrive at creative new understandings, this last trio of essays illustrates well just how productive it is to question kinship and gender as distinct fields of study. Along with the other articles, they take us a significant way toward the goal we set for this volume—to renew the intellectual promise of kinship and gender studies by reconstituting them as a single whole.

Toward a Unified Analysis of Gender and Kinship

Sylvia Junko Yanagisako and
Jane Fishburne Collier

THIS ESSAY attempts to draw together and advance the theoretical contribution that feminist rethinking of gender has made to our understanding of both gender and kinship.* Our answer to the question of what a feminist perspective has to offer the study of gender and kinship is that, above all, it can generate new puzzles and, thereby, make possible new answers.

A productive first step in rethinking any subject is to make what once seemed apparent cry out for explanation. Anthropologists inspired by the women's movement in the late 1960's took such a step when they questioned whether male dominance was a cross-cultural universal and, if so, why (Rosaldo and Lamphere 1974; Reiter 1975; Friedl 1975). By asking what explained sexual inequality, they rejected it as an unchangeable, natural fact and redefined it as a social fact.† A second step entailed questioning the homogeneity of the categories "male" and "female" themselves and investigating their diverse social meanings among different societies (Rosaldo and Atkinson 1975; Ortner and Whitehead 1981; Strathern 1981a). Once we recognized that these categories are defined in different ways in specific societies, we no longer took them as a priori, universal categories upon which particular relations of

*This paper was written after the 1982 conference on Feminism and Kinship Theory in Anthropology. We wish to thank Jane Atkinson, Donald Donham, Sherry Ortner, Roger Rouse, David Schneider, Judith Shapiro, Anna Tsing, and Harriet Whitehead for their helpful comments and criticisms. This paper is a contribution to the ongoing debate within feminist anthropology. The views we express are not necessarily shared by the colleagues whose comments and criticisms helped us to sharpen our arguments.

†Although we recognize that some anthropologists questioned the universality of Western concepts of gender before the late 1960's, we begin with the 1960's women's movement because it inspired the arguments we discuss in this paper.

gender hierarchy are constructed. Instead, the social and cultural processes by which these categories are constituted came to be seen as one and the same as those creating inequality between men and women.

In this essay, we suggest that the next puzzle we must generate and then solve is the *difference* between men and women. Rather than taking for granted that "male" and "female" are two natural categories of human beings whose relations are everywhere structured by their difference, we ask whether this is indeed the case in each society we study and, if so, what specific social and cultural processes cause men and women to *appear* different from each other. Although we do not deny that biological differences exist between men and women (just as they do among men and among women), our analytic strategy is to question whether these differences are the universal basis for the cultural categories "male" and "female." In other words, we argue against the notion that cross-cultural variations in gender categories and inequalities are merely diverse elaborations and extensions of the same natural fact.

We begin our essay with a critical review of a number of analytical dichotomies that have guided much of the literature on gender in anthropology and related disciplines for the past decade, and we conclude that they assume that gender is everywhere rooted in the same difference. Our point is that, in doing so, these dichotomies take for granted what they should explain. In the second section of this essay, we discuss commonalities between the assumptions underlying these dichotomies and the assumptions that have dominated kinship studies in anthropology since their beginnings in the nineteenth century. We argue that gender and kinship have been defined as fields of study by our folk conception of the same thing, namely, the biological facts of sexual reproduction. Consequently, what have been conceptualized as two discrete fields of study constitute a single field that has not succeeded in freeing itself from notions about natural differences between people. In the final section of the essay, we propose a multifaceted strategy for transcending the analytical categories and dichotomies that have dominated past studies of kinship and gender. Because the analytical program we suggest requires study of culturally constructed social inequalities, we begin with a critique of the concept of "egalitarian society." We then suggest an analytical program that entails explicating the dynamic cultural systems of meanings through which different kinds

of historically specific systems of inequality are realized and transformed.

Questioning Analytical Dichotomies in the Study of Gender

In questioning analytical dichotomies, we first examine those of
"nature/culture" (Ortner 1974), "domestic/public" (Rosaldo 1974),
and "reproduction/production" (see Harris and Young 1981). Each
of these has been said to structure relations between men and
women in all societies and, therefore, to offer a universal explanation of sexual inequality. Whereas the dichotomies of domestic/
public and nature/culture are more in line with structuralist perspectives, the distinction between reproduction and production
has emerged from a functionalist-Marxist perspective.

Second, we examine implicit dichotomies between women's and
men's consciousnesses. Scholars (for example, Rohrlich-Leavitt,
Sykes, and Weatherford 1975; Weiner 1976) seeking to correct the
androcentric bias in ethnographic accounts by advocating attention to "women's point of view" have posited a distinction between
men's and women's perspectives of social relationships. Arguing
that most anthropological monographs reflected men's views of
how their system worked, they suggested we correct this bias by
including women's accounts of social and cultural institutions in
our ethnographies. In contrast, Sherry Ortner and Harriet Whitehead (1981) have more recently proposed a focus on male prestige
systems, not as a way of correcting male bias, but as a way of understanding the cultural construction of gender. These latter authors, however, share with the former the notion that men and
women—as unitary and opposed categories—have different views
of how their mutual system works.

Domestic/Public and Nature/Culture

Ortner and Whitehead propose that the nature/culture and do-
mestic/public oppositions, along with the distinction between self-
interest and the social good identified by Marilyn Strathern
(1981b), derive from the same sociological insight: "that the sphere
of social activity predominantly associated with males encompasses the sphere predominantly associated with females and is, for
that reason, culturally accorded higher value" (1981: 7–8). The emphasis placed on any one of these specific contrasts, they suggest,

depends upon the theoretical interests of the analyst and the empirically observed "idiom" of a particular culture; however, "all
could be present without inconsistency; all are in a sense transformations of one another" (1981: 8).

Since these dichotomies were first presented a little over ten
years ago as explanations of universal sexual asymmetry, both the
domestic/public dichotomy proposed by Michelle Rosaldo (1974)
and the nature/culture opposition proposed by Sherry Ortner
(1974) have come under considerable criticism. Ortner's hypothesis that the symbolic association of a lesser valued "nature" with females and of a more highly valued, transcendent "culture" with
males is the basis for the universal devaluation of females has been
most persuasively and thoroughly criticized in Carol MacCormack
and Marilyn Strathern's volume *Nature, Culture, and Gender* (1980).
In their introduction to this collection of essays, MacCormack and
Strathern pose the crucial question, When can we usefully translate a symbolic opposition found in another culture into one found
in ours? Together the case studies in their volume argue that our na-
ture/culture opposition does not do justice to the range of symbolic
configurations of gender meanings found in other societies.

Strathern (1980), for one, builds a convincing case that the Hagen
opposition between "mbo" and "rømi" is not homologous to the
nature/culture opposition in our culture, but has both different
symbolic meaning and social consequences. The strength of Strathern's argument rests as much on her explication of *our* conception
of the nature/culture dichotomy as on Hagen conceptions. This
kind of effort has been too often slighted in discussions about the
universality of cultural features—whether the disputed features
are symbolic oppositions or social institutions such as "marriage"
or "incest." In other words, in many instances our erroneous assumptions about the concepts of other people are coupled with
erroneous assumptions about the simplicity or homogeneity of
our own cultural concepts. As Maurice and Jean Bloch point out,
we cannot assume that the terms we use in our own cultural discourse provide a straightforward, unambiguous analytical focus
(1980: 125).

Bloch and Bloch's historical analysis of the changing usage of
"nature" as a category for challenging the prevailing cultural order
in eighteenth-century France (1980) reveals a particularly crucial dimension that is missed by the claim for a universal nature/culture

opposition—a synchronic dimension that permits change. Like all universal structural oppositions, this one necessarily flattens dynamic transformations of meanings into static structural sameness. Consequently, it tends to impede the elucidation of the historical processes through which systems of meanings change.

This absence of a historical dynamic is closely tied to another problem inherent in the claim for a universal symbolic opposition. This is the problem of conceptualizing symbolic systems as if they exist apart from social action. Only if we construed symbolic systems as having a structure independent of social action could we claim that a symbolic opposition of gender categories is universal without claiming that a system of gender relations is universal. Such a view is the result of too dichotomized a vision of ideas and action. Thus, the issue is not whether the Hagen concept of "mbo" stands in relation to the Hagen concept of "rømi" as our concept of "culture" stands in relation to our concept of "nature," but, rather, whether mbo/rømi constitutes the same system of social relations in Hagen society as nature/culture does in ours. Put another way, the question we should ask is, What do these oppositions *do* for social relations and, conversely, how do people encounter these oppositions in their practice of social relations?

Whereas the nature/culture opposition draws on a Lévi-Straussian symbolic-structuralist perspective, the domestic/public opposition is more in line with a structural-functionalist perspective of the sort that has prevailed in the field of kinship studies. Michelle Rosaldo first construed the domestic/public opposition as the "basis of a structural framework" necessary to explain the general identification of women with domestic life and men with public life and the consequent universal, cross-cultural asymmetry in the evaluation of the sexes. At the core of this identification of women with domestic life lay their role as mothers: "Women become absorbed primarily in domestic activities because of their role as mothers. Their economic and political activities are constrained by the responsibilities of childcare and the focus of their emotions and attentions is particularistic and directed toward children and the home" (Rosaldo 1974: 24).

Although she did not initially draw a link between the domestic/public opposition and the distinction between the domestic domain and the politico-jural domain, which had long been employed in kinship studies (Fortes 1958, 1969), Rosaldo later (1980) acknowledged that link and its problematic theoretical implications (Yanagisako 1979). She came to share Rayna Reiter's (1975) view of the domestic/public opposition as an ideological product of our society and a legacy of our Victorian heritage that "cast the sexes in dichotomous and contrastive terms" (Rosaldo 1980: 404). As John Comaroff notes in this volume, such a dichotomous vision of society is logically entailed in a "universal asymmetry" thesis that relies upon an orthodox image of the form and content of the two domains. Conversely, arguments against the universality of sexual asymmetry and inequality have necessarily engaged in a critical reexamination of this image. As Rapp (1979) and Comaroff (this volume) point out, however, these latter efforts have encompassed a range of feminist theoretical perspectives.

Attempts to salvage the domestic/public opposition—which continue to accept the two categories as a valid description of a universal reality even though varying widely in their specific content and interpenetration—cannot escape the self-defeating circularity inherent in its initial formulation (Comaroff this volume). As Yanagisako points out in this collection, the claim that women become absorbed in domestic activities because of their role as mothers is tautological given the definition of "domestic" as "those minimal institutions and modes of activity that are organized immediately around one or more mothers and their children" (Rosaldo 1974: 23).

The a priori definition of the domestic domain by the mother-child relation is inextricably linked with the troubling analytical problems arising from its claim for universality. These are shared by the nature/culture opposition. As Karen Sacks (1976, 1979), Eleanor Leacock (1978), and Alice Schlegel (1977) have argued convincingly, those writers who assert the universality of sexual asymmetry encourage the search for biological causes, even though such writers explicitly emphasize social processes. In their contributions to *Woman, Culture, and Society*, Rosaldo and Ortner both proposed social causes for universal sexual asymmetry, as did Nancy Chodorow in her contribution to the 1974 book, but each author focused on the social construction of a biological "fact": women's capacity to bear and nurse infants. The obvious conclusion is that biological motherhood "explains" the universal devaluation of women. As Rosaldo herself later noted, a focus on universals makes us "victims of a conceptual tradition that discovers 'essence' in the natural characteristics" that distinguish the sexes, "and then declares that women's present lot derives from what, 'in essence,' women are" (1980: 401).

In summary, we suggest that Ortner and Whitehead's claim that the domestic/public and nature/culture oppositions are transformations of each other is valid (1981: 7–8), although not because these oppositions summarize, each in a way more suited to the theoretical interests of a particular analyst or the cultural idiom of a particular society, a universal structure of gender relations. Rather, domestic/public and nature/culture, like the reproduction/production distinction we discuss below, are variations of an analytical dichotomy that takes for granted what we think should be explained.

Reproduction/Production

In the last decade, several writers (for example, Eisenstein 1979; Benería and Sen 1981; Harris and Young 1981), attempting to develop a Marxist theory of gender while at the same time bringing a feminist perspective to Marxist theory, have argued for the need to develop a theory of relations of reproduction. Olivia Harris and Kate Young (1981: 110) note that the proliferation of studies in Marxist literature centered on the concept of reproduction reflects not only feminist concern with the status of women but, among other things, the concern of some Marxists to "break conclusively with economistic versions of a Marxism which places too great an emphasis on the forces of production" (see, for example, Hindness and Hirst 1975; Friedman 1976). Women have been cast as the "means of reproduction" in several Marxist discussions of the control of labor and its reproduction in both capitalist and precapitalist societies.

Claude Meillassoux's (1981) evolutionary theory of the domestic community is perhaps the most ambitious of these works in its attempt to build an analysis of the family into a Marxist analysis of imperialism. For Meillassoux, control over the labor of individual human beings is more important than control over the means of production in defining the relations of production in agricultural societies where productive forces are not highly developed. The reproduction of the domestic community of these societies is contingent upon the reproduction of human beings and, consequently, upon control over women, whom Meillassoux views as the means of that reproduction. In capitalist societies, on the other hand, capital is unable itself to reproduce the labor power necessary for social reproduction. Therefore, it must rely on both precapitalist modes of production, such as exist in Third World countries, and on the family—in particular, women's work in it, in industrial society—as the means of reproduction of labor power.

Feminists have strongly criticized two inextricably linked aspects of Meillassoux's theory: his analytical treatment of women and his concept of reproduction. They challenge his view of women solely as "reproducers" and his neglect of their productive activities (Harris and Young 1981; O'Laughlin 1977), which blind him to the ways in which the social constraints placed on women's productive activities, as well as the control placed on their reproductive activities, structure their oppression. They point to the ironic lack of attention to what is commonly called "domestic work" in a book dedicated to the analysis of reproduction.

These limitations in Meillassoux's work can be largely traced to the considerable ambiguity surrounding his use of the term reproduction, which conflates biological reproduction with the reproduction of the social system. For Meillassoux, kinship is the institution which at once regulates the function of the reproduction of human beings and the reproduction of the entire social formation (Meillassoux 1981: xi). This functionalist perspective also underlies his assumption—one common in much of the anthropological literature—that precapitalist societies are in static equilibrium. Thus, despite his interest in the evolution of social forms, Meillassoux ends up with a Marxist version of teleological functionalism in which "all modes exist to reproduce themselves" (Harris and Young 1981: 115).

Unfortunately, many critics attempting to compensate for Meillassoux's inattention to "domestic work" have employed a concept of reproduction similar to his. As a consequence, their work has also been characterized by conceptual confusion. These writers take as their starting point Engels's formulation of the distinction between reproduction and production. In contrast to Marx (1967: 566), who used these terms to describe a unitary social process, Engels tended to treat production and reproduction as two distinct, although coordinated, aspects of the process of social production: "This again, is of a twofold character: on the one side the production of the means of existence, of food, clothing, and shelter and the tools necessary for that reproduction; on the other side the production of human beings themselves, the propagation of the species" (1972: 71).

It is not surprising that Engels's formulation would receive so much recent attention from Marxist-feminist social scientists, as it is one of the few early Marxist statements offering an explicit approach to gender. Much of the literature on the subject of women and capitalist development, for example, employs this distinction. In their 1981 critique of Ester Boserup's neoclassical, comparative study of the role of women in economic development (1970), the economists Lourdes Benería and Gita Sen argue that we should attend to the role of reproduction in determining women's position in society. They rightly fault Boserup for her distinction between "economic activity" and "domestic work," which results in her excluding such activities as food processing—largely a female activity—from her description of economic activity in agricultural societies. Their concept of reproduction, however, proves more a liability than an asset. They define reproduction as not only biological reproduction and daily maintenance of the labor force but also social reproduction, that is, the perpetuation of social systems (Benería and Sen 1981: 290). Yet, in their analysis of the ways in which the status of women has changed with economic transformations, reproduction is reduced to "domestic work." Accordingly, when they discuss industrial society, they equate "housework" with reproductive work and assume the household is the focal point of all sorts of reproduction (Benería and Sen 1981: 293, 291).

The social historians Louise Tilly and Joan Scott also employ a similar distinction in their history of women's work in industrializing England and France. Reproduction is for them, by definition, a gendered category: "Reproductive activity is used here as a shorthand for the whole set of women's household activities: childbearing, child rearing, and day-to-day management of the consumption and production of services for household members" (Tilly and Scott 1980: 6). This unfortunate equation of reproductive activity with *women's* household activities excludes anything men do from the category of reproductive activity and, consequently, is blind to men's contribution to "childbearing, child rearing and day-to-day management of the consumption and production of services for household members." This, in turn, makes it impossible for Tilly and Scott to attain their goal of writing a history of the changing relation between the reproductive work of women and men. There can be no such history of change when, by their own definition, men do not engage in reproductive work.

The best attempt to clarify the confusion surrounding usages of the term reproduction and its relation to production is Olivia Harris and Kate Young's comprehensive review of the concept (1981). Having found fault with Meillassoux's concept of reproduction, Harris and Young propose to salvage it by isolating different meanings of the concept, which they see located at "different levels of abstraction and generality" and which "entail different types of causality and different levels of determination." "Here we have isolated three senses of the concept of reproduction for discussion which seem to us to cover the major uses of the term and to illustrate the confusion that has resulted from their conflation. We feel it is necessary to distinguish social reproduction, that is, the overall reproduction of a particular social formation from the reproduction of labor itself; and further to distinguish the latter from the specific forms of biological reproduction" (Harris and Young 1981: 113).

By teasing apart these different meanings of reproduction, Harris and Young do an excellent job of displaying the density and complexity of the concept. Yet, their attempt to place these meanings in distinct and analytically useful levels generates new problems. It becomes quickly apparent just how difficult it is for them to separate their notion of the reproduction of labor and their notion of social reproduction. They admit that: "to talk of the reproduction of labour is in itself perhaps too limited; it would be more accurate to talk of the reproduction of adequate bearers of specific social relationships, since we also wish to include under this category classes of non-labourers" (Harris and Young 1981: 113). Once the reproduction of labor slips into the reproduction of "adequate bearers of specific social relations"—a process that presumably includes such social categories as "males" and "females" as well as "lineage elders" and "capitalists"—it becomes indistinguishable from the process of social reproduction. That is to say, if "capitalists" are being reproduced, then relations of capital must be simultaneously reproduced; just as, if "males" and "females" are being reproduced, then gender relations must be reproduced.

As do all the authors who draw upon Engels's distinction between production and reproduction, Harris and Young locate the construction of gender relations—and, consequently, women's

subordination—in the reproductive process. The productive process, regardless of the particular mode of production it comprises,
is conceptualized as theoretically independent of gender considerations. Like the notion that relations of reproduction are more
homogeneous and unchanging than relations of production, this
line of thought grants the two spheres of activities an analytical autonomy that seems unjustified.

What lies behind the willingness of so many authors to overlook
the conceptual ambiguity and confusion of the reproduction/pro-
duction distinction and to remain committed to its usefulness for
understanding gender relations? Behind this distinction, we suggest, is a symbolically meaningful and institutionally experienced
opposition that our own culture draws between the production of
people and the production of things. When Harris and Young consider the reproduction of a particular social formation—which in
Marxist terms entails the reproduction of a particular mode of production—they do not see gender as relevant because, although
both women and men are involved in production, they do not appear to be involved as "men" and "women." In other words, their
gender attributes do not appear to be crucial in structuring their relations. Yet, Harris and Young see women as "women" and men as
"men" when they are involved in the reproduction of labor and biological reproduction because in our cultural system of meanings,
the production of people is thought to occur through the process of
sexual procreation. Sexual procreation, in turn, is construed as possible because of the biological *difference* between men and women.
The production of material goods, in contrast, is not seen as being
about sex, and thus it is not necessarily rooted in sexual difference,
even when two sexes are involved in it.

In this folk model, which informs much of the social scientific
writing on reproduction and production, the two categories are
construed as functionally differentiated spheres of activity that
stand in a means/end relation to each other. Our experience in our
own society is that work in production earns money, and money is
the means by which the family can be maintained and, therefore,
reproduced. At the same time, the reverse holds: the family and its
reproduction of people through love and sexual procreation are the
means by which labor—and thus the productive system of society—is reproduced. Although we realize that wage work, money,
and factories do not exist in many of the societies we study, we im-

pose our own institutional divisions and culturally meaningful categories onto them by positing the universal existence of functionally differentiated spheres of activity. In our folk model, we contrast
the following pairs, each linked, respectively, to the productive and
reproductive spheres:

material goods	people
technology	biology
male or gender neutral	female or gendered
wage work	nonwage work
factory	family
money	love

A means/end relation between the family and capitalism has prevailed in Western sociological thought, not only in the writings of
Marxist functionalists but in those of structural-functionalist theorists as well. In Talcott Parsons's theory of the family in capitalist-
industrial society (Parsons and Bales 1955), the particular form of
the family helps to reproduce the "economic system" by permitting
the social and geographic mobility required by an open-class, universalistic, achievement-based occupational system while still providing for the socialization of children and nurturance of adults. In
sum, both Parsonian structural-functionalist theory and Marxist-
functionalist theory posit a means/end relationship between what
they construe as the reproductive and productive spheres of
capitalist-industrial society.

At the bottom of the analytical confusion surrounding the repro-
duction/production dichotomy is a circularity similar to that which
has plagued the domestic/public distinction. Like the former analytical opposition, it leads us back to reinventing, in a new form,
the same dualism we were trying to escape.

Women's Consciousness / Men's Consciousness

One of the first changes called for by feminist scholars in the social sciences was the correction of androcentric views that had paid
little attention not only to women's activities and roles but also to
their views of social relationships and cultural practices. This feminist challenge was useful in calling into question seemingly natural social units. Among the social units taken for granted were the
"families" that anthropologists continued to discover everywhere
as long as they confounded genealogically defined relationships

with particular kinds of culturally meaningful, social relationships (Yanagisako 1979; Collier, Rosaldo, and Yanagisako 1982). The feminist questioning (for example, Collier 1974; Lamphere 1974; Harris 1981; Wolf 1972) of the assumed unity of families, households, and other sorts of domestic groups denaturalized these units by asking whether their members had the same or different views, interests, and strategies. The recognition of the diversity and, in some cases, the conflict of interests among the members of supposedly solidary groups opened the way to a richer understanding of the dynamics of these groups (for example, Wolf 1972; Yanagisako 1985) and their interaction with other social units.

At the same time, we have come to realize that correcting the androcentrism of the past without reproducing its conceptual error in inverted form requires considerable rethinking of our notions of culture and ideology. We appear to have left behind naive claims (for example, Rohrlich-Leavitt, Sykes, and Weatherford 1975) that female anthropologists intuitively understand the subjective experience of their female informants simply by dint of their sex. Likewise, we have rejected claims for a universal "woman's point of view" or a universal "womanhood." Marilyn Strathern has argued convincingly that "it is to mistake symbol for index to imagine that what Trobrianders make out of women identifies something essential about *womankind*. We merely learn, surely, how it is that cultures constitute themselves" (1981a: 671). Furthermore, we cannot assume that *within* a society there is a unitary "woman's point of view" that crosscuts significant differences in, for example, age, household position, or social class.

Despite this skepticism about the existence of a unitary "woman's point of view" in any society, the notion that there is a unitary "man's point of view" appears more resilient (for example, Ardener 1972). Because men are socially dominant over women, it is tempting to treat the cultural system of a society as a product of their values and beliefs and to assume that it is shared by most, if not all, of them. This assumption is implicit in the concept of a "male prestige system," which Ortner and Whitehead (1981) have proposed for understanding, among other things, the connections between gender and kinship.

Ortner and Whitehead suggest that in all societies the most important structures for the cultural construction of gender are the "structures of prestige." Moreover, because some form of male dominance operates in every society, "the cultural construction of sex and gender tends everywhere to be stamped by the prestige considerations of socially dominant male actors" (Ortner and Whitehead 1981: 12). "Women's perspectives are to a great extent constrained and conditioned by the dominant ideology. The analysis of the dominant ideology must thus precede, or at least encompass, the analysis of the perspective of women" (Ortner and Whitehead 1981: x). In the above quotations, Ortner and Whitehead assume that men's perspectives are not also constrained and conditioned by the dominant ideology. Instead, in the case of men, ideology and the perspectives of social actors are conflated. This, of course, assumes a priori that men and women have distinctly different perspectives, including different ideas about prestige relations.

The problems generated by this conceptualization of the dominant ideology are manifested in confusion about the analytical status of prestige structures. At times Ortner and Whitehead refer to prestige as a "sphere of relations," at other times as a "set of structures" on the same level as political structures, and at still other times as "a dimension of social relations" of all kinds of structures, including political structures (1981: 10, 12–13). They also speak of "prestige situations" (1981: 13). For the most part, however, they use the term "prestige structures": "The sets of prestige positions or levels that result from a particular line of social evaluation, the mechanisms by which groups arrive at given levels or positions, and the overall conditions of reproduction of the system of statuses, we will designate as a 'prestige structure'" (Ortner and Whitehead 1981: 13). Confusion about the status of prestige structures, moreover, leads to a tautological proposition about their relation to gender systems. Ortner and Whitehead contend on the one hand that the "social organization of prestige is the domain of social structure that most directly affects cultural notions of gender and sexuality," on the other, that "a gender system is first and foremost a prestige structure itself" (1981: 16).

Much of the confusion can be attributed to equating the dominant ideology with men's point of view. Even in those hypothetical cases where men as a whole are socially dominant over women as a whole and share the same values, beliefs, and goals, it seems a mistake to construe their perspective as more encompassing of the larger cultural system than women's perspective. For, like women's views, men's views are constrained and conditioned by the particular forms of their relations with others. The men and women in a particular society may construe women's ideas and experience as more restricted than that of men (see, for example, Yanagisako this volume), and this may be reflected in the appearance that men have certain kinds of knowledge that women do not. But, this appearance does not justify the analytical incorporation of women's views in a supposedly more inclusive male ideology. Our task, rather, should be to make apparent the social and cultural processes that create such appearances.

In the end, the concept of "male prestige system" tends to replicate the problems inherent in the domestic/public dichotomy. Because it too rests on the notion of an encompassing male sphere and an encompassed female one, it assumes that "domestic life" is "insulated from the wider social sphere" (although its degree of insulation may vary) and that "domestic life" is concerned with "gender relations" and "child socialization." Thus, for example, in discussing Marshall Sahlins's (1981) analysis of systemic change in post-contact Hawaii, Ortner writes, "To the degree that domestic life is insulated from the wider social sphere . . . , important practices—of gender relations and child socialization—remain relatively untouched, and the transmission of novel meanings, values, and categorical relations to succeeding generations may be hindered. At the very least, what is transmitted will be significantly—and conservatively—modified" (1984: 156–57).

Pierre Bourdieu's (1977) notion of "embodiment" offers a useful framework to counter the notion of conservative domestic spheres, detached from the public world of struggle and change. Domestic life, for Bourdieu, is not insulated from the wider social sphere. Rather, he argues that both gender relations and child socialization take place in a socially structured world. He writes that, for the child, "the awakening of consciousness of sexual identity and the incorporation of the dispositions associated with a determinate social definition of the social functions incumbent on men and women come hand in hand with the adoption of a socially defined vision of the sexual division of labor" (1977: 93).

Bourdieu's framework thus suggests that gender relations and child socialization—far from being insulated from changes in "meanings, values, and categorical relations"—are implicated in those changes. Indeed, the same point is suggested by Sahlins's analysis of change in Hawaii that Ortner discusses, for Sahlins describes how the struggle over novel meanings of hierarchy was simultaneously a struggle over chiefship and gender relations. For Hawaiians, understandings of the chief/commoner relation and the husband/wife relation were implicated in each other and changed together. Similarly, Yanagisako's essay in this collection shows how Japanese Americans' conceptions of the domains of husbands and wives changed along with their institutional model of the relations between family and society.

The reemergence of a form of the domestic/public dichotomy in the concept of "male prestige systems" brings us full circle and poses, in a particularly dramatic way, the question of why we keep reinventing this dichotomy or transformations of it, such as reproduction/production. If, as we have argued, these oppositions assume the difference we should be trying to explain, why do we find them so compelling? Why do they seem, as Rosaldo (1980) claimed even when she argued against using domestic/public as an analytic device, so "telling"?

The answer, we suggest, lies in our own cultural conception of gender and its assumption of a natural difference between women and men. To arrive at an understanding of that conception, however, requires that we first review some recent insights in kinship studies. As we will demonstrate, there are striking similarities between muddles in kinship studies and those that we have just discussed in gender studies. Kinship and gender, moreover, are held together by more than a common set of methodological and conceptual problems. They constitute, by our very definition of them, a single topic of study.

The Mutual Constitution of Gender and Kinship

Both "gender" and "kinship" studies have been concerned with understanding the rights and duties that order relations between people defined by difference. Both begin by taking "difference" for granted and treating it as a presocial fact. Although social constructions are built on it, the difference itself is not viewed as a social construction. The fundamental units of gender—males and females—and the fundamental units of kinship—the genealogical grid—are both viewed as existing outside of and beyond culture. In this section, we consider David M. Schneider's critique of the biological model that pervades and constrains kinship studies in order to suggest a parallel critique of gender studies.

Kinship and the Biological "Facts" of Sexual Reproduction

Among kinship theorists, Schneider (1964, 1968, 1972, 1984) has been the most consistent in refusing to take for granted what others have, namely, that the fundamental units of kinship are everywhere genealogical relationships. In his cultural analysis of American kinship (1968), Schneider first demonstrated that our particular folk conceptions of kinship lie behind our assumption of the universality of the genealogical grid. By explicating the symbolic system through which Americans construct genealogical relationships, Schneider denaturalized kinship and displayed its cultural foundations.

Most recently, in his 1984 critical review of the history of kinship studies, Schneider argues that, for anthropologists, kinship has always been rooted in biology because, by our own definition, it is about relationships based in sexual reproduction. When we undertake studies of kinship in other societies, we feel compelled to start from some common place, and that place has always been sexual reproduction. We do not ask what relationships are involved in the reproduction of humans in particular societies. Instead, we assume that the primary reproductive relationship in all societies is the relationship between a man and a woman characterized by sexual intercourse and its physiological consequences of pregnancy and parturition. The only time we bother to ask questions about reproduction is when we discover that the natives do not draw the same connections we do between these events, as in the case of the Trobriand Islanders, or when we discover that the natives permit marriages between people with the same genital equipment, as among the Nuer or Lovedu. In other words, we assume that of all the activities in which people participate, the ones that create human offspring are heterosexual intercourse, pregnancy, and parturition. Together these constitute the biological process upon which we presume culture builds such social relationships as marriage, filiation, and coparenthood.

The one major modification in kinship studies since the middle of the nineteenth century, according to Schneider, was the shift from an emphasis on the social *recognition* of the biological bonds arising out of the process of procreation to an emphasis on the sociocultural *characteristics* of the relations mapped onto those bonds (Schneider 1984: 54). Since this shift, kinship theorists have been adamant that they view marriage, parenthood, and all other kinship relationships as social relationships and not biological ones. Schneider argues convincingly, however, that for all the claims these writers make that they are speaking of social paters and social maters and not genitors and genitrexes, they have biological parenthood in mind all the time. This point is perhaps no more clearly illustrated than in the following statement by Fortes, quoted by Schneider: "The *facts* of sex, procreation, and the rearing of offspring constitute only the universal raw material of kinship systems" (Fortes 1949: 345, italics ours). For Fortes, as for the other kinship theorists reviewed by Schneider, these *facts* are unambiguously construed as *natural* ones.

Although it is apparent that heterosexual intercourse, pregnancy, and parturition are involved in human reproduction, it is also apparent that producing humans entails more than this. M. Bridget O'Laughlin (1977) put it very succinctly when she wrote, "Human reproduction is never simply a matter of conception and birth." There is a wide range of activities in which people participate besides heterosexual intercourse and parturition that contribute to the birth of viable babies and to their development into adults. These activities, in turn, involve and are organized by a number of relationships other than those of parenthood and marriage. Given the wide range of human activities and relationships that can be viewed as contributing to the production of human beings, why do we focus on only a few of them as the universal basis of kinship? Why do we construe these few activities and relationships as natural facts, rather than investigating the ways in which they are, like all social facts, culturally constructed? The answer Schneider has proposed is that our theory of kinship is simultaneously a folk theory of biological reproduction.

Gender and the Biological "Facts" of Sexual Reproduction

Schneider's insight that kinship is by definition about sexual procreation leads us to realize that assumptions about gender lie at the core of kinship studies. Moreover, not only are ideas about gender central to analyses of kinship, but ideas about kinship are central to analyses of gender. Because both gender and kinship have been defined as topics of study by our conception of the same thing, namely, sexual procreation, we cannot think about one without thinking about the other. In short, these two fields of studies are mutually constituted.

Gender assumptions pervade notions about the *facts* of sexual reproduction commonplace in the kinship literature. Much of what is written about atoms of kinship (Lévi-Strauss 1949), the axiom of prescriptive altruism (Fortes 1958; Fortes 1969), the universality of the family (Fox 1967), and the centrality of the mother-child bond (Goodenough 1970) is rooted in assumptions about the natural characteristics of women and men and their natural roles in sexual procreation. The standard units of our genealogies, after all, are circles and triangles about which we assume a number of things. Above all, we take for granted that they represent two naturally different categories of people and that the natural difference between them is the basis of human reproduction and, therefore, kinship. Harold Scheffler's (1974: 749) statement that "the foundation of any kinship system consists in the folk-cultural theory designed to account for the fact that women give birth to children" reveals that, for him, kinship is everywhere about the same biological fact. Although he recognizes that there are a variety of ways in which this "fact" may be accounted for in different societies, Scheffler, like most kinship theorists, assumes certain social consequences follow necessarily from it, including that biological motherhood is everywhere the core of the social relationship of motherhood (Scheffler 1970).*

Likewise, the literature on gender is sensitive to the many ways in which pregnancy and childbirth are conceptualized and valued in different societies and to the different ways in which the activities surrounding them can be socially organized. But, the conviction that the biological *difference* in the roles of women and men in sexual reproduction lies at the core of the cultural organization of gender persists in comparative analyses. As we argued in the previous section, the analytical oppositions of domestic/public, nature/culture, and reproduction/production all begin with this as-

---

*It is noteworthy that motherhood is the locus of many assumptions in feminist writing as well as in the nonfeminist kinship literature. However, in the feminist literature, the emphasis is more on the ways in which mothering constrains and structures women's lives and psyches (for example, Chodorow 1979), whereas in the nonfeminist kinship literature (for example, Fortes 1969; Goodenough 1970; Scheffler 1974), the emphasis is on the positive affect and bond that maternal nurturance creates in domestic relationships.

sumption of difference. Like kinship theorists, moreover, analysts of gender have assumed that specific social consequences necessarily follow from this difference between men and women. For example, the assumption that women *bear* the greater burden and responsibility for human reproduction pervades gender studies, in particular those works employing a reproduction/production distinction. Yet, this notion often appears to be more a metaphorical extension of our emphasis on the fact that women *bear* children than a conclusion based on systematic comparison of the contribution of men and women to human reproduction. In other words, the fact that women bear children and men do not is interpreted as creating a universal relation of human reproduction. Accordingly, we have been much slower to question the purported universals of the reproductive relations of men and women than we have been to question the purported universals of their productive relations. For example, as we have shown, in the literature on women and capitalist development, women's natural burden in reproduction is viewed as constraining their role in production, rather than seen as itself shaped by historical changes in the organization of production.

The centrality of sexual reproduction in the definition of gender is reflected in the distinction between sex and gender that has become a convention in much of the feminist literature. Judith Shapiro summarizes the distinction between the terms as follows:

[T]hey serve a useful analytic purpose in contrasting a set of biological facts with a set of cultural facts. Were I to be scrupulous in my use of terms, I would use the term "sex" only when I was speaking of biological differences between males and females, and use "gender" whenever I was referring to the social, cultural, psychological constructs that are *imposed upon these biological differences*. . . . [G]ender . . . designates a set of categories to which we can give the same label crosslinguistically, or crossculturally, because they have *some connection to sex differences*. These categories are, however, conventional or arbitrary insofar as they are not reducible to, or directly derivative of, natural, biological facts; they vary from one language to another, one culture to another, in the way in which they order experience and action" (1981: 449, italics ours).

The attempt to separate the study of gender categories from the biological facts to which they are seen to be universally connected mirrors the attempt of kinship theorists reviewed by Schneider (1984) to separate the study of kinship from the same biological facts. Like the latter attempt, this one seems doomed to fail, because it too starts from a definition of its subject matter that is rooted in those biological facts. It is impossible, of course, to know what gender or kinship would mean if they are to be entirely disconnected from sex and biological reproduction. We have no choice but to begin our investigations of others with our own concepts. But, we can unpack the cultural assumptions embodied in them, which limit our capacity to understand social systems informed by other cultural assumptions.

Although gender and kinship studies start from what are construed as the same biological facts of sexual reproduction, they might appear to be headed in different analytical directions: kinship to the social character of genealogical relations and gender to the social character of male-female relations (and even to male-male relations and female-female relations). However, because both build their explanations of the social rights and duties and the relations of equality and inequality among people on these presumably natural characteristics, both retain the legacy of their beginnings in notions about *the same natural differences* between people. Consequently, what have been conceptualized as two discrete, if interconnected, fields of study constitute a single field.

Our realization of the unitary constitution of gender and kinship as topics of study should make us wary of treating them as distinct analytical problems. As Schneider (1984: 175) points out, part of the "conventional wisdom of kinship" has been the idea that kinship forms a system that can be treated as a distinct institution or domain. Like "economics," "politics," and "religion," kinship has been posited as one of the fundamental building blocks of society by anthropologists (Schneider 1984: 181).* At the same time, neither should we assume that in all societies kinship creates gender or that gender creates kinship. Although the two may be mutually constituted as topics of study by *our* society, this does not mean they are linked in the same way in all societies. Instead, as we shall suggest below, we should seek rather than assume knowledge of the socially significant domains of relations in any particular society and what constitutes them. Having rejected the notion that

---

*Schneider attributes this to the mid-nineteenth-century attempt by anthropologists to establish the history or development of civilization as this was embodied in European culture, and to the notion that development proceeded from the simple to the complex, from the undifferentiated to the differentiated. To the extent that kinship, economics, politics, and religion were undifferentiated, a society was "primitive," "simple," or "simpler."

there are presocial, universal domains of social relations, such as a domestic domain and a public domain, a kinship domain and a political domain, we must ask what symbolic and social processes make these domains appear self-evident, and perhaps even "natural," fields of activity in any society (see Comaroff this volume).

Transcending Dichotomies: A Focus on Social Wholes

Understanding the folk model of human reproduction underlying the analytical categories and dichotomies—explicit and implicit—that have dominated both gender and kinship studies is the first step toward transcending them. The next step is to move beyond the dichotomies by focusing on social wholes. Instead of asking how the categories of "male" and "female" are endowed with culturally specific characters, thus taking the difference between them for granted, we need to ask how particular societies define difference. Instead of asking how rights and obligations are mapped onto kinship bonds, thus assuming the genealogical grid, we need to ask how specific societies recognize claims and allocate responsibilities. Our ability to understand social wholes, however, is limited by another analytic concept—that of "egalitarian society"—which, as used by many feminists and Marxists, once again bears the legacy of our folk notion of difference.

Questioning the Concept of "Egalitarian Society"

Anthropologists have used the concept of "egalitarian society" in two, somewhat contradictory, ways. Morton Fried coined the term to denote a particular form of organizing inequality. Given his assumption that "equality is a social impossibility" (1967: 26), he defines an "egalitarian society" as "one in which there are as many positions of prestige in any given age-sex grade as there are persons capable of filling them" (1967: 33). Not all people achieve valued positions. Fried, for example, writes that men in such societies "display a considerable drive to achieve parity, or at least to establish a status that announces 'don't fool with me'" (1967: 79). He thus reveals that some men fail, whereas women and youths never have a chance to "achieve parity." Given that Fried focuses on the organization of inequality, his usage of the term "egalitarian society" is misleading.

In contrast to Fried, many Marxist and feminist scholars use the concept of "egalitarian society" to denote societies in which people are indeed "equal" in the sense that they do not exhibit the class and gender inequalities characteristic of ancient societies and modern capitalism. These scholars define egalitarian societies less in terms of features they possess than in terms of features they lack. In arguing that the gender and class inequalities familiar to us today and from accounts of the past are the product of specific historical processes, these scholars suggest, usually by default, that the organization of gender and production in nonclass societies is not produced by history. Consequently, the social categories in nonclass societies are seen as reflecting "natural" human propensities, given particular environmental conditions (Jaggar 1983: 70).

For example, Gough, in writing on "The Origin of the Family," states that "marriage and sexual restrictions are practical arrangements among hunters designed mainly to serve economic and survival needs. In these societies, some kind of rather stable pairing best accomplishes the division of labor and cooperation of men and women and the care of children" (1975: 68). In this passage, Gough clearly assumes the existence of a "natural" difference between females and males that must be accommodated through a particular form of organization—through marriage and sexual restrictions—for human reproduction to be successfully accomplished. When writing about complex, inegalitarian societies, however, she observes that marriage and sexual restrictions reflect ruling class efforts to perpetuate class dominance. In sum, for Gough, the gap between nonclass and class societies is sufficiently wide to justify the use of two distinct theories of society: in the case of the former, an ecological-functionalist theory that portrays social restrictions as "practical arrangements" promoting the collective good among naturally different kinds of people, and in the case of the latter, a Marxist-functionalist theory that portrays social restrictions as hegemonic arrangements promoting the self-interest of the dominant group among socially constructed categories of people.

Feminists arguing against the universality of sexual asymmetry are presently the most active proponents of the concept of egalitarian society. Not only do they believe that such societies once existed, but they consider the concept our most effective rhetorical strategy for establishing that biology is not destiny (Sacks 1976; Sacks 1979; Leacock 1978; Schlegel 1977; Caulfield 1981). They argue that assertions of universal sexual asymmetry—such as those by Rosaldo (1974), Ortner (1974), and Fried (1975)—legitimize a search for biological causes. Consequently, to posit the existence of sexually egalitarian societies is to obviate such a search before it begins.

Eleanor Leacock, in an important article positing the existence of sexually egalitarian societies (1978), argues that Western observers have failed to recognize such societies because their ability to understand egalitarian socioeconomic relations is hindered by concepts derived from the hierarchical structure of capitalism: "The tendency to attribute to band societies the relations of power and property characteristic of our own obscures the qualitatively different relations that obtained when ties of economic dependency linked the individual directly with the group as a whole, when public and private spheres were not dichotomized, and when decisions were made by and large by those who would be carrying them out" (1978: 247). In particular, Leacock criticizes our tendency to interpret a sexual division of labor as hierarchical—our inability to imagine that men and women who do different things might be "separate but equal" (1978: 248).

In seeking to counter anthropological accounts portraying women in band societies as subordinate to men, Leacock suggests that men and women were equally "autonomous." Men and women may have engaged in different activities, but women "held decision making power over their own lives and activities to the same extent that men did over theirs" (1978: 247). Leacock writes that she prefers "the term 'autonomy' to 'equality,' for equality connotes rights and opportunity specific to class society and confuses similarity with equity" (1978: 247).

Substituting "autonomy" for "equality," however, does not free Leacock from the problems inherent in using concepts based on the hierarchical structure of our own society. "Autonomy," as used in our cultural system, is not a neutral term. As Sandra Wallman observes, in Western social science, "behavioral differences between men and women have generally been attributed *either* to natural, and therefore, essential differences in biology, physiology, genetics *or* to cultural, and therefore non-essential impositions, the fortuitous demands and/or accidents of a social system and the dialectics of history and/or the human mind" (1978: 21, italics hers). In other words, our folk system posits that behavioral differences not explained by culture must be due to nature, and vice versa. As a result, by claiming a freedom from outside constraints, "autonomy" inevitably invokes notions of biological destiny.

Leacock surely did not intend to portray women in band societies as acting out their biological natures when they engaged in women's work. But by failing to treat "men" and "women" as cultural constructs and in accepting the difference in their activities, Leacock suggests this position by default (see Strathern 1978; Atkinson 1982). Leacock's notion of "autonomy" can be read in two ways, but neither avoids the implication of biological destiny. If we interpret her statement that women "held decision making power over their own lives and activities" to mean that women could decide what they wanted to do, then we are faced with the question of why women all decided to do women's tasks rather than doing what men did. Why did women not decide, like good Marxists, "to hunt in the morning, fish in the afternoon, rear cattle in the evening, [and] criticize after dinner" (Marx and Engels 1970: 53)? The obvious answer, given Leacock's failure to investigate the social and cultural factors shaping women's decisions, is that women "naturally" wanted to do women's tasks, just as men "naturally" wanted to do men's tasks. If we adopt an alternative reading of Leacock's statement and conclude that women "held decision making power over their own lives and activities" *only* "to the same extent that men did over theirs," we are left with the question of what it means to "have decision making power" over one's own life. In this reading, women and men appear equally constrained to take up only sex-appropriate tasks. But the social and symbolic practices through which they are constrained are not discussed, suggesting, again by default, a "natural" division of labor by sex.

In summary, however useful the concept of "egalitarian society" may be for denaturalizing gender in class societies, it raises many of the problems we encountered in our discussion of the analytic dichotomies of domestic/public, nature/culture, and reproduction/production. By positing a past Eden in which women and men were "autonomous," we assume precultural, natural differences as the bases for the sexual division of labor.

Analyzing Social Wholes: Meanings, Models, and History

Given our tendency to reinvent the analytic dichotomies that limit our ability to understand gender in our own and other societies, we need an explicit strategy for transcending them. The one we propose in this final section of the paper rests on the premise that there are no "facts," biological or material, that have social consequences and cultural meanings in and of themselves. Sexual intercourse, pregnancy, and parturition are cultural facts, whose form, consequences, and meanings are socially constructed in any society, as are mothering, fathering, judging, ruling, and talking with the gods. Similarly, there are no material "facts" that can be treated as precultural givens. The consequences and meanings of force are socially constructed, as are those of the means of production or the resources upon which people depend for their living.

Just as we reject analytic dichotomies, so we reject analytic domains. We do not assume the existence of a gender system based on natural differences in sexual reproduction, a kinship system based on the genealogical grid, a polity based on force, or an economy based on the production and distribution of needed resources. Rather than take for granted that societies are constituted of functionally based institutional domains, we propose to investigate the social and symbolic processes by which human actions within particular social worlds come to have consequences and meanings, including their apparent organization into seemingly "natural" social domains.

We begin with the premise that social systems are, by definition, systems of inequality. This premise has three immediate advantages. First, it conforms to common usage. By most definitions, a society is a system of social relationships and values. Values entail evaluation. Consequently, a society is a system of social relationships in which all things and actions are not equal. As Ralf Dahrendorf (1968) notes, values inevitably create inequalities by ensuring rewards for those who live up to valued ideals and punishments for those who, for one reason or another, fail to do so. Every society has a "prestige structure," as Ortner and Whitehead (1981) presume. A system of values, however, is not "male," and in analyzing any particular society, we must ask why people appear to hold the values they do.

Second, the premise that all societies are systems of inequality forces us to separate the frequently confused concepts of equality (the state of being equal) and justice (moral rightness). By presuming that all societies are systems of inequality, we are forced to separate the study of our own and other people's cultural systems of evaluation from considerations of whether or not such systems meet our standards of honor and fairness.

Finally, the premise that all societies are systems of inequality frees us from having to imagine a world without socially created inequities. We therefore avoid having to assume social consequences for "natural" differences. If we assume that all societies are systems of inequality, then we, as social scientists, are forced to explain not the existence of inequality itself but rather why it takes the qualitatively different forms it does.

In defining "egalitarian society" out of existence, however, we do not propose a return to the hypothesis of women's universal subordination. Rather, the premise that all societies are systems of inequality forces us to specify what we mean by inequality in each particular case. Instead of asking how "natural" differences acquire cultural meanings and social consequences (a strategy that dooms us to reinventing our analytic dichotomies), a presumption of inequality forces us to ask why some attributes and characteristics of people are culturally recognized and differentially evaluated when others are not. This requires us to begin any analysis by asking, What are a society's cultural values? And what social processes organize the distribution of prestige, power, and privilege? We may find that in some societies neither cultural values nor social processes discriminate between the sexes (that is, a nongendered system of inequality). But this conclusion must follow from an analysis of how inequality is organized.

Given our premise that social systems are systems of inequality, we propose an analytical program with three facets. These facets are arranged not in order of theoretical importance but in the sequence we feel they should be employed in any particular analysis. Some researchers, depending on the particular question or type of society that is the topic of study, may find another sequence preferable or may choose to focus on one facet more than the others. But, we suggest, no attempt to analyze social wholes can proceed very far without employing all three.

The Cultural Analysis of Meaning. The first facet of our program entails an analysis of cultural systems of meanings. Specifically, we must begin by explicating the cultural meanings people realize through their practice of social relationships. Rather than assume that the fundamental units of gender and kinship in every society are defined by the difference between males and females in sexual reproduction, we ask what are the socially meaningful categories people employ and encounter in specific social contexts and what symbols and meanings underlie them. Just as Schneider (1968) questioned, rather than took for granted, the meanings of blood, love, and sexual intercourse in American kinship and their influence on the construction of categories of relatives, so we have to question the meanings of genes, love, sexual intercourse, power, independence, and whatever else plays into the symbolic construction of categories of people in any particular society. This analytical stance toward gender is well summarized in the following statement by Ortner and Whitehead: "Gender, sexuality, and reproduction are treated as *symbols*, invested with meaning by the society in question, as all symbols are. The approach to the problem of sex and gender is thus a matter of symbolic analysis and interpretation, a matter of relating such symbols and meanings to other cultural symbols and meanings on the one hand, and to the forms of social life and experience on the other" (1981: 1–2). By attending to the public discourses through which people describe, interpret, evaluate, make claims about, and attempt to influence relationships and events, we can extract the relatively stable symbols and meanings people employ in everyday life.

These symbols and meanings, as will be stressed in the next section on systemic models of social inequality, are always evaluative. As such, they encode particular distributions of prestige, power, and privilege. However, because they are realized through social practice, they are not static. As will become apparent when we discuss the importance of historical analysis, we do not assume cultural systems of meaning to be timeless, self-perpetuating structures of "tradition." Yet, even when the meanings of core symbols are changing, we can tease apart their different meanings in particular contexts and, thereby, better understand the symbolic processes involved in social change (Yanagisako 1985; Yanagisako this volume).

Once we have investigated the various ways in which difference is conceptualized in other societies—including whether and how sex and reproduction play into the construction of differences that make a difference—we can return to examine the biological model that defines gender in our own society. In other words, just as our

questioning of the domestic/public dichotomy as the structural basis for relations between men and women in other societies has encouraged us to question its analytical usefulness for our own society (Yanagisako this volume), so we can ask what a conception of
gender as rooted in biological difference does and does not explain
about relations between men and women in our society. Having
recognized our model of biological difference as a particular cultural mode of thinking about relations between people, we should
be able to question the "biological facts" of sex themselves. We expect that our questioning of the presumably biological core of gender will eventually lead to the rejection of any dichotomy between
sex and gender as biological and cultural facts and will open up the
way for an analysis of the symbolic and social processes by which
both are constructed in relation to each other.

The cultural analysis of meaning, however, cannot be isolated
from the analysis of patterns of action. We do not view systems of
meaning as ideational determinants of social organization or as solutions to universal problems of meaning and order. Rather, we
conceptualize the interrelated, but not necessarily consistent,
meanings of social events and relationships as both shaping and
being shaped by practice. Our refusal to dichotomize material relationships and meanings or to grant one or the other analytic
priority derives from our conceptualization of practice and ideas as
aspects of a single process.

Systemic Models of Inequality. Ideas and actions are aspects of a
single dialectical process, and we understand this process by focusing on how inequality is organized. Because we assume that cultural conceptions are voiced in contexts in which, among other
things, people make claims, provide explanations, try to influence
action, and celebrate the qualities they use when creating relationships, we understand cultural conceptions by focusing on what
claims may be made, what things explained, what actions influenced, and what relationships forged. In order to understand what
people talk about, we must ask what people may want or fear. And
so we must understand how inequality is organized in any particular society.

The second facet of our analytical strategy thus requires the construction of systemic models of inequality. These models are of a
particular type. Following Bourdieu (1977), we analyze a social sys-

tem not by positing an unseen, timeless structure but rather by asking how ordinary people, pursuing their own subjective ends, realize the structures of inequality that constrain their possibilities. This is why the first facet of our strategy requires an analysis of the commonsense meanings available to people for monitoring and interpreting their own and others' actions. But this analysis of meaning must be followed by an analysis of the structures that people realize through their actions. Because we understand the commonsense meanings available to people not by positing an unseen, timeless culture but rather by exploring how people's understandings of the world are shaped by their structured experiences, we must move back and forth between an analysis of how structures shape people's experience and an analysis of how people, through their actions, realize structures.

Although a systemic model of inequality may be constructed for any society, developing a typology of models aids in the analysis of particular cases. In the end, as we will discuss in the next section, each society must be analyzed in its own, historically specific terms, but a set of ideal typic models helps us to see connections we might otherwise miss. All attempts to understand other cultures are, by their nature, comparative. It is impossible to describe a particular, unique way of life without explicitly or implicitly comparing it to another—usually the analyst's own society or the society of the language the analyst is using. Since comparison is inevitable, it seems more productive to have a set of models available for thinking about similarities and contrasts than to have but ourselves as a single implicit or explicit standard of comparison.

In suggesting that we need to develop several ideal typic models, we echo those feminists who similarly advocate developing a typology of societies to aid in the analysis of particular cases (see Etienne and Leacock 1980). We may define social systems as systems of inequality, but like feminists who posit the existence of "egalitarian societies," we recognize that our ability to understand social relations in other societies is hindered by our "tendency to attribute to [others] the relations of power and property characteristic of our own" (Leacock 1978: 247), even as our hierarchical division of labor makes it difficult for us to imagine that men and women who do different things might nevertheless be "separate but equal" (Sacks 1976). We thus agree with feminists who posit the existence of "egalitarian societies" that we need models capable of distinguishing among qualitatively different forms of social hierarchy.

In seeking to develop such models, however, we do not view either technology or socially organized access to productive resources as determining traits (see Collier and Rosaldo 1981: 318; Collier this volume; Collier n.d.). Given our assumption that no biological or material "fact" has social consequences in and of itself, we cannot begin by assuming the determining character of either the forces or relations of production. We therefore do not classify societies according to technologies—such as foraging, horticulture, agriculture, pastoralism, and industry (for example, Martin and Voorhies 1975)—or according to social relations governing access to resources—such as egalitarian, ranked, and stratified (Etienne and Leacock 1980) or communal, corporate kin, and class (Sacks 1979).

An example of the kind of model of inequality we are proposing is Jane Collier and Michelle Rosaldo's ideal typic model of "brideservice" societies (1981). The classification scheme employed in this essay and others (Collier 1984; Collier this volume; Collier n.d.) uses marriage transaction terms—brideservice, equal or standard bridewealth, and unequal or variable bridewealth—as labels for systemic models, treating marriage transactions not as determinants of social organization or ideas but rather as moments when practice and meaning are negotiated together. Marriage negotiations are moments of "systemic reproduction" (see Comaroff this volume) in those societies in which "kinship" appears to organize people's rights and obligations relative to others. Societies with different bases of organization will have different moments of "systemic reproduction."

Just as we do not posit determining traits, so the kind of understanding we seek is not linear. Rather, the type of model we propose traces complex relationships between aspects of what—using conventional analytical categories—we might call gender, kinship, economy, polity, and religion. The principal virtue of such models is that they provide insights into the cultural meanings and social consequences of actions, events, and people's attributes by tracing the processes by which these elements are realized. Such systemic models privilege no domains over others. Unlike Ortner and Whitehead, who advocate a focus on "male prestige-oriented action" as the key to understanding gender relations in any society (1981:20), we suggest that "prestige systems" also need explanation. When men, for example, talk as if male prestige is generated through activities that do not involve relations with women, such as hunting and warfare, we ask why men make such statements and what social processes make them appear reasonable. A "brideservice" model suggests that—at least in societies of foragers and hunter-horticulturalists—people celebrate "Man the Hunter" not because male prestige is actually based on hunting, but rather because hunting is a principal idiom in which men talk about their claims to the wives whose daily services allow them to enjoy the freedom of never having to ask anyone for anything (Collier and Rosaldo 1981).

Because systemic models specify the contexts in which people articulate particular concerns, such models can help us to understand the apparently inconsistent meanings we discover through cultural analysis. In their analysis of "brideservice societies," for example, Collier and Rosaldo (1981) suggest why male violence is feared even as it is celebrated, why women who contribute as much or more than men to the diet do not emphasize their economic contribution but rather stress their sexuality, why bachelors are lazy hunters when sex is portrayed as the hunter's reward, and why notions of direct-exchange marriage coexist with the belief that men earn their wives through feats of prowess. Systemic models, by allowing us to understand such apparent inconsistencies, provide the analytic tools necessary for overcoming our own cultural bias toward consistency. Once we understand that force is both feared and celebrated, for example, then we are no longer tempted to ignore one aspect or choose which one is more empirically valid.

Although models provide conceptual tools for analyzing social and cultural systems, they, like the cultural analysis of meaning, are but one facet of our strategy. If our aim is to understand real people, model building can never be an end in itself. Because models are necessarily abstract, to the degree that we succeed in building a systemic model, we cease to illuminate the particularities of any given historical society. It is not, as has often been claimed, that systemic models of the sort we are proposing are inherently static. Because these models rest on the assumption that social structures are realized and cultural conceptions voiced by people pursuing their own subjective ends in social worlds of inequality, competition, and conflict, the potential for change is inherent in every action. Systemic models appear static, however, because they are designed to answer the unstated question of why societies appear to change as little as they do given the constant possibility of change. Models thus tend to reveal how those in power use their power to preserve their positions of privilege.

Historical Analysis. The third facet of our analytical strategy is motivated by our belief that change is possible in all social systems, regardless of their particular configuration of inequality. We thus need an explicit strategy to counterbalance the emphasis on social reproduction in our systemic models, so that we can see how social systems change and, at the same time, better understand the processes that enable them to remain relatively stable over time. A historical analysis that interprets current ideas and practices within the context of the unfolding sequence of action and meaning that has led to them provides this balance. Such an analysis broadens the temporal range of our analysis of social wholes by asking how their connection with the past constrains and shapes their dynamics in the present, whether that connection is one of relative continuity or of radical disjunction. In other words, whereas historical analysis is of critical importance for understanding societies and communities that are undergoing dramatic transformations (for example, Sahlins 1981; Yanagisako 1985; Collier 1986), it is of no less importance for understanding societies characterized by seeming social and cultural continuity (R. Rosaldo 1980). For, given that change is inherent in social action, the reproduction of social systems requires no less explanation than does their transformation.

The kind of historical approach we are proposing will enrich our cultural analysis of meaning by broadening the range of symbols, meanings, and practices to which we relate concepts of value and difference. Our proposal to link historical analysis with symbolic analysis rests on the premise that we cannot comprehend present discourse and action without understanding their relation to past discourse and action (Yanagisako 1985). The relevant context of specific cultural elements, such as "marriage," "mother," "blood," or "semen," is not limited to current practices and meanings, but includes past practices and their symbolic meanings. For example, the meanings of "equality," "duty," and "love" in the conjugal relationship may be shaped by the past character of conjugal relationships as well as their present ones and by the way in which past and present are symbolically linked (Yanagisako this volume). Likewise, the meaning of "agnatic" ties at any one period may be shaped by the uses to which such ties were previously put (Comaroff this volume). All these analyses argue that we must know the dialectical, historical processes through which practices and meanings have unfolded if we are to understand how they operate in the present.

Similarly, grounding our analysis of social wholes and fashioning our systemic models of inequality within particular historical sequences will enable us to see how the dynamics of past actions and ideas have created structures in the present. Relationships suggested by our systemic models can be tested in a dynamic context and, if necessary, modified or refined. By taking such a historical perspective on the constitution of social wholes, we avoid assuming that present systems of inequality are the timeless products of identical pasts; instead, we question whether and how these systems developed out of dissimilar pasts (Lindenbaum this volume; Smith this volume). We can see how aspects of ideas and practices, which in our systemic models seem to reinforce and reproduce each other, also undermine and destabilize each other.

A historical perspective also highlights the interaction of ideas and practices as dialectical, ongoing processes and so avoids the teleological bent of those models that seek a single determinant, whether material or ideational, for social reproduction. A good example of how historical analysis can help us transcend the dichotomization of ideas and practices can be seen in the anthropological literature on the sexual division of labor. As Jane Guyer (1980) notes, much of this literature has tended to emphasize either the material, technological determinants of the sexual division of labor or its cultural, ideational determinants. Yet, she points out, "the division of labor is, like all fundamental institutions, multifaceted. Within any particular society, it is an integral part of the ideological system, economic organization, daily family life, and often the political structure as well. . . . In any one case, all these dimensions reinforce each other, so that the current structure seems both heavily overdetermined and ultimately mysterious since it is difficult to assign weight to any one factor over another" (1980: 356).

Guyer's comparative analysis of historical developments in the sexual division of labor and organization of production in two African societies offers a useful alternative to unidimensional views of the division of labor. She shows how the development of cocoa as a cash crop in two societies initially characterized by different sexual divisions of labor and organizations of production brought about different changes in these and other aspects of social organization.

Finally, to return to the beginning of this essay, historical analysis can help us to transcend the analytical dichotomies and domains that we have argued have plagued gender and kinship studies. Historical studies (see Comaroff, Lindenbaum, Maher, Rapp, Smith, and Yanagisako this volume) reveal how seemingly universal, timeless domains of social structure are created and transformed in particular times and places.

Conclusion

At the beginning of this essay, we suggested that feminism's next contribution to the study of gender and kinship should be to question the difference between women and men. We do not doubt that men and women are different, just as individuals differ, generations differ, races differ, and so forth. Rather, we question whether the particular biological difference in reproductive function that our culture defines as the basis of difference between males and females, and so treats as the basis of their relationship, is used by other societies to constitute the cultural categories of male and female.

Past feminist questions have led to the opening up of new areas for investigation, even as such investigations have raised new problems and questions. By doubting the common assumption that sex and age are "natural" bases for the differential allocation of social rights and duties, feminist scholars paved the way for studies of the social processes that granted men prestige and authority over women and children. Yet feminists' attempts to provide social explanations for perceived universal sexual asymmetry used the analytic dichotomies of domestic/public and nature/culture that themselves became problematic.

Doubts concerning the analytic utility and cultural universality of these dichotomies led, in turn, to studies of the social and cultural processes by which the categories of masculinity and femininity are constituted in particular times and places. Yet, as we have suggested, some of these studies raised a new set of questions. Attempts to replace the inherently gendered dichotomies of domestic/public and nature/culture with the distinction between reproduction and production, and the positing of "male prestige systems," have revealed our tendency to rediscover gendered dichotomies. Similarly, attempts to argue that men and women have not everywhere and at all times been unequal have given rise to the concept of "egalitarian society," a concept that, if not complemented by a cultural analysis of personhood, implies, by default, a "natural" basis for sexual divisions of labor.

Now, we suggest, our problem of continually rediscovering gendered categories can be overcome by calling into question the universality of our cultural assumptions about the difference between males and females. Both gender and kinship studies, we suggest, have foundered on the unquestioned assumption that the biologically given difference in the roles of men and women in sexual reproduction lies at the core of the cultural organization of gender, even as it constitutes the genealogical grid at the core of kinship studies. Only by calling this assumption into question can we begin to ask how other cultures might understand the difference between women and men, and simultaneously make possible studies of how our own culture comes to focus on coitus and parturition as *the* moments constituting masculinity and femininity.

It is not enough to question the universality and analytic utility of our implicit assumptions about sex differences. Rather, we need specific strategies to help us overcome our tendency to reinvent gendered analytic dichotomies. In this essay, we have argued for the need to analyze social wholes and have proposed a three-faceted approach to this project: the explication of cultural meanings, the construction of models specifying the dialectical relationship between practice and ideas in the constitution of social inequalities, and the historical analysis of continuities and changes.

The commitment to analyzing social wholes is one we share with all the contributors to this volume. Not everyone might agree with our questioning of the difference between women and men, or with our three-faceted approach to analyzing social wholes, for we formulated both notions after the conference. Nevertheless, we believe that this volume provides a good illustration of the insights to be gained from a commitment to holistic analysis.

Finally, we have no illusions that the strategy we propose will resolve all the issues we have raised. We know that we, too, can never be free from the folk models of our own culture, and that in questioning some folk concepts we privilege others. We expect that the studies we hope to generate by questioning the difference between women and men will, in time, reveal their own problematic assumptions. These will generate new questions that will, in turn, give rise to new strategies and new solutions.

Part One

The Transformation of
Cultural Domains

Sui genderis: Feminism, Kinship Theory, and Structural "Domains"

John L. Comaroff

The classical distinction between the domestic and politico-jural domains has loomed large in feminist critiques of established anthropological concepts and categories. But it has done so in many different ways, some of them mutually contradictory. At one extreme, an entire sociology of gender relations has been built on the alleged universality of this distinction (Rapp 1979: 508ff). At the other, it has been rejected on two quite different counts: either that the form of the domestic and politico-jural spheres varies widely across cultures (for example, Rogers 1975; Quinn 1977; Rosaldo 1980), or that their very existence is a figment of Western capitalist ideology (for example, Nash and Leacock 1977). Clearly, such differences lie behind a number of controversies in women's studies, from theoretical discussions of the "universal fact" of sexual asymmetry to debates over the nature of female power in specific social systems.*

The problem of structural domains is equally significant in the past and future of anthropology at large and in the analysis of family and kinship in particular. The distinction between the domestic and politico-jural, the private and public, is usually associated with Fortes's portrayal of "traditional" society (for example, Fortes 1969), but it appears throughout Western social theory. Moreover, the tendency to view economy and society as consisting in a series of dichotomous "spheres" is as common in Western folk models as it is in the social sciences. There is an already large and varied body of criticism directed at the notion that social organization is every-

*Various drafts of this chapter have been read by Jane Collier, Jean Comaroff, Kathleen Hall, Jean Lave, Carol Nagengast, and Terence Turner. I wish to thank them for their valuable critical comment.

where "a balance . . . between the political order . . . and the familial or domestic order, . . . a balance between polity and kinship" (Fortes 1978: 14ff). Some argue less about the existence of the domains than about their diversity; others assert that, far from being a structural given, these spheres are a specific historical product that demands explanation (see Yanagisako 1979).

Given the significance of the distinction between the two domains for both feminist scholarship and kinship theory, it is useful to examine (1) the critiques of the distinction itself and the images of society built upon it, (2) efforts to revise or reject it entirely, and (3) the general implications of such efforts for the analysis of gender and kinship, economy and society. How, in sum, does the problem of structural domains stand to be "rethought" *sui genderis*?

II

One of the earliest theoretical concerns in feminist writings was the universality of sexual asymmetry. As Rogers has noted, those who sought to confront established preconceptions within the palpably androcentric discipline of anthropology seemed to face a binary choice: "to elucidate the means by which women have universally 'been denied the opportunity of taking the lead,' [or] . . . to demonstrate that . . . women (as a category) are not universally subordinated by men" (1978: 24). For those who sought to explain, in sociocultural terms, why "sexual asymmetry is a universal fact of human societies" (Rosaldo 1974: 22), the domestic/public distinction became a transcendent, suprahistorical principle of social organization.* Not only was the division between these domains "taken as a description of social reality" (Rapp 1979: 508), but it came to stand for an embracing class of oppositions, as if all were aspects of one super-dichotomy. Thus the contrast between the domestic and politico-jural was equally one between informality and formality, nature and culture, private and public, family and polity—and female and male.

It is arguable that this view of society was logically entailed in the universal asymmetry thesis, at least as posited in the book most commonly associated with it, *Woman, Culture, and Society*. For, if women are assumed everywhere to be subordinated *as a category* because of sociocultural rather than physical facts, it follows that

---

*See, for example, the essays of Michelle Rosaldo, Nancy Chodorow, and Sherry Ortner in *Woman, Culture, and Society* (1974), although Rosaldo (1980) later amended her views.

the genders have to be assigned to different spheres, one dominant and encompassing, the other dominated and encompassed. Hence, not only must all social orders become binary systems, but men must, by definition, be associated with the overarching, regulatory institutions of society—the politico-jural "domain"—while women are located within its incorporated units, those of the domestic "domain."

It follows that efforts to challenge the universal asymmetry thesis would demand a reexamination of orthodox anthropological images of the form and content of the two domains. Such efforts have by no means been uniform, however (Rapp 1979: 508ff). Not only do they reflect the theoretical diversity in feminist discourse, but they vary in the degree to which they explicitly depart from received wisdom.

Studies at one extreme accept the domestic/public distinction itself but reconsider the substance and functional significance of each domain. For example, Rogers does not contest their existence, nor does she dispute the general association between the public sphere and maleness (1978: 146). Rather, she argues that the "meaning of the public sphere" must be "radically revised." For in domestic-centered communities, such as European peasantries, the family is the key economic, political, and social unit, and power in the private sector is of greatest import. There are many variants of this argument, usually backed by studies of peasant or "traditional" societies. These studies prove that there is great diversity in household relations, and that many social and material functions hitherto attributed to politico-legal institutions may occur within the domestic context. Hence, aside from their obvious corollaries for the analysis of women's status (Quinn 1977), these studies negate the premise that the substance of structural domains is universal or historically invariant.

They also raise another problem, that of the relationship between the domains. As Tilly notes (1978: 167), this relationship is not constant over time and space; she describes as useful Lamphere's very general thesis (1974) that the domestic and public sectors differ in their degree of overlap or segregation. In evaluating the ethnography of the Middle East, Nelson extends the same point by drawing the (now commonplace) inference that the received contrast between the domains is an unwarranted imposition of the categories of Western social science (1974: 552). Evidence of the fact that women often exercise public power and transact relations between households leads her to three conclusions: first, that the taken-for-granted association of women with the private/informal/domestic and men with the public/formal/political is false; second, that the metaphoric use of "private" to describe the domestic and "public" to describe the political is thus misleading; and, third, that the domains, being articulated by the purposive action of women, take on their social content by virtue of their interrelationship. Nonetheless, although Nelson challenges the public/private dichotomy as both sociological concept and culturally relevant distinction, like Tilly she does not deny the existence of the spheres themselves.

A yet more radical reformulation of the problem has it that the public sector emerges only as an outcome of domestic and inter-household relations (Jayawardena 1977; Sudarkasa 1976). This resonates with the more general argument that the existence of the domains cannot be presumed from the first. For example, in hunter-gatherer societies there simply is no distinction between the domestic and public; that distinction must, therefore, be the product of some historical transformation. For Draper (1975), who is concerned with Bushmen, it is sedentarization, which leads to the creation of households differentiated by material interests. For others, it is the development of agriculture (Boserup 1970; Martin and Voorhies 1975), hastened by the introduction of cash cropping and wage labor under colonialism.

A more complex argument is propounded by Sacks (1975) and Reiter (1975). According to Sacks's analysis of African prestate systems, domestic and public statuses depend on property and productive relations, but the distinction between domains is not especially marked. With the rise of states and the formation of classes, as ruling cadres come to expropriate surpluses, the separation of domestic and public sectors becomes an enduring feature of the social order. The former, in effect, becomes the "private" locus of the reproduction and sustenance of labor power; the latter, the conduit along which surplus value flows and is regulated. Reiter (1975) also attributes the emergence of the two spheres to the rise of states and the concomitant displacement of former kinship functions. Under industrial capitalism the distinction is sharpened, for the integrity of the nuclear family, like the segregation of home and workplace, is central to its ideology. In a later essay, Reiter notes again that the distinction is primarily ideological. More-over, "ideologies are powerful cultural statements which simulta-neously mask and reveal contradictions that grow out of necessary productive social relations. . . . Such contradictions are [not] uni-versal between domestic and public domains. Rather, they are cre-ated in historically specific times and places when resource rela-tions between households and large politico-economic arenas become problematic" (Rapp 1979: 510).

In sum, critics of the classical conception of the domestic and politico-jural domains fall along a continuum: those who recon-sider the substance and functions of the domains, without ques-tioning their sociological reality or the relationship between them; those who acknowledge the existence of these domains, but stress the variability of their interconnection; and those who view their emergence as an historically specific phenomenon, often arising from transformations in political economy, and who treat them as problematic social forms and ideological representations. An anal-ogous range is evident in debates over the nature of kinship and the family. In a review essay, Yanagisako (1979) cites Goody's model (1973, 1976) of the relationship between productive technologies, marriage, and devolution as one which speaks to the diversity of domestic arrangements without questioning the universality of the nuclear family or its encompassment in politico-jural institutions (1979: 171ff). She then discusses historical studies (for example, Kent 1977; Davis 1977) that reveal new subtleties in relations be-tween family and extradomestic structures, and, finally, recent ef-forts to prove that the content and constitution of domains can be established only by analyzing total political economies over time (1979: 192).

The cogency of these parallel lines of criticism is reinforced by the fact that Fortes's very conception of the domains was flawed from the outset. On one hand, he warned against reifying the domestic/ politico-jural distinction, stating that "the actualities of kinship re-lations and behaviors are compounded of elements derived from both" (Fortes 1969: 251). Yet, on the other, he insisted that they are "analytically and indeed empirically distinguished" even where apparently fused in a single kinship polity (1978: 14ff). But surely there is a discontinuity here. If the domains appear to be fused in some cases (as among Australian Aborigines) and clearly segre-gated in others (the paradigmatic West African instances), both their content and their articulation must be variable. Further, when the features separating the spheres are not visible, they can *only* be discriminated by being objectified, tautologically, in terms of "universal" analytic categories. Even when the domains are, in Fortes's terms, quite distinct, the same problem arises: how can kinship relations and behavior be divided into two discrete spheres—given that they are actually compounded of elements of both—without reifying those spheres and carving up social reality by heuristic fiat?

III

It is one thing to debate the universality or variability of the domestic and public domains, their historical specificity or cultural relativity, but quite another to decide finally what they are. In the past, they have been treated as fields of relationship, as sets of roles, as social and spatial contexts of activity, as niches in the division of labor, and as ideological constructs. More recently, three alternatives for rethinking their form and interconnection have emerged with particular clarity. Not surprisingly, each corresponds broadly with one of the major lines of criticism discussed above. For descriptive purposes, I shall typify them as the comparative, transactional, and systemic solutions.

The comparative solution, an emphatically empiricist one, starts with the notion that the categories "domestic" and "political" *do* describe a very general reality. Each sphere comprises relations and activities which may be identified by their sociospatial contexts; however, their content and articulation vary widely. In some societies, the domestic sphere may indeed be composed of residentially bounded nuclear families—the locus of socialization, production, and reproduction—whereas the public domain is the encompassing arena of politico-legal and economic regulation; in others, both the folk distinction between the two and their content may be quite different. But the discovery of such differences is primarily a problem of comparative ethnography. Once we set aside androcentric preconceptions (according to feminists) and ethnocentric illusions about the universality of the human family (according to some critical sociologists), we will gain a deeper insight into the real essence of, and diversity in, domestic structures. Allegedly, this will yield better taxonomic and morphological models and so disclose the "factors" underlying patterns of regularity and variation.

Lest this approach be dismissed as a straw person, I should note that it corresponds to the practice of much positivist sociology. The critiques, mentioned earlier, that call for more nuanced comparisons of the content and interrelationship of the domains clearly follow its logic. So, too, do many cultural relativist and multifactorial studies of gender relations and family organization (see Quinn 1977; Yanagisako 1979).

Pervasive as it may be, this approach to "rethinking" concepts has generated a large body of criticism. I shall draw just one strand from it and let the matter rest. The comparative alternative, with its positivist roots, implies that data may be gathered in such a way that, once unworthy assumptions are set aside, the facts will speak out. Yet, as has repeatedly been noted, there are neither facts nor any basis for their interpretation without a preexisting conceptual repertoire. Of course, having decided that the domains do describe a concrete reality with definite properties, proponents of this alternative *have* made a theoretical election. But it is a circular one. For, on one hand, the very object of the comparative solution is to account anew for the nature of these domains; in other words, to regard them as an empirical problem. Yet, on the other hand, because they are *already* presumed to exist very widely, they are treated as analytic categories through which human activities and relations may be classified. As a result, the comparative solution can only affirm what has already been assumed—that is, that the distinction between the domestic and politico-jural is an intrinsic, if variable, fact of social existence.

The transactional solution, in contrast, does not assume the reality of the domains. Rather, it takes as its touchstone the fact that members of society engage, as a matter of course, in the transaction of value of various kinds, a process that generates both structural arrangements and culture as an order of negotiated values (Barth 1966). Moreover, these structural arrangements are, at least potentially, in constant flux; ongoing exchanges—primed by past interactions—may just as easily alter fields of relationship and cultural priorities as reinforce them.

This approach would argue, then, that family and household organization is not determined by cultural rules or by enduring social principles, and is neither static nor uniform. It is the product of chains of transactions among living persons. Thus, insofar as there is a domestic domain, it is purely a descriptor of the overall regularities generated by human actors as they navigate their lives. Similarly, the public domain is shaped by exchanges within and between families; from this standpoint, it *does* appear as an extension of intra- and interhousehold transactions.

This solution would appear to have undeniable appeal. In principle, it distinguishes clearly between analytic subjects (exchange, transaction) and predicates (fields of relations, values), as well as between explanatory constructs (interaction, emergent property) and descriptors of social regularity (family, household, public sphere). Also, it does not deny women a role, as autonomous actors, in fashioning their world; and, far from presuming the universality of domestic organization, it seems to account for diversity within and across societies. Finally, it does not rely on an a priori opposition between the domains; inasmuch as these are useful labels, they are simply heuristic tools.

This solution is implicit in feminist analyses that hold that women's status is molded by intentional action and interaction; that the domestic domain is more than the locus of reproduction and socialization; and that the public sector is a product of interhousehold exchanges undertaken primarily or in part by women. It is also represented in methodological individualist sociologies of the family. Nevertheless, despite its appeal, the transactional approach has been censured on several grounds: for its unremittingly utilitarian conception of *homo economicus* as a rational actor, free to enter into self-interested transactions without the constraints of class, gender, or anything else; for its arbitrary selection of exchange as the generative source of culture and society; for its circularity in treating value as both the motivation for, and a product of, interactional processes.

Although it is indefensible to treat the domains as invariant, the converse is no more acceptable. For if domestic and political structures *were* purely the product of individual transactions, it would be difficult to explain their continuity, in particular societies, over the long run. After all, familial arrangements, for all their diversity, tend to have deep institutional and ideological foundations; they are not the object of perpetual reinvention. This is not to deny that processes of transaction have the capacity to realize concrete social forms, or that they may alter the content of relations and values. Moreover, individuals may indeed perceive their contexts as presenting them with more or less free choices, and may see their own actions as being primed by pragmatic interest. But to view social orders, analytically, as the outcome of cumulative exchanges confuses the world of subjective appearances with the structures and forces that produce it (Comaroff and Roberts 1981: 31ff).

The systemic solution posits that the domestic domain—its form and substance, as well as its relationship to the public sector—is conditioned by the total social order of which it is part. This alternative is the most difficult to typify, partly because it is the least developed in either feminist discourse or kinship theory. In addition, it has several potential variants. At the risk of oversimplification, I shall explore two of these, both of radical origin and orientation.

One variant builds upon Meillassoux's (1972, 1975) and Terray's (1972) characterizations of precapitalist orders as systems of domination (see also Bourdieu 1977) in which processes of production and reproduction shape household and interhousehold arrangements. For Meillassoux, the essence of such systems lies in elders' control of the labor of youths and the fertility of women, largely through their monopoly of marital exchanges. This claim and the criticisms it has raised are familiar enough not to require reiteration. More to the point, some scholars have drawn useful insights from it. Thus, Collier (n.d.) argues that political economies are indeed orders of institutionalized inequality; that marriage exchanges, of both objects and services, are not only the means by which various forms of material dependency and power are realized but also moments of social reproduction; and that the processes that yield asymmetries are masked in positive cultural values, such that those who suffer subordination conspire in their own predicament. Collier's analysis of three classical Plains Indian systems indicates that marital exchanges, productive structures, and household relations also vary systematically with contrasts in politico-legal organization. In other words, the nature of the domestic domain and its relationship to extradomestic institutions are shown to stem from the total constitution of historically specific political economies.

This solution, again, offers a clear prescription for addressing the domestic/public dichotomy. It suggests that this dichotomy may be grasped by examining the underlying structures that reproduce concrete social arrangements, for it is these structures that fashion the observable relations and ideologies subsumed in such "institutions" as the "household" and "public sector." Where discrete domains occur—and their existence is no longer taken for granted—they are not to be understood by analogy to Western forms; they must be analyzed, in their own right, within their appropriate historical and cultural contexts.

For all its obvious promise, however, this alternative remains provisional. It deals with prestate, precapitalist formations of limited range and accounts only for their reproduction, not for their transformation in response to either internal processes or external forces. What is more, it evokes a vision of economy and society in which human action is determined entirely by existing structures. I shall return to these points after discussing the second variant of the systemic approach.

This variant, which grows out of the radical feminist writings of Sacks (1975), Reiter (1975; Rapp 1979), and others, also holds that the content of the domestic sphere and its articulation with the public domain are determined by the particular social order of which it is part. But the major concern here is with the broad sweep of human history. Where it is found, goes the argument, the private/public dichotomy expresses specific social contradictions and values (Rapp 1979: 510ff); it is an ideological construct that originates in "necessary productive . . . relations" but in disparate proportions over time and space.

Neither Sacks nor Reiter accords the dichotomy any great significance in prestate or preclass systems. Although Sacks notes that domestic relations are affected by the disposition of property, the organization of public and domestic labor, and the orientation of production to use or exchange, she holds that "the domestic and social spheres of life are not really independent" in such systems (1975: 228). For Reiter, prestate societies are based on two sets of ties, kinship and location. In them, there is an incipient "sexual division of labor: kinship-as-politics belongs to men, kinship-as-household-organization belongs to women. It is here that I see the basis for an elaborate distinction between private and public domains in state . . . societies" (1975: 276). Anthropologically orthodox though this may sound, Reiter is in fact arguing that the domains are foreshadowed, but not realized, in prestate orders. With the simultaneous rise of states and classes, the development of distinct sectors is an ineluctable—if uneven—process: "A state system must be structured to ensure that the acquisition of resources by an elite is institutionalized, and is, to a large extent, accepted. . . .

One of the mechanisms that underwrites the control of a central power over the minds of its population is the separation of society into public and private spheres. State structure and its functions are defined as public. . . . Reproducing and sustaining those people whose labor and goods are essential to that structure is defined as a private function" (1975: 277–78). In contrast to prestate society, where economy, polity, and religion are all "familized," "in state society, these spheres emerge as separate and public while the family becomes privatized" (1975: 278).

This distinction, then, represents a "cultural expression of the real relations in peoples' lives," relations of subordination and the exploitation of the many by the few. Whereas the specific ideological substance of such relations depends on the mode of state formation—and is mediated by prior cultural forms (Rapp 1979: 510ff) —some division between public and private spheres inevitably results from the growth of centralized polities. This process occurs in "early and archaic states" but reaches its apotheosis under industrial capitalism (1975: 279). Sacks develops a similar theme but focuses more directly on the transformation of relations of production—and, by inference, the extraction of surplus value—involved in class formation. The latter process, which accompanies the rise of production for exchange and demands the constant regeneration of labor power, leads to a bifurcation of domains: men come to be located in social production (in the public sector) and women are confined to domestic work for "private" use, which underwrites the sustenance and renewal of labor power. It is thus that the modern family, as economic and social unit, assumes its ideological and organizational character, and structures of gender and class inequality are defined.

Like the other variant, this one suggests that comparative systemic analysis will establish why, in different places and epochs, the domains assume such varying character. Even though the first addresses prestate/preclass society while the second focuses on state/class polities, both see domestic and family organization as an historical product; and, just as the second variant does not deny that domestic arrangements in prestate systems differ according to existing relations of production, exchange, and inequality, the first does not hold that a distinction between domains is a necessary feature of such systems. There is, in sum, little in either that would contradict the other.

In light of the shortcomings of the comparative and transactional

solutions, might we then conclude that the systemic alternative sat-
isfactorily resolves the problem of "rethinking" the distinction between the domains? A synthesis of its variants certainly seems to
offer a persuasive way to treat the problem in comparative perspective. It distinguishes carefully between Western *ideological* constructs, whose roots it illuminates, and units of analysis that may
explicate similarities and variations in social systems; it shuns universalistic assumptions about the human family and gender asymmetries, the origins of societal forms, and the utilitarianism of *homo
economicus*; and, ideally, it integrates the historical, structural, and
cultural analysis of the interconnections between domestic arrangements, relations of gender and class, and systems of production and exchange.

All this amounts to a heady program: what might be its limitations? Although I concur with many aspects of the systemic approach—above all, its focus on total formations and their historicity—I maintain three reservations. First, this solution still remains
largely schematic and leaves much as yet unspecified. Second, the
radical dichotomy between prestate, preclass systems and state
structures echoes the division of human societies into binary
categories—hot/cold, complex/simple, open/closed—so common
and so commonly criticized in anthropological imagery (Goody
1977: 1ff). Thus, precapitalist orders are viewed as being capable
only of reproducing themselves, they are ("kinship") societies to
which history happens under the impact of external forces, not
ones which have a historicity of their own. This has many implications, one of which is especially salient here. If such systems *are*
only capable of their own reproduction, it follows that social practice can do nothing but realize existing structures. But it is not only
in prestate contexts that practice is thus ordained. The account
given of the rise of states and classes implies that social action and
sociocultural transformation are determined in a similarly mecha-
nistic vein. Insofar as people make their own history, they do so as
marionettes acting out a structurally scripted tableau.

This, immediately, evokes a number of great debates—between
normative and interactionist sociology; between what Worsley
(1980) dubs "systems" and "Promethean" Marxism; and between
structuralist and phenomenological culture theories. For now, the
point is simply that the systemic approach stands in danger of egre-
gious reductionism until it provides some basis on which to deal

with the variabilities in social systems of a single "type"; with the potential of human actors to transform their social orders; with the effect of preexisting sociocultural forms on the historical destiny of any society; and with the subtle changes wrought by a society's encounter with alien systems, especially under colonialism. These clauses are all of a piece. They are the essential demands of a dialectical representation of historical systems—and of the social and material relations entailed in them.

Third, although I agree that the emergence of the domestic/public dichotomy accompanies processes of class formation, its exclusive association with the rise of mature states may be misleading, for the complex dynamics of noncapitalist orders may thereby be ignored or obscured. The following ethnographic case not only makes this specific point but illustrates my argument for a dialectical approach to the analysis of structural domains, family and household organization, and gender relations. This case describes the social system of the Tshidi Barolong, a South African Tswana people, at three periods in their history.

IV

The Tshidi chiefdom of the early twentieth century may be analyzed at two levels. At one level, it consisted in the social and material forms of a lived-in world, a world of values and interests, conventions and relations, conflicts and constraints. From within, it was perceived as a negotiable and individualistic universe. Despite an elaborate administrative hierarchy and a repertoire of norms to govern interaction, relations and rank were frequently contested, and groups and alliances were seen to reflect coincident interest. Beneath these surface forms, at another level, lay an order of constitutive principles—at once a *langue* of signs and categories and a set of organizational forms—that structured social and economic arrangements and inscribed a contradiction at the core of both sociocultural order and political economy.* This contradiction not only motivated social action, but underlay the everyday workings of the system at large.

Two ethnographic facts illuminate the contradictory character of

---

*See, for example, Comaroff (1982) and Comaroff and Roberts (1981). Limitations of space make it impossible to offer annotation in support of this summary account. The early twentieth-century data and their documentary bases are discussed in Comaroff (1973), Comaroff and Comaroff (n.d.), Comaroff (n.d.), J. Comaroff (1985).

the sociocultural order. First, Tshidi relational categories were founded upon an irreducible opposition between agnation and matrilaterality. This opposition had wide symbolic and pragmatic ramifications. In its social aspect, agnation signified ties of rivalry and inimical interest between ranked, but broadly equal, individuals; in fact, descent groups were little more than genealogically defined status orders, seniority in them determining access to position throughout the administrative hierarchy. In this respect, agnation, and the rules of rank it embodied, provided the cultural terms in which men had necessarily to negotiate and legitimize their standing. In addition, the agnatic nexus was linked ideologically with public activity: it was a male context wherein actors sought to "eat" each other by material and mystical means. By contrast, matrilaterality was female-centered and associated with the house and its confines. Unlike agnatic relations, which were always ranked and subject to management, matrilateral relations were unranked and morally nonnegotiable; they connoted supportiveness and complementarity, often between unequals.

The full salience of these categories can be understood only in light of the second ethnographic fact: Tshidi encouraged all forms of cousin marriage, including marriage with a father's brother's daughter. The general implications of such endogamic unions are well known: they transform agnatic relations into multiple bonds that are at once agnatic, matrilateral, and affinal; they blur the boundaries of descent groups and segments within them; they place the onus for the contrivance of social, political, and economic relations on the household; and they individuate the social field. However, for the Tshidi, among whom cousin marriages wove an especially dense web of overlapping connections, this yielded a paradox: how were these multiple bonds to be reconciled with the radical opposition between agnation and matrilaterality? After all, the two modes of relationship entailed not merely different but mutually exclusive social conventions.

The simple answer is that they could not be reconciled. The contradiction between cultural categories and social realities demanded that the Tshidi manage relations, and reduce them to some definition, in the contexts of everyday life. Nor was this a matter of volition; individuals were compelled to designate others as senior or junior agnates, matrilaterals, affines, or outsiders. It follows that these labels reflected the negotiated content of relations. Thus, if two households came to be in a clearly hierarchical relationship—if their bond was unequal enough to preclude rivalry—a matrilateral label was applied; if they were in a more equal and competitive relationship, agnatic terms were used, relative seniority signifying the "state of play" between them. Affinity was stressed in a partnership of symmetrical interest, and remote agnation described ties that had lapsed or had never existed. Of course, the parties involved could contest and try to renegotiate their bond; such efforts were a pervasive feature of social life.

This illuminates the dualistic nature of Tshidi society. Since its construction made relations inherently ambiguous and contradictory, Tshidi could not but act on their world, and so appear as social managers; the social and ideological stress on individualistic, utilitarian management was entailed in the logic of the system itself, not in some "very general [human] motive" (Leach 1954: 10). And yet, because relations always came to be labelled according to their negotiated content—and thereby defined with reference to received cultural categories (agnation, matrilaterality, etc.)—they ultimately did conform to normative expectation. For instance, the Tshidi claim that a man and his mother's brothers never fight was true; if they had fought, they would have been agnates, not matrilaterals. Similarly, although position and office were often contested, the outcome was always rationalized according to the rules of agnatic rank that underpinned the administrative hierarchy. As a result, the social universe could appear both as a structured order of relations and as a fluid social field.

The construction of that universe also shaped intentional activity and the values to which it was directed. Thus, the negotiation of agnatic rank was expressly motivated by its capacity to determine rights in people and property. But, whereas agnation charted the distribution of social and material resources, matrilateral relations were crucial to political success: without matrilateral connivance, there was little prospect of coping with, let alone "eating," agnatic rivals. The creation of strong ties of this kind, therefore, was perceived as a primary objective. If they could be secured by transforming agnates into client matrilaterals—and there were recognized means for doing so—all the better. From an individual standpoint, it gave the senior party subordinates where before he had antagonists; for the client, it might provide access to wealth and influence that were otherwise unavailable. Predictably, the production of inequality in this vein was seen as the optimal outcome of social management, at least by those, usually of the ruling cadres, who succeeded in harnessing it to their own ends. From the analytic perspective, its consequence was the replacement of competitive relations among ranked—but broadly equal—agnates with ties of complementary and unequal interest.

Inasmuch as the contrivance of relations held the key to property and position, marriage and affinity were seen to offer a ready context in which such relations could be negotiated. The structure of conjugal choice, in fact, reflected the major avenues of social management open to males. Three options were entertained and, because affinity involved a potential partnership between households, each had different connotations: unions between unrelated spouses implied the attempt to forge alliances beyond the field of close kin; those between spouses defined as matrilaterals entailed the perpetuation of existing relations of complementarity; and those between spouses defined as agnates opened the way for rivals to seek to reduce each other to (matrilateral) clientage. While managerial activity was not confined to the sphere of marriage and affinity, this range of choice indicates that social practice had three paradigmatic moments: the creation of new alliances between equals; the reproduction of inequalities; and the effort to transform ties of relative equality into asymmetrical ones.

As this suggests, the Tshidi system contained contradictory tendencies toward hierarchy and egalitarianism. Moreover, these two tendencies had to be realized in some measure *relative* to each other; and, since this could not remain constant, the social universe was always in flux. Clearly, the constitution of the system could not determine the precise contours of the everyday world at any moment in time: that depended on social practice. And practice, in turn, was conditioned as much by the exigencies of political economy as it was by the signs and categories of the sociocultural order.

The Tshidi political economy was also founded on a contradiction—in this case, between the centralized controls over the community vested in the chiefship and the social ecology of production. Ideally, all households were domiciled in villages and dispersed to their fields for the agricultural cycle. The regulation of annual movement was a chiefly prerogative which, albeit in the productive disinterest of the population, was closely protected by ruling cadres wherever possible. A century earlier, women had been assigned to cultivation, gathering, and domestic work; young men and serfs had hunted and herded cattle, the prime medium of symbolic and material exchange, under the direction of free adult men. However, the introduction of the plow and enforced labor migration changed this pattern and, by 1900, the household cultivated together as a group. The tendency of the prevailing social order to individuate domestic units was also reflected in relations of production and property; and it was visibly reinforced by the effects of colonialism and capitalist penetration.

Furthermore, when larger cohorts of workers were needed, reciprocal arrangements were usually made between households. Such reciprocities rarely involved agnatic rivals, but matrilaterals were a reliable source of aid. Indeed, powerful men could sometimes establish a semipermanent work force, and generate surpluses, by exacting labor from matrilateral clients, other "partners," and serfs. As this implies, social management had a direct expression in economy: just as the individuation of households was reflected in material relations, so the "eating" of people amounted to the social production of a labor force. And yet, because the universe was highly fluid and competitive, it was difficult for anyone to sustain a position of prominence: the emergence of individuated inequalities was not itself a sufficient condition for the rise of a stable dominant class, save under specific conditions.

Although relations of production emphasized the primacy of households, residential arrangements and chiefly control over seasonal movement constrained domestic activities. The Tshidi themselves saw these centralized constraints to be inimical to their interests in two respects. First, in a dryland ecology with marginal and uneven rainfall, the timing of arable operations is critical. Each day that passes between the first rains and the start of plowing lowers final yields. Given that the decision to allow dispersal depended on rainfall at the ruler's holdings, his announcement always was unduly late for many throughout the territory. Second, by regulating domicile and movement, a chief could ensure that selected workers gave tributary labor on royal lands before they scattered, thereby causing them yet greater loss. That the Tshidi were acutely aware of this is proven by their repeated enumeration of the advantages of perennial dispersal and by their haste to establish permanent rural homes whenever they could.

Still, the contradiction between centralization and decentralization was not simply an opposition between chief and populace. The village was the arena of social management, so that all activities conducted in pursuit of property and position affirmed existing sociospatial arrangements. The contradiction inhered, rather, in the *structure* of Tshidi economy and society. But it was pragmatically expressed in the political context, in which chiefly legitimacy was the constant object of evaluation and negotiation (see Comaroff 1975). Folk theory had it that the rights of chiefs, as measured in the willingness of the populace to execute their commands, varied according to their proven performance, and it is certainly true that the extent of their authority fluctuated widely within and between reigns. Significantly, when a ruler suffered a cumulative loss of legitimacy and surrendered control over executive processes, he would eventually be unable to regulate domicile and movement. It was then that households were apt to scatter, returning only when centralized authority was reestablished.

I stress, however, that power relations and executive control were not determined purely by rhetorical exchanges or political debates. Rather, their logic derived from the dynamic interrelationship of political economy and sociocultural order. Chiefly dominance and centralization in the political economy both necessitated and conditioned the sociocultural tendency toward hierarchy; decentralization and weak rule were linked to the tendency toward the egalitarian individuation of the social field (Comaroff 1982; Comaroff and Comaroff n.d.).

For example, when the social field was highly individuated, it was difficult for any ruler to exercise effective political control, for such control required the allegiance of high-ranking men who themselves commanded lower order constituencies. But when a measure of hierarchization existed, a chief could build a power base by making alliances with influential persons, by subordinating some of his close kin, and by dividing rivals within his own descent group. If successful, this permitted the placement of allies in important offices and consolidated a faction of "chief's men" for whom executive centralization, the extraction of surpluses, and the management of processes of chiefly evaluation became common cause. These allies might then exploit their positions to extend fields of unequal relations around themselves and to expand their economic enterprises.

Such activity, in turn, led to an increasing emphasis on asymmetrical alliance and to the encompassment of households within larger productive units and relations of material inequality. If, then, the emergence of a centralized political economy depended, initially, on the prevailing state of the social field, any movement toward centralization itself altered that field. Conversely, processes at the center could lead in the other direction: strong political opposition to a regime might weaken chiefly control and fragment the social field, thus allowing the population to disperse.

This schematic account of the Tshidi world has several interrelated implications. First and most broadly, it underscores the indissolubility of sociocultural order and political economy within a total system, a system whose underlying principles expressed themselves as categorical oppositions in culture, as contradictions in structure, and as unavoidable demands for action in social experience. In short, these principles motivated—in the dual sense of "impelled motion" and "gave meaning to"—everyday practice. And practice imparted form to social, productive, and political relations. Since such relations necessarily varied over time and space, it becomes clear, second, why Tshidi society took on diverse appearances—sometimes hierarchical and centralized, at other times individuated and egalitarian, with a weak authority structure at its core. These were contrasting transformations of a historical system with a complex constitution. The latter was not invariant either: it changed in response to both internal processes and external forces. Third, this account reveals how ideologies of egalitarian individualism and hierarchical centralism could coexist in the Tshidi universe. Both were partial representations of the manner in which the everyday world was constituted, each being an expression of one tendency within its contradictory scaffolding. In this sense, ideologies were neither "autonomous" nor "determined." They were an integral part of Tshidi society and its historicity, an irreducible element in the process whereby contradictory structures primed human action and were thereby fashioned into living relations.

The more specific implications of this ethnography flow from the fact that the nature of the "domains," family and household arrangements, and gender relations varied with the fluctuating Tshidi world. Such variations may be described, if only initially, in ideal-typical terms. When that world was highly centralized and hierarchical, the division between public and private sectors was well developed, and social life was marked both by extensive institutional activity and by an intense concentration on agnatic politics. This is not surprising: the production of inequality involved the contrivance of rank, and rank, to have currency, had to be situated in the administrative apparatus of the state. Since seniority in that apparatus gave access to public value—control over people and property, courts and councils, labor and land—a centralized state, agnatic politics, and a developed public sector were inseparable. Significantly, too, the elaboration of this sector was conditioned by its contrast to the domestic sphere: just as the cultural order opposed agnation to matrilaterality, so social practice underwrote a complex interdependence between them. Indeed, Tshidi held that the negotiation of agnatic relations by men depended on the backing of their matrilateral kin and the women who bore the linkages with them, the secretive strategizing associated with the privacy of the homestead, and the strength of the household itself. Hence, an active public sector placed great stress on the closure of the domestic unit—and on social and ritual efforts to protect it from intrusion—and sharpened the division between spheres.

By contrast, under conditions of decentralization, the public domain barely existed. Much of the populace dispersed and took little part in communal activities. During such periods, office-holding was largely a nominal affair, for the state apparatus was virtually moribund. Tribute could not be exacted, assemblies were rare and poorly attended, legislation had little prospect of execution, new administrative units were not created and existing wards became inactive, and agnatic politics were subdued, their context and the values to which they were addressed having been displaced. The major form of extradomestic interaction was the exchange of labor and goods and, for some, involvement in Christian sects with structures strikingly similar to domestic units.

The contrast was also expressed in family and domestic organization. In the decentralized mode, households varied in composition but were rarely nuclear or polygamous units; many included siblings and their families, aging parents, and other kin. In this mode, too, the rate of cousin marriage was low, which meant that a dense network of multiple ties was less likely to envelop the household. Thus, the managerial quality of the social field was reduced, and the mechanisms that integrated and stratified domestic units within the overarching polity were eclipsed. As a result, these units were as liable to interact with others on the basis of residential proximity as kinship.

Within the group itself, moreover, the division of labor by gender and age was less sharply drawn. Ranching was still done mainly by men and domestic work by women, but agricultural tasks were undertaken together by everyone present. Decisions about the use of resources also tended to involve all adults, not just the male head, and heritable property was commonly managed for most of the developmental cycle. Although the head had final control over the assets and members of the household, he usually shared it with his wife. In fact, given patterns of migrant labor, the unit was likely to remain under her jurisdiction for long periods during his absence and after his death.

In a centralized universe, however, households were more tightly incorporated into the administrative hierarchy of the state, each being part of an agnatic segment, a ward, and a section. Under such conditions, the activities and decisions associated with domestic groups in an individuated field became the concern of the segment or ward. Since an officeholder's power depended on his ability to control the flow of everyday life, headmen brought as much as possible within the purview of their courts and councils, bodies composed of male household heads. This produced a contradiction between the autonomy of domestic units and the demands of the state; it also engendered conflicts of interest among these units, since their access to value depended on the negotiated status of their heads. Thus, patterns of reciprocal exchange gave way to efforts to create debt and redefine rank; noncoincidentally, rates of kin marriage were high, households were enmeshed in multiple bonds demanding management, and disputes and sorcery allegations were frequent.

Domestic relations were also affected. For example, units were smaller during periods of decentralization because a married couple had to set up its own residence in order to obtain land and initiate the male's social career. Also, in situations of plural marriage, sons sought early independence to gain an advantage over half-siblings in their struggles for heritable assets and status. Fathers also had cause to encourage their offspring to leave; a man with adult sons and sons-in-law on whom to call for aid and support was greatly advantaged.

But the most stark effect lay in the division of labor itself. While Tshidi were resident in the village, the allocation of tasks by gender and age was unequivocal: women did domestic work, young males husbanded stock, and adult men engaged in managerial enterprises and public activities. During the arable season, however, social inequalities mediated relations of production. Affluent household heads stayed at the center, in order to advance their careers there, and their wives, children, and clients were sent out to cultivate. Poor families toiled together, much as in periods of decentralization; however, if they were in need or debt, males would go away to work and leave women to plow alone. Of course, this limited their yields and so reinforced inequalities and proto-class differences. In short, in a centralized field, the division of labor was sharper, and, because households were entailed in a structure of relations that drew males to the public arena and women to domestic and agricultural work, it was marked by gender and age asymmetry. Men tended to wield tight control over the household and take decisions on its behalf, and leadership passed directly to male heirs rather than through widows.

The degree of centralization also had a clear impact on the tendency toward gender asymmetry. Under decentralization, when the public sector was absent and the integrity of domestic units was emphasized, this tendency was largely invisible: the division of labor was less markedly sex-linked; women participated in decision-making processes, which usually took place in the household, and exercised control over their own conjugal choices; males and females were not rigidly separated in everyday social life; and the proportion of female-headed units was high. The more centralized the political economy, however, the greater the gender asymmetry. Most significantly, women were debarred from public arenas and confined to the house and the marginality of the fields; they could not manage cattle, the premier medium of transaction; they were treated as minors and excluded from decision-making at all levels; and their marriages were arranged by others.

In summary, gender and age asymmetries inhered in the very logic of a centralized universe. The elaboration of the state apparatus not only yielded a distinction between public and private spheres but also integrated households into a ranked administrative hierarchy according to the conventions of agnatic seniority. This meant that the social and material situation of any household depended on the status of its head, which made the negotiation of men's position the central theme of the political process. Men were drawn into the public sector to manage their resources on behalf of their households—in particular, their children's marriages, their cattle, and their arable wealth—whereas women and youths were relegated to the production of those resources. If males failed in their managerial activities, they too were excluded from the public sector and forced to alienate their labor. If they succeeded, they increased the resource base of the household, accumulating both wealth and clients.

I have discussed the nature of domains, family and household organization, and gender relations in terms of ideal-typical contrasts in order to demonstrate that these were interdependent elements of a total, dynamic social system. But precisely because this is so, it is necessary next to examine the dialectics of that system. For, from the perspective of the Tshidi, relations within and between households, their political and economic encompassment in the state, and the exigencies of gender and age were not abstract correlates of their social order. They were the lived-in forms of the everyday world. As such, they contained, in microcosm, all the contradictory features of that world and were at once the arenas for, and the objects of, social practice in response to the status quo.

This was vividly exemplified, in a centralized universe, in the reaction of poor commoner and junior royal men to the constraints imposed on them by chiefly regulation of movement and by their subordination in a network of unequal relations. Essentially, two alternatives presented themselves. One was to seek advancement by slowly renegotiating their rank in relation to erstwhile seniors. But in order to do so, they had to gain the support of their wives, adult children, and matrilateral kin through cooperation or coercion (Comaroff and Roberts 1981: chaps. 5, 6). Either way, this involved making the domestic unit—replete with gender asymmetries and a highly segregated division of labor—into a political base for males in the public arena. The effect of such activity within and upon households, even where it failed, was to affirm the centralized state.

The other alternative was to withdraw entirely from the social field. Although this was easiest when a regime was weak and could not hold people at the capital (Comaroff 1975), a household head could always resist centralization by not participating in ward affairs. A strong headman might avert this, but, if enough groups withheld their involvement, the officeholder's loss of authority might be so great that the ward would become politically inactive, thereby weakening the state at large. In its social aspect, a strategy of withdrawal entailed the avoidance of agnatic interaction and kin marriage, with all their inevitable embroilments. Above all, though, this strategy depended on, and in turn affected, domestic organization itself, for it required a distinct division of labor, modes of property holding, and familial politics. This confirms Nelson's point that the conflation of the private with the domestic and the public with the political is misleading. The construction of household relations, here as elsewhere, was a profoundly political matter. Indeed, the politics of the family and politics in the public sector always condition each other.*

The same analysis is applicable to gender relations. If we view the Tshidi world from a female standpoint, two considerations stand out. First, the greater the degree of centralization, the more acutely women in general suffered inequality. And, second, insofar as women cooperated, voluntarily or not, in the male-centered politics of interhousehold relations, most were placed in a position whereby they contributed to their own subordination. Like men, in other words, they were confronted by a contradiction, if a somewhat different one, that primed their action. Again, this was mediated by status differences. For a woman in a subordinate household, the options were clear, if not always palatable: either she supported her husband's managerial efforts—and there were compelling reasons to do so, despite the costs—or she could try to persuade him to adopt a strategy of withdrawal. When a man eschewed this second option, his womenfolk could challenge him with their noncooperation (and perhaps that of their children and kin) or the dissolution of the union. The outcome of such interactions depended on circumstance, but the fact that they occurred at all indicates that gender and household politics were two sides of one coin; they entered equally and complementarily into the internal dynamics of the system. To be sure, women's responses to the

---

*I have illustrated the point with respect to social practice in a centralized universe. However, the converse processes may be demonstrated for a decentralized social field; for an ethnographic example, see Comaroff (1982).

contradictions in their position had as great an impact on the social field as did men's.

In affluent households, the alternative to participation in the political process was not withdrawal; hence, women's strategies for shaping their lives and relations were different. Two factors affected their options. First, wealthy units could depend on client labor, which decreased their reliance on cultivation by wives and daughters; in addition, they tended to build their fortunes on cattle and other forms of wealth. Women in these households could thus resist participation in agriculture if they so desired. Second, the wife of a powerful man had strong potential sanctions against him: she was a vital link to his affines and, in the web of ties woven by cousin unions, to his allies and rivals. As a result, she could intervene either to threaten those ties or, conversely, to influence her kin to aid her husband's managerial efforts. Women who played the role of broker in this way often emerged as potent forces in intra- and interhousehold relations. Of course, the fact that some women became prominent did not remove gender asymmetry as a generic property of centralized polities. These women remained jural minors; and inasmuch as they became powerful—and contributed to the dominance of their households over others—they abetted the reproduction of a centralized order and the predicament of female members of subordinate units. As elsewhere, class and status differences created a situation in which the resolution of contradictions by individual women reinforced gender inequality at large; the only way to reduce that inequality was to subvert centralization itself.

In sum, then, the construction of gender relations was inseparable from the workings of the total system. It was an integral part of the process whereby the principles underlying the Tshidi social order motivated action and so fashioned concrete relations of widely varying and ever-changing contours. Before summarizing the implications of all this for the conceptualization of domains, for kinship theory, and for the analysis of gender, however, I must place these ethnographic data in broader historical context.

It goes without saying that the Tshidi system at the turn of this century was not an isolated "precapitalist formation." Like all societies for much of their history, it had been shaped alike by its own internal dynamics and by its encounter with external forces. A cen-

tury before, prior to settler or colonial penetration, the tendency toward centralization was more firmly entrenched, more regularly
reproduced, than that toward decentralization.* This is not to say
that the contradiction between these tendencies was absent—although it was not identical in content—or that it never produced a
fragmented polity. Tswana chiefdoms did disappear, and sometimes reappeared, of their own accord, and there is record of a
number of acephalous communities in the region. Nor is their history reducible to a pattern of oscillation of the sort described by
Leach (1954) for Highland Burma. The transformations of these
polities over the long run, due both to their interior working and to
their external relations, simply did not conform to a regular, me-
chanical movement between polar forms of social organization.

However, there were specific factors—stemming from the interaction of the Tshidi with the contemporary outside world—that favored hierarchy and chiefly dominance: the control exercised by
ruling cadres over the spoils of war and raiding, especially serfs and
cattle; the royal monopoly of cross-regional trade; and the existence
of alliances, military and marital, with other dynasties. Although
chiefs could never eliminate the tendency toward individuation
and were always vulnerable to enmities that could split the polity,
Tshidi society was more stratified in the early nineteenth century
than it was to be later. Gender and age asymmetries were highly
marked and symbolically inscribed in rites that were submerged in
periods of decentralization and were to disappear under colonialism (J. Comaroff 1985).

Inequalities also took on the form of class differences, differences
in access to the means of production and redistribution. For the
control of serf labor and trade goods by senior royals and commoner headmen—through the crucible of the chiefship—underwrote the subordination of the rest of the citizenry. Indeed, by supporting executive dominance, such controls further facilitated the
exaction of tribute and the hierarchical integration of domestic
units into the polity. All this, moreover, promoted rivalries among
households over rank—rivalries often intensified by kin marriage
and always rationalized with reference to agnatic status. It also encouraged patron-client relations between groups of unequal stand-

*For accounts of the Tshidi social order in the early nineteenth century and full
supporting documentation, see J. Comaroff (1985), Comaroff and Comaroff (n.d.),
and Comaroff (1973).

ing, expressed through the loan of cattle. In short, all the features of centralization were evident during much of this earlier era, and its realization was favored, if not guaranteed, by an external context that gave a dominant class the means to control the flow of value.

In the remaining years of the century, the Tshidi were gradually absorbed into the concentric spheres of colonial domination: the subcontinental economy, the British Empire, and the expanding world system. From the native perspective, this process had three interrelated facets. The first was the presence of missionaries, which had both a material and an ideological aspect. For the Tshidi not only were subjected to a Methodist vision of "civilization" shaped by English industrial capitalism but also were introduced to the plow and other technical innovations. The immediate impact of Christianity, as measured by numbers of converts or by the removal of such "barbarisms" as bridewealth and polygyny, was distinctly equivocal. But, in the long run, it laid the ground for important transformations. Specifically, the church became an alternate focus for political mobilization and for the rise of an anti-chiefly faction; the leadership of the congregation, equipped with mercantile and clerical skills, became the core of a small local bourgeoisie; the coming of the plow sharpened the contradiction between the demands of household production and centralized constraints, altered the division of labor by drawing men into agriculture, and facilitated cash cropping; and the ideological justification of the Protestant work ethic and the worth of money prepared the Tshidi for the labor market.

The second facet of the encompassment of the local system lay in the expansion of the regional economy and the growth, from the late-nineteenth century, of its mining and industrial sectors. The effects of this expansion on rural comunities are by now familiar: it led to the proletarianization of much of the black population, to their impoverishment and restriction to reservations from which labor migration could be regulated, and to the origins of modern apartheid. The means by which this situation was contrived, its bases in coercion and mystification, are well documented. Above all, they depended on the third facet of the process, the political agency of the colonial and post-colonial regimes.

Although the Tshidi had themselves sought imperial protection from Boer settlers, the establishment in the 1890's of a crown colony over the southern Tswana hastened their absorption into the sub-continental system. The British administration, followed by an independent South Africa in 1910, not only hastened the entry of Tshidi into the labor market by imposing taxes and levies but also had an impact on internal political processes. "Indirect rule" left the constitution of the polity intact, but it put an end to war and raiding—and, with it, the access of ruling cadres to their major external source of wealth and power, cattle and serfs. In addition, their trade monopoly was subverted by white merchants, who bought and sold grain and stock on terms disadvantageous to local producers. And, finally, chiefs were reduced from tribute receivers to tax collectors, from the judges in their own legal order to lower functionaries in a state judiciary, from politicians to civil servants.

These ideological, economic, and political agencies gradually eroded the mechanisms underlying centralization. Nonetheless, those mechanisms were not immediately removed: ruling cadres still enjoyed greater wealth than others, monopolized the allocation of land and authority, and dominated local political institutions. Some also earned new forms of income from trade and salaried work, and forged alliances through such arenas as the church. Furthermore, the cultural terms of social management—kinship categories, marriage arrangements, and so on—remained largely intact. Hence, although the indigenous political process was undermined—its demography altered by migrant labor and its content diminished by overrule—its principal *forms* were perpetuated. Nonetheless, as it became increasingly difficult to sustain a centralized order, the contradictions in the system became more acutely manifest. Thus, by the early-twentieth century, the dynamics of centralization and decentralization, of domestic organization and gender relations, of the private and public domains came to assume the character described above. For, as external processes took their course, the changes they wrought were incorporated into the cultural and practical logic of the Tshidi system.

The Tshidi world underwent further transformation as it was drawn yet more tightly into the regional political economy. Especially after 1948, the South African state asserted increasing control over such diverse features of everyday life as marriage and divorce, local legal procedures, and ranching practices. It also continued to denude chiefs and headmen of power, thereby undercutting the political order that had given form to internal social processes.

Moreover, by imposing additional levies and by allowing pressure on land and erosion to reach unprecedented levels, it seriously undermined agricultural and pastoral production. Established forms of social practice finally lost their salience; there was no point in social management, and hence in agnatic rivalries or kin marriage, once its context and material bases had been eliminated. As this implies, the mechanisms underlying hierarchical centralization disappeared entirely. Yet the rationale for perennial dispersal—optimal household production in a dryland ecology—had also been eclipsed. With the ebbing prospect of yielding subsistence crops from infertile soil, many households ceased plowing or did so on a very small scale. Thus, by the 1950's, the local system was no longer workable, its constitutive principles no longer able to motivate relevant forms of action. What remained was an impoverished community with no choice but to depend for survival on migrant labor.

This had a direct impact on the construction of domains, domestic arrangements, and gender relations. With the removal of the local political machinery, administrative units ceased to function as a public sector; wards and sections were reduced to mere residential neighborhoods, the archeology of a vanishing order. Insofar as the public sphere persisted at all, it was a creature of the South African regime, an imposed bureaucracy of "tribal authorities" and assemblies to which the Tshidi were peremptorily summoned, ostensibly to discuss policy. Few attended, though, most expressing their resistance in silent nonparticipation and in the one form of collective action allowed blacks under the law, Christian rituals (J. Comaroff 1985).

Equally marked transformations in domestic and gender relations were reflected in the division of labor. Since most men had become wage laborers, they were removed from the household and from its limited productive efforts for much of the time. Women, who were not allowed to join their husbands in the cities, had either to enter employment—usually as farm hands or domestic servants in nearby towns—or to eke out an existence through cultivation; the regulation of black wages made it impossible for households to live on the income of male "breadwinners." Consequently, families were divided for long periods and rarely lived as domestic units, which generally consisted of women and their children, or grandparents and grandchildren, with other kin and visiting husbands occasionally present. Like the household's strategies for economic and social survival, its membership, though typically female-centric, was a situational response to external pressure. Demonstrably, the removal of men to cities and the consignment of women to the rural "home" was a deliberate state policy that not only hindered the rise of a permanent black proletariat in "white" South Africa and depressed labor costs but also assured the reproduction of a conveniently placed reserve army of workers.

Under these conditions, too, gender relations were no longer the product of internal processes. Men and women had become proletarians and peasants, complementary fractions of an underclass within an overarching structure of inequality. Notwithstanding the association of women with the rural domestic sector and men with urban wage labor in the public sphere, their relations cannot be reduced to the language of symmetry or asymmetry, equality or dominance. All alike were caught up in an historical movement wherein the contradictions of a prior order gave way to those of an intrusive capitalist state—all, that is, except the small bourgeoisie which, unafflicted by the need to alienate its labor power, earned an income locally from trade, salaries, and commercial farming on the large holdings accumulated during the preceding century. This bourgeoisie had long been identified with the mission church and its ideology, and maintained a pattern of domestic and gender relations that resembled middle-class England more than anything to be found among the Tshidi.

v

This historical sketch is far from exhaustive. Still, by revealing the workings of the Tshidi system over both the short and long term, it encourages us to recast our understanding of the public and domestic domains, family and household organization, and gender relations. Indeed, the Tshidi case affirms and amplifies the conclusions of my earlier critical discussion. It underscores the irremedial limitations of the comparative and transactional approaches: since neither addresses the subtle dialectic of structure and practice that gives form to all historical systems, both reduce social existence to a shadow of its true complexity. Likewise, the analysis speaks to the twin dangers of the systemic alternative. First, it repudiates the notion that the distinction between public and private spheres can occur only in capitalist or mature state formations; more generally, it warns against reducing noncapitalist orders to such caricatures as the self-reproducing "kinship society," the "tributary mode of production," or the "domestic community." And, second, by demonstrating that it is motivated human activity that realizes and transforms social arrangements, it establishes that the social process is *not* mechanically determined by structure. How, otherwise, do we account for radical fluctuations in the lived-in universe, for the processes that bring about these fluctuations, or for the contradictions that underlie them?

One last critical point warrants repetition. At the outset, I noted that social science imagery typically conflates the domestic/politico-jural distinction with other oppositions, such as private/public and family/polity. The Tshidi ethnography shows that this is misleading and that the classical conception of these domains is no longer defensible. Domestic relations are always affected by the exigencies of political economy, just as wider political and economic structures are predicated on the division of labor and the production of value within the household. The dynamics of historical practice weave together these two dimensions of the social system, a process that not only imparts substance to the domains but also establishes the very terms of their existence. The implication is that the emergence of a distinction between private and public sectors does not denote a "balance" between the domestic and the politico-jural, kinship and polity. Rather, it indicates a specific mode of vertical integration whereby elementary social units are incorporated in higher-order structures. And it is the *manner* of their incorporation that determines the ideological and social content of each domain.

Let me elaborate. Above all else, the Tshidi ethnography suggested that the distinction between domains was a function of the hierarchical centralization of the social world. For centralization entailed, by its very nature, an opposition between an encompassed ("domestic") sphere, the source of social value, and an encompassing ("public") sector in which the flow of that value was negotiated and regulated. Of course, the use of the terms "domestic" and "public" to describe these domains is an arbitrary use of Western folk categories. The former, put in more general terms, refers to culturally constituted units of production and social reproduction, the latter to the apparatus by which they are integrated into a centralized political economy. They are, in other words, distinct and complementary levels of a hierarchical social universe.

At the same time, the articulation of these levels and the content of the "domains" are not always the same. The precolonial Tshidi world, even at its most centralized, differed markedly in these respects both from its neocolonial counterpart and from capitalist Europe. In the first, households were integrated within higher-order structures through the politics of chiefly dominance, an ongoing process that generated a hierarchical field of relations and was buttressed by a specific division of labor. In contrast, centralization in the neocolonial context rested on a house forcibly divided: on the segregation, by a repressive state machinery, of men into the industrial labor market and women into the rural sector, where they cultivated for use and entered local employment. These two modes of centralization yielded quite different domestic forms, similar, perhaps, only in their position at the lowest level of systems in which the production of value was regulated from above.

This fact affirms the suggestion that the "domestic" is defined less by its intrinsic nature than by a total order of social and material relations. The point is underlined by considering the social architecture of mature capitalism, where centralization involves the commoditization of production and labor power, the organizational and ideological ascendance of market forces and, in variable measure, the executive agencies of the state. This, in turn, generates yet another transformation: the "domestic" becomes synonymous with the nuclear family and is subsumed into the division of productive and reproductive labor so familiar in the folk imagination of the West. Significantly, this transformation is found, in the Tshidi context, among the bourgeoisie, in whose collective consciousness the moral and social value of the monogamous family is deeply engraved.

Here, then, are three contrasting instances of centralization—the precolonial, the colonial/neocolonial, and the industrial capitalist—each with differently constructed "domains." But these are not taxonomic types, frozen in time. For, the very fact of hierarchical centralization implants a contradiction at the core of *any* social order, a tension that primes human action and, through it, shapes the surface contours of economy and society. Among the Tshidi, where the contradiction cast household autonomy against the structures of state authority, these contours were inherently fluid. The "domains," family and kinship arrangements, and gender relations—inseparable elements in the dialectics of social life—varied predictably along with related patterns of devolution and succession, communal ritual, and residence. Thus, an understanding of the logic of this covariance clarifies both short- and long-term diversities in household and family relations; the dynamics underlying the division of labor and gender asymmetries, and their connection to political processes; and the impact of practice, male and female alike, on the world.

This study of Tshidi thus confirms the significance of feminist critiques of orthodox anthropological percepts and concepts, and illustrates an analytic method in response to the vital challenge they pose. Creative anthropological discourse on any aspect of social being—be it family and kinship or gender relations, polity or economy, culture or ideology—depends finally on the ability to reveal the subtle logic of total social systems and their historicity.

Mixed Metaphors: Native and Anthropological Models of Gender and Kinship Domains

Sylvia Junko Yanagisako

THIS ARTICLE explicates native and anthropological models of gender and kinship domains in an attempt to locate them in a specific historical process of transformation.* I begin by bringing together two sets of analytical oppositions—each of which has occupied a central place in its field of study—to better display their common theoretical underpinnings as aspects of the same model of kinship and gender. The two analytic oppositions are the distinction between the "domestic" and the "public" spheres, which Michelle Z. Rosaldo identified as the structural framework necessary for arriving at an understanding of a universal sexual asymmetry, and the distinction between the "domestic (familial)" and the "politico-jural" domains, which Meyer Fortes identified as a heuristic framework for understanding kinship in all human societies. Although they share the same label for one of their categories, these two oppositions might seem to constitute rather different frameworks of analysis. One was formulated, above all, to address the problem—which has been traced at least as far back as Lewis Henry Morgan's research—"of how kinship and polity are interconnected in tribal society" (Fortes 1969: 219). The other was proposed as "a universal framework for conceptualizing the activities of the sexes" (Rosaldo 1974: 23). In the past decade, however, we have begun to recognize the gender model underlying our kinship analyses and the kinship model underlying our conception of gender domains (Yanagisako 1979; Yanagisako and Collier, this vol-

*This paper has benefited greatly from the comments of Jane Atkinson, Maurice Bloch, James Boon, Jane Collier, Donald Donham, Frank Dubinskas, James Fernandez, Jack Goody, Yukiko Hanawa, Thomas James, Marilyn Strathern, and Anna Lowenhaupt Tsing.

ume). Hence, we have become both more conscious and more suspicious of the parallels between the heuristic devices of what are purportedly different fields of study motivated by different analytic intentions.

The gendered character of the domestic/politico-jural opposition is reflected in Fortes's conception of the different types of normative premises regulating the two domains. Indeed, for Fortes, the defining feature of each domain is the character of its normative premise. Underlying the politico-jural domain are jural norms guaranteed by "external" or "public" sanctions that may ultimately entail force. The domestic or familial domain, in contrast, is constrained by "private," "affective, and moral norms, at the root of which is the fundamental axiom of prescriptive altruism" (Fortes 1969: 250–51). At the core of the domestic domain in "primitive societies" is the "matricentral cell" of a mother and her children (Fortes 1958: 8), which is the source of the affective and moral convictions permeating the entire sphere. The biological, reproductive, and inherently female core of the domestic domain is perhaps most apparent in the following admittedly speculative aside by Fortes:

If a person who is not a kinsman is metaphorically or figuratively placed in a kinship category, an element, or at least a semblance, of kinship amity goes with it. It is conceivable—and I for one would accept—that the axiom of amity reflects biological and psychological parameters of human social existence. Maybe there is sucked in with the mother's milk, as Montaigne opined, the orientation on which it ultimately rests. But this is not my subject (Fortes 1969: 251).

Although the biological and psychological parameters of human social existence and, in particular, the processes through which mothering generates kinship amity may not be Fortes's subject, assumptions about them pervade his conception of the domestic domain and its articulation with the politico-jural domain. It is hardly surprising, therefore, to find that other anthropologists have emphasized the reproductive, biological ("natural") constraints of the domestic domain. Raymond Smith, for example, suggested that "matrifocality" can be observed in the domestic relations of a wide range of societies because "mothering, or child-rearing, is the central activity of the domestic domain and is productive of the intense relations which pervade it" (1973: 140). For Maurice Bloch, "domestic kinship" is characterized by natural constraint, which is negated in the politico-jural domain (Bloch 1977: 291).

Finally, the gendered nature of the opposition is apparent from its usage by researchers who assume that female activities are "domestic" activities and groups in which females are found are "domestic" groups (Bender 1967: 498), whereas activities and groups from which females are excluded (or in which their participation is limited) belong to the politico-jural or some other extra-domestic domain. Evans-Pritchard, for one, excluded "the relations between the sexes and between children and adults" from his analysis of Nuer social structure because they "belong to an account of domestic relations rather than to a study of political institutions" (Evans-Pritchard 1940: 178).

Although Rosaldo (1974) drew no explicit link to Fortes's distinction or to any particular institutional model of kinship in her initial formulation of the domestic/public opposition, she later came to recognize the existence of that link along with its troubling analytical consequences (Rosaldo 1980). If she still found domestic/public "as telling as any explanation yet put forth" of universals in sexual asymmetry, she also traced its roots to a "Victorian theory [that] cast the sexes in dichotomous and contrastive terms, describing home and women not primarily as they were but as they had to be, given an ideology that opposed natural, moral, and essentially unchanging private realms to the vagaries of a progressive masculine society" (Rosaldo 1980: 404).

Despite Rosaldo's reconceptualization of her initial proposal and her misgivings about a distinction that, following Reiter (1975), she came to view as the ideological product of a particular social formation, the domestic/public contrast continues to be used in anthropology and related disciplines as if it constituted an empirically observable, uniform difference in the orientations and interests of men and women in most, if not all, societies (Yanagisako and Collier, this volume). Ortner and Whitehead (1981: 7), for example, suggest that the domestic/public distinction is one of the "sets of metaphorically associated binary oppositions" that recur frequently in gender ideologies. Like the nature/culture opposition (Ortner 1974) and the contrast between "self-interest" and the "social good" (Strathern 1980), the domestic/public formulation is said to derive from the central sociological insight "that the sphere of social activity predominantly associated with males encompasses the sphere predominantly associated with females and is, for that reason, culturally accorded higher value" (Ortner and Whitehead

1981: 7). Which one of these oppositions appears in the idiom of a particular culture is said to be an empirical question. However, "all could be present without inconsistency; all are in a sense transformations of one another" (Ortner and Whitehead 1981: 8).

In this article, I hope to shed further light on the "gender" opposition of domestic/public and the "kinship" opposition of domestic/politico-jural by analyzing them together. For by examining the interpenetration of models of kinship and polity and models of gender domains, we may see more clearly their relation to particular social formations and historical transformations. Such clarity is of crucial importance, because failure to recognize these models as the products of a particular culture undergoing a particular historical transformation can lead to faulty analysis of cultural oppositions that emerge from cultures undergoing different transformations. As Strathern (1980) and others have convincingly argued with regard to the nature/culture opposition, we cannot assume that the terms we use "identify straightforwardly a genuine analytical focus" (Bloch and Bloch 1980: 25); rather, we need to examine our own concepts and the historical processes that have produced their ambiguities and their social implications.

My attempt at such an examination here reverses anthropological convention by using "native" explications of gender domains to illuminate anthropological models of gender and kinship. This reversal is less presumptuous than it might appear, however, given that my natives have participated—albeit in a particular way—in the same historical processes out of which our analytic oppositions have emerged. By allowing two generations of Japanese Americans to explicate anthropological categories, I hope to ground a rather sweeping hypothesis about the transformation of conceptions of gender and kinship in Western industrial-capitalist states in the daily discourse of the members of a middle-class, urban community in northwestern America.

The Two Generations: Issei and Nisei

Japanese Americans are one of those rare populations in which historical events have rendered kinship-defined generations identical with birth cohorts. The political history of Japanese immigration to the United States created relatively discrete, nonoverlapping generations. The concentration of the marriages of the first generation during the period from 1907 to 1924 in turn concentrated the births of the second generation and created a distinct bimodality in the age structure of the pre–Second World War population. Second-generation marriages were similarly concentrated and so produced a third generation—the vast majority of whom were under thirty in 1970. The discreteness of the generations continues to be recognized by Japanese Americans and is reflected in their usage of distinct terms (Issei, Nisei, and Sansei) for each generation. In this article, I will consider only the first two generations: Issei and Nisei.

Like other Japanese American communities on the West Coast, the Seattle community originated in the 1890's with the immigration of young and, for the most part, unmarried men from farming households or small-town, entrepreneurial households in the southern prefectures of Japan. During the initial "frontier period" of the community from 1890 to 1910, these men worked primarily as wage laborers. Between 1910 and 1920, the number of males decreased as a result of the "Gentlemen's Agreement" between the United States and Japan, which was intended to halt any further immigration of Japanese laborers. In an historical irony of unintended consequence, however, the decrease in the male population was more than compensated for by the arrival of wives and brides and, shortly thereafter, high birth rates.

The period of marriage and family building among the Issei coincided with the economic boom accompanying U.S. entry into the First World War. In Seattle, the Issei moved quickly to establish small retail businesses and services catering to the large influx of white workers as well as to the Japanese farmers in the surrounding rural areas. Whether marriage preceded or followed the movement from wage labor for any individual Issei, for the Seattle Issei as a whole, marriage was historically linked with the shift to entrepreneurship. But the expansion of the community was short-lived. The growing anti-Japanese sentiment that already had led to the passage of discriminatory laws in California brought about similar restrictions in Washington. In 1921, the state of Washington passed the Anti-Alien Land Law denying foreign-born Japanese the right to lease or own land. A year later, in *Takao Ozawa* v. *United States*, the U.S. Supreme Court upheld the ineligibility of Japanese immigrants to citizenship through naturalization. After passage of the Immigration Act of 1924 halted immigration from Japan, the economy of the Seattle Japanese American community was further crippled and its population growth limited to the births of the second generation.

Up until the Second World War, the Seattle Issei presented a collective tale of small-business enterprise in early-twentieth-century America. In the 1930's, two-thirds of Issei men and women were self-employed entrepreneurs in "trades" or "domestic and personal services" (Miyamoto 1939:71). Their businesses were restricted to a narrow range of service-oriented enterprises, including hotels for single workingmen, groceries, grocery stands, produce houses, restaurants, greenhouses, gardening services, barbershops, laundries, and peddling routes. Less than twenty percent of the Issei were wage earners at the outbreak of the Second World War.

The predominance of small-business enterprise among the Seattle Issei encouraged high rates of female participation in income-earning work during the childbearing and childrearing years. Fifty percent of Issei wives worked in family businesses or wage-earning jobs during their first year of marriage, and this percentage rose until it reached a peak of 75 percent in the twentieth year of marriage.* Within this general rise in the percentage of women engaged in income-earning work in addition to their own housework, patterns of work in family business and work for wages showed different trends. There was an increase in the percentage of women working in family businesses, but a decline in the percentage of women working for wages. Women whose husbands were entrepreneurs worked more continuously in productive activities than did women whose husbands were wage earners (Yanagisako 1985).

The events following immediately upon the outbreak of the Second World War destroyed the community's entrepreneurial character. The imprisonment of the Japanese population on the West Coast, immigrant Japanese citizens and second-generation U.S. citizens alike, resulted in the forced sale or abandonment of businesses and the liquidation of assets. From studies of the "relocation camps" and of the resettlement period that followed the camps' closure in 1945, we know of the disruption of family life, the decline in the first generation's political and parental control, and the fi-

---

*These figures are based on a sample of 24 Issei married couples interviewed in Seattle between 1973 and 1975. For more information on the study, see Yanagisako 1977 and 1985.

nancial and social hardships Japanese Americans faced trying to re-
build their communities. We know, too, that the majority of the Japanese Americans who returned to Seattle after the war did not
resurrect their businesses, but instead moved into wage and salaried employment (Miyamoto and O'Brien 1947).

By the end of the war, the majority of Issei men were over fifty-
five years old; the majority of Issei women were in their late forties
and early fifties. Most of the couples who had small family businesses before the war were forced back into the unskilled, low-
paying jobs in which they had started their work histories in America. Less than a third of the men and women in my Issei marriage
sample who had been self-employed entrepreneurs at the outbreak
of the war were in the same line of business in 1946, one year after
the war had ended and the camps had closed. Two-thirds of the
men were unemployed or had taken wage-earning jobs as janitors,
kitchen helpers, and handymen. A third of the women were unemployed housewives, and half of the women had become domestic servants, seamstresses in garment factories, and cannery
workers.

After the war, the children of the first generation, who by the
1960's surpassed whites in median school years completed, moved
into predominantly white-collar, managerial, and professional occupations. In Seattle today, there are higher percentages of college
graduates, white-collar employees, and professionals among Nisei
men than among white men. Less than 29 percent of second-
generation men are self-employed businessmen. Nisei women
evince even lower rates of self-employment; the vast majority of
employed Nisei women are in secretarial, clerical, and low-level
managerial positions. Because of the dramatic turn of events
caused by the wartime imprisonment and its aftermath, Nisei
wives in different marriage cohorts (prewar, wartime, resettlement, and post-resettlement) exhibited very different rates of employment (from 8 percent to 93 percent) during the first year of marriage. Over time, however, these four Nisei marriage cohorts
converged toward the same pattern of female employment: a
steady decline in the percentage of wives employed until the tenth
year of marriage (when it reaches a low of around 15 to 20 percent)
followed by a steady rise to the twentieth year of marriage (when it
reaches a peak of around 65 to 75 percent).

Issei Gender Domains in Marriage: Inside and Outside

Marriage for the Issei is above all a relationship that brings together the different, but complementary, gender domains of women and men, which, in turn, are conceptualized in terms of the opposition between "inside" and "outside." By far the most common way for the Issei to describe the responsibilities, activities, and concerns of spouses is to say that wives take care of things "inside" the house, home, or family and that husbands take care of things "outside" those spheres. When using English, the Issei say "inside the house," "inside the family," or "inside the home" in reference to the wife's domain, and "outside the house," "outside the home," or "outside the family" in reference to the husband's domain. When Japanese is spoken, the phrases "uchi no koto" (things inside, things indoors, or things of the household) and "soto no koto" (things outdoors or outside) are used to describe this opposition. Sometimes, however, only the wife's domain is clearly specified as including matters inside the house, home, or family; the husband's domain is said to include "everything else."*

*The phrase "uchi no koto," which several of the Issei used to describe the responsibilities of wives, can be interpreted in several ways. "Uchi" can be translated as "the inside," "the interior," or "one's house," "one's home," or "one's household." The addition of "no" (possessive marker) and "koto" (things) makes it possible to interpret "uchi no koto" as referring to things physically inside the physical structure of the house, things indoors in general, or things *of* the home or household (and not necessarily physically inside them). Similarly, "ie no naka no koto" can be interpreted in a number of ways depending on whether "ie" is taken to refer to the physical structure of the house, a home, a household, or a family. As it can mean any of these things or all of these things at the same time, it would be a mistake to pin our interpretation on any one literal, and narrow, translation.

The same is true of the meaning of the English phrases "inside the house," "inside the home," and "inside the family," which the Issei used to define the domain of wives. Here, as well, there is some ambiguity as to whether that domain is a physically circumscribed one (the interior of the physical structure of the house or the property on which the home sits) or a more socially circumscribed one (the relations within the family). In this paper, my explication of the meaning of such phrases as "inside the home" and "uchi no koto" is *not* the sum of my explication of the literal, dictionary definitions of each of these phrases and their constituent words. Rather, it is my analysis of the sum of the Issei *usages* of all these phrases—English and Japanese—in their discussion of the conjugal relationship and the domains of wives and husbands. For the above reasons, I have not emphasized the literal definitions of terms such as the Japanese term of reference for one's wife (kanai)—which means, literally, "inside the house"—and the term of reference for another man's wife (okusan)—which means the person (honorific, "san") of the "interior" or "depths" (oku).

In its most narrow sense, the opposition between the female inside sphere and the male outside sphere reflects the spatial location of tasks around the home that wives and husbands assume. Everything inside the walls of the house is said to be the responsibility of women; everything outside the walls is the responsibility of men. Women do the dishes, cook meals, iron, sew, and clean everything in the house. Men do yard work, maintain the external appearance of the house and its structural soundness, and wash and repair the automobile. The division of indoor and outdoor tasks extends to work in the family business. If a couple had operated a hotel, for example, the wife took care of cleaning everything inside the building, and her husband took care of the exterior. If they operated a laundry, she worked in the back room, and he made the deliveries.

The spatial referent of the opposition has another broader meaning. Here, the boundary between "inside" and "outside" divides familial space from non-familial space. Both the home and family business are considered "inside," first, because they are controlled by the family. Thus, although a woman's work in the family business brings her in contact with people outside the family, it does so in a space that is controlled by the family and, thereby, separated from the non-familial world. Second, in interactional terms, work in a family business remains "inside" to the extent that a woman interacts primarily with family members or people with whom the family is familiar, even if she does so outside the home. A major disadvantage to women of work outside the family in wage-earning jobs is the necessity to interact with non-kin and strangers (employers, clients, fellow workers).

The outside domain of men comprises both the sphere of extra-familial activities and the interstice that links the household to individuals, groups, and institutions outside it. Politics, community organizations, and the construction of a social world outside the household are the proper concern of men, who bear the ultimate responsibility for the security and reputation of their households in that social world. A husband's activities outside the household provide him with a broad network of relationships—primarily with other males—that establishes his family's identity in the community. A wife needs no such extrafamilial relationships because her social identity is derived from her place within the family and from the public statuses of other family members.

There is yet another level of contrast between "inside" and "outside" within the household itself, however. The "inside" encompasses specific tasks like child care, housecleaning, and any of the routine, day-to-day chores that are considered necessary for the operation of the household but of little consequence for the family's relations with the larger social world. Thus, "inside" also refers to "small" actions of lesser consequence—including making minor purchases and decisions. Whereas women may pay bills and make daily purchases for the upkeep of the household, large and extraordinary financial decisions and decisions in the family business are left to men. Likewise, the care and supervision of small children, whose actions have little impact on relations outside the household, are viewed almost entirely as the responsibility of mothers. But when children begin to interact with the world outside the home, their behavior becomes the fathers' concern. Fathers, therefore, should make decisions about their children's education and occupations and their participation in churches, social clubs, and other community organizations.

Finally, "inside" and "outside" symbolize the different motives and orientations of women and men. Above all, a woman's proper motive for action is to provide for the well-being of her family. Indeed, motive appears to be the ultimate criterion for evaluating the gender correctness of female behavior. The propriety of a woman who goes outside the home to work or to engage in any social activity is judged according to whether she is acting out of concern for the family or seeking to satisfy other interests. As one Issei man stated, "If [a wife] wants to work because her family needs the money that's fine, but if she wants to work just to kill time or get out of the house, that's her problem." Accordingly, a woman who operates in the world outside the family, such as the woman who was a successful entrepreneur, says that her ambitions are motivated solely by her desire to provide for her family.

Men's actions, of course, are also subject to evaluation on the basis of intention. But because men are expected to have a broader range of concerns than women have, they can engage in a wider range of activities with a wider range of people without having to justify their actions. No Issei man I interviewed felt the need to attribute his strivings for wealth or social advancement solely to concern for his family. Although men are expected to share these concerns, they are also expected to have other (potentially competing) concerns arising from their wider sphere of relationships outside the family. Thus, it is acceptable for a man's motives for financial gain to derive not only from his commitment to his family but also from his desire for public acclaim in the community.

Furthermore, the boundaries of the male domain are comparatively vague and more difficult to locate, because "outside" is an expansive category that can only be defined in contrast to "inside." As I mentioned earlier, several of the Issei said that wives took care of everything inside the house, home, or family and men took care of "everything else." The image conveyed by these statements is of a bounded female sphere, clearly delimited by a male sphere that is unbounded, except by the excluded female elements, and expandable.

Ideally, marriage is the harmonious coordination of these different, but complementary, gender domains. Each spouse fulfills his or her proper responsibilities without interfering in the other's domain. Men should not engage in housekeeping and child-care activities: women should not represent the household in its relations with the community. If a woman steps beyond her sphere, it is because she has been compelled to do so, either by her husband's failure to meet his responsibilities properly or by unusual circumstances.

Although the Issei consider the two domains to be complementary, they do not consider them to be equal. From Issei men's point of view, the female inside sphere is encompassed by the male outside sphere and, therefore, is subject to male authority. A wife may be mistress of her own sphere, but her husband is master of the whole, and she must follow the direction in which he leads the entire family. His knowledge of the world outside the family as well as within it is thought to give him a broader base upon which to make decisions and shape strategies. In the best of all possible marriages, a man does not have to intervene in his wife's sphere, because she constantly adjusts her actions to his. If she does not, he should correct her. He may be compassionate and understanding, but more important, he must exercise firm leadership as head of the household.

Women's notions about the control over the two domains and the relations between them are close to men's, if a bit more ambivalent. On the one hand, they emphasize the necessity of male leadership. A good Japanese wife, they affirm, is quiet, reserved, nonaggressive, and somewhat subservient. Above all, she is constantly loyal and obedient to her husband, who ideally is a responsible and wise leader. On the other hand, they emphasize that a good husband also gives his wife the freedom to manage her sphere without meddling or close monitoring. In addition, he keeps her informed of important matters affecting the family and confides in her so that they have a mutual understanding of their affairs. Although ultimately he makes the decisions, he is considerate of her concerns and wishes and does not bully her into submission. Thus, although they accept the legitimacy of male authority and men's right to make decisions that women may not like, Issei women often complain about the inconsiderate manner in which a particular husband exercises that authority.

"Japanese" and "American" Marriage

The preceding conceptions of marriage emerge from Issei accounts of their own marriages, which they categorize, for the most part, as "Japanese." "American" marriage,* a category in which the Issei place the marriages of their children the Nisei, is entirely different; indeed, it is defined in symbolic opposition to "Japanese" marriage. "Japanese" marriage is rooted in "giri" (duty); "American" marriage is based on (romantic) "love." "Japanese" marriage is enmeshed in a structure of obligations to parents and family; "American" marriage is free from these burdens. The freedom to choose one's own spouse is, for the Issei, the key symbol for the freedom, the lack of constraint and restraint, that characterizes "American" marriage in general and renders it the antithesis of "Japanese" marriage.

The opposition between "American" and "Japanese" marriage is even more central to the Nisei's discourse on marriage. Indeed, Nisei notions about marriage and the terms in which they evaluate their own marriages can be understood only within the framework of this symbolic opposition. When they describe their own marriages, Nisei invariably contrast them with "Japanese" marriage— a model that they perceive to have been both the rule and the practice in Japan and that they consider the marriages of the Issei to represent. "American" marriage they perceive to be the dominant shape of the marriages of their middle-class, white American con-

---

*"American" was the adjective the Issei used most frequently to refer to this category of marriages. The term "hakujin" (white people) was also used occasionally.

temporaries.* Sansei (third-generation) marriages are also ad-duced as illustrative cases of "American" marriage, particularly among older Nisei who have married children.

In the Nisei's view, their own marriages are a compromise be-tween the all too whimsical and dangerously unstable "American" marriage and the emotionally ungratifying and often burdensome "Japanese" marriage. "Love" and "affection" have been brought into the conjugal relationship, but not at the expense of "duty" and "commitment." The Nisei marriage, unless it is a marriage gone wrong, is said to blend the best elements of the opposing "Japa-nese" and "American" types. The capriciousness of romantic love and its inherent instability are balanced in Nisei marriage by the stabilizing force of ethical "duty." One chooses one's spouse on the basis of romantic and sexual attraction, albeit tempered by sound judgment. But once "love" has brought a couple together and they marry, it becomes more than just an emotional state. It is trans-formed into an emotional commitment. After marriage, "love" is not merely the physical and romantic attraction between two unique individuals, but the mutual commitment of husband and wife to fulfill each other's needs and desires for intimacy and af-fection, to care for each other materially and physically, and to em-brace happily all their conjugal obligations.

Nisei Gender Domains in Marriage: Work and Family

The unity of husband and wife—a unity so deeply felt that some Nisei say that a spouse is "just like a part of me" or "an extension of myself"—is not dependent upon constant interaction, shared activities, or expressions of affection. It is good for a husband and wife to spend time together, to "learn to play together," to "go out together," to demonstrate their affection, and to provide each other with companionship. A spouse is, in a sense, one's "best friend." But this does not mean that a couple should spend all, or even a ma-jority of, their evenings together, or that they should share the same activities. Indeed, for the Nisei, it is important that each spouse maintain a sense of his or her individuality and separate identity.

*Here again I use the adjective "American" to label the construct of marriage that the Nisei oppose to "Japanese" marriage, because it is the term most frequently em-ployed by the Nisei. However, the Nisei also use the term "hakujin" (white people) and "Caucasian" to refer to this category of marriages.

The Nisei conception of the unity of husband and wife is best described as a model of organic solidarity constructed out of a functional division of labor. The terms the Nisei use repeatedly to talk
about the domains of husbands and wives are "work" versus "family" or "home." Men's concerns and responsibilities are said to lie
in the area of work. The foremost duty of a husband is to work to
support his wife and children. Women's domain is that of the family or home. To the Nisei, a woman's role as homemaker entails
more than just cooking, cleaning, and providing for the physical
well-being of her husband and children; it literally entails transforming a house into a home. As the central node in the family's
communicative network, a wife should be aware of her husband's
and children's needs, activities, and feelings. Because the most important part of her "job" as wife and mother is to "take care of the
children," she is responsible for monitoring their behavior as well
as making routine decisions about their activities. Men, too,
should be concerned with and interested in their children and
should try to "be in touch with them," but their concern with
"work" exempts them from having to have detailed and up-to-date
knowledge of their children's lives. Hence, fathers feel free to admit
a certain ignorance of and detachment from their children without
the fear of criticism or the guilt experienced by mothers.

Women, of course, can also work outside the home, but this activity is considered secondary to their job as homemaker and
mother and, at least ideally, a matter of choice rather than duty.
Everyone agrees that it is acceptable and, in some instances, desirable for a woman to work after her children have grown up and are
independent. Although there are differing opinions about when
this critical point is reached, Nisei agree that a woman should not
work as long as any of her children are of preschool age. Nisei
women place great value on the experience of mothering. For them,
the greatest drawback of an income-earning job is that it takes them
away from constant interaction with young children. Several
women explained that mothers with jobs "miss so much," even if
their children are well cared for. Returning home tired from work
reduces a woman's capacity to enjoy her children and her "experience of being a mother." For this reason, women say, the best job
for a mother who must work is one that allows her to be at home
when the children return from school, even if this job is only part-
time, with little security and reduced earnings. Furthermore, a

woman returning home at the end of the day wants to leave all concern for "work" behind so that she can devote her full attention to her family. If she has been away for the entire day, it is all the more necessary that she be "there for her family" when she returns home—that is, fully available to minister to their needs. So a Nisei woman who is an elementary school teacher and the mother of a preschool child explained that she no longer brought her "work" home as she used to before her child was born, because when she is at home now her "job is to be a mother."

What the Nisei say in some contexts about the work domain of husbands and the home domain of wives depicts them as equally important, complementary sets of functions that must be fulfilled if a marriage and a family are to survive. People often speak of men's income-earning work and women's housework and child care in terms that portray them as functionally different, but structurally equivalent, activities. For example, when the Nisei say that it is a wife's "job" to take care of the family and the home, they convey a sense of symmetry in the domains of men and women. A marriage functions smoothly if each spouse does his or her "job." Hence, although it is husbands who should work at income-earning jobs while their wives should take care of the family and home, in another sense both husbands and wives have jobs. As several women put it when they discussed the conjugal division of labor, "He has his job and I have mine."

The equivalence of men's work and women's work is also conveyed in the Nisei's comments about men's assistance with housework and child care. Neither men nor women feel it desirable for a husband to share equally in the housework or even to do a significant portion of it. After all, they explained, a man goes to work and does "his job," so he should not have to come home and do "his wife's job." For a husband to provide more than infrequent help with the housework, therefore, unbalances what the Nisei view as an equitable division of labor. What a husband must do to earn a livelihood is equivalent to what a wife must do to maintain the upkeep of the home and children.

The logic of this equation would seem to break down when a wife takes on a full-time job, for then it would appear that she is doing twice her husband's work. On the few occasions when I confronted Nisei informants with this problematic extension of their equation, their response was either to admit the inequality—often in a half-joking manner, as when one man said, "Well, I guess that's just women's lot"—or to explain that if a woman "chooses to go to work" then she must be ready to shoulder the burden of both job and housework.

The sense of equivalence and symmetry imparted by the Nisei's discussions of the work domain of husbands and the family/home domain of wives extends to their use of the terms "inside" and "outside." In contrast with the Issei, the Nisei employ these terms in fewer contexts and in ways that convey a narrower range of meaning. For the Nisei, "inside" and "outside" refer to physical space, and they are used primarily to talk about the sexual division of tasks around the home.* Men are considered responsible for the upkeep of objects and areas that are physically outside the house, including the yard, automobile, garage, and the exterior walls and roof of the house. Everything inside is the responsibility of women. No hierarchical structure is implied by the Nisei's use of these terms. "Inside" and "outside" are spoken of as two *adjacent* spatial domains, and neither men nor women convey the sense that one is subsumed by the other.

The Nisei are quick to make known their rejection of the "Japanese" devaluation of females. Husbands and wives, men and women, they claim, are equally valuable human beings. Yet, at the same time, the Nisei are of the opinion that the husband should "lead" in the marriage. He should act as the "head of the family" and "be strong." In particular, he should represent the couple and the family in community affairs. This does not mean that men have the right to make decisions by themselves, or even that they should have a greater say in decisions affecting the couple or the family. A few women said that they liked to be "subordinate" and wanted their husbands to handle all the important affairs, although they were defensively apologetic about being "a member of the old school of thought." Other women said that they found it difficult to be submissive to their husbands and could not accept "Japanese" ideas about female subordination. They were especially critical of their Issei fathers' attitudes toward women, which they portrayed

---

*Another context in which "inside" and "outside" surface in Nisei discussions of the conjugal relation is when people say that men "go out to work" (i.e., work at income-earning jobs) whereas women "stay at home." Yet, here again it is the work/home contrast that appears more salient to the Nisei conception of male and female domains than the inside/outside contrast.

as "feudal." But although they rejected the devaluation of women and the male dominance they associated with Issei marriage, even these women said that a husband should "lead" in a marriage.

Wives' comments show that they believe they play an important part in the construction of male leadership: if they lean on their husbands, their husbands will be strong, but if they take the lead too often, their husbands will become weak and dependent. A woman commented, "In the papers I read about men getting less and less able to make decisions and relying on their wives. I think this is the consequence. The more you [a wife] boss, the more the man will back up into the corner. Someone has to be the primary one to make decisions."

The conviction that "only one person can be the boss" is the inevitable conclusion of the Nisei's discussions of authority and power in marriage. In fact, they offer little else than this to explain or legitimate male leadership. No one ever expressed the view that men are inherently stronger or natural leaders, or that women are naturally submissive. On the contrary, the idea that male leadership and strength is a contingent social phenomenon, dependent upon women's eliciting behavior and their consent, is a clear thread that runs through the comments of the Nisei.

The limits of male leadership in marriage are defined by the "rights" of wives, the most important of which are knowledge, participation in decision making, and autonomy. First, a wife has a right to know about the couple's current financial situation, their prospects for the future, and any strategies or plans a husband may have that could affect the couple and their children. Second, a wife has a right to express her opinion and to have it seriously considered before any family decision is made. A husband should involve his wife in the decision-making process by talking the matter over with her before he takes any action. Finally, a wife has a right to a degree of autonomy in her life. Not only should she be allowed a free rein in running the house, but she should have freedom of movement and freedom to purchase items she wants either for herself or for others, within reasonable limits. It was these latter two "freedoms" that Nisei wives mentioned most often as signs that their marriages had changed for the better over time. Freedom of movement means that a wife is not held accountable to her husband for her activities while he is at work. If she fulfills her housekeeping and childrearing duties, she can spend her remaining time as she sees fit. Freedom to purchase means that a wife does not have to justify to her husband every penny she spends. Men and women agree that a wife should have some leeway to buy personal items and gifts and to go out with her friends, within reason.

The freedom of wives to spend money, however, must be considered in relation to their husbands' freedom to do the same. And this opens up some rather murky Nisei notions about marriage, namely those concerning the ownership and control of the incomes of husband and wife. On the one hand, the Nisei express a strong commitment to joint ownership and control over any income earned by husband or wife. What a husband earns plus what a wife earns, if she has a paying job, is automatically part of their conjugal fund. Marriage, the Nisei claim, is after all a relationship based on complete sharing and unity. One's earnings are not thought of as one's own; they belong to the couple. A married man does not work for himself; he "works for his family," and what he earns goes into the common fund. The same is true of his wife's earnings. This is why the Nisei say they have joint checking accounts, joint saving accounts, or both. Common ownership applies not only to current earnings but to past earnings and inherited wealth that may be in the form of savings, investments, or property. As one husband summarized it, "What's mine is hers, and what's hers is mine."

Yet, the Nisei say other things that belie this notion of equal ownership. Husbands say that on occasion they make large purchases without consulting their wives beforehand or that they simply announce their intention of doing so. Wives say they do not feel free to make such purchases, whether or not they are themselves bringing in earnings. Those who are not employed say they do not feel free to spend "his money." Those who are explain they still feel they are using "his money" because their husbands earn more.

The reluctance of wives to spend more than fifty dollars or so extends to buying gifts for their husbands. Men think it generous to buy lavish presents for their wives; women feel uneasy being generous with "his money" even if he is the recipient of their generosity. Likewise, Nisei husbands and wives judge a husband's generosity by the amount of money he "gives" his wife to spend. No one ever spoke of a wife's generosity in allowing her husband the freedom to purchase independently or to use either his or his wife's

earnings. Hence, men are not only accorded "leadership" in financial decisions, but in a sense they are seen as owning the couple's
money because they earn all or most of the joint income.

Socio-Spatial and Functional Metaphors of Gender Domains

Both the Issei "inside/outside" opposition and the Nisei "family/
work" opposition might be classified as variations of a universal
opposition between a female "domestic" sphere and a male "public" sphere (Rosaldo 1974), or between an "encompassing" male
sphere and an "encompassed" female sphere (Ortner and Whitehead 1981). To classify them as such, however, would be to obscure
what renders them different key metaphors of gender oppositions
with different normative implications. "Inside" and "outside" are
the core symbols of a metaphor of socio-spatial opposition with an
inherent hierarchy of authority. "Work" and "family" are the core
symbols of a metaphor of functional differentiation of labor that
says nothing about authority.

The Issei's metaphor of gender opposition chiefly concerns the
relative placement of men and women—their activities, relationships, and orientations—in a hierarchy of social space. Men are located physically, socially, and motivationally between women and
the world outside the home. Women constitute an interior that men
both shield from and link with an encompassing social order.

The Nisei opposition of "work" and "family/home" constitutes a
model of gender based on labor specialization. The central concern
here, and the critical difference between men and women, lies in
the kind of work they do, that is, in their respective "jobs" or functions. The core feature of the male domain is the earning of income;
"his job" is productive work. The core feature of the female domain
is homemaking and mothering; "her job" is reproductive work.

The Nisei are not particularly concerned with the relative location of men and women in social space. It is not because income-
earning work takes women outside the home that it poses a problem for the Nisei. When the Nisei say "women should stay at
home," they invariably add "with the children" or "when the children are young." As we saw, the Nisei reject as "feudal" the restrictions that the Issei placed on the physical mobility and social activities of women. Accordingly, they claim the right of a wife to "get
out of the house" and do what she pleases as long as she has done

"her job." Women's right to participate in social activities outside the home and family undermines a socio-spatial division of gender domains.

That a functional division between income-producing work and non-income-producing reproductive work does not define Issei gender domains is apparent in their discussions of work. The labor of wives in family businesses is construed as work inside the family and is not conceptually opposed to housekeeping and child-care tasks. Labor in family-operated enterprises, moreover, is conceptually differentiated into inside female tasks and outside male tasks. As long as Issei women engaged in inside work and did not enter into outside spheres, income-producing work was not experienced as problematic. What was problematic and what Issei women resented most of all was having to work outside the family—and, hence, being placed in inappropriate social space—during the periods of marriage when they had no children at home as well as during the periods when they did.

A comparison of Issei and Nisei women's accounts of early married life reveals the secondary role that reproductive functions play in defining the Issei female domain. We have seen that Nisei mothers consider mothering of young children to be a "full-time job" in which they must be constantly available to provide nurture and care as well as to foster children's emotional and intellectual development. This functional conception of motherhood is not articulated by Issei women, whether or not they engaged in other work while their children were young. The Issei women whose infants or young children were sent to Japan did not report any regret or concern about not being able to raise them. They missed their children, but none of them said they missed fostering their development. Indeed, a couple of these women said that, in order to work, they had chosen to send their young children back to Japan. Another Issei woman, whose two sons were cared for by her adoptive mother during working hours, said it made no difference to her whether she worked in the family's laundry business or "watched the boys." At the risk of oversimplification, it may be said that the Issei place emphasis on motherhood (a social identity and relation) rather than on mothering (fulfilling childrearing functions).

The different ways in which Issei and Nisei conceptualize the domains of men and women are linked with, and have different implications for, their conceptions of authority and leadership in marriage. Embedded in the Issei conception of the male outside domain and the female inside domain is a structure of authority. The male domain's symbolic expansiveness and association with the larger social order in which families are located gives it precedence over a female domain limited to the narrow confines of familial experience. Male authority in marriage, as in society in general, is based upon the priority of the expansive over the restricted, the encompassing over the encompassed, the knowledgeable over the ignorant, the experienced over the inexperienced, and the extrafamilial (i.e., communal and societal) over the familial interests and concerns. Hence, along with describing the content of two socio-spatial domains, "inside" and "outside" define the hierarchical relationship between those domains and the people who occupy them.

In contrast, the Nisei conception of "work" and "family" does not assign greater priority to either domain or set of functions. Nisei discourse on gender domains in marriage grants each spouse authority over his or her functionally differentiated but equal sphere. It is true that what the Nisei say about male "leadership" appears to grant husbands greater authority over the whole of marriage and the family and, thereby, to subvert this model of equality. That inconsistency—to which I will return in the final section of this paper—generates contradictions that subvert men's authority even while it enables them to exercise financial power over their wives. To comprehend those contradictions, however, we must first consider the source of these metaphors for separate gender domains.

Core Metaphors of Gender and Kinship

The Issei's socio-spatial and hierarchical ordering of gender domains bears a striking resemblance to the ideological separation of society into gendered private and public spheres, a division that has been linked to the development of modern European, industrial-capitalist states (Ariès 1962, Reiter 1975) and that, according to Rosaldo (1980), has made its way into anthropology via Victorian social theory. According to Reiter:

One of the mechanisms that underwrites the control of a central power over the minds of its population is the separation of society into public and private spheres. . . . In pre-state societies, economy, polity, and religion are all familized; in state societies, these spheres emerge as separate and public while the family becomes privatized. . . . As the state gains hege-mony over kinship-based organizations, its political, religious, and mili-tary elites increasingly define service to the public realm as having legiti-macy and high status. . . . In the process of elite classes legitimizing service to their ends, it is the sphere that is extra-local, and male, to which prestige is attached. A distinction that was functionally based on the di-vision of labor by sex and its geographical expression becomes trans-formed into more distinct public and private arenas. The state then uses the distinction to assert its own legitimacy and to devaluate the authority of kinship groups. While I would assert that early and archaic states all needed to transform kin-based organization to serve legitimized, public ends, it is clearly in the development of industrial capitalism in modern states that the division into public and private domains is most radical (Reiter 1975: 278).

Given that cultural distinctions, such as gender constructs, are the "products of specific historical and cultural transformations" and "must be examined with great caution in their own right" (Bloch and Bloch 1980: 25), we might ask how the Issei came to ac-quire such an ideology of gender, family, and state, if, indeed, that is what their inside/outside metaphor represents. Were we to at-tempt to explain the Issei's adoption of American gender and kin-ship and polity models as part of an "acculturation" process, we would have to marvel at the amazing receptiveness that has en-abled them to incorporate that model in the very core of their family relations. And, if they so willingly embraced European-American models of gender domains after their arrival in America, why do they not label their conjugal relations as "American," rather than claiming for themselves a "Japanese" form of marriage?

We might adopt a rather different stance and hypothesize that a generalized metaphor of encompassed/encompassing spheres is the inevitable ideological product of all processes of modern capitalist-industrial state formation, whether French, American, or Japanese. The Japan in which the Issei grew up at the turn of the century was, after all, undergoing just such a transformation pro-cess. Moreover, the eight years of schooling that, on average, Issei men and women alike had completed upon arrival in the United States took place in an educational system that has been described as a "far more rationalized, secular, and *state-oriented* educational system than existed at that time in most of the West" (Reischauer 1974: 137, my emphasis).

By analyzing the early history of the formation of the modern Japanese state by the leaders of the Meiji Restoration, we can see that the Issei illustrate neither an acculturation tale of immigrants who discard the useless baggage of "Japanese" cultural concepts of gender and kinship upon their arrival in the New World, nor an overdetermined tale of immigrants who find that identical metaphors of gender and kinship have been independently produced by their native and adopted countries, whose histories have been shaped by the same ideology of a capitalist-industrial elite. For the leaders of the Meiji Restoration not only were intent on transforming Japan into a modern capitalist state but also were convinced that the best way to protect Japan from penetration by the Western powers was to modernize her along Western lines. That entailed more than the acquisition of Western (particularly American) technology and military organization; it meant also the incorporation of Western political theory—in particular, French and German models of local government and jurisprudence. Indeed, the battle between the two camps of jurists who worked on Japan's 1890 civil code has been described as a struggle between French and German schools of jurisprudence (Sansom 1943). The Meiji reformers self-consciously incorporated Western legal concepts and codes defining the rights as well as the duties of citizens, because they were "fully aware that *nothing* would more favorably impress the nations of the West than a constitutional form of government . . . with representative institutions and clear and just legal procedures like [those] of the West" (Reischauer 1975: 143).

Among the codes developed during the last three decades of the nineteenth century were those defining the authority of the household head—including his authority to determine the place of residence of members of his household, to expel members from the household if they defied his authority or threatened its good name, and to select his children's spouses. The latter practice had not previously been the custom among the peasants, who allowed their children to select their own spouses (Befu 1971: 50). The "rules of the Japanese family"—including the authority of the (male) household head—which the Issei were taught as part of their "moral training" in a state-controlled educational system were a blend of Western European and elite (samurai) Japanese ideologies of gender, kinship, and polity.* Hence, if today these rules are viewed by

*For discussions of the incorporation of Western European concepts of polity and family in the formation of Meiji ideologies of the state, see Befu 1971, Fukutake

the Issei as quintessentially "Japanese" and as both "Japanese" and "feudal" by their children, we can clearly see how quickly the past can be transformed and "tradition" created.

In contrast to the Issei model, the Nisei's differentiation of the spheres of work and family seems to reflect the separation of production from kinship-defined units in industrial-capitalist society. The pervasiveness of this metaphor of gender domains among Americans (at least middle-class Americans of the Nisei's birth cohort) suggests that the Nisei adopted it along with the rest of their cohort in the classroom and through the popular mass media. Although the Nisei grew up in households that were still engaged in income-producing activities and in which mothers engaged in productive work as well as reproductive work, the concepts of family, work, and gender they learned were rooted in a society in which the *ideological* separation of production from family had already been accomplished. Given that the Nisei's social mobility and their eventual acceptance into the "middle-class"* was accompanied by a shift from family business to salaried and wage employment, they may well have been strongly influenced by the symbolic association of this family/work model with the American middle class and national identity.

Each generation's model of gender domains, I am suggesting, was learned along with an institutional model of society—more specifically, an institutional model of family and society. That institutional model was, in turn, inherently gendered. Hence, depending on the context, we could describe such a model as a gendered model of the institutional domain of family and kinship or as an institutional model of gender domains. I will refer to it hereafter as a model of gender and kinship. It is this homology of gender domains and institutional domains (for example, female is to male as household is to state) that is so well epitomized by the core metaphors of inside/outside and family/work and that in turn endows these metaphors of opposition with symbolic power. They help people not only to make common sense of their relationships in

---

1967, Dore 1958. The inside/outside metaphor promulgated by the Meiji state, of course, was built upon a Confucian social metaphor that had prevailed in elite Japanese conceptions of polity, family, and gender long before the Meiji era.

*The Nisei as a group not only are predominantly "middle-class" according to the American folk concept of class (a socio-economic status dependent on income, education, and occupation) but are categorically perceived to be "middle-class" by themselves and others—at least on the West Coast, where they are concentrated.

marriage, in the workplace, in the community, and in interactions with the state but also to analyze institutions and cultures in ways that mutually reinforce the logic of the gender relationships in each.

The recognition of the homology and mutual reinforcement of concepts of gender and kinship in society, however, also underscores the point that inside/outside and family/work constitute two different core metaphors of gender and kinship with different normative implications and, indeed, different meanings of gender opposition and the place of family in society. The Issei inside/outside metaphor models an opposition between family and state, private and public, female and male that is fundamentally about the boundaries of authority in a nested system of authority. Just as the household defines the boundaries of state interference into the domestic domain, so the inside, female domain defines the boundaries of male interference into the affairs of women. Women, men (as heads of households), and the state are located in increasingly expansive, encompassing circles.

The Nisei family/work metaphor models an opposition between female reproductive labor and male productive labor, which in turn is symbolically associated with an opposition between love and money, cooperation and competition, expressive and instrumental activity. It is not a model of kinship and polity and the boundaries of state or male authority, but a model of functionally differentiated sets of activities that stand in relation to each other as means toward an end. Indeed, the lack of an inherent structure of authority or hierarchy of value is reflected in the fact that, depending on context, either gender—or that gender's domain—can be cast as the support for the other. Quite commonly when speaking about "the family," the Nisei refer to "work" as the means of family existence. Men go to work "to support the family," and, as a couple of Nisei men put it, "without the family, work has no meaning." Likewise, men are the "means of support" of women. Yet, in the context of talk about "work" and particularly about "careers," "family" and the nurturant affection and homemaking services provided by women are said to enable men to "do a good job." Here, the means and the end are reversed, and, in a sense that corresponds to a Marxist model of the reproduction of labor in the "domestic community" (Meillasoux 1981), family and women are conceptualized as the means of the reproduction of work (see Yanagisako and Collier, this volume, for a critical review of the reproduction/production distinction).

As analysis of Issei and Nisei concepts has shown, seemingly subtle differences between metaphors of gender and kinship can underlie significant differences in the meaning of family and that which it opposes, as well as significant differences in the meaning of gender domains. In the final section of this paper, I will propose that these different meanings and the different norms linked with them suggest a historical process of transformation in gender and kinship models in American society. First, however, I return to the anthropological categories most often applied to these models.

Anthropological Categories as Mixed Metaphors

Like the oppositions of domestic/public and domestic/politico-jural in anthropology, Japanese American models of gender domains are also models of kinship and society. Hence, if our analytic categories of kinship are inherently gendered, and our analytic categories of gender reflect an institutional model of kinship and social structure, we might simply congratulate ourselves on having successfully captured native concepts in our heuristic concepts and leave it at that. Yet, my discussion of the different meanings underlying Issei and Nisei metaphors of gender and kinship raises the question, do these differences underlie anthropological categories as well? The answer I suggest below is that both domestic/public and domestic/politico-jural oppositions combine a socio-spatial metaphor of authority with a labor-specialization metaphor of differentiated functions. In short, each is a mixed metaphor.

Rosaldo explicitly states that the domestic/public opposition organizes an *institutional* model of gender domains:

An opposition between "domestic" and "public" provides the basis of a structural framework necessary to identify and explore the place of male and female in psychological, cultural, social, and economic aspects of human life. "Domestic," as used here, refers to those minimal institutions and modes of activity that are organized immediately around one or more mothers and their children; "public" refers to activities, institutions, and forms of association that link, rank, organize, or subsume particular mother-child groups (Rosaldo 1974: 23).

Domestic/public draws upon a socio-spatial image of a "hierarchy of mutually embedded units" (Rosaldo 1980: 398) to explain the general identification of women with domestic life and of men with public life and, hence, a universal, cross-cultural asymmetry in the evaluation of the sexes.

Yet, it is the biological role of women as mothers that lies at the root of these identifications: "Women become absorbed primarily in domestic activities because of their role as mothers. Their economic and political activities are constrained by the responsibilities of child care, and the focus of their emotions and attentions is particularistic and directed toward children and the home" (Rosaldo 1974: 24). Here, the logic of the causal link between women's reproductive function and their identification with domestic life rests upon an a priori separation of "domestic activities" from "economic and political activities." A division of the social world into an inward-oriented, particularistic sphere and an expansive, universalistic sphere is conflated with a less explicit division of human activities into functionally differentiated domains: that of "domestic" (reproductive) activities and that of "economic" (productive) and "political" activities.

The double image produced by considering domestic and public spheres as both a functional division of social activity and as a nested hierarchy of social space is perhaps best illustrated by the following statement: "Although varying in structure, function, and societal significance, 'domestic groups' which incorporate women and infant children, aspects of childcare, commensality and the preparation of food can always be identified as segments of a larger, over-arching social whole" (Rosaldo 1980: 398). In a telling unevenness, reproductive functions stand in opposition to an encompassing social order in a model of gender and polity that Rosaldo had come to recognize as constituting "an ideological rather than an objective and necessary set of terms" (1980: 402).

Whereas Rosaldo came to view the domestic/public opposition of gender domains as an ideological distinction that had devolved on anthropology from our nineteenth-century predecessors, Fortes continued to view the domestic/politico-jural opposition as a *heuristic* distinction that had evolved in anthropology as we refined the insights of our Victorian predecessors. According to Fortes (1969: 36), Morgan perceived in *Ancient Society* that even though the tribe was based "on the selective recognition of kinship relations, it was a civil, that is, a political unit, rather than a domestic unit"; Radcliffe-Brown (1952) formally recognized the jural dimension of kinship and descent institutions, and "the major advance in kinship theory since Radcliffe-Brown, but growing directly out of his work, has been the analytical separation of the politico-jural domain from the familial or domestic domain within the total social universe of what have been clumsily called kinship-based social systems" (Fortes 1969: 72).

Fortes was very clear that the critical feature differentiating the two domains is the type of normative premise that regulates each. The politico-jural domain is governed by jural norms guaranteed by "external" or "public" sanctions that may ultimately entail force; the domestic domain is constrained by "private," "affective," and "moral" norms, at the root of which is the fundamental axiom of prescriptive altruism (Fortes 1969: 89, 250–51). Likewise, Fortes was adamant on the point that "this is a methodological and analytical distinction. The actualities of kinship relations and kinship behavior are compounded of elements from both domains and deployed in words and acts, beliefs and practices, objects and appurtenances that pertain to both of these and to other domains of social life as well" (1969: 251). Thus, even when the two domains are fused and structurally undifferentiated in a single "kinship polity," as in Australian societies, "the jural aspect of the rights and duties, claims and capacities embedded in kinship relations is clearly distinguished" from the domestic aspect (Fortes 1969: 118).

A somewhat sharper image of domains emerges, however, from Fortes's assignment of entire categories of genealogically defined relationships to one or the other domain. Scheffler (1970: 1465) notes that Fortes has "a tendency to treat social relations ascribed by reference to relations of common descent as though they were necessarily 'politico-jural relations.'" Conversely, Fortes assigns ego-oriented, cognatically defined relations to the domestic domain. In the following statement about the matrilineal Ashanti, he relegates entire social relations, rather than aspects or elements of those relations, to either the politico-jural or the domestic domain:

An Ashanti father's model field of kinship relations has two parts. On the one side is his wife and children, on the other a sister and her children, the two being residentially separated. In relation to his children he conducts himself solely in accordance with norms of the familial domain. These entitle him, for example, to chastise his children if they misbehave. In relation to his sister's children his behavior is ruled more strictly by reference to the politico-jural domain, the source of his lawful rights over and duties towards them. This corresponds to a field of social relations that extends beyond his domestic field—it includes his lineage, the village political authorities, and the chiefdom of which he is a citizen. Thus, if we take such a person's total field of kinship relations, we find that its management involves compliance with norms that emanate from two distinct and in some ways opposed domains of social structure (1969: 98).

The last two sentences in the preceding quotation not only convey a geographical image of increasingly expanding "fields" of relations but also add the dynamic of opposition and, thus, bring domestic/politico-jural categories even further in line with a sociospatial model of the boundaries of authority.

At the same time, a model of functionally differentiated sets of activities underlies Fortes's concept of domain: "Each sector—which I call a domain—comprises a range of social relations, customs, norms, statuses, and other analytically discriminable elements linked up in nexuses and unified by the stamp of *distinctive functional features* that are common to all (1969: 97, my emphasis). In our society, Fortes claims, we have no difficulty in distinguishing the domain of the law—"judges and courts, police, prisons and lawyers" (1969: 97)—from that of the family. If, as Fortes claims, a domain is "not merely a classificatory construct" but a "matrix of social organization," it is also clearly more than a heuristic category defined by its normative premises. It appears to have an institutional and functional basis as well.

For Fortes, the functional core of the domestic domain—as was argued in the first section of this article—is biological reproduction. The "reproductive nucleus" of the mother-child unit generates the "affective and moral components" found in interpersonal kinship relations (Fortes 1969: 191). "The nodal bond of mother and child implies self-sacrificing love and support on the one side and life-long trust and devotion on the other. The values mirrored in this relation have their roots in the parental care bestowed on children, not in jural imperatives. Their observance is dictated by conscience, not legality" (Fortes 1969: 191). Just as it is a mistake to view the politico-jural aspects of kinship as an extension of the affective, moral norms of familial relations (the error committed by Malinowski), so Fortes argues that it is a mistake to view the moral and affective components in interpersonal kinship relations as a sanctioned construct of the lineage. Fortes limits the range of relationships shaped by moral conscience and sentiment but traces them to the same source, namely, the mother-child bond. Affect extends into society only far enough to bound the sphere of relations that is not constructed by politico-jural principles. To put it another way, the affect, extending from biological reproduction, limits the penetration of "external" authority into familial relations—whether that external authority is the lineage or the state.

If both the domestic/politico-jural distinction and the domestic/public distinction mix metaphors of a hierarchy of social space and a functional division of social activity, it might be argued that in doing so they appropriately incorporate the two metaphors that best summarize the structural and conceptual oppositions that have resulted from the separation of productive and reproductive functions in modern industrial-capitalist states. In other words, a case might be made that even though the historical specificity of these categories renders them inappropriate tools for analyzing gender and kinship in other societies, they might be useful for analyzing gender and kinship in our own society. Analytic metaphors, however, should help us to explicate native metaphors in ways that clarify the specific historical and cultural processes out of which they emerge. They should also enable us to recognize processes of change. By unself-consciously mixing a metaphor of socio-spatial opposition with a metaphor of functional differentiation, the domestic/public dichotomy and the domestic/politico-jural dichotomy obscure a cultural transformation that, in the concluding section below, I suggest has occurred not only among Japanese Americans but among other members of industrial-capitalist societies.

The Historical Transformation of Gender and Kinship Domains

The experience of the Japanese Americans whose metaphors of gender domains have been explored in this article appears to support Reiter's (1975: 281) hypothesis that the "radical separation of home and workplace in industrialism" leads to the "privatized kinship realm [being] increasingly defined as women's work." At the same time, however, I would argue that the ideological shift accompanying the separation of home and workplace (a shift that may have facilitated it) has transformed, rather than reproduced or buttressed, conceptions of gender domains and gender hierarchy. The shift from a cultural model of socio-spatially differentiated gender domains to one of functionally differentiated gender domains has indeed resulted in kinship being increasingly defined as "women's work"; but it has also undermined the authority of men in the family at the same time as it has reconfigured the relationship between family and society. In other words, the shift has caused not so much an increasing separation of male and female spheres and of private and public spheres as a reconceptualization of what constitutes those spheres and structures their relations.

I base this hypothesis on my analysis of the different meanings and normative implications of Issei and Nisei core metaphors of gender and kinship. I suggest that the transformation in metaphors we have seen in these two generations represents the general experience of members of advanced, capitalist-industrial states in which production is increasingly separated from the household and family. For, although the Issei and Nisei hold attitudes shaped by a particular history of emigration from the nascent Japanese industrial state and by their social mobility in a postwar advanced-industrial economy, they were affected by the same sociopolitical dynamics that influenced a large sector of the population in America and other industrial-capitalist states. The Issei's acquisition of the model of state, household, and male spheres of authority fashioned by the Meiji government as the institutional basis of their modern nation-state and disseminated through state-controlled schools parallels the experience of many other peoples caught up in the ideological processes accompanying modern state formation. Likewise, the Nisei, along with the rest of the members of their cohort in America and in other advanced industrial-capitalist societies, acquired a gender and kinship metaphor of functional differentiation that prevailed in the mass media and in the public schools.

This change in models of gender and kinship spheres in America and other industrial-capitalist societies, I suggest, has been accompanied by a decline in culturally legitimated male authority in the family similar to that experienced by Japanese Americans. Earlier, I stated that whereas the Issei inside/outside metaphor models an opposition between family and state, female and male, and private and public spheres that establishes a hierarchy of authority, the Nisei family/work opposition says nothing about authority. The absence of a hierarchical structure of authority in the family/work opposition is demonstrated by the Nisei's ability to characterize each sphere as the means of support for the other. Family/work as a core metaphor of gender opposition, therefore, has distinctly different normative implications for the relations between husbands and wives than does inside/outside.

What the Nisei say about a husband's "leadership" and his prerogative in spending money from the conjugal fund might appear to counter my argument for such a transformation in gender concepts and hierarchy. Far from demonstrating continuity between Issei and Nisei conceptions of gender and hierarchy, however, the Nisei's talk of male leadership in marriage points to the disjunction between those conceptions and the contradictions generated by their historical succession. When they attempt to explain the husband's role as leader, the Nisei rely on ad hoc justifications that contradict the normative implications of their model of functionally differentiated but equal male and female spheres. When they offer that men need to lead to satisfy their "male egos"—a claim made by men as well as by women—they seem to explain male leadership more as a response to a psychological need (and one that might readily be changed by altering socialization practices) than as a dictate of a social, or even a biological, order. When, on rare occasions, they justify male leadership by pointing to men's greater familiarity with the world of finance, politics, and community affairs, they would seem to draw upon an Issei socio-spatial model of authority. But an inside/outside metaphor has little symbolic power for the Nisei in justifying gender hierarchy or, indeed, hierarchy of any kind. For one, it is an Issei metaphor of gender hierarchy that the Nisei have rejected as "feudal" and "oppressive." For another, it is a metaphor of the authority of the community over the family and of the family over the individual. The Nisei have at best a strong ambivalence toward such a hierarchical model of self, family, and society, for it represents for them a "Japanese" notion of authority that they have struggled against in their relations with their parents.

Moreover, the Issei's inside/outside metaphor does not explain male leadership in marriage for the Nisei because the "outside" they perceive in opposition to the "inside" of their families today is not a sphere of overarching political authority, but the world of the workplace and the marketplace. It is an economic world rather than a political one, and, as such, it offers individuals material rather than sociopolitical resources. The socio-spatial metaphor of their parents does not work to legitimate hierarchy in marriage for the Nisei because the functional metaphor of family/work has transformed not only their conception of gender domains but their conception of the social world in which families are located. An image of an external polity from which men, through their connections with it, draw their authority no longer exists, for it has been obscured behind an image of the workplace.

Above all, Nisei men's leadership in marriage is of questionable cultural legitimacy inasmuch as it is explained by their greater earnings. When they attribute husband's prerogatives to their greater earnings, the Nisei grant men *power* that derives from money rather than *authority* that derives from men's rightful place in an ordered, social world. The source of male power is not a higher sphere of authority and societal integration, but a sphere of market relations. This economic world of material resources, although it provides funds necessary for the support of the family, by no means has priority over the family. Indeed, the sphere of money and market relations is characterized by aspects from which the family must be protected. As the primary income earners, men both gain prerogatives by providing the financial support that protects the family from the harsher world of the marketplace and, at the same time, call into question the legitimacy of those prerogatives by basing their special privilege on control of money. For, men's greater control of the conjugal fund subverts the unity of the conjugal bond that it represents and, along with that, the Nisei notion that love and complete sharing is what marriage is all about.

Although the mixing of a metaphor of socio-spatial hierarchy with a metaphor of functional differentiation is highly problematic for the Nisei's conceptions of their conjugal relations, the mixing of these metaphors is even more problematic for anthropologists' analyses of gender and kinship relations. As mixed metaphors, neither the domestic/public opposition nor the domestic/politico-jural opposition are of much help in teasing apart the subtle, but socially significant, differences in folk metaphors of gender and kinship domains. A recognition of these differences and a comparison of their sociopolitical contexts provides a way to trace the historical processes through which both native and anthropological metaphors emerge and are transformed.

Toward a Nuclear Freeze?
The Gender Politics of
Euro-American Kinship Analysis

Rayna Rapp

THE FIELDWORK STORY I am about to tell illustrates the presence of the past in the present of one anthropologist.* In exploring kinship patterns among recent urban migrants in southern France, I discovered that even questions about kinship that are seemingly inspired by feminism may be premised on androcentric assumptions. That lesson propels me from Provence toward a general examination of the way we study kinship as anthropologists who are also native participants in the culture that sets up the terms of our study. In bringing together a series of theoretical questions and wide-ranging cultural examples, I hope to show how the questions we ask about gender and family arrangements set limits on the answers we are able to discover. Such limits then mask hegemonic thinking—our own as anthropologists as well as that of our Euro-American informants—about how kinship systems operate and how they change. In the case I will describe, a set of assumptions concerning the centrality of male-headed nuclear families blocks recognition of innovation in kinship patterns. To better understand how both anthropologists and their Euro-American informants think about family life, I propose a "nuclear freeze." Only when we deconstruct these classic assumptions will we be able to see the shifting symbolism, the creativity, and the continuities that people inscribe in the realm of kinship.

*Grateful acknowledgment is made to the Wenner-Gren Foundation, which supported my fieldwork in Provence in 1980. Earlier versions of this essay benefited from the comments of Eric Arnauld, Judith Friedlander, Susan Harding, Shirley Lindenbaum, Ellen Lewin, Ellen Ross, Marilyn Strathern, Roger Sanjek, Eric Wolf, Sylvia Yanagisako, Marilyn Young, and other conference participants. I thank them all and absolve them of any responsibility for the shortcomings in the final version.

When I returned to southern France in 1980, I planned a classic migration study with a feminist twist. I would trace the entire cohort of young adults who had grown up in the tiny village of Montagnac, 90 kilometers northeast of Marseille, where I had conducted fieldwork a decade earlier. All but four of the 33 young adults had left the village, and my sample of 29 ex-villagers was easy to locate with the help of parents and grandparents still living in Montagnac.

Initially, I wanted to investigate the migrants' transition from village to urban life, from peasantry to wage work, and, especially, from a sexually segregated to a more sexually integrated culture. Like so many of their Mediterranean neighbors, these Provençals grew up in a world where men traditionally participate in a rich public life of agrarian labor exchange, political activity, and an elaborate ethos of male sociability, including styles of recreation and intricately developed oration. Women, whose social life is focused in the domestic domain, traditionally use their extended female kin networks to share child care, work skills, stories, and cultural knowledge. Raised in such a sex-segregated world, but currently living in a rapidly expanding milieu without the familiar village squares, male-only cafés, boules courts,* and neighborhood circles of female relatives, would new urbanites construct a cultural language and way of life that bridged the separate male and female worlds of their youth? Would new experiences with cities, with wage labor in sectors nonexistent in the village, with public culture at once more distant and bureaucratic than the village square have an impact on the meaning of family life? These were the questions I contemplated as I tracked down the urban migrants.

Although a few villagers were far-flung, most were easy to locate and interview. With the exception of three in Paris, one in Corsica, and one in New York, all had settled short distances from home: six lived in Marseille; one was in nearby Toulon; three lived in neighboring Digne or Manosque, small cities of 15,000 and 20,000, respectively; and the remaining fourteen lived and worked in tiny towns of 2,000 to 5,000 inhabitants—such as Gréoux, Riez, Moustiers, and Volx—each about a half-hour's drive from Montagnac.

---

*The game of boules is the most popular public sporting event in southern France. Like Italian bocce, and somewhat like English lawn bowling, boules is traditionally played by teams of men, surrounded by a highly engaged audience.

The cultural meanings of such short migrations are properly the subject of other essays.*

At first, change seemed apparent everywhere. Young men whose fathers still tilled the soil earned their livings as bank clerks, gas station owners, postal employees, electricians, and plumbers. Young women whose mothers had never worked for wages brought home regular paychecks as secretaries, pharmaceutical factory workers, nurse's aides, and child-care workers. The great majority—25 of 29 ex-villagers—were married, only one couple endogamously. Of the eleven male migrants, eight were married to women who worked outside the home, and seven had young children. Of the fourteen female migrants, thirteen were married. Six were what the French delicately call "sans profession," women in the "housewife" category who perform a multitude of labors like childrearing, farming, or working in family businesses; seven worked for wages outside the home. All but one of the thirteen had young children.

I had gone on a fishing expedition for change in kinship patterns and consciousness. What I actually found was a great deal of continuity. Despite adjustment to female paid employment, these young couples experienced a smooth transition from villager to urbanite—their new homes, new work, new consumer culture did not appear to separate them, in their own minds, from the generation they had left behind in the village.

This was especially true for the women, who thought of themselves as living as their own mothers did. And although France has perhaps the most comprehensive set of institutional arrangements for child care in the West, especially crèches for toddlers, only one of the young wives was using public day care. All the rest relied on kinship aid. In a complex and contingent pattern of migration, they had situated themselves within walking distance of mothers-in-law and siblings; some had even moved mothers-in-law into their block of apartments. Whereas a village woman had traditionally relied on her mother for informal help with her children, the urbanite now enlisted a wider circle of kinship aid during her formal working hours.

This pattern allowed for a reassuring continuity of consciousness among villagers separated by age and distance. Of course, such a

*Other essays exploring these patterns are Rapp 1986 and Rapp forthcoming.

pattern depends on close migration and the dynamic growth of small and medium-sized towns with expanding service-sector employment, especially for women. It is also reinforced by the "urban bias" in the marriages that village migrants make: they usually marry someone whose family lives in a town or small city and settle there. Young villagers-turned-urbanites can appropriate old symbols of hearth and home to new ends. The activities and emblems of home and children remain solidly female-centered and are increasingly shared with women of the husband's family, especially his mother. Women can rely on their mothers-in-law and identify with their mothers, even as they live lives "objectively" quite different, filled with food processors, urban schools, and automobiles. This transformation can be experienced as continuity because the scale and pace of urbanization permit some semblance of control over neighborhoods, housing, and networks, so that affines can move in and out together. The social reproduction of kinship networks here supports sex-segregated culture, which then helps to make the "new woman's" life as a wage earner possible.

It is striking that neither my informants nor I coded the switch from reliance on a woman's mother to reliance on her mother-in-law or on a widened circle of kin as a "change." We all saw the continuity of nuclear family life and the use of female-centered "extensions" as the core of a stable kinship pattern. I would argue that continuity in kinship forms is easier to see than change as long as people live in nuclear families. Such male-headed, bounded units are central to Euro-American kinship patterns and to the anthropologists who study them. We are accustomed to putting the paterfamilias at the jural and cultural center of our definitions of family structure. All other forms of domestic organization are then labeled as extensions of or exceptions to "the family," defined as husband, wife, and children. As long as Provençal migrants live as members of nuclear families, neither they nor I find it remarkable that the women have shifted and widened their extended kinship relations. We thereby miss an important opportunity to see how people actively (if sometimes less than consciously) appropriate their key cultural relations and turn them to new ends.

Of course, this ongoing process of refashioning the language, norms, and relations of family life has a long history in Euro-American cultures. When we turn to the lively literature on the history of family life in England, France, and the United States, we can see how hegemonic family forms—in this case, male-centered, nuclear family forms—have been created and transformed. Anthropologists studying Euro-American family life would do well to consider some of the lessons this history suggests.*

An obvious first lesson is that the definitions and cultural importance of family units change over time. In England, for example, a narrowing of the co-resident kin group and a transformation of its authority structure accompanied Puritan moral reforms, which made the male head of the household responsible for all his dependents.† What Lawrence Stone labels "the restricted patriarchal nuclear family" was in part the creation of the divine-rights jural system, which considered fathers and dependents to be analogous to monarchs and subjects. Rewriting this political script gave a context for redrawing the family as "a little commonwealth" in the seventeenth century. By the nineteenth century, with the increasing separation of home from workplace and the normative removal of women and children from productive and public life, families became "havens in a heartless world."

In France, the primacy of conjugal nuclear units came later, perhaps with less political and cultural force. Among bourgeois and noble peoples, "family" referred to houses or lineages, not co-resident domestic groups, well into the eighteenth century. The more restricted meaning of the term emerged fully only in the nineteenth century, undoubtedly strengthened by the Napoleonic reforms.‡

In America, the father's role as "family governor" was an aspect of "the little commonwealth" model that settled New England.§ By the late eighteenth century, families became more private, defined in distinction to, rather than in the context of, the state. Nineteenth-century reforms—first through charity, later through welfare—used the language of familism to stress a father's responsibility for his wife and children. Such language was used to criti-

*Here I am concerned with what Barrett (1980, Chap. 6) has called "the ideology of familism," not with a thorough survey of family history. For an overview, see Laslett 1965, Laslett ed. 1972, Flandrin 1979, Rosenberg ed. 1975, Stone 1977, and Tilly and Scott 1978. For critical review essays, see Pleck 1976, Rapp, Ross, and Bridenthal 1979, and Mitteraurer and Sieder 1982.

†English family history is discussed throughout the pages of *History Workshop Journal*. See also Fox-Genovese 1977, and Goody, Thirsk, and Thompson eds. 1976.

‡For French family history, see Flandrin 1979, Goubert 1977, and Segalen 1983.

§For American family history, see Gordon ed. 1978, Cott 1977, Zaretsky 1982, Gutman 1976, and Demos 1970.

cize first Southern and Eastern European immigrants for their extended family structures and, later, American Blacks for their responses to poverty. Families as social units are in continuous flux.

A second and related historical lesson is that the cultural meaning of "the family" is shaped in the broad context of politics and economics. Although not simply a reflex of these spheres, the cultural domain of kinship does incorporate, reflect, and transform the social forces within which it is embedded. From a patriarchate to a little commonwealth to a haven in a heartless world, the conjugal unit has responded to changing notions of appropriate roles for family members and yet maintained a reassuring sense of stability in the language of kinship. Thus, a familial role like "father" appears constant, but its meaning shifts up and down class lines, responds to political transitions, and summarizes current cultural thinking about such "distant" institutions as the labor market, the health care system, and the courts. As a key symbol, the family is not a realm apart, despite the heritage of nineteenth-century thinking to the contrary.

Third, the cultural meaning of family life not only reflects large-scale political and economic forces but also provides some of the normative "glue" that holds other institutions, and public policy, together. The language of family life is highly political. It is used to blame the poor for their lack of respectability in turn-of-the-century New York or "Outcast" London. It also informs the discourse on how the evolving social services redistribute responsibilities between the private sector and the state in twentieth-century France. And, of course, it is key to the struggles over civil rights for Black Americans following Daniel Moynihan's 1965 report, *The Negro Family*. Cultural meanings flow in many directions, radiating in, out, and around the institutions we Euro-Americans bound as normative nuclear families, overflowing and legitimizing public policies and attitudes through the language of familism.*

Fourth, Euro-American family life defines the intersection of gender and generation. It provides a language linking sex and age groups in patterns of hierarchy and dependence, authority and obedience, spoken in the etiquette of generosity and responsibility. The domain of kinship overlaps with other arenas—such as the

*For New York, see Stansell 1982. For "Outcast" London, see Jones 1974 and Alexander 1976. For France, see Donzelot 1979. On the politics of Black American family life, see Staples ed. 1971.

workplace, the schools, and the fashion industry—in which the cultural meanings of men and women, children and adults, are spelled out. Yet, it is still the primary locus for the reproduction, transmission, and transformation of cultural notions of gender and generation. We thus inherit as Euro-Americans a notion of womanhood intimately linked to maternity, of fatherhood connected to economic responsibility, and of childhood defined in terms of malleability and potential development. The three are not innocent of historical struggles. The cultural meaning of womanhood, for example, has been transformed by the images deployed in the "cult of true womanhood," feminism's "social housekeeping," the psychological reforms of "companionate marriage," and most recently the growing economic importance of "working mothers." These social movements and discourses all made claims on family life and its reform.* We Euro-Americans consider the male-headed and autonomous nuclear family to be normative, but it is also a symbolic, historical creation that reflects a particular cultural construction of gender and generation. When we take this unit as stable and central to Euro-American cultures, we lose sight of the activities, choices, and struggles out of which the definitions of family relations and norms flow.

When male-headed nuclear families are uncritically accepted as normative (by native informants as well as anthropologists, who are usually also native informants), all other kinship patterns are relegated to a lower status as extensions of or exceptions to the rule. Yet, we know that "fictive kinship" and extended matrifocality are crucial to the survival and reproduction of some kinship systems. Among Afro-Americans, for example, friends are often turned into brothers, sisters, aunts, and cousins, a tactic that increases social solidarity under conditions of economic and social fragmentation.† And a pattern of "informal matrifocality" is now emerging throughout the American class structure among the rapidly increasing population of women and children living without males in their households.‡

Even in Montagnac, where nuclear families remain intact, it can

---

*For American women's history, see Cott 1977, Cott and Pleck eds. 1979, and Kerber and Mathews eds. 1982.

†For classic descriptions of this pattern, see Stack 1974 and Liebow 1967.

‡Lewin (forthcoming) makes this argument most forcefully for American family structure.

be argued that men and women live in "different families," the men's more bounded, the women's open to female-centered, diffuse extensions.* Throughout the twentieth century, when village women married, they often relied on their mothers for aid. This pattern was most dramatically illustrated when a peasant woman sent an "extra" child to live with her own mother, thus saving expenses and redistributing child labor and social solidarity. Such supplementary, or alternative, patterns of kinship are usually centered on women and their kin relations to one another. The reasons for this "female bias" within a kinship system that is officially male-centered are worth discussion.

Sylvia Yanagisako (1977) made a major contribution to the analysis of such configurations when she urged us not to automatically accept women's roles as "affective" and therefore linked to kinship. Among the Japanese-Americans she studied in Seattle, women cement social relations among households and across generations. Both women and men consider this "community work" to occur "inside" the home, with which women are symbolically associated; yet, it is highly social and structural. If men did it, it might well be perceived as belonging to the "outside" realm in which they operate. Yanagisako's analysis of Japanese-American kinship pushes us to see the symbolism of gender divisions and not to reduce informants' beliefs to a naturalized outgrowth of women's universal mothering. The biological facts of maternity do not automatically propel women toward domesticity, nurturance, and extended kinship organization; these are cultural, not natural, attributions.

When anthropologists assume the identity of women and the domestic domain, we reflect, rather than analyze, a prime piece of Euro-American cultural ideology. Unproblematic acceptance of the domestic/public opposition replicates and legitimates the sense that women and families are biologically rooted. In associating women with unchanging biological reproduction and nurturance and setting these activities in a sphere apart from the rest of society, we inherit the assumptions of our Victorian predecessors. To the Victorians, the monogamous, privatized, male-headed nuclear family appeared to be a major achievement of Western civilization, conceptualized in opposition to the impersonal forces of state and market (Rosaldo 1980; Collier et al. 1982). In our own thinking, the

*This is the central thesis of Reiter 1974.

value judgments are overtly removed, but their cultural map remains, separating and labeling as male and female the spheres of workplace and home, labor and leisure, production and reproduction, money and love, public and domestic, and rationality and nurturance. We too easily accept these cultural antinomies as necessary outcomes of the gender division of labor, without considering the social relations that provided their context and which they in turn sustain. "Separate sphere" ideology flourished along with campaigns to remove children and women from production that accompanied the rapid spread of mass urbanization and factory-based wage dependency for men. This is the context in which Victorian understandings of the centrality of the nuclear family developed.

This cultural imagery now has serious social and political effects, as contemporary feminists have been quick to point out, for it naturalizes both women's activities and values. To the extent that the realm of paid work provides value (cultural because economic under capitalism), women's labors are symbolically depreciated. Indeed, as Sandra Harding has pointed out, the very categories of modern economics—Marxist as well as neoclassical—are sex biased. "Production" as a Euro-American category of analysis refers to the creation of wealth in things, and not in people. Activities surrounding the production of people (unpaid, and labeled "reproductive") are not culturally work, and they create no value.*

The naturalization of domestic labor associated with unpaid women's work has several important consequences. "Hidden in the household," this work appears unrelated to the "larger" circuits of economy, polity, and culture.† Household activities are then perceived as unchanging; they are easily and falsely universalized, reduced to breeding and feeding. Debates about household morphology and function then begin to replicate the problems in earlier exchanges on the nuclear family: we *can* locate such bounded units and observe a core of universal activities inside them, but we have already mislabeled and decontextualized the unit we create as we study it.‡

*See Harding 1981; for an alternative reading of a cultural system where reproduction creates value, see Weiner 1979, 1980.

†For discussions of the economics, politics, and history of women's work in the home, see Fox ed. 1980, Luxton 1980, Malos ed. 1980, and Oakley 1974.

‡This point is made in Harris 1981.

In recent years, several anthropologists have attacked the false naturalization of households from a variety of perspectives.* This form of ethnocentrism is a particularly vexsome problem in studies of underdeveloped economies, which rely heavily on household analysis. As Roger Sanjek has pointed out, we need to see households as more than mere tables of personnel and activities (Sanjek 1982). We must take into account the form and content of production, social reproduction, consumption, sexual union, and socialization of children—highly variable factors that respond to political and economic, as well as kinship, relations. One reason we have difficulty seeing the political and cultural dimensions of households more clearly is that their ideologically naturalized labors are assigned to women as part of general reproduction in Euro-American culture. We then speak of female-centered extended kinship as it binds households together, having already assumed the form and content of the units under discussion.

"The family" is a key symbol in American culture; everyone grows up in its shadow. (See Schneider 1968, 1972; Yanagisako 1978.) And despite its cultural privatization, there is much evidence that the domain of kinship is deeply implicated in the realm of current political symbolism in American culture. In a world in which household life has undergone continuous transformation, Americans actively appropriate, refashion, and legitimate their experiences in family language. Thus, the term "single mother" has come to validate the shared experience of millions of American women whose families might previously have been labeled "broken." A symbol in transition, "single mother" no longer designates a mother of an illegitimate child but a divorced mother whose family follows the pattern Ellen Lewin calls "informal matrifocality," a recent adaptation to spiraling divorce rates. Likewise, "working mother" condenses formerly disparate symbols—one normative for the public domain, one for the private domain—to rename and legitimate the presence of female wage earners in masses of American households.† "Gay marriage" is another label reflecting changed social experience that has made a less successful bid for legitimation in family language. Behind such cultural claims for

---

*Overviews of the household literature are provided in Wilk and Netting 1984, and in Yanagisako 1979.

†A useful discussion of how elements of kinship symbolism change is found in Yanagisako 1975.

recognition couched in kinship language lie demands for social services, civil rights, and general institutional support for such "new families."

And it is both kinds of claims—for cultural legitimation and social support—that have become central to American political discourse about family life in the 1980's. The New Right came to electoral power in part by mobilizing a "pro-family" voting bloc aimed at combating the "breakdown of the family," by which it meant any challenge to the normative, male-headed nuclear family. Much of its discourse has focused on abortion rights of women, homosexuality, and teenage sexuality. I believe these three issues are so potent symbolically because they speak to the loss of patriarchal kinship authority over relations of gender and generation. The New Right, of course, speaks the direct language of patriarchy, hoping to reprivatize kinship authority in the hands of the male household head. However, it has cast the symbolic mantle of patriarchal authority over institutions far removed from "the family" itself: its social programs aim to return government-funded services to the private sector, to entrust factory workers' health protection to their employers, and to leave school curriculum and busing decisions to "the community." What Rosalind Petchesky has labeled "corporate reprivatism" is thus a social agenda that speaks the political language of patriarchal family life.* Struggles over the definition of normative family life and its transformations are thus intertwined with political metaphors and mobilizations.

In discussing the seeming continuities of family life in Provence, and its discontinuities in America, I have been arguing for a deconstruction of our assumptions about kinship units. When we assume male-headed, nuclear families to be central units of kinship, and all alternative patterns to be extensions or exceptions, we accept an aspect of cultural hegemony instead of studying it. In the process, we miss the contested domain in which symbolic innovation may occur. Even continuity may be the result of innovation.

The young women who used to live in the female world of Montagnac and now depend on their urban mothers-in-law have been active participants in the appropriation of old kinship elements to new ends. They have substituted reliance on a diffuse network of

---

*The analysis of corporate reprivatization and the crisis of patriarchal family structures come from Petchesky 1981 and 1984.

siblings and mothers-in-law for reliance on mothers and sisters; yet, for them, a reassuring continuity exists. Their experience of cultural change occurs in the context of the urbanization of small cities in southern France, under conditions that allow them to enter wage labor and to face new stresses on parenting at a pace conducive to symbolic reproduction. They have little control over such conditions, although they clearly benefit from them. Short distances of migration and the possibility that several siblings and groups of in-laws will find themselves in the same small town allow minor kinship innovations to mask the discontinuities of migration. Despite their own sense of continuity, migrants have not "simply" kept their nuclear families and their female-centered, extended networks intact in their move. Rather, they have actively adapted old symbolic elements and sociabilities to make sense out of new contexts. What is continuous is their reliance on the authority and aid of elder kinswomen and their choice of child care in the female-centered domestic domain.

This sense of continuity is missing among many Americans experiencing "family breakdown." I might argue that the rapid rate of entry of women, especially mothers of young children, into the labor force; the precipitous shift in industrial and service-sector employment around the country; and the rise of movements since the Second World War explicitly aimed at sexual liberation have all contributed to the present contest over the cultural meaning of family life. Kinship has become more overtly politicized as the material conditions of sexuality, marriage, and maternity are transformed. We then experience a family transformation that is culturally labeled a decline. Once again, people are actively attempting to rework the symbolic elements at their disposal, in some cases to claim legitimacy for new family experiences, and in others, to deny it. And the outcome of these struggles is very much up for grabs.

In 1972, David Schneider told us, "One must take the natives' own categories, the natives' units, the natives' organization and articulation of those categories and follow their definitions, their symbolic and meaningful divisions, wherever they may lead. When they lead across the lines of 'kinship' into politics, economics, education, ritual, and religion, one must follow them there and include those areas within the domains which the particular culture has laid out" (Schneider 1972: 51). I believe we need to follow and transcend that advice. The hegemony of male-headed nuclear families and exceptionalism of female-centered extended kinship networks are both products of our specific history. To study the future of Euro-American kinship, we have to break through our mystification of its past. As cultural actors as well as anthropologists, we can only accomplish this task by taking gender politics seriously.

Sewing the Seams of Society: Dressmakers and Seamstresses in Turin Between the Wars

Vanessa Maher

THE POLITICO-JURAL domain in a class-stratified society is the product of the relationships among that society's various classes, even if one class is dominant. To elaborate on such a statement, I would be forced to present an analysis of legitimacy and consensus, class antagonism and hegemony, which I do not intend to pursue here but which is implicit in much that follows.

Classes that differ in their relationship to the management of social and economic resources may divide up the domestic and the politico-jural domains between men and women in different ways. For example, during the period under discussion, working-class families considered the management of family earnings to be the responsibility of the *materfamilias*; in bourgeois or noble families, it was the father who managed the family patrimony. It could be said that the first function is domestic, a matter of feeding and clothing the family, whereas the second concerns the deployment of resources in such a way as to create political alliances and to consolidate economic power. However, it was working-class mothers who took to the streets to protest the price of bread after the First World War and set off the famous occupation of the Fiat factories in Turin in 1920. Were they acting in the domestic or the politico-jural domain? Fulfilling female roles or usurping male ones? Judgments of the time differed according to the class of the speaker.

According to the census figures, the proportion of women registered in the regular Italian workforce (including all sectors of the economy) dropped from 48.6 percent to 28.6 percent of all workers between 1861 and 1911. This trend was clearly reflected in the industrial workforce, in which women—employed mainly in textiles and in food and tobacco processing—outnumbered men at the end of the nineteenth century. Their position then worsened as the twentieth century opened a period of "protective legislation" that tended to emphasize the priority of women's maternal and familial roles. Women's chances for regular employment were thus whittled away, and many were pushed into occupations that were increasingly underpaid and exploitable, such as outwork.

With the specter of postwar unemployment looming, women's courageous struggles to save their factory jobs were viewed resentfully, even by the male leaders of their labor organizations, who accused them of "leaving their homes" to compete with men for employment.

However, as Rayna Rapp has remarked in this volume, the separation of home from workplace that took place in industrializing countries during the nineteenth century, and the progressive expulsion of women from the regular workforce during the twentieth, did not put an end to women's work. Rather, such work was placed outside the sphere of paid contractual labor and thus rendered of little or no "value."

The fact that male trade union leaders, even before the advent of the Fascist regime, believed women properly belonged at home should not be taken to mean that they thought women should not work. Rather, it was women's extradomestic work that was considered admissible only when women were motivated by necessity and when they were not competing with men on the labor market. Reasoning along parallel, if not identical, lines, Liberal and Fascist legislators sought to "protect" only those women working on industrial premises outside the home. Women working at home were fulfilling their "natural" domestic calling. Such work "could be extremely exhausting, without time or age limits (e.g., agricultural labor, outwork, or work in the family workshop), but after all, it took place within the family as a natural accompaniment of domestic work and so did not entail exploitation and dishonor as did extradomestic work under a factory boss. Much better to be under the household boss, in an authoritarian and rigidly hierarchical family structure like that outlined by the current (Fascist) Civil Code" (Galoppini 1980: 47–58). Thus we find that both bourgeois and working-class women were expected to stay at home, where the latter were to carry out both their own domestic work and that of bourgeois families or to produce goods for the commodity market.

My hypothesis is that although all classes tend to associate "domestic" with women and "politico-jural" with men, the definitions they give to these spheres of action differ. The use that is made of this association is the same, however. It is normative and designed to maintain a specific power relation between men and women, in which women are subordinate to men.

However, as with all norms, this one is most apparent when violated. In this article, I will try to show how seamstresses in Turin played on the ambiguity in sexual roles created by the combination of different class practices with a single social norm. Their experience between the wars seems to point to a tug-of-war over gender and class prerogatives, in which the contenders knew alternate fortunes; the real interpenetration of the domestic and political, the private and public, the inside and the outside, shows up to a greater or lesser extent. However, it is not surprising that those working-class women who benefit least from such normative separations treat them with nonchalance.

The history of Turin seamstresses and dressmakers is intimately intertwined with the political and social history of the city and, indeed, of northern Italy. The presence of the Savoy monarchy's court at Turin and the growth of a flourishing natural textile industry in the Piedmont contributed to the importance of Turin's fashion industry in the second half of the nineteenth century and the first half of the twentieth. Most important was the link between fashion and Turin's rapid industrialization and social change. The life histories of many women who subsequently became famous in the city's political history note their beginnings as seamstresses.

My research has entailed a series of unstructured interviews with 24 dressmakers and former dressmakers about their lives and work histories, interviews conducted in their homes, workshops, or boutiques between 1981 and 1982. I came to know these women through friends and acquaintances closely tied to Turin dressmakers as relatives or clients, through the textile workers' union, and through members of the Union of Italian Women (UDI) who had helped to reorganize the "Circolo delle Caterinette," or "Seamstresses Circle," after the Second World War. This account of the seamstresses' experience between the wars relies on interviews with ten dressmakers and four UDI militants born before 1930 and on published biographies of dressmakers born between 1890 and 1910 (Serra 1977; Cavallo 1979–80; Noce 1977).

Seamstresses in the Atelier

Until the Second World War and for some years after it, down-town Turin was the scene of feverish sartorial activity, a center of fashion second only to Paris, from which it took many of its cues. The owners of the most important ateliers would journey to Paris to buy designs and then travel throughout Italy, collecting orders from houses of fashion and dressmakers. Designs would be bought, borrowed, or "stolen" by the lesser ateliers and workshops and so filter down to the dressmaker working on her own at home for a clientele of neighbors.

The intensity of work in Turin, then, varied according to the seasons of Parisian fashion and was especially high during the autumn and spring. During these periods, the number of seamstresses working in the ateliers increased by over a third, but during the *stagione morta*, the dead months of January, February, and August, all of them, even regular employees, were sent, significantly, home. However, rarely could their families do without their earnings, and those who could not find work in smaller workshops, which had a more modest clientele and were less affected by changes in fashion, would sew at home for neighbors or do mending until the atelier opened again.

The seamstresses were young, and most were unmarried. In fact, as a rule, they were fired upon marriage. Most entered the ateliers at about age thirteen or fourteen after having attended school for three or four years and then working as apprentices for a self-employed dressmaker, often a family friend or neighbor. But others were taken into the *grand atelier* even younger to work as *piccinin*, the little girls who picked up pins, bought thread, or carried parcels from atelier to client. Although an 1886 law concerning the work of women and children forbade the employment of children under nine years old, dressmakers considered themselves a special case. "An institution for the creation of luxury garments cannot be considered an industrial establishment," protested one employer in 1900 (Merli 1972: 23).

A rigid hierarchy regulated the seamstress's career. Only after her initiation as a *piccinin* or *cita*, when she learned to make her way through streets she had never seen before and through houses very different from her own, would she be admitted to the rank of *seduta*, or "seated worker," and trained to sew hems.

Rarely would she be directly or explicitly taught those skills on which her progress up the ladder of tasks and pay depended. It was a matter of "stealing with the eye" (*bisognava rubare coll'occhio*), a training in the imitation of gestures and attitudes that would be essential to the future dressmaker, whose task it was to manipulate social appearances. For the first three or four years in the atelier, the seamstress received nothing but token payment for her work. However, when she reached the grades of *aiutante* (assistant) and *lavorante* (dressmaker), she would be compensated idiosyncratically according to her *bravura* or "cleverness." (The term *bravura* has moral overtones and also means "good behavior.") In addition to owners, large ateliers included a *première*, or principal dressmaker, who worked directly with clients and was responsible for fittings; a *coupeur*, or cutter, usually male; and a *directrice*, or manager, responsible for work coordination and employee discipline. There were also *mannequins* who modeled the dresses.

Few seamstresses reached the ranks of *première* or *coupeur*. One reason was that most seamstresses would marry and then be fired; the *première* tended to be an older woman past the age of marriage. More important, the *première* and the *coupeur* were careful to guard the skills they controlled—the ability to establish confidential and appropriate relationships with rich clients—for this knowledge could render the *lavorante* capable of becoming an autonomous rival.

However, some informants suggested that the seamstresses themselves saw the atelier only as a place to prepare for married life. Most married couples first lived with one spouse's parents (usually the husband's) for a couple of years, and then moved to their own home, where the wife would have enough to set up her worktable and receive clients. The ambition to set up an independent business, to be able to choose one's own clients and hours of work, must nevertheless be viewed as an ambiguous one, induced in part by circumstances, in part by the material and moral restrictions on married women working outside the home.

Most dressmakers remember the period spent in the atelier as a time not only of freedom and gaiety "because we were young," but also of cruel privation and grinding work, which was paid too little to be considered a livelihood. As one dressmaker reported, "To get married was the only thing for a woman; from the economic point of view, she couldn't keep herself." And when she got married, she could no longer meet the inflexible demands of the atelier, since there were others at home, equally inflexible.

Conditions of work in the ateliers had been the subject of scandal for decades. Merli's account of working-class conditions in Italy at the turn of the century cites a number of sources between 1902 and 1906 that decry the tragic situation of the seamstresses. According to these sources, the sewing establishments, commonly called "schools" by their owners, made the girls work eighteen or twenty hours a day, and often on Saturdays and Sundays when the season of high fashion was approaching. In Turin the windows were blacked out so that no light could be seen from the outside and the illegal night-work could be kept hidden from prying eyes.

Professional diseases were rife among the seamstresses. The sources mention deformation of the spine, tuberculosis, eye disease, and a high frequency of miscarriages and menstrual troubles, since the use of the pedal-machine was known to cause damage to the reproductive organs (Merli 1972: 241–42, 251, 254).

An inquiry into the health of seamstresses in Turin in 1911 showed them to be increasingly anemic, especially in their early twenties, and in an overall state of health worse than that of a comparable sample of textile workers (Allaria 1911).

Although there was a gradual improvement in working conditions, such as the provision of heating at the employer's expense, the close personal relations between employers and seamstresses, which laid the latter open to emotional blackmail and bound them to their exploiters by expectations of loyalty, and the shrinking of the employment opportunities for women—in part as a result of the decline of the textile industry, in part as a result of Fascist legislation—made such improvements difficult to perceive until the early 1960s. In 1963, for example, a law was introduced that forbade the dismissal of women workers upon marriage, which up until then had been a matter of course (Società Umanitaria 1962).

Seamstresses' Age and Social Position

Since most seamstresses married at about twenty-five, they spent little more than ten years in the ateliers. Perhaps their adolescence explains their peculiar position, as a category of workers, with respect to the rest of society.

To begin with, the seamstresses were usually referred to by the diminutive form *sartina*, which carries connotations both of youth and of incomplete professional training. According to the stereo-type, they were not only young but elegant and *graziose*, dainty, inclined to amorous dallying. Their work, dedicated to the en-hancement of female charm, was seen as a kind of extension of their exquisitely feminine nature and a demonstration of worldly wisdom.

Informants themselves tended to describe a lifetime's grueling and poorly paid work in terms of a "passion": "It is really a kind of work which engages your mind. It is not just a question of physical effort, and to be able to do it, you must really have a passion for it; if not you can't do it." "Passion" is a term that belongs to the private sphere of the affections, but it also points to the voluntary artistic and creative side of the work in which its practitioners take great pride. The term itself indicates a contradiction that repeatedly emerges in the lives of the seamstresses even after they have left the atelier: that between family and professional commitments, be-tween a private and a public identity. The word "passion" evokes the self-forgetfulness or "prescriptive altruism" considered appro-priate to the performance of women's family roles. The seamstress who applies this attitude, learnt for family use, to her work in the atelier is a docile and profitable employee. However, it is also a source of professional pride and knowledge, such that she fashions a public identity that is anomalous in gender and class terms.

One dressmaker described the opposition of her mother's neigh-bors to her entering an atelier: "It was sheer perdition! They said: 'You can't send her to an atelier; they're such equivocal places!' But it wasn't." That the atelier was perceived as a place of "perdition," "equivocal," suggests that here we are dealing with a social space that was anomalous and interstitial with respect to social structure.

Spatial and Social Relations: Inside and Outside, High and Low

Turin, like many of the cities of Central Europe, betrays in its ar-chitecture the strength of the ideal of separating private and public life, but also the importance of the outdoor "social drama." The center of town is an important arena for the negotiation of prestige, with its covered arcades that permit strolling even in bad weather, its *piazze* surrounded by cafés and wine houses, its benches for sitting outside on warm evenings, its ice cream parlors, cinemas, and dance halls. Above all, the streets and squares in Italy are where the social order is represented, mocked, undermined, and renegotiated in the symbolic interaction of religious processions, political demonstrations, carnivals, festivals, and masquerades. And dress—dressing up, dressing to please, dressing to impress, dressing to frighten, dressing in fancy costume—is an essential part of this representation.

A person's dress, at least up until the Second World War, indicated a claim to social precedence and civil rights (Saraceno 1979–80). Women workers, for example, did not wear hats, although middle- and upper-class women did. Delicate materials and dainty shoes were the prerogative of women who could command a carriage or, later, an automobile. But despite these norms, movement out of doors always presents an occasion for making social claims, since this sphere is outside the control of intimates whom such claims could affect directly. Such claims, sustained by appearance alone, are made within a public framework. If collectively stated, they may be a means of testing political boundaries and of claiming social space. The claims and counterclaims to precedence and respect turn the public arena into a vortex of tensions into which everyone is drawn willy-nilly. In Turin, and perhaps in Italy in general, part of the skill of self-presentation lies in trapping the glance of the passerby and compelling respectful notice. One of the most obvious means of doing so is by one's dress. But the exchange of glances entails not only the notice of the aesthetic aspect of a person's appearance but also the appraisal of his or her social condition. A person's dress fits him or her for moving in certain social circles, in certain places, on certain occasions and not others.

It is the knowledge of the finer details of the symbolism of dress in relation to social circumstance which the seamstress acquires in the atelier and which, because of its changing and esoteric nature, is the basis of her power vis-à-vis the members of other social categories. The dressmaker's clients depend on her not only for the execution of their requirements but for their very formulation. The dressmaker knows not only how to collocate her clients symbolically within the social system, but also, unlike many of the other members of her own class, how these symbols should be used in different contexts—that is, the manners that go with the clothes. In Roland Barthes's terms, she possesses knowledge of costume as well as of dress (Barthes 1982).

It seems to me that if we add to this knowledge the technical capacity to produce clothes, considered as symbols, the dressmaker is seen to be in a position to create new relationships between symbols and referents or new referents for existing symbols. This happens, for example, when she invents new designs for other people, or when she makes fashionable clothes for herself, following designs she has come across in an atelier. It is my hypothesis that the deployment of prestigeful symbols, held generally to correspond to economic and political power in the politico-jural domain, by people whose power lies in esoteric knowledge of matters considered proper to the domestic domain, may actually change social relations, in particular those between the sexes and between classes, or other groups of higher and lower status.

In the discussion that follows, I intend to consider the seamstresses and dressmakers of Turin first in their capacity as "ritual experts," trained in the manufacture of the symbols with which the social order articulates in the public sphere. Second, I will consider them as participants in that social order, who use their symbolic and technical knowledge to subvert it and create enclaves of anomalous social relations, in which they enjoy certain freedoms. Finally, I will consider the social tensions to which their activity gives rise and their implications for social structure, or more exactly, for the relations between the classes and the sexes in Turin.

Dress and Undress: The Dressmaker and Her Clients

Common to the relationship between a woman and her dressmaker and that between a woman and her doctor is the central importance of the body. A woman faces both professionals in a state of undress, which establishes a "private" relationship similar in its secrecy and intimacy to relationships among family members or between sexual partners. In a world in which a woman gains the consideration of others above all as a function of her sexual attractiveness, her dress rehearsal in front of the mirror (the other which anticipates all others) with the dressmaker as witness and adviser, is a tense and revealing moment. Apart from the knowledge that the dressmaker acquires of her client's person—her body in its perfection or imperfection—she frequently comes to understand, and to share, to a certain extent, her client's emotional and relational concerns.

The dressmaker often demonstrates great sensitivity for the circumstances for which she is dressing her client and for the way her client wishes to appear in them. The client, on the other hand, often shows signs of dependence: "staying with" the same dressmaker for decades, coming to see her on any pretext, telephoning her to recount her woes. And the interest is reciprocal, as the following dressmaker's account indicates:

When I take up a fashion magazine—and really I'm a nobody, I'm just a working woman—but as I leaf through that magazine, and I see a dress I like, I know that sooner or later I'll make it for a client, because I know who ought to wear that dress. . . . I link it straightaway to a person, and if I don't manage to make it for myself, I make it for someone before the season is over. Because it is something that seizes me, and somehow I succeed in convincing my clients, and those of them that have been coming for many years know that already. They come here with the material and they say, "Think about it, then you decide what to do with it." And it is the only way because if they come saying "I want this dress" we start off badly because I don't feel like doing it.

This same dressmaker said how much she enjoyed making wedding dresses:

Perhaps because you participate in this moment, in the euphoria which it gives you, and perhaps you go to the wedding feast, and they toast the dressmaker. That made me cry once; it was lovely, a marvellous thing. You see, that girl was a secretary, but her husband was a notary, and her in-laws were all notaries from way back. And that was a fine wedding and so was the wedding dress. I had copied a design of Nina Ricci's; it was lovely and everyone liked it very much, with a turban head-dress. We try to add something personal, otherwise I say, "Go and buy it already made."

In this context, one could tentatively advance the hypothesis that the wedding dress—and perhaps dress in its public and ceremonial aspect, in general—is a dominant symbol in Victor Turner's sense: "The symbols as I have affirmed, produce the action, and dominant symbols tend to become the centers of focalization of the interaction. The groups mobilize around them, venerate them, carry out other symbolic activities near them and add other symbolic objects to them. . . . Generally these groups of participants indicate important components of the secular social system, like the families and lines of descent" (Turner 1967: 47).

The process by which the dressmaker, using personal knowledge voluntarily or involuntarily conveyed to her, contributes to the social and personal identity of her client, is one in which she often displays more worldly (or ceremonial) knowledge than does the latter. She handles the social system in its symbolic aspect, and this function creates in the client a strong sense of dependence and complicity. But it is in the atelier or rather during the years spent in the center of town and in contact with people of all statuses and walks of life, that the seamstress acquires this knowledge, which will be necessary for establishing successful relationships with her future clients. Yet, in the atelier, she experiences the contrast between her own relation to these symbols of status and that of the rich clients. Whereas the bodies of the latter are cossetted and adorned, her own is abused and neglected. Much of the behavior of the seamstresses and later of the dressmakers appears to be in rebellion against this situation and indicates that they used all the means available to them to modify it.

The Body in the Atelier

Battles between employers and workers over the question of workers' physical needs come under the heading "conditions of work." In the atelier, these battles take on the extra significance of struggles over social worth and identity, given the contrast between the suppression of the seamstress's physical requirements and the elevation of the client's person, ever present in the form of a dummy proportioned to her size and shape.

The seamstresses I interviewed vividly remember episodes in which they were physically neglected. One remembers that a girl with acute menstrual pains was not allowed to interrupt her work for ten minutes. Another remembers being forced to sit for hours on a broken stool and then, when she had difficulty, being struck on the back by the *directrice*, who told her, "You're not here to lie down." A third remembers her indignation when as an apprentice she was told to deliver a hat late in the evening to a client who needed to wear it to the Royal Theatre: "I began to say to myself, 'Just look at that. I still have to have my supper and everything, and she is there just waiting for me and making herself elegant in her fine evening clothes, just waiting for her hat to go to the theater.'"

Although it is their relation to production that determines the seamstresses' status, they are well aware that they are producing the *symbols* of status on which a woman without real power in the politico-jural domain is highly dependent for public consideration. Since they are familiar with both "costume" and "dress," they are as capable as anyone else of displaying such symbols and enjoying the benefits of public consideration—if they can escape the social sanctions that would prevent them from usurping the prerogatives of other classes.

The mannequin, although she is a worker and shares the social origins of the seamstresses, receives attention as a physical person, and in this way may claim a higher social status. When the Labor Inspectorate carried out an inquiry into the health of workers in the dressmaking establishments of Turin in 1911, they noted that the mannequins refused the appellative of *operaia* (worker), and claimed that of *signorina* (young lady). *Signorina* indicates an unmarried lady, and to a certain extent holds out the prospect of becoming *signora*, married lady of means. In fact although many of the seamstresses had *amici*, friends and lovers from other classes, the girls they cited as having married into another class were often mannequins.

However, marriage out of their own class constituted a part of the seamstresses' and dressmakers' dream. Its incidence was rare but the fact that it did occur is a symptom of the permeability of class particularly in a society subject to rapid social and economic change.

In the seamstresses' stories of work in the atelier, the clients appear somewhat ridiculous, their fat dummies the butt of the workers' obscene jokes. The young and pretty seamstresses mocked the dignity supplied by "costume" to those clients whom they did not consider dignified or socially superior. Because of their symbolic knowledge, the seamstresses were a continual challenge to the upper classes' monopoly on certain kinds of appearance.

For this reason, their employers tried to prevent them from acquiring the whole trade, as mentioned above. The cutting out of a design was a key part of its realization, and in most ateliers this task was carried out by a man who couldn't sew or by the owner herself. But the seamstresses made copies of the designs, outlining them on fine tissue paper with the chalk for marking hems and smuggling them out under their clothes. One woman recounted that she had copied a skirt with three side pleats for herself and for her sister, a simple enough design. Imprudently, she wore it to work, and the manager of the atelier was so furious that she cut it to bits. Other seamstresses said that they knew that they would be fired if they were caught smuggling a design or wearing it near the center of town: "If a great lady saw a little seamstress with a dress like hers, there was trouble!" Nevertheless, the seamstresses were recognized as a group that dressed with taste and elegance. "There were working-class girls who had learned to sew, who wore a nice little hat, two or three stylish garments, and you couldn't see they were poor."

Perhaps even more important was the fact that the seamstresses filtered the top fashion designs down through the dressmaking trade and, to a certain extent, acted to regulate fashion as a system of social differentiation. One milliner who worked in a fashionable atelier told me that she was never out of work in the "dead season" because the small workshops took her on, hoping she would betray the secrets of the coming fashions. An even greater threat to the ateliers was the seamstresses' habit of keeping their dressmaker friends and relatives in touch with the fashions in the ateliers and of taking on clients in their neighborhoods after working hours. In some ateliers, seamstresses were forbidden to have their own customers, and since the manager and even the owners were often of the same milieu as their employees, they were able to have them watched. The diffusion of designs meant that new ones had to be introduced to act as symbols of social distinction. However, it was this function of the seamstresses that created a demand for their skill in the rest of society.

The Dressmaker and the "Quartiere Popolare"

The Liminality of the Atelier

My discussion of the seamstresses and dressmakers of Turin has begun, as did many interviews with my informants, with the most "visible" phase in their lives: their work in the center of town in the fashionable ateliers, those that dominated appearance in the public arena. This period in their lives is remembered as the most exciting and romantic, characterized in the popular imagination by stories of amorous relations between university students and pretty seamstresses. However, although this colorful and contradictory picture of the dressmaker's years in the atelier is arresting, it captures only a small part of her working life, the years from early adolescence to marriage. The peculiar characteristics of this period have led me to describe it as liminal. During this time, young women tended to transgress class boundaries, to evade the domestic and private norms considered proper to their sex, to work within an anomalous assembly of female peers, to experience female sociality outside the home and among non-kin, to take part in the obscene and carnivalesque joking characteristic of the atelier, to avoid male control of relations among women. In fact, they refer frequently to dreams and masquerade in descriptions of their work and the fine garments they produced. Finally, it was clearly a time and place for training, technical and social, and the acquisition of knowledge, social and sexual.

The following description of atelier life by Teresa Noce, later a famous trade unionist and Communist militant, is to a certain extent a stereotype; many ex-seamstresses describe their experience in these terms.

Although I didn't know how to sew at all, I liked the work straightaway. It seemed new, exciting (*appassionante*). It wasn't easy like ironing, because here it was a question of creating lovely, elegant, filmy things. All the workers loved the work. They wanted to get married but not to leave off working after marriage. Their dream was to set up on their own.

Through the talk of these seamstresses, I discovered love for the first time. All of them had boyfriends and while they worked, they talked freely of them. The other apprentice Marcella took charge of my sexual education. I knew very little. She unveiled many mysteries to me, and explained things that I hadn't understood until then. First of all, the mystery of woman, because she already had her menstrual periods and so could procreate, whereas I was still a girl (child—*bambina*). Thanks to Marcella's instruction, when I became a woman too, I did not go through a trauma like many other girls did (Noce 1977: 11).

The use of words like "mystery" suggests that such knowledge, like the more technical knowledge acquired in the atelier, was regarded as esoteric. It is knowledge that bourgeois and aristocratic women—who were supposed to be virgins at the time of marriage and who did not have similar opportunities for spending time with their peers far from parental control—probably acquired much later, if ever.

To grasp the significance of the atelier as a place in which the seamstresses passed a liminal period of their lives and to understand its relation to social structure, we must take into account not only the network of relations in which seamstresses were involved before marriage but also those they set up after marriage. We should consider not only the terms of the network but also the nature of the exchanges within it. After marriage, most dressmakers went on working for forty or fifty years, although this work was not memorable for society at large. Perceived as domestic, private, indoor work, it is nevertheless the main bulk of production in the dress trade.

Work, Leisure, and Sociality in the "Quartiere Popolare"

In the last quarter of the nineteenth century, the population of Turin increased by 243,000 people, and another 199,000 were refused residence. To accommodate the new immigrants, mostly workers from the countryside, whole new residential areas were built on the edges of the city; thus, the relation of center to periphery took on precise class connotations. The new *quartieri* were indicated by the term *borgo*, and it is generally to these *borghi* that we refer when we use the term *quartieri popolari*.

When analyzing the class origins of the seamstresses, we should take into account the fact that many workers were also artisans part-time or at some phase in their lives and that the shopkeepers in the *quartiere* were also part of the workers' network of social relations and shared the same set of cultural assumptions. Although only two-thirds of the seamstresses' fathers were identified as workers, the artisans and shopkeepers who made up the remaining third may have been enjoying merely a temporary ascendancy; many artisans expected their daughters to marry workers. The Italian phrase *quartiere popolare* seems more apt for this community than "working-class neighborhood," for it reflects a fluidity of occupational status typical of Italian productive organization until quite recently and particularly marked between the wars (see also Gribaudi 1983; Levi et al. 1978).

In the words of Massimo Paci, an Italian sociologist well known for his research on the Italian labor market, the late-nineteenth-century productive structure based on small workshops and outwork was "considered to be functional to the need of the developing national manufacturing industry to make the best use of what was perhaps its only real resource: an abundant and cheap labor force. The other factors of production were organized around this fundamental resource. . . . There is much evidence that the entrepreneurial class was well aware of the advantages of this kind of organization of productive life" (Paci 1982: 23, 24).

Fascist economic policies favored the emergence and reinforcement of a sharp dualism between the traditional sectors manufacturing textiles, clothing, food, and wood byproducts, in which employment was increased by emphasizing casual labor and by exploiting the contribution of part-time farmers, and the relatively advanced sectors comprising chemical and engineering industries, in which the state had a stronger incentive toward productive concentration.

In addition to this dualism in production, which placed dressmakers and most of the artisans in the *quartiere popolare* in the sector of high labor inputs and relatively low-priced products, there was also a dualism in consumption.

The *quartiere popolare* must be seen as an environment with a high concentration of different skills, a chronic scarcity of capital, and a negligible circulation of money. The exchange of goods and services within the *quartiere* enabled many people to make a living and to acquire goods that would have been too expensive for them to buy. For example, the woman who sold dressmakers' finishings was often linked to her customers as a client.

However, perhaps it is legitimate to view the pool of skills in the *quartiere* as a collective resource on which almost everyone had some claim—and toward which everyone had an obligation. Boys would be apprenticed to their fathers' workmates, or girls would go to "learn" from dressmakers working at home—neighbors, relatives, or friends of their mothers. Thus, although the dressmaker's immediate concern was her family and primary kin, her relation to the other women she met in the shops and the streets would involve her in a series of exchanges, such that she came to be a key figure in the neighborhood. Moreover, the dressmaker's skills and the contacts she maintained with women who continued to work in ateliers would permit her to cultivate a richer clientele who paid cash and whose business in some cases promised her real social mobility. The social world of the client occasionally became fused with that of the dressmaker to the extent that the latter's children became part of it, attending the university and becoming teachers, architects, or even professors.

All the dressmakers, in fact, talked of the friendship and affection linking them to their clients and within which they experi-

enced an essential equality. Although most dressmakers with atelier training potentially attract both neighborhood and rich clients,
their choice of clientele is often conditioned by the occupations of
other members of their families. For example, one widowed dressmaker was supported by business from her secretary daughter's
workmates. Family members may restrict as well as expand business, however, as commonly happens when a worker husband
feels threatened by his wife's rich clients and forces her to drop
them. After the First World War, in particular, many husbands ob-
jected to their wives attending to clients after working hours when
they were at home. The husband not only felt his preeminent right
to his wife's services to be threatened but also resented his wife, in
his presence, representing the household to members of other
households and other classes (see Cavallo 1981). That is, she was
assuming a public role that was normatively his as head of the
household. Such a husband might well accept his wife working
outside the home.

In order to understand the way in which the dressmaker was
conditioned by the economic and political roles of other members
of the household, it will be useful to take a brief look at the developmental cycle of the domestic group in which she was involved.

The Household in the Quartiere Popolare

The single household in Turin between the wars was a unit in
which resources were pooled. Earners "put their earnings in the
family," to translate the Italian expression literally. To a certain extent, the members of the family were subordinate to rules of consumption accepted within the group but not common to all its
members; girls as smaller earners received half the pocket money
to which their brothers were entitled. However, it should be emphasized that the resources of members living within the household were not the only ones that could be called upon. In fact,
primary kin, living in other households, were expected to be associated in a close if secondary way in its material well-being.

As children married, they would live for a short while with their
parents until they found a home of their own. However, their new
apartment was most often nearby, and until the newly married
dressmaker had children, she would often visit her parents' house
to help with domestic tasks and any outwork in which members of
the household were engaged. One does not have the impression of

a brusque or drastic separation between the dressmaker and her kin. On the contrary, their lives continued to weave in and out of one another.

In all cases in which a mother outlived her spouse, she would go and live with one of her daughters, often the dressmaker who worked at home and who would take care of her. By contrast, a widowed father generally refused to relinquish his position as head of the household. As long as both parents were alive, they stayed in their own house, even if the mother were too ill to cope with housework, and their daughters visited daily to take care of their needs.

It is possible that a mother's desire to have her daughters learn a trade reflected her need to facilitate their and her obligations as housekeepers rather than her hope that they could earn an independent living. Indeed, most seamstresses said that their fathers had decided to train them as dressmakers and some fathers seem to have had greater ambitions for their daughters than their mothers had. One father, for example, planned for his three daughters to set up a business together; he, in his old age, would have organized the delivery side. However, the marriages of all three daughters apparently put an end to his project. Many workshops and even ateliers were indeed run by two or three sisters; a quarter of all those listed in the Commercial Catalogue of 1919 had this structure. Given the low capital investment necessary for setting up a workshop, this was one way of providing family members with more lucrative employment than could be had *sotto padrone* and of maintaining the family fund undivided.

The Place of the Dressmaker in the Family Economy

Of all family members, it is usually the dressmaker who looks after the old and ill. Yet it is also the dressmaker who is best equipped to help out the family when other members are not contributing income. A woman can be put to work at her labor-intensive workbench, and men can rely on her earnings when still in school, unemployed, or in debt.

The "family" tasks of the seamstress or dressmaker seem far less related to the care of children than to housekeeping and its close relation, stop-gap earning. Of the sixteen women in my sample who worked in this period, seven had no children, six had one child and three had two. Yet perhaps their sense of having a sure and constant market for their skills, however badly paid, during the whole course of their lifetimes promotes the description many dressmakers give of themselves as "independent."

It is difficult to derive such an epithet from their financial circumstances, for their earnings are often barely enough to cover the living expenses of one person, let alone the rent of a house. They are forced to live with their family of origin or with a wage-earning husband and in a position subordinate to the household head. However, in more general terms, this self-description reflects a confidence in their capacity to support themselves under any circumstances, a pride in their skill, and an assurance of their ability to enter into advantageous relationships with non-kin or neighbors, that is, to act in the public sphere without needing a male mediator. And it is this capacity that is penalized within marriage and proves to be a source of tension within the family, since it contrasts with the accepted hierarchy not only within the family but also outside it.

At this point, it might be illuminating to review the normative categories to which the dressmakers are supposed to conform. "Public" and "private" have a different extension to "inside" or "outside" the household, for women's private networks include kin living in other households. In a more confusing way, a dressmaker's private circle also includes some of her clients of whom she speaks in affectionate terms, although her husband may regard them as outsiders related to her only by contract. It may also include neighbors, to whom she acknowledges a moral bond. Therefore, there are many discrepancies between the real activities and social relations of dressmakers (and perhaps of other women too) and those ideally attributed to them in the social construction of gender identity. And if we accept the existence of a network of "extradomestic" relationships among women, kin, and neighbors— relationships that do not concern only the affective or "reproductive" functions—the dichotomies of "domestic/political," "private/public," and "inside/outside" become difficult to apply in a sex-linked way.

As Rayna Rapp points out in her article in this collection, unpaid activities are not carried out exclusively within the family, if indeed the latter can be regarded as a bounded entity. Further, if "domestic" refers to the sphere of "human reproduction" and so to maternal functions, why should it be a "female" sphere in generic terms, unless it is constructed around culturally rather than biologically defined roles (see Edholm, Harris, and Young 1977; Harris 1981)? And if the domestic unit is represented in the politico-jural sphere by its male head, how do we conceptualize the relations of women across domestic units? And how, in the case of the dressmakers and seamstresses, do we conceptualize the relations of women with men outside the domestic unit? For it is perhaps this aspect of their behavior that offers the most striking contrast to social norms for gender identity.

Geographical Mobility and Gender in Turin

In order to point out the distinctiveness of the behavior of the seamstresses in Turin, it will be useful to plot the movements of other segments of the city population. As girls in primary school, and after marriage, working-class women tend to be confined within their own *quartiere*, where they often seek flats for their married daughters. As adolescents and as unmarried women, they move out of the *quartiere* to go to work. Boys are more mobile, both as youngsters within the *quartiere* and as adolescents attending evening school and frequenting, to some extent, the center of town. However, the factories in which men work and the artisans to whom they are apprenticed are likely to be in their own *quartiere*. Married men are closely tied to the neighborhood; they may meet at a wine house for a drink after work but rarely go out at night (see Gribaudi 1983).

The town center is the place for offices, shops, and public buildings such as the university, and for the more elegant places of entertainment: theaters, cafés, cinemas, dance halls. It is frequented by people of leisure and, during regular working hours, by middle- and upper-class men, university students, and working-class adolescents. The latter two groups also frequent the riverbanks and the riverside parks, roaming in bands that often engage in savage fights.

The seamstresses were the only category of women, apart from a few secretaries and the shop assistants, to work in the center of town. Certainly, they were the most numerous. Perhaps to a greater extent than their male working-class peers, they frequented middle-class precincts, cafés, and theaters. Given their irregular hours and their distance from home, their behavior during and after working hours was subject to few controls. Often they would go dancing, informing their fathers that they would be late at work. Their mothers regularly aided them in this subterfuge, sometimes accompanying them to the dances and helping them in other ways to elude their fathers' somewhat distracted eye.

This was the period of love affairs between seamstresses and university students. The latter were also going through a liminal phase in which they were subject to few "domestic" controls but not yet integrated into the professional and institutional framework of their class. Superficially, this kind of relationship might appear similar to that between the *senoritos* of Alcalá described by Pitt-Rivers, and young women of the pueblo.

If the behaviour of the *senoritos* [of Alcalá] conforms less strictly to the morality of the pueblo, it is because they escape the full force of the moral sanctions of the community. They demand, at the same time, a stricter mode of conduct from their women-folk. . . . In effect these restrictions virtually exclude any young woman who is regarded as a social equal, and in this way the manifestations of anti-social sex are projected outside the circle of local upper-class society (Pitt-Rivers 1971: 118).

There seems to be some evidence that the young seamstresses did not regard their relations with the students as a matter of "anti-social sex," and indeed the term *amico*, often used to describe a student lover, suggests a more complex relationship than does *innamorato* or *amante*, which have middle-class, extra-conjugal implications.

Many of the attitudes that seamstresses convey in their accounts of relationships with students have already been noted in other contexts: a sense of independence, a desire for knowledge, a certain aspiration to social mobility, a demand for equality, and a considerable nonchalance toward the norms that defined proper behavior for their sex. In particular, they exhibited a certain lucidity about social and class relations, which prompted one dressmaker to say that she thought the seamstresses got far less involved than the students, although in the popular myth the seamstress dies of a broken heart when her student lover gets his degree and abandons her to marry a woman of his own class. As the following interview excerpts demonstrate, the seamstresses' accounts of these affairs contrast sharply with this stereotype:

They talk a lot about the girls today, but we were wide awake; perhaps it was because we went to work at twelve years old, and so we always had a lot of boys paying us attention. You see, it was like that. I began to go around town very early and so you get used to such things.

You see what happened. They were very pretty girls, very elegant and fine with nice manners, because they were used to working and talking with those ladies, and so they liked the students, and the middle-class boys liked these girls too, and so there were always problems.

There were so many problems; for example the fear of being pregnant, of pregnancy and with the families as they were then, the work and everything.

To be sincere, at that time, we were romantic; we liked love to be like that. At that time, we were in young company, we had met boys of good family who were marvelous, and now when I hear of certain things happening, they seem impossible. At one time they behaved like real gentlemen. We went out together, it was lovely because we were all friends (*amici*).

Then there were many students around, we had a thirst for knowledge, we always frequented the students. We learned a lot of things because they were at the university, and you see that means we really had a thirst for knowledge; it was always like that.

Then there were some workers who studied, certainly my brother did, but there were also workers who had very little culture, but we had a great desire for culture and we wanted to get to know these boys [the students] also to learn to speak Italian well [because at home the seamstresses spoke Piedmontese dialect].

In my opinion, I think it right that they want to be equal [*uguagliarsi* is almost "get equal"], frequent people in order to know more about things.

And then we didn't have the problem of getting married; it irritated us to hear people talking of marriage; it wasn't our problem. When you have a work qualification, what happens? You are always independent and then you create, you really choose. Not that they told you to marry that one, but we didn't agree to. We chose him ourselves, also because we were already at work.

By pursuing these relationships, seamstresses were transgressing both gender and class boundaries, creating a tension throughout the social order. Unlike women of other classes, they attended theaters and frequented cafés in groups, without male escorts; they circulated outside their social milieu and did not observe the middle- and upper-class restrictions on premarital sexual activity. It is not surprising that relations between students and workers were hostile, nor that it was the student's womenfolk who tended to prevent him from marrying his *amica*, whom they treated with contempt and described as a "loose woman," whatever her real virtues. These are only some of the sanctions that operated to restore class boundaries.

The Seamstresses' Ball

However, it was the students themselves who felt uneasy about the seamstresses' challenge to gender boundaries. It is perhaps this uneasiness that was expressed in the students' ribald behavior at the Seamstresses' Ball "Feste delle Caterinette," held every year on November 25th, the feast day of their patron, St. Catherine. This celebration was an important public appearance for the seamstresses, treated with all seriousness.

Various firms and shops would contribute their products or lengths of material, which the seamstresses would use to create a fashion parade that took place in an elegant ballroom, usually in the center of town.

We all went with the students to the Valentino Park, in the evening you saw all the students with bunches of flowers because it was the seamstresses' day. . . . [We went] always [to] the Valentino, and then there was a great ball, there was a fashion parade. . . . It was a romantic thing, everyone knew there was this big party, and so everyone made herself a new dress, a new hat, there was such a coming and going and then it was wonderful the way these girls were dressed. And so we went to this party and there was the ball and afterward the fashion parade. We went, all the girls who worked in our workshop, and there were the boys from the faculties of medicine and engineering and all the faculties of the university, with their hats [feathered three-cornered fancy-dress hats], then they used to wear these hats. Then there was the ball and when we came out there were all the couples in the Valentino. Because in Turin at that time we used to go to take a walk [*fare la passeggiata*] in the Valentino, or in the via Roma.

The ball was the scene of the seamstresses' reappropriation of their own creations. Here they paraded in the latest fashions. Here they celebrated their art and its authorship, normally claimed by the owner of the atelier or by the client who reaped a harvest of prestige and admiration. The seamstresses were normally invisible. The visible ones were the rich ladies who "consumed" their work. At the ball, the seamstresses not only "consumed" their own work, but did so with the maximum publicity. Moreover, they did so in their own name, not as part of the public identity of a man.

The seriousness of the seamstresses, who still keep photos of the occasions and describe them in nostalgic and triumphant tones, contrasts with the students' ribaldry. They used to come in "fancy dress" and enact a number of jokes. One of these was the attempt to carry off the girl whose dress and whose beauty had won her the title of "Caterinetta of the Year." She symbolized, in other words, the seamstresses' claim to represent themselves in the public arena. More often the students' "jokes" were directed at the dresses of the girls, the means of their distinction. They surrounded a girl and threatened to set her tulle dress on fire with their cigarette lighters, or they tore the winning dress off the "Caterinetta of the Year."

In such cases, it seems to me that their aim was not so much to humiliate the girl (as it was, perhaps, in cases where men stripped girl strikebreakers) as to reduce her to her "private" identity, to strip her of her pretensions to appear in public. It was an attempt to destroy the ceremonial aspect of the occasion and turn it into one that recalled the relations of maximum informality and intimacy to which they wished the seamstresses to confine themselves. It was also, to a certain extent, a sexual assault, sanctioning the seamstresses' organizing their own public appearance without the male company that made it legitimate.

Conclusion

In my study of the lives and work of seamstresses and dressmakers between the wars, I have found it impossible to use the gender-linked dichotomies domestic/political, private/public, and inside/outside as descriptive or otherwise heuristic categories. It seemed rather that these were folk categories used by social actors and legislators in situations where, for example, the behavior of the seamstresses and dressmakers tended to challenge existing hierarchies and power relations. That is, the dichotomies have a normative function serving to guarantee to certain social groups the personal services and surplus value produced by others.

John Comaroff's article in this collection comments on the ideological nature of the dichotomy between domestic and political and points out that, within capitalist systems, the separation of home and workplace is essential to this representation. The point I wish to make also echoes one made in 1980 by Michelle Rosaldo, who suggested that the terms "domestic" and "public" (here in my sense of "politico-jural," referring to activities rather than to social relations) are used to evaluate activities in a way that gives the former less weight than the latter. In their sex-linked version, they are used to describe women's activities as "domestic" and men's as "public," whatever their real nature (Rosaldo 1980). The same is true to a certain extent and at certain points in Western European history for the nature/culture dichotomy (Bloch and Bloch 1981).

Women are taught that the activities proper to their sex are of secondary importance, and men are taught the opposite. Further, women are portrayed as continuing to perform the same "domestic" tasks over time, while men are portrayed as "making history" in the political field. In pointing out that the domestic-politico-jural dichotomy is both normative and evaluative, I suggest that it is an important instrument of women's subordination. Women's activities in all classes should be dedicated toward enabling men's work and sociality and reproducing the family.

However, for working-class men, "home," with its connotation of personal service by the women of the household, means the satisfaction of physiological and emotional needs; for bourgeois men, it is a place to receive society, to exhibit. To a certain extent, a bourgeois wife and mother is supposed to participate in the exhibition of her husband's and her children's superior social status, rather than to cater to their physiological needs. Hence, dress assumes great importance.

It seems to me that, in both cases, we are dealing with a further dichotomy of normative import, between private and public social relations. In general, the representation of women is subsumed by men in their own public aspect. However, as Edholm, Harris, and Young (1977: 26) remark: "Women do not naturally disappear; their disappearance is socially created and constantly reaffirmed. Often men's solidarity is created precisely on the basis of the absence of women. . . . Keeping women out of public roles is in fact a positive and time-consuming aspect of social organization."

Although rendering women invisible entails, to a certain extent, "shutting them away," the concepts of public and private seem to me to be less spatial than relational concepts. Public relations are impersonal, often contractual, and to a certain extent representational. Generally, they are governed by a formal etiquette or even ceremonial of which dress forms a part. "Private" signifies a closed set of personal relationships in which behavior is informal and seg-regated from the public gaze. Here again, the dichotomy is ideal, and these sets of relations interweave in a generally unacknowl-edged way.*

The last dichotomy that occurs repeatedly in the social construc-tion of gender identity in Western Europe is that of inside/outside. This division does not coincide with private/public, nor with do-mestic/political, but the overlap is important. Women are sup-posed to stay at home. The social tensions deriving from the fact that many working-class women do not do so during at least a part of their lives are clearly seen in this account of the seamstresses' experience.

These dichotomies, which appear to be implicit in much of the literature of the time—and indeed have not disappeared since fem-inists pointed out that "the personal is political"—are also reflected in the way the dressmakers I interviewed treated *casa*, that is, home or house:

There was that kind of mentality that at a certain point it was a good thing that woman learned a skill because she could work at home and look after her house. . . . Even my father used to say to me, "Oh yes, it's a good thing that you learn a skill; at least you won't go outside the house. Be-cause I know what it means to go and work under a boss. . . . " Nowa-days, it is all right that these girls go outside the house, that they should study, create a world of their own. But then it was like that, and unfor-tunately one's husband was like that too, even if he had seemed so ad-vanced. But he said: "I can see these secretaries who work with me. I see them; there's no point. That's fine that you're at home. You look after the children; if you want to make some little thing, you can." And in the mean-time, the woman is kept under, even if we never said so. But anyway she is shut up within four walls, the children, husband. Then at the end you had a little freedom in this work, which perhaps you even liked doing. Once you left off that, it was all over.

I think several themes emerge quite clearly from this dialogue: the normative content of *home* and *house*; the contraposition of in-side and outside, husband and boss, private and public; the dis-regard for women, such as secretaries, who challenge these dis-tinctions; and the roles of husbands and fathers in enforcing the whole. Female labor should be devoted to the household, accord-

*Rayna Rapp Reiter tends to treat this distinction as empirically rather than nor-matively based and consequent on state organization. See "Men and Women in the South of France," in Reiter ed. 1975.

ing to an ethic of "prescriptive altruism." Work outside the house for money is in many accounts associated symbolically or explicitly with prostitution. The key issue in the attempts, particularly by men, to confine the seamstresses and dressmakers to certain spheres of activities and relationships appears to be the control of their services and the surplus value they produce.

Thus husbands and fathers intended their wives and daughters to work "inside," to "look after the house and children," rather than to provide services to their employers. Husbands opposed their wives' working for clients if it detracted from their personal comfort and prestige. Upper-class women opposed marriages between their male relatives and dressmakers. Such marriages had an equalizing effect that threatened bourgeois women's access to the services of women of lesser means. Students and employers attacked the dressmakers' appropriation of their own skills for their own benefit, rather than using them for the greater prestige of male companions or upper-class women.

It is clear that such sanctions were applied not only to dressmakers but to all women during the period in question. Male trade unionists advised female industrial workers to "go home" and leave their jobs to the men. Yet women continued to work. The sanctions applied to their work were low pay and lack of legal and social recognition, which guaranteed their dependence on male earnings and protection, in exchange for which their personal services were forfeit.

Power relations within the city were expressed in territorial terms that determined who should occupy which social roles and who could command which services in which context. The rivalry between adolescent workers and students was exacerbated because it was indeterminate which group had the clear right to command the seamstresses' female services. It is this element—the possibility of upper-class men marrying poorer women and the challenge offered by the latter's male peers—which differentiates a class society such as that of Turin from societies based on hierarchies of caste or race, such as those in the Caribbean described by Raymond Smith. Marriage to someone higher in the racial hierarchy was not possible for the slave mistress in the latter context, and her male peers could offer no challenge to the white man's claim to her sexual and domestic services.

Where the domestic and private spheres are subordinate to and encompassed by the political and public spheres, social ideology enjoins women to serve men and the lower class to serve the upper class. In the last analysis, state institutions tend to reinforce these normative arrangements in favor of upper-class men. To this extent, the normative distinction between a female "domestic" and a male "political" sphere would seem to be a male fiction that many women disappoint in practice and deride in speech.

In this article, I have tried to indicate how, partly through conscious effort and partly through the nature of their work and their key role in the representation of the social order, the seamstresses and dressmakers in Turin came to obscure the relationship between the symbolic articulation of the classes and the sexes and their actual interaction. In this way, they created anomalous enclaves of social relations, within which they enjoyed certain freedoms. These freedoms were tolerated by society as long as the seamstresses were in liminal positions in society, or as long as they were in a liminal period of their lives. However, since they were linked to a skill that the dressmaker continued to practice and to a social identity that she never completely relinquished, they tended to contribute to the fluidity of gender and class relations. The areas of uncertainty are those marked by explosions of conflict: between men and women within the family, between men of different classes (students and workers), between women of different classes (seamstresses and their upper-class lovers' mothers), between men and women of different classes (students and seamstresses). It is remarkable that it is in precisely these areas that the dressmaker set up relationships within which she exercised a certain power and claimed equality. Certainly, her alliances with other girls in the atelier and with other women inside and outside the family provided her with a certain coverage. As one dressmaker said, "We were the first feminists."

Part Two

The Politics of Marriage

Hierarchy and the Dual
Marriage System in West Indian Society

Raymond T. Smith

The Problem and Theoretical Considerations

The Caribbean has always been a test case for theories of the family and woman's role in society. High illegitimacy rates, unstable conjugal unions, and a high proportion of female-headed households pose a problem for theories which assume that nuclear families are necessary in all societies and that men are the natural heads of families. Those theories generally adopt the distinction between "domestic" and "politico-jural" domains, assigning women to the one and men to the other. Because of its deep roots in European culture, that distinction continues to be a preoccupation of modern feminist writing, but the Caribbean case shows that it obscures more than it illuminates.

In the period after 1945—the period of postwar nationalist sentiment, the phenomenal expansion of social science research, and a general yearning for change—broad agreement was reached on "the facts." Negro, black, Afro-American, or lower-class (the terms were often used interchangeably or linked together, as in "Negro lower-class") family relations were said to be characterized by unstable conjugal unions, a high incidence of illegitimate births, and a high proportion of female-headed households. Sharp differences in the explanations of why this should be so, coupled with the acrimonious nature of the debate, concealed a surprising level of agreement on unstated assumptions.

Virtually all investigators treated the "Negro lower-class" as an entity that could be defined (if somewhat imprecisely) and bounded for purposes of discussion. Apart from Melville J. Herskovits, who saw contemporary family forms as reinterpretations of surviving African forms, social scientists assumed that deviations from a normal family pattern were the product of class position or poverty. It was agreed that even lower-class West Indians value a Christian, monogamous family life, and that they would like to live as the middle-class was believed to live. The conclusion was inescapable: circumstances prevent them from establishing stable families. They are forced to "stretch their values," as one writer put it (Rodman 1963). The middle-class was believed to be quite different—to be the cultural heirs of the British colonial upper-class—although little or no attempt was made to understand the actual social practices of the class to which the eighteenth- and nineteenth-century whites belonged or to examine the exact genealogy of the modern middle-class.

It has always been assumed that upper-class West Indians had a family life that was essentially "English" and that it was very different from the disorganized conjugal and family patterns of the black and colored population. This article will show that the apparently "English" upper-class was intimately involved in the creation and maintenance of a system of marriage and domestic relations that embraced all sections of the population. It has been customary to think of a "normal" system of legal, Christian marriage from which certain sections of the population deviated for one reason or another: because slaves were forbidden to marry legally; because of poverty; or because of the persistence of other cultural forms. I argue that these supposed "deviations" are an integral part of one marriage system that included alternate forms appropriate to different class and racial groups, or to certain inter-class and inter-racial relations. I refer to this as the "dual marriage system."

Structure and Function

The idea that the lower-class is deviant (both historically and in the present) was reinforced by another set of shared assumptions, theoretical this time, concerning the functional necessity of a "nuclear family relationship complex" in all human societies. Talcott Parsons (1955) gave a plausible account of why this should be so, George Peter Murdock (1949) declared that the nuclear family is found in *all* human societies, and Meyer Fortes (1949, 1958, 1969, 1978) refined Bronislaw Malinowski's view of family dynamics, integrating it with new ideas about the "kinship polity," or external politico-jural domain. The analysis of West Indian family structure in the period after the Second World War was informed by this developing structural-functional theory, and the results were used, in turn, to validate and support that theory (see Fortes 1953: 3–8; Fortes 1956: xiii; Fortes 1969: 255, 259; Parsons 1955: 13, n. 11).

Structural-functional theories of the family and kinship now face mounting criticism. Attempts to save, and even improve, them either refine definitions to accommodate marginal cases—such as the Nayar and the Ashanti—that threaten the idea of a universal nuclear family, or they seek to break apart clusters of variables tied together by previous theorists. The most notable attempts are those of Jack Goody and Terence Turner. Goody has redirected attention from the "necessary functions" of nuclear family relations to what are supposed to be the actual "similarities in the way that domestic groups are organized throughout the whole range of human societies" (Goody 1972: 124). Taking note of some empirical complications, he has left intact the essential features of the functional model proposed by Fortes and Parsons (see R. Smith 1978a: 338–39). Turner's reformulation is more theoretically ambitious, attempting to synthesize the work of Meyer Fortes, Claude Lévi-Strauss, Talcott Parsons, and Jean Piaget by making their several "contributions" part of a more abstract model, which he hopes will rise above the low-level confusion of family and domestic group and embrace a wide range of empirical variation by redefining it as "surface structure" produced by "generative mechanisms" (Turner 1976). It is impossible to do justice to Turner's complex text here, but he too ends up arguing for certain substantive "reference points"—sexuality, the life cycle, the mother-child dyad—that are always culturally "appropriated and transformed." The analysis remains faithful to Parsons's view that family and domestic groups perform essential functions, "the replacement and integration of individuals into the society as socially and psychologically mature adults, and, at the level of social organization, the regeneration of the social groupings within which these functions are accomplished" (Turner 1976: 440). Revisionist structural-functional theories such as these carry forward the idea of domains, the primacy of the mother-child relationship, and, ultimately, the linking of sex role distinctions to domain distinctions.

Feminists analyzing West Indian family life tend to adopt this paradigm, and many writers are preoccupied with the idea of a "value stretch." Most feminists try to correct male bias by focusing on women and their problems. Since lower-class women bear the brunt of economic deprivation and the responsibility for child care, they remain the center of attention. Although it is agreed that "family life and the domestic domain [are] spheres of particular importance and relevance to female status" (McKenzie 1982: vii), increased attention is being paid to the resources women are able to—or are forced to—mobilize from wage labor, from productive economic activity such as farming, or from "external networks."

Some feminist criticisms of domain distinctions have been simplistic to a fault, suggesting that the whole idea of domains is invalid just because men have roles in the domestic sphere and women engage in market activities (see, for example, Bourguignon 1980: 338). A major exception is Verena Martinez-Alier's 1974 analysis of marriage patterns in nineteenth century Cuba, which argues that the hierarchical relation among races, and not poverty or males' inability to provide for their families, produces the "sexual marginalization" of women (see R. Smith 1978a: 349–50 for further discussion). It also reinforces a concern with class relations that was evident in some earlier studies.

Cultural Analysis and History

The racial hierarchy has not disappeared, and it continues to affect marriage and the family, as can be shown from studies carried out under my direction in Jamaica, Guyana, and Trinidad over the past fifteen years or so. These studies collected extensive genealogies, detailed family histories, and material on occupation, education, race, and social status.* Other case materials, collected to supplement wide-ranging survey data (Roberts and Sinclair 1978), or to stress subjective factors in understanding familial behavior (Brodber 1982; Gonzalez 1982), also throw new light on interclass linkages and the dual marriage system. My view of Caribbean kinship assumes that ideology, or culture, is an important part of the system of social relations and not a mere rationalization of them. I

---

*Publications based on these studies include Alexander 1976, Alexander 1977, Alexander 1978, Alexander 1984; Austin 1974, Austin 1979, Austin 1984; DeVeer 1979; Fischer 1974; Foner 1973; Graham and Gordon 1977; R. Smith 1973, R. Smith 1978a, R. Smith 1978b, R. Smith 1982a, R. Smith 1982b.

argue that a creole kinship structure was established in the for-
mative stage of West Indian society, and that women occupied a peculiar position in it. Although they were jural minors and linked
ideologically to "domestic" activities, they played crucial economic,
political, and status roles; these social roles and the meaning of
"domesticity" itself are part of a unique social formation that was,
and is, West Indian creole society.

Marriage and Concubinage

From the beginning of the development of the slave regime, a
marriage system was in place that included both legal marriage and
concubinage, a system in which the elements were mutually and
reciprocally defining and which articulated with the racial hierarchy. White men married white women but entered into non-legal
unions with women who were black or "colored," that is, of mixed
race. The laws governing marriage, legitimacy, and inheritance
were, in all the English colonies, based upon English common law,
but each colony introduced significant modifications to deal with
the particular circumstances of a slave regime.* The term "concubinage" is a general one, contrasting with "marriage" in terms of
legality, but it includes practices ranging from short-term sexual relationships that did not involve co-residence to permanent unions
that differed from marriage only in terms of the legal status of the
spouses and children. While a few lower-class white women migrated to the colonies—usually as indentured servants—and some
of them bore out-of-wedlock children resulting from casual unions,
the overwhelming majority of non-legal unions were between
white men and black or colored women, and between those
women and black or colored men. Slaves were almost always forbidden to marry or to become Christianized. The incorporation of
free blacks and colored people into the churches was extremely uneven prior to the beginning of the nineteenth century, depending a
great deal upon local circumstances and the waxing and waning of
missionary efforts. It is difficult to generalize because of the many
exceptions that were made. For example, in Jamaica during the

---

*Little attention has been paid to the precise structure of colonial law and its ef-
fects upon marriage and inheritance. Pioneering work was carried out by Linda
Lewin in Brazil (unpublished manuscript), and more recently Mindie Lazarus-Black
has made a detailed study of the relation between legal statute, the judicial process,
and family structure in Antigua, West Indies.

eighteenth century it was possible for the illegitimate children of wealthy planters to be declared legally white by an act of the Assembly, thus entitling them to inherit property and to enjoy all the social status of free whites. When the number of such special acts became excessive, and appeared to be a threat to the slave regime itself, a law was passed limiting such possibilities. Throughout all the variation however, the central opposition between legal marriage and concubinage, and its association with the racial hierarchy, remained the same. Indeed an act of the Assembly declaring a person of color to be "white" merely reflected the existence and strength of the system itself.

This system did not arise and continue just because it was useful or practically necessary. It is often supposed that a shortage of white women forced white men to take concubines for "natural" reasons, a supposition that does not survive close examination. The cultural system did indeed invest concubinage with a degree of "naturalness" in contrast to the "civilized" institution of marriage, but that is part of the data not of the analysis. Marriage to a white woman did not preclude nonlegal unions with black or colored women, nor was it permissible for a white woman, even if single or widowed, to indulge in "natural" sexual relations with a black or colored man.* The limits of possible action were contained within the structure of the meaning of the system, and at its core was the set of contrasted meanings attaching to marriage and concubinage. Far from being anarchic, this was a finely regulated system in which the meaning of different types of union was, and is, widely recognized.

Because the dual marriage system permitted white men to have "outside" unions with black and colored women, while being married to white women, it wove a complex tapestry of genetic and social relations among the various segments of creole society. Once established (in the earliest period of settlement of the New World), it was capable of ordering conjugal relations outside the simple black-white conjunction; it could generate the forms of sexual and conjugal behaviour appropriate to equals and unequals of all kinds.

*Isolated cases of marriage between colored men and white women (they were extremely rare) are interesting precisely because they indicate the extent to which property and class could override racial barriers. This was always a latent possibility, reflecting the contradiction between class and color values, and its existence called forth much racist rhetoric (see Brathwaite 1971 and Long 1774).

In its most general form it embodied the rule that men marry status equals and have non-legal unions with status inferiors; since slaves were property, slave men and women could only engage in non-legal relations. The legal and overt bases of status differentiation are vastly different today, but the general structural principles of the marriage system are not.

I have not attempted to establish structural continuities in detail, but my analysis recognizes the pivotal role played by women, and their status concerns, in maintaining the dual marriage system in both historic and modern periods. Just as the slave or Free Coloured woman accepted concubinage for the benefits it might confer upon her and her children, so today lower and working class women accept non-legal conjugal relationships in place of the idealised norms of legal marriage because they believe that they "cannot do better," a belief that derives from their self-conception as "poor sufferers" in a social system that continues to be hierarchical in its most basic structure. Middle-class West Indian women of all races have, since the latter part of the nineteenth century, been the most vocal opponents of "outside" unions, but they implicitly accept the supposed inevitability of male extra-marital affairs. However, it is wrong to explain a structured system of social practices in terms of the motives of the individuals who act within it; the motives themselves are partially derived from the structure that sustains and reproduces them. In this case the dual marriage system is an integral part of a structure that has been, in its most general form, persistent over a long period of time. In order to understand its nature I will now look more closely at the range of practices found during the crucial period of the formation and development of the system. That is, during the period of slavery. The exposition moves between data from archival research and modern field study.

The Genesis and Nature of the Dual Marriage System

Racial and Class Hierarchies in the Slave Regime

Upper-Class Whites. The tentative nature of domestic life among the earliest West Indian settlers may be gauged from the following inventories of two Barbados estates in 1635: "A Captain Ketteridge had five white servants, a Negro slave, and six hundred acres, yet his total household furnishings consisted of an old chest, six hammocks (the Negro slept on the ground), some empty barrels, a broken kettle, an old sieve, some battered pewter dishes, three napkins, and three old books. Mathew Gibson, with four servants, possessed even less: a chest, a cracked kettle, two pots, several barrels, a sieve, a glass bottle, and a pamphlet without covers" (Dunn 1972: 54). By 1680, sugar cultivation using slave instead of indentured labor had already supplanted the incipient tradition of European small farmer agriculture. The population of Barbados, and of the other British colonies such as Antigua, St. Kitts, Nevis, and Montserrat, grew rapidly, as did that of Jamaica, acquired from Spain in 1655. Although these were not true settler colonies, the increased immigration of upper-class white women meant that family life was possible, and by the early eighteenth century there was already a creole white population. White women of lower social status who came to the colonies as domestic or indentured servants sometimes married the owners of small plantations, thus moving up in the social scale.

Wills and parish registers in Jamaica show that, contrary to much speculation in the literature, there was an orderly social life among white settlers, with proper Christian celebration of births, marriages, and deaths. Because the creole white population was small, cousin marriage seems to have been common—as it was in other New World colonies (Farber 1972; Lewin 1981)—and the high mortality rate resulted in multiple marriages and complex families with half siblings. In an interesting discussion of the descendants of Dr. Robert Dallas—a prominent eighteenth-century landowner, physician, and member of the Jamaican Assembly—Michael Ashcroft (n.d.) mentions cousin marriage, arranged marriages, and elopement as well as the existence of extra-marital unions and "outside" children among whites themselves.

What kind of people were these West Indians? Janet Schaw, visiting Antigua in 1774, reported on the character of the white inhabitants, declaring the creole women to be

the most amiable creatures in the world . . . amazingly intelligent and able to converse with you on any subject. They make excellent wives, fond attentive mothers and the best housewives I have ever met with. Those of the first fortune and fashion keep their own keys and look after everything within doors; the domestick Economy is entirely left to them. . . . A fine house, an elegant table, handsome carriage, and a croud of mullatoe servants are what they all seem very fond of. . . . While the men are gay, luxurious and amorous, the women are modest, genteel, reserved and temperate (Andrews and Andrews 1923: 113).

By the second half of the eighteenth century, the "great houses" of wealthy West Indians had come to constitute important statements about the wealth, power, and prestige of their owners, who devoted much time to entertaining. The "domestic life" of the West Indian upper-class cannot be equated with anything so mundane as cooking or childrearing. These activities were delegated to the large numbers of servants, almost all black or colored slaves or freedmen, who lived in or near the main house, constantly at the beck and call of the whites for all kinds of purposes (see Buisseret 1980 on "great houses").

On small plantations with few slaves, the owners' wives generally took an active part in running the property. A widow might be left in a position that forced her to take over management or to remarry quickly—not so easy when properties were entailed. For example, when Robert Elbridge died around 1727, he left his share of the Spring Plantation in Liguanea, Jamaica, to his wife Mary for her life. Upon her death it was to revert to his lawful heir, who happened to be his elder brother's daughter's husband. Other persons having shares in the plantation agreed to Mary's managing it for the rest of her life, which she did with considerable skill. As she wrote rather angrily to the legal heir, Henry Woolnough, on June 20, 1739, in response to his veiled hint that she was not playing straight with the plantation accounts, "I have laboured on this plantation for 12½ years and Can prove by the Accounts that I have made more money of it and Saved more than ever was under any person Management" (BRO: AC/WO 16[17]e). Mary Elbridge was not unusual; many of the 4,000 white settlers on small Jamaican farms in 1792 (mostly cattle, ginger, pimento, coconut, and coffee properties) were women (Brathwaite 1971: 146).

Dunn has noted that English colonists in Barbados were "not transferring to the tropics the strong family structure they established in . . . mainland America" (Dunn 1972: 109–10). By "strong family structure," he means households established through stable, legal marriages that comprised parents, large numbers of legitimate children, and few servants. The West Indian pattern is different because of slavery and the existence of concubinage alongside marriage. Concubinage was found in Britain, of course;

it was common enough for members of the upper-class, not excluding royalty, to have large numbers of bastard children. In the West Indies, the practice was much more widespread and inextricably intertwined with the special nature of the social hierarchy.

When Janet Schaw referred to the creole men as "amorous," she was noting the most important feature of the kinship system. These men

have their share of failings, the most conspicuous of which is, the indulgence they give themselves in their licentious and even unnatural amours, which appears too plainly from the crouds of Mullatoes, which you meet in the streets, houses and indeed every where; a crime that seems to have gained sanction from custom. . . . The young black wenches lay themselves out for white lovers, in which they are but too successful. This prevents their marrying with their natural mates, and hence a spurious and degenerate breed, neither so fit for the field, nor indeed any work, as the true bred Negro. Besides these wenches become licentious and insolent past all bearing (Andrews and Andrews 1923: 112).

Janet Schaw's indignation is directed more toward the black "wenches" than to the white men and contrasts sharply with the view that their irregular unions were the result of coercion, or even rape. Some recent literature on slavery and the origin of the modern black family has revived the image of white slaveowners or overseers raping slave women, forcing them against their will to submit to brutal sexual advances and perhaps tearing them away from slave lovers or husbands. Yet this image, which gained currency in the antislavery literature of the eighteenth and nineteenth centuries, does not accord with most contemporary accounts or with the picture Barry Higman painstakingly put together from Jamaican plantation records. His study shows that black women who bore children for white men rarely had black children prior to the birth of their first child of mixed race and were likely to continue bearing colored children. His conclusion is that there is little evidence of women being torn away from slave husbands: "It was very rare for a slave woman to bear children darker than herself. . . . Mulatto, sambo and black women . . . sometimes had children of different colours at different stages of their lives. For all these women the movement was from white towards black fathers. . . . It would appear that the process of miscegenation followed rules known and obeyed by the whites as well as the slaves and that direct physical compulsion was perhaps unimportant relative to the psycho-social imperatives" (Higman 1976: 152–53).

By contrast, there is much evidence that the "laying out" that Janet Schaw observed became institutionalized. For example, in the 1820's, a man who presented himself as a "Slave Driver" who had put aside the whip to take up the pen described the following scene in a work of fiction: "[The young plantation employee, Marly,] was interrupted by a rather strange form of application, from an elderly negro woman, accompanied by a young negro girl about sixteen or seventeen years of age, who she said was her daughter, requesting Marly to take this young girl for his wife,—the girls who live with the white people being so called" (Anonymous 1828: 80). Twenty years earlier Henry Bolingbroke had observed in Demerara that every European male in the West Indies finds it necessary to provide himself with a "housekeeper, or mistress": "The choice he has an opportunity of making is various, a black, a tawney, a mulatto, or a mestee; one of which can be purchased for 100£ or 150£ sterling, fully competent to fulfil all the duties of her station. . . . They embrace all the duties of a wife, except presiding at table; so far decorum is maintained and a distinction made" (Bolingbroke 1809: 26–27). Bolingbroke was not the only writer to mention that "housekeepers" did not preside at table, so we may infer that this symbolic activity was reserved for the wives alone. However, it was not essential for a man to have a wife in order to establish himself as a man of substance and a lavish host; his housekeeper was not to preside at table (we do not know how rigorously this rule was observed), but she was responsible for the household and its hospitality.

William Codrington, later to become the first baronet of the Codrington line, was grandson of the first of the West Indian Codringtons. Until about 1715, William was resident at Betty's Hope, his plantation in Antigua that had a complement of 322 slaves (125 men, 126 women, 41 boys, and 30 girls). Just before he left Antigua in 1715 to return to England and the life of an absentee, William Codrington wrote a long and detailed letter of attorney to The Hono. Wm. Byam, Esq., Mr. Jos. Jones, and Capt. John Lightfoot, who were to be entrusted with the care of his properties. The four pages of closely written instructions, preserved in Sir William's letter book, state his wishes regarding the running of his estates and the treatment of his house servants who are, presumably, slaves.

I earnestly desire that Babe, Judy, Beck and Florah be not molested or troubled in their Grounds or provisions by anybody much more my own people, and that they live alltogether there and that Beck and Florah they have each one barrel of beef and 200 lbs of good salted cod fish. . . . That they have always the Negroes they have now. That the above wenches have particular care taken of them when sick and to have anything they want from my Plantation Doctor. . . . That Sackey's Sary be kept in the house at Betty's Hope and that her child might be cloathed as may be proper. . . . That Unoe the wench who lived with my Couz Bates be always kept in the great house which is what Mr. Bates desired of me about 2 hours before he dyed. That Moll and Unoe be allways kept at the great house at [my adjacent plantation] The Cottin and no others. That my two boys Quashie and Johnoe Ham be put to the Carpenter's trade.

The instructions go on and on, and Codrington keeps reverting to Babe, Judy, Beck, and Florah and to his boys Quashie and Johnoe Ham: specifying the horses they shall be allowed to use, providing for their passage to England should they wish to "come home," and repeatedly reminding his attorneys that "the wenches are not to be ill-used by anybody and you have nothing to do with the house Negroes" (GRO 347: C2).

Once back in England, William married Elizabeth, daughter of William Bethell, owner of considerable estates in Swindon, Yorkshire. She brought to the marriage not only her own "fortune" or dowry but also an alliance between Sir William and her brother Slingsby Bethell, a powerful London merchant, member of Parliament, alderman and lord mayor of London. The four sons and three daughters she bore him inherited their father's property and status. He did not forget his Antigua connections, for we find him writing again in 1717, complaining that his instructions have not been followed properly and repeating that only Babe, Judy, and Florah are to live in the great house and to have all its keys. It is possible that he visited Antigua again sometime between 1722 and his death in 1738, but nothing is yet known of the fate of those he mentioned in his 1715 instructions.

For a man as wealthy as William Codrington, the possibility of settling down permanently with a slave or free colored woman was quite remote. However, he left behind an elaborate establishment at Betty's Hope and The Cottin. The days of Captain Ketteridge and Mathew Gibson were long past. The 1715 inventories show the houses to be well furnished and equipped; the lists of items shipped from Bristol to Betty's Hope include 100 Delft plates, 30 jelly glasses, sweetmeat plates, sconces, and large numbers of prints, looking glasses, damask curtains, tablecloths, and napkins.

Assuming that the "wenches" referred to by name were either house slaves or free colored servants (Moll and Unoe are listed elsewhere as "House Negroes," but Babe, Beck, Judy, and Florah cannot be identified as such), they obviously enjoyed positions of trust and must have been skilled in the management of a large household. At least one of them had children by William Codrington, and it is not unlikely that other children by other white men, perhaps attorneys or managers with their own creole wives, formed part of this large ménage.

As this example clearly shows, the West Indian marriage system included alternative forms of union that mutually defined each other and related directly to the color class hierarchy. This does not mean that class differences in marriage were unimportant. For the upper class, marriage meant alliance between status equals, and its specific values included permanence, religious sanction, and the maintenance and reproduction of status; concubinage was defined in terms of "service" and patronage.

The question is whether this structure dominated the whole of West Indian society and whether those lower in the social scale attached different values to that structure. To answer that, and the larger question of how we can understand the relation between structure and process, we must look first at the other social elements in slave society and then consider the change in the relationship between classes effected by the abolition of slavery.

Slaves. Female members of the slave field gangs differed most from upper-class white women. On a large West Indian plantation, sex was not a primary factor in deciding how labor was to be divided. The "great gang," engaged in the hardest labor, was made up of the healthiest men *and* women working side by side in the fields. Many aspects of "domesticity" were communal. The main meal of the day was prepared by cooks and served to the field gangs; small children were taken care of by old women while their mothers worked (breaks being given for breast-feeding); medical care was provided by the plantation physician and his slave assistants in the hospital; rewards and punishments were dispensed by the overseer.

This invites reconsideration of the supposed universal necessity of domestic groups and nuclear families, but it does not mean that slaves had no domestic life, no independent fields of action, or no norms in their kinship relations. The cultivation of provision grounds and the marketing of vegetables and small stock were important slave activities even in the seventeenth century. Slaves would not allow their owners to arrange the details of their sexual lives and would not be bound to lifelong unions arbitrarily arranged by the master. Conversion to Christianity and Christian marriage practices made little headway until the first decades of the nineteenth century, but slaves had their own customs.

In 1776, Adam Smith recorded that Greek and Roman as well as West Indian slaves "were hindered from marriage. They may cohabit with a woman but not marry, because the union between two slaves subsists no longer than the master pleases. If the female slave does not breed he may give her to another or sell her. Among our slaves in the West Indies there is no such thing as a lasting union. The female slaves are all prostitutes, and suffer no degradation by it" (A. Smith 1978: 451). Adam Smith's view from the top of the system is echoed in recent work by Orlando Patterson (1969: 159–74; 1982: 139–43), although there is no evidence that slaves regarded their own familial relations in these terms.

In his detailed discussion of the Montpelier and Shettlewood estates in early-nineteenth-century Jamaica, Higman identifies three major categories of family and household organization among slaves, categories which he believes have wide validity. In the first type of household, formed largely by old people, and Africans without kin, slaves lived alone or with friends. In the second, the "great majority of the 70 percent of slaves who did possess family links lived in simple family households, most of them nuclear units" (Higman 1976: 168). In the third type, favored mostly by Creoles, slaves lived in extended family households. Although believing this third category to be "relatively unimportant" (a conclusion based solely upon its infrequent occurrence in the house lists), Higman provides information based on more than simple counts of who lived in which house. At Montpelier and Shettlewood, "ten of the groups of 'families and dependents' [were] occupying two or three houses. Most of the latter were type 2 housefuls, containing coloured and skilled slaves; they generally had the use of relatively large areas of provision grounds and possessed considerable numbers of livestock. It is evident that these slaves had more than one house not because of their numbers but because of their privileged occupations and relative prosperity" (Higman 1976: 168–69). This fascinating information pertains to the elite of the slave population. Some of these families could have been based on the privileged position of men who had polygynous extended family households, although it seems that actual polygynous compounds were rare. It is more likely that drivers, skilled tradesmen, and the like were able to build up extended family units in which both men and women played important roles as the nucleus of household groups. At the same time, the dominant males established unions with women in other places, thus creating households that appeared to be both female-headed and matrifocal. Women played a crucial part in creating and maintaining this structure because they too were selectively entering unions with men resident in other households— some of them white men.

Lower-class Whites and Free People of Mixed Race. The number of unions between white men and black or colored women may have been small, as was the number of households resulting from these unions, but their importance is much greater than their frequency of occurrence would suggest. They embodied the structural contrast between legal and nonlegal unions, and the households were archetypically matrifocal. Contemporary observers said frequently that the colored women's preference for unions with white men made it impossible for colored men to marry. This is an exaggeration; both marriage and Christianization gained among free colored people during the nineteenth century as civil rights were gradually extended under pressure from Britain. What is important is that black and colored men in positions of prestige, either members of the slave elite or freedmen, reproduced the whites' pattern of marital behavior. That is, they might marry—either legally or according to some customary form (Smith 1956: 171–72)—but they would also have "outside" unions, and those usually with women of lower status in the racial hierarchy (see Higman 1976: 146–47).

We now have a great deal of information about social and plantation hierarchies, the role played in their creation by the sexual unions of white men with black and colored women, and the emergence of the population of mixed racial origin as an important element in those hierarchies. But an analysis of modern West Indian kinship is incomplete without an account of the history of the "colored middle class" and of the ideologies created in the course of its emergence as the politically dominant element in West Indian life.

"Lesser whites" such as overseers, bookkeepers (a local term used for field supervisors), and skilled tradesmen on large plantations, were usually recruited as single men and forbidden to marry so long as they were employed, presumably on the assumption that marriage would distract them from their duties and require a larger outlay for housing. Almost all soon acquired a mistress (not least to nurse them back to health when they succumbed to tropical disease). Most often the woman was a slave, also forbidden to marry because of her status as property, and any children that resulted from their union shared the mother's slave status. Although slaves, these "Persons of Colour" were set apart, believed to be unsuitable for field labor. The men were usually apprenticed to skilled tradesmen and the women employed as domestic servants, washerwomen, or seamstresses. Fathers often tried to improve the status and life chances of their bastard children; how much of that effort was prompted by the mothers we shall never know.

For example, John Hugh Smyth of Bristol gave permission on a number of occasions between 1765 and 1797 for slaves to be manumitted on his Jamaica plantation, The Spring, by having them replaced with new slaves. On September 3, 1765, he wrote to his attorneys, "As you think letting Mr. SEWARD put an able Negro on the estate in place of the Mulatto girl will be an advantage, I readily acquiess in granting her freedom." Again on May 1, 1797, he wrote to Hibbert and Taylor, his attorneys, "As you recommended and Messrs Rothley and Stratton have consented I can have no objection to authorize you to join in manumissing [sic] the Negro Woman Slave named Margaret and her Mulatto Son named Peter on condition the proposal made by the Executor of the late Mr. Stewart's will be complied with in placing in their room two prime new Negroes" (BRO: AC/WO 16[37]).

Not well endowed with property (by definition), white men with low status were oriented toward material and social improvement, observing the hierarchical distinctions of race and servitude with scrupulous care. They attached the same value to marriage as did the upper class; when plantation employees formed long lasting liaisons with colored women, marriage was rare even if the man managed to leave plantation employment and acquire a small property of his own. Although such unions and attempts at manumission were common and continued through the slavery period, it is not clear that the unions created a "family," and it is certain that "domestic groups" were not always constituted thereby.

The free colored population comprised slaves who had been manumitted because they had performed faithful service (usually as house slaves) or because they were the offspring of nonlegal unions, plus those born to free colored parents. Free status was a prized and jealously guarded possession, not easy to maintain if one was black in a slave society that equated blackness with servitude. If legal status distinguished the free colored from the slave, "complexion" separated the colored from the whites and imposed other civil disabilities. Those disabilities did not bar the free colored from legal and Christian marriage, but their position in the status hierarchy caused them to experience the marriage system in a different way.

Women of mixed race, slave or free, were preferred as concubines by white men, and so long as the slave regime persisted these women were disposed to prefer a nonlegal union with a white man to marriage to a colored man. In 1794 Bryan Edwards discussed the situation of the Jamaican free colored population at some length, remarking that the women are often accused of incontinency for accepting the position of kept women without entertaining the hope of marriage. But "in their dress and carriage they are modest, in conversation reserved; and they frequently manifest a fidelity and attachment towards their keepers, which, if it be not virtue, is something very like it. The terms and manner of their compliance . . . are commonly as decent, though perhaps not as solemn, as those of marriage; . . . giving themselves up to the husband (for so he is called) with faith plighted, with sentiment, and with affection" (Edwards 1794, II: 23). His explanation for their behavior was complex but as interesting as most of those we find today: "Excluded as they are from all hope of ever arriving to the honour and happiness of wedlock, insensible of its beauty and sanctity; ignorant of all christian and moral obligations; threatened by poverty, urged by their passions, and encouraged by example, upon what principle can we expect these ill fated women to act otherwise than they do?" (Edwards 1794, II: 22).

Other observers noted that colored women, exploited though they might have been, seemed to enjoy considerable freedom: "Though the daughters of rich men, and though possessed of slaves and estates, they never think of marriage; their delicacy is such, for they are extremely proud, vain and ignorant, that they despise men of their own colour; and though they have their amorous desires abundantly gratified by them and black men secretly, they will not avow these connections" (Moreton 1790: 124–25, quoted in Brathwaite 1971: 177). This passage draws attention to the important and neglected fact that colored women often had white fathers who were powerful, rich, *and* sufficiently interested in the welfare of their children to leave them substantial property. To what extent these men concerned themselves with their daughters' unions—or left this matter to the mothers—we do not know. Mavis Campbell reports that a white man entering into a union with a free woman of color often signed a bond, similar to a marriage settlement, providing for her maintenance in case of death or separation (Campbell 1976: 53ff). A colored woman who was mistress of a white man probably had her own household and more freedom to come and go than if she were married. Colored women also seemed to have dominated huckstering, small shopkeeping, and the management of hotels and inns.

Although social convention depicted the slave, colored, and white groups as discrete social entities, in fact "segments" were defined, differentiated, transformed and dynamically interrelated through a series of exchanges and interactions. One can never find the "essence" of each group. An African became a Negro only in the context of the slave regime, just as a creole or a mulatto acquired his or her social being only in this particular social formation. Field slaves learned to speak creole English quickly; the customs and manners of the upper classes were not unknown to them, just as the creole whites were well versed in the speech patterns, "superstitions," music, and folklore of the slaves. These were small societies, but all groups did not converge upon a uniform culture; new modes of conflict and distance developed out of the cleavages and contradictions of creole society, and the constant influx of new immigrants was absorbed with difficulty. But a distinct society was created, and upon its basis, modern social forms were built.

Structural Reproduction and Transformation in the Nineteenth Century

We have seen that the West Indian system of kinship and marriage was an extension in cultural logic and social action of the dominant structural element in creole society, the racial hierarchy—an element that pervaded every aspect of social life, economic, political, religious and domestic. In the late eighteenth and early nineteenth centuries, that society began to feel the impact of profound changes taking place in Europe: the rapid growth of industrial production, the increasing power of the bourgeoisie, the expansion of overseas enterprise into new areas of the world, and the triumph of new political ideologies espoused in the American and French Revolutions. When, in 1791, a West Indian visitor wrote a letter from New York where she, her mother and husband had recently arrived as "Travellers of Observation in this Land of Equality and Independence," she was being ironic but also communicating the complex sentiments of the West Indian planter class; admiration for colonists willing to stand up to Britain over unjust taxation, and fear of the consequences of espousing doctrines of freedom and equality in a society based on slavery (GRO 351: D1610, C22).

The gradual decline of the mercantile system, the emergence of powerful interests dedicated to the destruction of the slave regime, and the changing patterns of world trade and world markets eventually were to transform many aspects of the internal economy of West Indian colonies. Those movements cannot be discussed here, nor is there space to detail the ways in which the planter class managed to maintain its domination and ensure that structural change in the racial hierarchy and in the economic system were more apparent than real (see Hall 1959; Brathwaite 1971; R. Smith 1982b; Campbell 1976; Heuman 1981). Instead, we may take the most dramatic of the apparent changes and examine their implications for kinship.

The Ending of Slavery

The abolition of the slave trade in 1807 set in train a series of demographic changes, the most important of which was the rapid increase in the proportion of people of mixed race in large colonies such as Jamaica (Higman 1976: 153). As the economics of tropical agriculture shifted, and as opportunities increased in the expanding economies of Europe and in new areas of enterprise such as Australia, New Zealand, southern Africa, and North America, the proportion of whites in the West Indian population began to fall. The cessation of African immigration ensured that the black population was predominantly creole by the 1830's, except in areas of new settlement such as Demerara, Essequibo, Berbice, and Trinidad.

Missionary activity, gathering momentum from about 1820, hastened the creolization of the slave population. Slavery was abolished throughout British possessions in 1838, following a few years' transition to wage labor. The event was experienced as a great transformation, ideologically at least, even though social relations changed at a very slow pace indeed. Two aspects of this change are particularly relevant to our discussion of kinship.

Suddenly there ceased to be any distinction in law based upon race, color, or servile status. On September 21, 1834, the secretary to the lord bishop of Jamaica issued an order instructing all parishes to use the same registers of births, marriages, and deaths for the whole population since all were now free. An order-in-council announced in the *London Gazette* of September 8, 1838, set out procedures for marriage in the colonies and confirmed the validity of the marriages of slaves, or even of free colored people, solemnized prior to emancipation. If people had married de facto, provision was now made for them to solemnize the union simply by signing a declaration (*London Gazette*, No. 19656: 2004–5). There was no rush to legalize unions. But over the next forty years or so, there was an important shift in the position of the various groups in the class system, and nothing is more interesting than the changing position of the colored woman.

The free colored population had attained a prominence and new political significance in many colonies long before the abolition of slavery. As early as the latter part of the eighteenth century, there had been advocates of the automatic manumission of colored slaves and the extension of more civil rights to qualified people of color. Many free colored people were themselves owners of slaves, since the bequest of a few slaves was a favorite means of granting a continuing (and perhaps increasing) source of support. But despite their privileged position and economic importance, this group did not become a significant and active political force mediating between white and black until the 1830's (see Campbell 1976; Handler 1974; Heuman 1981).* By 1850 a proportion of the

---

*It is interesting that there was a sudden increase in the reported number of colored people in Jamaica from 40,000 (10.8 percent of the total population) in 1834 to 68,000 (18.1 percent of the population) in 1844. This remarkable increase is almost certainly due to the reclassification of people previously reported to be "slaves" (see Smith 1982b: 104).

colored population was firmly established as a new elite, the vanguard of the so-called "coloured middle-class." Prominent members of this group were active in politics, in journalism, and in such professions as law, but not all colored people were suddenly elevated into an economically based "middle-class." The reality is different and has a great deal to do with the complexity of today's relation between race and class.

Free colored and free black people who owned small numbers of slaves or small plantations faced the same economic problems that white planters faced once slavery had been abolished and as the markets for tropical produce became constricted. As the upper levels of the society came to be filled with expatriate officials, managers, and professionals, the class status of the creole white and colored population began to converge. This took time, and the process intertwined class and kinship factors in a complex way.

The changes of the mid-nineteenth century also began to produce a literate, devout core of churchgoers from the ex-slave population, the "peasantry" often referred to at the time as the stable foundation of the new order. They were generally small farmers growing minor crops such as coffee, ginger, arrowroot, plantains, pimento—crops traded through middlemen who became prosperous produce dealers. In Jamaica, banana was to become the favored crop after the North American market opened in the 1870's.

Most of the ex-slaves constituted an impoverished rural proletariat, and even those who managed to acquire some marginal cultivable land found it little different from the "provision grounds" to which they had had access as slaves. They still had to work for wages on the surviving plantations and engaged in an increasingly bitter struggle over the conditions and rewards of their labor. Those with land suitable for semisubsistence farming appeared to be cushioned from the full force of industrial discipline, but it is a mistake to think of them as peasants working only occasionally for wages. Their lives were shaped by the plantation system, and the legacy of resentment created by the whites' refusal to permit a radical transformation of the society and its economy is embedded in much of present-day West Indian life.

Changes in the Dual Marriage System and Class Structure

Was the marriage system transformed during this period, and if so, in what ways? The rich planters of the eighteenth century were mostly gone by about 1850, soon to be replaced by corporate capital, operating larger, consolidated plantations staffed by "expatriates." Many European and creole whites continued to operate small plantations, especially in Jamaica and Barbados. Preliminary historical research strengthens the impression, derived from genealogical study, that an upwardly mobile colored population and the downwardly mobile remains of the white planter class converged in the formation of the modern West Indian "middle-class." In Jamaica, at least, both groups became increasingly urban from the mid-nineteenth century onward, leaving the less successful family members in the rural areas. The continuing vitality of the dual marriage system, linked in complex ways to the changing definitions of status and class, resulted in a new concern among the upwardly mobile with *lower-class* "illegitimacy," a concern that has lasted into the present. That concern was a displacement onto the lower-class of issues that were central in the life of the middle-class. In order to understand it one must follow the changing structure of class itself, which will also throw light on the question of whether the marriage system was transformed or not.

Wills filed in the Jamaica Island Record Office show that the custom of open concubinage of white men and colored women did not end with the abolition of slavery. The will of "John Smith, a native of Scotland now residing at Cape Clear Pen in the Parish of Metcalfe" (formerly and subsequently St. Mary) and styling himself "Planter" was entered at the Island Record Office on January 22, 1870 (JIRO: Wills, Lib. 131, f. 88). In it he leaves to Bridget French Kilkelly, now residing at Cape Clear, "one hundred pounds sterling and one moiety or half share of my table knives, silver forks, silver spoons, furniture," and other goods. However, it is his "natural daughter, Janet East, daughter of the said Bridget French Kilkelly," who is to be his residual legatee after various monetary bequests are made to nephews and nieces in Scotland and in Canada. This natural daughter is married to one Patrick East and is the mother of John Smith's grandchildren, John Slater East and Isabella East. Although it is possible that Bridget French Kilkelly is white, the chances are very much against it. No attempt has been made to follow the subsequent career of John Smith's grandchildren, but it is reasonable to infer that they moved into the emergent middle-class, a class increasingly preoccupied with respectability and increasingly based in urban bureaucracy.

More characteristic, perhaps, is the fate of the O'Sullivan family of Clarendon, Jamaica, as revealed in Albinia O'Sullivan's diary covering the years 1872 and 1873 (IJMC: MS 1604). This small leatherbound book contains little in the way of diary entries but quite detailed copies of letters sent and received by the daughter of John Augustus O'Sullivan of Highgate Park, Jamaica, and formerly of Richins Park, Buckinghamshire, England. At one time provost marshall of Jamaica and owner of considerable acreage and two houses in St. Catherine, O'Sullivan died in June 1871, leaving three daughters and five sons by his late wife Jane, daughter of Sir Charles Taylor of Cothrell in County Glamorgan, Wales. Albinia's diary begins with an accurate and complete transcription of her father's will (entered JIRO: Wills, Lib. 131, f. 202, Nov. 7, 1871), which leaves 100 acres to each of the four younger sons and a grandson; a house and the income from a £5,000 life insurance policy to the daughters; and the residue of the estate—including pictures, books, family heirlooms, and the family great house at Highgate Park—to his eldest son and heir, Augustus.

The letters that follow reveal the family's plight. Augustus, who has taken holy orders, emigrates to Nova Scotia with his wife and children. In a letter dated May 17, 1872, he urges his brothers and sisters to join him, rent a farm, and make a new start: "Tell [the boys] to come to Canada. Put Pride in their pockets or leave it in a yam hill and go to work like 1000^{ds} of others are daily doing in a few years they may be sure of having a thriving farm each of their own and a jolly wife apiece to churn butter make cheese too. I implore them not to waste their lives in Jamaica." They declined this invitation, and indeed it is not long before Augustus brings his family back to Jamaica with plans for revitalizing the old Highgate Park property—with the capital of his brothers and sisters. The problem is that they do not have enough capital; indeed, Albinia and her sisters have been obliged to sell the piano and sundry other possessions just to keep going. Brother Edward, who lives in Four Paths, is so hard up that he has to walk four miles to his office each day; brother George is trying to make a go of cattle farming; the most successful brother is living in Richmond Park and has a steady job in business, but he cannot afford the £40 to £50 per annum that it would cost to send his son Benji to be educated by a private tutor in Kingston.

Again, although I have not followed the O'Sullivans' fortunes further, interviews with the living descendants of similar families suggest that in many cases the more energetic and successful family members moved to the urban areas or even migrated to North America, leaving behind a deteriorating property on which the others struggled along, having "outside" children, and sometimes even marrying darker-skinned partners (see Craton 1978 for an excellent discussion of cases of this kind). Such marriages were contrary to the structural principles of the system, and yet they certainly occurred, particularly in the rural areas where decreasing numbers of whites, downwardly mobile in economic terms, were absorbed into the colored population.

Illegitimacy Redefined as a Class Problem

Because very few slaves married before about 1830 (relaxation of the laws barring slave marriages was uneven until the institution of apprenticeship in 1834), "illegitimacy" was a meaningful concept only among the rich. Certainly it was not defined as a social problem, since it was an integral part of the whole slave system. In the approximately 150 years since the ending of slavery, illegitimacy rates have remained high and remarkably stable. In Jamaica, for example, the rate has varied between 60 percent and 70 percent of live births ever since reliable records were first kept in the 1870's. As George Roberts points out, these rates have been tied to the marriage rate, which is quite low (1957: 288). Many lower-class West Indians defer marriage until they have several children, but this is not just a system of deferred marriage pending the accumulation of resources for a proper ceremony. Simple "economic" theories have been employed to explain West Indian patterns of kinship and marriage, converting the "problem" of illegitimacy into an exclusively lower-class matter, but many errors could have been avoided had Bishop Enos Nuttall's statement of 1886 been noted.

In the mid-1880's there was an upsurge of sentiment in Jamaica favoring legislation to mitigate the evil of illegitimacy and check immorality. Led by clergymen, it is fair to assume that its most active supporters were the influential members of their congregations, among whom women of the new middle-classes were prominent. Partly a colonial reflection of the social purity and antiprostitution movement in Britain (see Walkowitz 1980), it nonetheless addressed what was coming to be seen as a local problem. During 1885, the governor of Jamaica received a number of petitions expressing concern over illegitimacy. One, from a conference led by Bishop Nuttall, suggested the enactment of a law containing the following provisions:

That, so far as possible and practicable, registration be made of the father of every illegitimate child.

That some Public Officer in each district (to be defined) be charged with the duty of securing such registration, and be held responsible for the taking, or causing to be taken, the necessary steps preliminary to registration.

That among such preliminary steps should be the proving of such paternity before competent authority in all cases where such paternity is not acknowledged by the father.

That every mother of an illegitimate child be required, under penalty, to give information to such Officer with a view to the ultimate registration of the father of such child.

That it also be made the duty of such Officer to see to the strict carrying out of the Law for the maintenance of illegitimate chidren in every case where there is an attempt to evade the obligations imposed by that Law (IJMC: MST 209, No. 13, p. 2, minute signed by H. W. Norman, Governor).

The governor declined to take action on these proposals, saying that they would be impossible to carry out in practice. The bishop was provoked into writing a pamphlet entitled "Public Morality: An Appeal, by the Bishop of Jamaica" (IJMC: MST 209, No. 13). In the course of a lengthy reply to the governor, Bishop Nuttall declared, "Let no man drag into this debate questions of class and colour, or suspect this agitation of any class sympathies or antagonisms. It is a question of the social life of a whole people. It has nothing to do with class. The immoral lives of numerous Englishmen, Scotchmen, and Irishmen in Jamaica, for generations past, are quite sufficient to silence those who want to get rid of this subject by the convenient insinuation that the blame for our present condition of things rests exclusively upon them [the lower-class]" (p. 4).

His warning was quite forgotten, and over the ensuing years marriage came to be the mark of "middle-class" status, whereas the lower-classes were considered to have "disorganized" family relations marked by unstable marriages and high illegitimacy rates. It was precisely the colored women with middle-class status who now became the most vocal critics of vice and immorality and the most staunch defenders of the sanctity of marriage. However, their indignation was largely directed against the immorality of the lower-classes and they accepted with relative passivity the continuing "outside" unions of their own menfolk.

Despite this newfound concern in the West Indies for respectability, the dual marriage system itself did not change; there was just a reallocation of positions within it. The pattern of men forming "outside" unions with women of lower status did not disappear; indeed it is an intrinsic part of present-day life. The dual marriage system is not a faint memory from the past but a living reality (R. Smith 1978a; R. Smith 1978b; R. Smith 1982a). It continues to disturb, but not destroy, relations within middle-class families. The woman who feels its full impact is the lower-class woman of limited means attempting to raise several children, forced to work if and when she can, and often passing through a series of unions with men who appear to be as transitory as the white bookkeepers of slavery days.

It is remarkable that social scientists should have adopted the class view of this system, attributing its major characteristics to poverty, adaptation, even African culture—anything, in fact, but its obvious relation to the overall structure of class society itself. Several aspects of the contemporary system make it difficult to understand the way in which the dual marriage system operates. Because it had its genesis in the relations between high status men and lower status women there is a tendency to suppose that such interclass relations would be necessary for it to continue, and that it is the nonlegal unions of such men and women that constitute the system. This is not so. Although cross-class nonlegal unions continue to be common, the phenomenon of primary interest to sociologists and social planners alike is the coexistence in the lower-class of legal and nonlegal unions, and the high proportion of illegitimate children born to lower-class women. Only a small proportion of these children are fathered by middle- or upper-class men.

Once the system was in place the structure became more general than the specific practices that gave it birth. If one considers the situation within the free colored population during slavery it is evident that the rule enjoining marriage to a status equal and nonlegal union with an inferior had to be implemented in a way different from that found within the white group. Whereas white women did not (with few exceptions) enter nonlegal unions, colored women were reputed to prefer concubinage with a white man over marriage to a colored man. Within the colored group, the principles embodied in the dual marriage system were transformed into the rule that legal marriage and concubinage were *alternative forms* even between status equals. For black slaves legal marriage was forbidden and by virtue of that fact was institutionalised *for them* as a superior form. After emancipation some white men continued to have colored mistresses but the white population declined rapidly in most colonies while the class position of the colored group was greatly improved through the growth in professional and bureaucratic employment. The whole system was shifted down one register, so to speak, without any basic alteration. For blacks, who were now enjoined to marry, the rule of marrying a status equal was conjoined with the conception of legal marriage as a sign of superior status. In other words, the structure was compressed within the confines of the lower-class in such a way that a lower-class man could use any status factor, even masculinity itself, as the basis for insisting upon a casual rather than a legally sanctioned union. However, there could be no exact correspondence between status and marriage type within the lower class; the dual forms of marriage became intra-class alternatives with the superior form sometimes being entered into late in life as the crowning event of a long relationship.

Although I have used language that implies rational choice, the system was not the end-product of a series of individual choices; if anything, it shaped and guided those choices. Outside unions between lower-class women and middle-class men are easy to document for the recent past (see R. Smith 1982a for details), but the following case illustrates the continuing relation between hierarchy, including gender hierarchy, and kinship, even when the individuals concerned are of the same economic class.

The Case of Alice Smith

Alice Smith is a thirty-seven-year-old single mother with six children by four different men.* She was born illegitimate in rural Jamaica and after her mother "walked out on us," as she puts it, she moved to Kingston to live with her mother's father, Conrad Drew, and his wife Carlotta Drew, whom Alice called "Aunt." Within about a year, her father entered another union with a Miss Parris,

---

*The ethnographic present is 1969 when the interviews took place.

who was living near Kingston, in a rural part of St. Andrew, and Alice and one of her brothers stayed with them on and off for two years. Her older sister lived in another rural area, probably as an "adopted" live-in servant. Alice, unable to get along with her step-mother, was brought to stay with a group of people she refers to collectively as "the relatives them." They were a miscellaneous collection of her father's kin living in a rundown area of Kingston on land that had "come down from the old people them." In Jamaica, such land is "family land," on which no member of the kindred can be denied accommodation. There she slept in a big room with her father's sister's daughter, her husband, and all their children.

Alice Smith's first child was born when she was sixteen. When a second child was fathered by the same man, she moved out of that room. However, she still lives on the same family land, in a shack of her own. Like most West Indian women, she has worked all her life, first as a domestic servant and then in a dry-cleaning plant. The father of her first two children lives with the mother of his other children, having contributed virtually nothing to the support of Alice's children. The father of the next two lives with his aunt; like the first, he did not actually live with Alice. The father of the fifth child lives with another woman. Alice's discovery of this relationship hastened the breakup of her arrangement with this man, but they remain on good terms; he visits his daughter, and if Alice needs repairs to the house, he usually does them. The father of her baby had not been around since Alice was eight months pregnant, but during our interviews, he began to visit again. He claimed to have stayed away because one of Alice's children had been rude to him by not saying "good night" when he arrived. This exquisite sensibility was only part of the story; it turned out that another woman had just had a child by him—this in addition to his three children in the country and an older daughter at school in town.

Alice Smith is no more resentful of what seems to be blatant sexual and economic exploitation by the fathers of her children than are other informants. One spoke, without regret, of the "upstanding man" who "fall me" as a young girl (R. Smith 1982a: 124). Men and women alike will declare that it is in the nature of men to need more than one woman—especially West Indian men—whereas a woman can be satisfied with one man. If women enter multiple unions, they are impelled to do so not out of natural desire but out of practical necessity. It sounds very much like the contrast drawn by Janet Schaw in the eighteenth century between creole white men and women, except that today lower-class women are forced into multiple unions in the search for a stable relationship with an adequate provider.

This case was chosen deliberately because it does not quite fit the received view of matrifocal kinship structure, where the mother-daughter relationship provides a stable domestic core to which men are loosely attached. Alice Smith is not atypical; many children grow up away from their mothers, and not infrequently with female relatives of the father. This does not alter the ideological link between domesticity, female sex roles, and maternity; indeed, Alice Smith's bitter regrets about her own childhood are ample proof of where the cultural stress is placed. Nor is Alice Smith atypical in the number of her unions and "sets" of children. She differs from the middle-class woman who passively accepts male infidelity. Lower-class women are fully aware that a lower-class visiting "boy friend" who has other relationships is unlikely to be an adequate source of support.

Feminist concern over the plight of lower-class West Indian women is not misplaced, especially concern for those women who have been uprooted from rural communities in which they had the support of networks of kin and are now struggling to make ends meet in the cities and towns. However, that concern should not lead automatically to the conclusion that high illegitimacy rates and multiple unions signify either "disorganization" or "adaptation." Even less should one conclude that mother-focused families, or even families in which the father does not share a household with the children, lead to deficiencies or disabilities in the children. The modern West Indian middle-class is well aware of its origin in "irregular" unions (Alexander 1977: 431–32), although it may not recognize equally clearly its own contemporary deviations from a so-called "normal" nuclear family pattern. Nor is it always recognized that many of the most ambitious, creative, and successful West Indians have been the children of outside unions with "irresponsible" fathers and hard-working, dedicated mothers. When those fathers have passed on to their children some advantage—be it wealth, color, education, or preferential treatment in gaining employment—it has not mattered a great deal that the children were illegitimate and brought up in a matrifocal household, and that has been true from the days of slavery to the present. The true disadvantage in the West Indies has been to be black and poor.

Conclusion: Feminist Issues and Caribbean Data

The Matrifocal Family

The aspect of Caribbean society that has most attracted the attention of feminist theorists has been the matrifocal family, in which women are salient in domestic affairs and men, in the status of husband-father, are marginal to the close bonds between mothers, children, and daughters' children (R. Smith 1956). Caribbean mothers, unlike those in the classic matrilineal societies, have not been under the politico-jural domination of brothers and mother's brothers, and therefore the Caribbean data seem to pose new questions about the universality of familial and kinship roles, and the ability of women to sustain viable family units without men in the status of husband-father, or avuncular protector. I have discussed elsewhere the nature of the dual marriage system and its implications for social policy in the contemporary Caribbean (R. Smith 1982); here I will concentrate on its relation to some theoretical issues in feminist writing.

Natural Functions

Much discussion in the feminist literature has focussed upon biological givens, upon the apparently irreducible facts of human nature. The matrifocal family is easy to interpret as a reduced, but still natural, form of the nuclear family, a form that continues to fulfil all the functions of the family through the heroic efforts of, in George Lamming's graphic phrase, "my mother who really fathered me" (Lamming 1953: 11).

Feminist theory has moved beyond this point, as is evidenced by the articles in this volume. Whatever the irreducible facts of biology may be, they are incorporated into social and cultural systems in ways that are, if not infinitely varied, remarkably diverse. Biology does not determine social and cultural arrangements; attention has been shifted elsewhere, most notably onto an examination of the economic and class factors that combine with gender, kinship, marriage, and family. It is here that the history of interpretation of Caribbean data is valuable in emphasizing the errors of economic determinism.

Economic Determinants

In New World colonial societies, the social and cultural systems that developed over time were, and are, more than epiphenomena of economic exploitation. Economic activities and economic class position certainly affect kinship, family, and marriage. Just how profoundly they do so is shown by Verena Stolcke's study of immigrant coffee workers in Brazil (1984). Recruited as families from Germany, Switzerland, and Italy, these workers initially were sharecroppers, operating in a system of labor relations which—despite its exploitative features—used families as units, thus reinforcing many aspects of "traditional" family structure such as paternal authority and a sexual division of labor. Today those coffee workers are transformed into a semiurban proletariat selling their labor on a daily contract basis and being trucked to work sites. The demand for female labor and the fragmentation of the old family work teams have changed the internal relations of the family, change reminiscent of industrializing England, where unemployment altered men's traditional role (Engels 1958; Smelser 1959; Anderson 1971).

Chattel slavery in the West Indies was an extreme form of economic exploitation; we have seen that writers from Adam Smith to the present have assumed that it was destructive of family relations. But all labor systems, including slavery, have to be seen in a wider context of social and cultural organization. Stolcke's coffee workers are affected by many things other than their participation in the labor market. Some of the changes that she reports, such as intergenerational conflict, may be due to urbanization and a closer integration into a Brazilian creole way of life. Lancashire cotton operatives, for all the trauma of male unemployment and the demand for female and child labor, did not experience a complete breakdown of family relations. In the Caribbean, despite the disrupting effects of plantation labor, Hindu and Muslim immigrants were not prevented from achieving a new equilibrium in family relations which differs in important ways from that of Afroamericans (Smith and Jayawardena 1959; Jayawardena 1960; Jayawardena 1962; R. Smith 1957; R. Smith 1963). Slavery, and the societies in which it was embedded, were more than systems of labor relations.

Class Relations

In her article in this collection on seamstresses and dressmakers in Turin, Italy, Vanessa Maher has provided us with a penetrating insight into the complexities of establishing and maintaining class differences, and into the relation between work, class, and female roles in a small—though crucial—sector of Italian urban society. The cultural distinction that she, and her informants, make between the "outside" world of work and public life and the "inside" domain of private, domestic, and essentially feminine activities has always been a feature of West Indian life as well—as we have seen. These cultural distinctions have not altered the fact of women's labor outside the home. There are some interesting parallels between Turin seamstresses and the colored women of eighteenth- and nineteenth-century West Indian society. Like the *sartina* of the Turin atelier, colored housekeepers, personal maids, and seamstresses were given privileged entry to the domestic domain of the higher classes. They too were renowned for their extravagance in dress. Colored women were in great demand at balls, where they partnered white men, and they played a prominent part in masquerades and festivals (Wright 1937: 243–47). However, for the colored woman, be she slave or free, this was not just a liminal phase between childhood and a settled life married to a man of her own class. Colored women, and men, may have been anomalies in a cultural system that posited pure races, but it was precisely because of their kinship connections and color that they were able to establish themselves as the nucleus of a new middle class. The complicating factor of race makes the comparison of Italy and the West Indies particularly interesting. It shows that supposedly universal distinctions of "public" and "private" domains, linked to hypothetical societal functions, fail to capture the complex realities involved; they mean different things in the two cases. As Stolcke (1981) has pointed out, the subordination of women in class society is largely derivative from an ideology of natural inequality that persists within the formal egalitarianism of bourgeois society. In societies founded on racist ideas, such as those of the Caribbean, one would expect colored and black women to be doubly subordinate; once on the grounds of race and once because of their femininity. But we have seen how colored women, like the *sartina*, penetrated the class world of the dominant groups. Whereas the Italian woman eventually returned to her natal class and married an equal, the colored woman was the matrix of a new social element capable, once economic and political conditions were right, of emergence as a new class. Those women bore and raised their children in the archetypical matrifocal family, without legal attachment to the fathers of their children and without the social commitment that such attachment implied. But these were the families identified by Higman as being among the elite of the plantation slave and free colored labor force.

Class and the Dual Marriage System

A double standard of sexual behavior—freedom for men to have outside affairs while women are obliged to remain faithful—is found in both Europe and the Caribbean. It is tempting to see this double standard as part of "nature," necessary for the continued operation of any society since men are naturally promiscuous while women must be confined to a stable domestic environment to make social reproduction possible. Not only is the assumption false, but this case shows the importance of the context in which double standards develop.

Europe and the Caribbean are each affected, in different ways, by the development of capitalist economies and the social relations created by those economies. The prerequisite for a fully developed system of extramarital concubinage is a class system in which lower status women are available as mistresses, a condition that certainly prevailed in both areas. In Europe, prostitution and concubinage existed alongside concepts of family honor that required sexual restrictions on women; therefore, prostitutes, kept women, and the mothers of illegitimate children were dishonored and socially marginal. Despite Adam Smith's pronouncements (and those of later writers), there were few "prostitutes" among West Indian women either during slavery or after, although some real prostitution occurred. Honor was closely related to race, and for all the fulminations against them of people like Edward Long (1774), people of mixed race—illegitimate or not—enjoyed more social honor than their black kin. By the same token, they had less social honor (even if of legitimate birth), than the most ignorant, illiterate white. Once these differing structural principles are understood, comparison is more meaningful.

Social science has measured all kinship against the standard of modern Euro-American bourgeois nuclear family structure. It has been argued, with much plausibility, that this family form—along with its associated concepts of "public" and "private" domains—is produced by capitalism and is reduced to performing the special functions of social reproduction and providing a "haven in a heartless world." The theory of the isolated nuclear family is an accurate representation of the situation of the bourgeoisie in developed capitalist societies.

Although the Caribbean and Latin America have been influenced by developments in North America and Europe, the material base is not the same and the ideology of the nuclear family has played a very different role in dependent and peripheral areas—a role closely linked to the maintenance of a different system of social relations and social hierarchy.

The dual marriage system of the West Indies is not a particular manifestation of European norms and deviance, nor is it the inevitable outcome of economic organization, to be changed solely by improved economic conditions. Its curious tenacity derives from its being embedded in a social formation with its own integrity and its own historical development. It demonstrates the variability of family structure and gender roles, while also showing the importance of ideology as a constituent element in that structure.

Rank and Marriage:
Or, Why High-Ranking Brides Cost More

Jane Fishburne Collier

IF THE WOMEN and men in all parts of the world who make marriages and other unions are themselves creations of particular societies, then analyses of marriage must be based on analyses of entire social systems (Rosaldo 1980; see also Comaroff, Maher, and Smith in this volume).* Women everywhere have fathers, brothers, husbands, and possibly male lovers, but the tensions and obligations they experience in close relationships with men vary from society to society, as do women's goals and means for achieving them. Thus, the feminist anthropologist studying cross-sex relationships must examine how systems of social inequality structure the powers, liabilities, ambitions, and fears that women and men bring to their encounters.

To do this, we need models capable of distinguishing both degrees of social inequality and the qualitatively different ways privileges and obligations may be organized. In "Politics and Gender in Simple Societies" (1981), Michelle Rosaldo and I developed such a model for analyzing gender relations among egalitarian hunter-gatherers and hunter-horticulturalists who validated marriages through brideservice and sister-exchange. This paper furthers that project by proposing a model for analyzing ranked but acephalous classless societies† in which marriages are validated through ex-

*This paper was prepared for the conference on Feminism and Kinship Theory held at Bellagio, Italy, in August 1982. The present version has benefited from the comments of Jane Atkinson, Nancy Donham, Shirley Lindenbaum, and Sylvia Yanagisako. The research for this paper was supported by a grant from the National Science Foundation (BNS 76-11651) to study "Stratification and Legal Processes."

†I write of "acephalous," ranked societies because I do not want to include societies commonly called chiefdoms. Some other acephalous, ranked societies that appear to share the cluster of elements discussed in this paper are the Yurok of

changes of gifts that vary in amount according to family rank.* I will illustrate the model with examples drawn from the Kiowa of the Great Plains.

The Kiowa were unique among bison-hunting Plains societies in recognizing social ranks (Hoebel 1954: 170). They "distinguished three semi-formalized named ranks into which one was born" (Richardson 1940: 15), as well as a category of outcasts. The Kiowa also shared several features of other ranked, acephalous societies, such as the "Gumsa" Kachin of Highland Burma, analyzed by E. R. Leach (1965). The Kiowa, like the Kachin, appear to have considered wife-takers to be inferior to those from whom they took wives. A Kiowa man "might never refuse a request from" his wife's brother, father, or other senior male kin, and it was a "great disgrace" for a man to make a request of these affines (Richardson 1940: 66). There is also evidence that Kiowa legal fines varied by rank. A high-ranking person appears to have demanded more when injured and to have paid more when fined as the offender (Richardson 1940: 114–17). And, as I will suggest, it seems reasonable to assume that marriages between high-ranking brides and grooms were validated with more lavish gift exchanges than were marriages of low-ranking couples.

There is also evidence that the three "hereditary" Kiowa ranks, like "Gumsa" Kachin ranks, "were not sharply demarcated: there was a gradual shading of one into the other and there were gradations within each" (Mishkin 1940: 37). Among the Kiowa, individual rank appears to have been as negotiable as it was among the Kachin. Jane Richardson, for example, describes the Kiowa as a "braggadocian society" (1940: 19), thus suggesting that they, like the Kachin, had to state continually the rank they claimed. In a world where ranks are not sharply demarcated by outward signs, people must tell others what they want others to believe.

These societal features—the ranking of wife-givers above wife-takers, graded fines, variable bridewealth, negotiable rank, and

---

California (Kroeber 1926) and perhaps other peoples of the Northwest American Coast (Drucker 1965); the Ifugao of the Philippines (Barton 1919); the peoples of Western Malaya (Gullick 1958); and the Kpelle of Liberia, whom Gibbs describes as having three "incipient classes" (of men): "wife-lenders, wife-keepers, and wife-borrowers" (1965: 215).

*This model for analyzing ranked acephalous societies is one section of a larger project to develop ideal typic models for analyzing three types of classless societies (J. Collier n.d.). The analysis presented here is thus a condensed version of a longer, more complete account.

bragging—are found, of course, among many groups, but it is their clustering that concerns me here. If, as I believe, this cluster of features or similar combinations can be found in several acephalous ranked societies, then a systemic model of the kind developed here may provide a tool for understanding all such ranking processes.

Information on the Kiowa comes primarily from data collected in the summer of 1935 by the Ethnology Field Study Group of the Laboratory of Anthropology of Santa Fe, under the direction of Alexander Lesser (Mishkin 1940: v). Like other anthropologists studying Plains societies at the time, members of the group were less interested in analyzing how the Kiowa adapted to reservation life than in reconstructing the social system as it existed before 1869, when the Kiowa were defeated and confined to Fort Sill. Despite the paucity of ethnographic information on Kiowa culture (the only major works to come out of the Ethnology Field Study Group are two published dissertations [Richardson 1940; Mishkin 1940] and one unpublished thesis [D. Collier 1938]), and despite its being based on informants' recollections, there are two advantages to examining this society when devising an ideal typic model of how a ranking system based on "variable bridewealth" might have worked.* First, the Kiowa are one of three Plains societies for which there is systematic information on social conflict (Richardson 1940). Such information is indispensable for understanding inequality, because it is in situations of conflict that inequality is revealed, negotiated, realized, or resisted. Second, the Plains provide a natural laboratory for analyzing differences among acephalous classless societies. The peoples who lived there during the eighteenth and nineteenth centuries came from different cultural and ecological backgrounds but faced similar problems as they adapted first to mounted bison hunting† and then to warfare with

*The analysis of specific societies, such as the historic Kiowa, and the development of ideal typic models are inherently contradictory objectives. To the degree that a society is analyzed in all its historic specificity, the analysis loses its utility as an ideal type, and to the degree that an ideal type is created, it ceases to give an accurate portrayal of any specific society. In this article, my aim is to suggest an ideal typic model. As a result, I present a necessarily deficient account of historic Kiowa society.

†In describing Plains peoples as bison hunters, I am following most ethnographers, but evidence suggests that their economies were far more complex. The Kiowa, for example, enter written history in the 1740's as long-distance traders, involved in trading horses and Spanish manufactures from New Mexico for agricultural produce (and guns?) with Arikara villagers on the Missouri River (Hyde 1959: 139).

whites moving westward (Oliver 1962). Kiowa men, and their counterparts among the Comanche to the south and the Cheyenne to the north, all hunted bison and raided for horses, but male (and female) labor was divided differently in each group. An examination of the similarities and differences among the Comanche, the Cheyenne, and the Kiowa thus illustrates the ways in which qualitatively different forms of social hierarchy are realized in the actions of women and men.

This paper is divided into three sections: an examination of the part marriage transactions played in the rise of the Kiowa ranking system; an analysis of how the wider system of inequality shaped Kiowa marital and affinal tensions; and finally, a discussion of the theoretical framework underlying my analysis and a brief comparison of the Kiowa with the Comanche and the Cheyenne that indicates the advantages and disadvantages of an ideal typic model for analyzing ranked acephalous societies.

The Marriage System

All ethnographers of Kiowa society agree that "war record was the single most important determinant of status in Kiowa life" (Richardson 1940: 14). "If any debate arose over the relative position of two individuals rather closely matched, it was usually settled by a recitation" of the contestants' brave deeds, followed, if necessary, by a recitation of "the number of captives and horses taken, and the horses given away" (Richardson 1940: 16). Any analysis of the Kiowa ranking system must therefore begin with an attempt to identify the factors that enabled some men to accumulate more war honors, captives, and horses than others.

The most obvious factor was the division of male labor by rank. Low-ranking men were, "for the most part, compelled to specialize in the prosaic activities, hunting, camp duties, etc." (Mishkin 1940: 62). They had poor war records because they had few opportunities to join raiding parties (Richardson 1940: 15). High-ranking men, in contrast, had many opportunities to acquire outstanding war records. Because they had low-ranking men to hunt and herd for them, they and their sons could pursue military careers (Mishkin 1940: 62).

The immediate question, then, is why some men worked for others, particularly since such an arrangement condemned them and their sons to low rank. What social mechanisms "compelled" low-ranking men to specialize in duties that kept them far from the battlefields where honors, captives, and horses were won? Because Kiowa had neither capitalist nor feudal relations of production, the answer to this question must be found in the way marriage transactions served to organize labor obligations among men.*

Jane Richardson's account of Kiowa affinal relations yields two significant insights into the labor ranking system. First, she describes the tie between a man and his wife's brother as "a fixed and unalterable one-way relation called the 'downhill' relationship. H[usband] was downhill from WB [wife's brother] in that H might never refuse a request from WB. A man was also downhill among others to his father-in-law and his parallel fathers-in-law" (1940: 66). Second, Richardson writes that "the poorer class constituted a desirable labor group, and there was considerable competition among the different *topadok'i* [band headmen] for these followers. One important formal mechanism to induce persons to join one's family was to give one's daughter or sister to some energetic though poor young man" (1940: 6). Both these passages suggest that Kiowa men worked for (or were not supposed to refuse requests from) their wives' male kinsmen. An analysis of Kiowa rank must thus begin with an examination of how men acquired wives.

*The question underlying this paper—why did some Kiowa men work for others?—is borrowed directly from Mishkin (1940). The answer I propose, however, is very different from his. Mishkin's answer presumes "private property," the ability of owners of the means of production to deny nonowners access to the resources needed to sustain life. Mishkin's argument, briefly summarized, is that the introduction of horses into what was once an egalitarian hunter-gatherer society led to the development of a distinction between "haves" and "have-nots," between men who were first successful at capturing horses and those who were not. This original distinction was perpetuated—according to Mishkin—because men without horses could not hunt bison or transport their belongings without borrowing from relatives who, in return for the loan of horses, required that borrowers "hunt for their benefactors or turn over part of their kill as well as spend considerable time herding horses for them" (1940: 45). Horse borrowers had to work for other men and so had few opportunities for acquiring horses of their own. Horse owners were freed from the drudgery of hunting and herding, and so were able to join many raiding parties, acquire many horses and war honors, and set their sons on the path of military careers. Over time, this division of labor between men who did and did not have horses led to the development of an hereditary elite—an aristocratic caste (1940: 63). The most direct evidence for refuting Mishkin's unstated assumption of private ownership of the means of production comes from the Kiowa's closest neighbors on the Plains. The hunting-gathering Comanche, who acquired horses before the Kiowa, did not develop an hereditary elite. It is also obvious that the Kiowa lacked the coercive state apparatus necessary for enforcing private property.

The most complete description of Kiowa marriage customs is provided by Donald Collier:

Marriage is of four kinds, two types by family arrangement and two by elopement. In the *first*, which will be called regularly arranged marriage, the boy's family approaches the girl's family and if accepted initiates a gift exchange between the two families. Both sides help to establish the married couple in housekeeping, and maintain friendly relations through continued gift exchange. In the *second* type, the girl's family picks out a deserving young man and gives her to him. There is no initial gift exchange between the two families, although later there usually is. The boy lives with his parents-in-law and works for them. This form of marriage is often preferred for his daughter by a wealthy man who wants assistance in herding his many horses and providing for his large family. In the *third* form, a boy and girl elope and go to the tipi of his father or some other of his relatives. The girl's family retaliates by raiding the property of the boy's family, later making gifts in return for what they have taken. The *fourth* form is the elopement of a married woman. The deserted husband retaliates by shooting horses of the man who has stolen his wife, and occasionally by doing physical injury to the fleeing couple. The first and third forms of marriage are the most frequent (1938: 11–12).

Because this account says little about the organization of labor obligations, it must be supplemented by an analysis of how the marriage system influenced other aspects of Kiowa life, such as the residence of newlyweds.

Newlyweds tended to settle in the band of the higher-ranking family (Richardson 1940: 12; D. Collier 1938: 12). Mishkin, for example, writes that a couple's band membership might be determined by "the relative wealth and rank of the two families," with "the poor being attracted to the *topotoga* [band] of the rich" (1940: 27). Although ethnographers tend to refer to "wealth" as a measurement of the number of horses in a family's herd, it is clear that, for the Kiowa, "generosity in giving horses was vastly more important than the possession of horses" in determining wealth (Richardson 1940: 14).* It thus seems reasonable to imagine that gift

---

*"Ownership" is never a relationship between a person and a thing. It is always a relationship between people in respect to things (or other people). "Wealth," therefore, implies very different possibilities in different social systems. In this paper, I suggest that, for Kiowa, horses had "value" only to the extent that men gave them away to validate kinship relations, and so to acquire the "sisters" and "daughters" whose husbands could not refuse in-laws' requests. In Kiowa society, the men most able to muster large numbers of horses or other valuables for giving away were not necessarily those with the largest herds (see Mishkin 1940: 42), but rather those with many "wife-takers" to command.

exchanges at marriage provided a major, if not the major, opportunity for assessing a family's wealth; the amount of gifts each family provided thus was very likely an important factor in determining a married couple's residence. Furthermore, it seems reasonable to assume that if "ideally, every male brought his wife to live in his *topotoga* and every female brought her husband back to her band to increase its size and political supremacy" (Mishkin 1940: 27), then the Kiowa would expect families to demonstrate as much "wealth and rank" as they possibly could by giving as many marriage gifts as members could muster.

Clearly if the kinsmen of a youth seeking a bride hoped to attract the newlyweds to their band, then they would have to take into account the number of gifts required, a factor dependent on the "wealth and rank" of the prospective bride's family, that is, on that family's ability to return gifts. To Kiowa contemplating marriage, therefore, brides must have appeared to vary in "price" according to the wealth of their families. No member of the 1935 Ethnology Field Study Group reports that high-ranking brides "cost" more than low-ranking ones, but other scholars discuss Kiowa marriage in the language of buying and selling and suggest that high-ranking men demanded more for their daughters than low-ranking ones (see Mayhall 1962: 110; Mooney 1898: 232; Wharton 1935: 146; Battey 1875: 328).

In his study of the "Gumsa" Kachin, Leach reports that "Kachin formal theory is that brideprice is adjusted to the standing of the *bride. . . .* [but] in every [documented] case the scale of the brideprice, as measured by the number of cattle, corresponds to the ranking status of the bridegroom" (1954: 151, italics his). Although no ethnographer of Kiowa society reports that a groom's rank was measured by the quality and quantity of valuables his family gave his in-laws, there are at least three reasons to think this must have been the case. The first has already been discussed. If the relative "wealth and rank" of the two families "might be determinative" of a couple's postmarital residence, then knowledge of a couple's residence and of the bride's rank allowed people to infer the rank of the groom.

Second, there is reason to believe that a husband's labor obligations correlated with his band membership. If a Kiowa man was obliged to comply with every request from his wife's brothers, father, or senior male kinsmen, then it is easy to imagine that the number and kind of requests a man received varied according to his residence. A man who lived in a band far from his wife's kin must have received few requests, and those he did receive were probably for horses or other goods. In contrast, a man who lived in his wife's band probably had to spend some of his time honoring his in-laws' requests for help in hunting or herding. As a result, men whose kin had not provided enough gifts to attract the newlyweds to their band must have worked for their in-laws, a sign of low rank. Men who lived far from their wives' kin, in contrast, probably gave horses, a sign of high rank.

Finally, there is reason to believe that the Kiowa expected a man to marry the highest-ranking woman he could afford, and so used his choice of a bride as a quick indicator of his rank. It seems reasonable to imagine, for example, that if Kiowa brides appeared to vary in "price" according to the wealth of their families, then outsiders would assume that a man who took a bride from a poor family did so because his kin were not able (or not willing) to muster the gifts needed to obtain a bride from a wealthier one. The amount a groom's family "paid" would thus be treated as an indication of the groom's wealth (i.e., his personal access to valuables for giving away).

The process of gift exchange between families characterized the two most common forms of Kiowa marriage described by Donald Collier—marriages initiated by family arrangement or by elopement—but not the form in which a wealthy man "gave" his daughter or sister to a youth in exchange for the youth's labor.* When writing about "gifts" of women, Collier uses words that suggest that *any* man with a marriageable daughter or sister might select a low-ranking male as her husband in order to gain access to labor. Wealthy men with large families and herds of horses practiced this form more often than poor men, Collier implies, simply because the former were more likely to want help in hunting and herding. But "wealth" in Kiowa society did not consist in having many horses. It consisted in giving many horses away (Richardson 1940: 14). Access to labor was thus the basis of wealth; it was by hav-

---

*Although ethnographers write that wealthy men "gave" daughters and sisters to poor men who agreed to join their bands, it will soon become apparent that Kiowa men did not "give" away women as they gave away horses. However, at this point in my argument, I will adopt ethnographers' usage in order to distinguish between "giving" and "marrying," two different processes.

ing others herd and hunt for them that some men were able to spend time raiding for horses and acquiring war honors. If any man could give away a daughter or sister to gain access to labor, why didn't all men arranging marriages seek out poor but energetic grooms?

To pose this question is, of course, to find its answer. In Kiowa society, giving daughters or sisters to poor youths was "often preferred" by wealthy men because they alone had this option. A poor man who tried to give his daughter or sister to a poor youth would not, by definition, be giving her away, but rather would be following one of the more standard forms of marriage. If, as I have suggested, men were expected to marry women of equal or higher rank, with the relative ranking of families established through the amount and quality of gifts exchanged, then a poor man who gave few gifts to the kin of his daughter's or sister's groom would be suspected of having few valuables to give, and therefore of being equal to the poor youth the woman married. As a result, only men of proven wealth could give women away and so acquire youths to work for them.*

As should now be obvious, I am suggesting that Donald Collier's second type of marriage established the basic system of male labor appropriation in Kiowa society. It was the relationship that organized the unequal division of labor between men. Wealthy men, freed from the drudgery of herding and hunting by the youths to whom they had given women, could devote their time to rustling more horses, acquiring war honors, and setting "their offspring on the path of military careers" (Mishkin 1940: 62). Similarly, the poor youths who had accepted the daughters and sisters of these wealthy men were expected to hunt and herd for their benefactors. Such low-ranking youths could not escape poverty not only because they had few opportunities to raid for horses or glory, but also because the products of their labor belonged to others.

My analysis so far suggests that poor youths would prefer to marry the daughters and sisters of other poor men because, as grooms whose families had provided gifts nearly equal to those re-

---

*Put differently, only "wealthy" men could "give" sisters and daughters in return for labor because only they could put poor youths in the position of being practically unable to return nearly equal gifts. In social systems where "high-ranking brides cost more," poor men who are allowed to live with women from high-ranking families incur unrepayable debts—that is, they become "debt-bondsmen" for life.

ceived, they would be subject only to occasional requests from wife's brothers. Yet some youths did, by accepting "gifts" of women from wealthy men, willingly enter a relationship that condemned them to long-term servitude. Why? The answer lies partly in the practice of polygyny and partly in the fact that a man's status was measured by the quantity and quality of gifts his family exchanged with the family of his bride.

Richardson writes that "polygyny was reserved only for [men] of high status" (1940: 12) who married women from both high-ranking and low-ranking families. Each high-ranking man had to acquire a bride of equal rank in order to prove his wealth by exchanging many gifts with affines. And high-ranking men acquired secondary wives from low-ranking men who hoped for patronage. Because the "downhill" relationship obligated a man to honor requests from his wife's kin, a low-ranking man whose sister or daughter married a man of high rank could expect to have his requests honored as long as the high-ranking man acknowledged the union.* In the long run, the secondary marriages of high-ranking men must have created a shortage of brides of equal, or slightly higher, rank for poor men, since there is no evidence that age of marriage differed greatly for boys and girls (see Mayhall 1962: 122).

At the same time, the fact that people measured a man's status by the rank of his bride put each man into the position of trying to marry as high-ranking a bride as he could afford. Kiowa families of all ranks thus faced the problem of allocating scarce resources among marriageable children, each of whom hoped for as lavish a gift exchange with affines as possible. Given the competition within families, some children were destined to lose, and it seems reasonable to assume that disobedient sons, orphans, and captives were more likely to be disowned by their natural or adopted families than obedient natural sons. And because such disowned youths had no means of acquiring marriage gifts by themselves (the Kiowa lacked a wage system and low-ranking men who joined

---

*The marriages of low-ranking women to high-ranking men were probably true marriages validated by gift exchanges. As long as the woman's low-ranking family demanded a reasonable amount of gifts from her husband, the arrangement was mutually beneficial. The woman's family gained access to horses for giving away, and her husband gained a wife and children to work for him. But because high-ranking men had little difficulty in finding substitute wives, a high-ranking man whose wife's kin became too demanding could sever the relationship by returning the woman to her father (D. Collier 1938: 90).

raiding parties were assigned camp tasks), these outcasts became the "poor" men who had to accept gifts of women from high-ranking families or remain wifeless.*

Polygyny by high-status men must have created not only a short-age of equal-status brides for low-ranking men but also a system of ranking within polygynous families. If high-ranking men had wives of different ranks, then some children must have had more powerful and prestigious mothers than their half brothers and half sisters. The most powerful mothers could ensure that many gifts were given away at weddings of their children, who thus appar-ently inherited their mothers' high rank. The children of lower-ranking wives would inherit a ranking status somewhere between their father's high rank and their mother's low one. And if, as I sug-gested earlier, "brideprice" appeared to vary according to the standing of the bride, then the amount of a mother's "brideprice" would appear to be the major determinant of her children's standing.†

Finally, given differences in power among co-wives, it seems rea-sonable to imagine that a polygynous man would not give away his full sister or his daughter by a high-ranking wife but rather his daughter by a lower-ranking wife or the daughter of one of his mother's co-wives. Polygyny, therefore, must have created a set of lower-ranking women that wealthy men could give to poor men who lacked access to the valuables needed to marry properly.

In summary, the Kiowa marriage system appears to have offered men three distinct ways to wed a previously unmarried woman. The first, by which others were evaluated, was marriage by gift ex-

---

*Although informants apparently told ethnographers that wealthy men sought out "deserving" or "energetic" poor youths as recipients for sisters or daughters, it seems more reasonable to imagine that the most "deserving" poor youths—that is, those whose families were willing to help them acquire brides—married the avail-able daughters of poor men. Those youths whose families had disowned them or who lacked families, such as captives and orphans, would thus be most likely to accept gifts of women. It is easy to understand, however, informants' description of the selection process. First, it must have been necessary for wealthy men to seek out deserving and energetic youths among the disowned, orphaned, and captive, and second, the youths who were given women probably had to project these qual-ities in order to retain access to female services.

†No ethnographer of Kiowa society writes about the status of children born to the women that high-ranking men "gave" to poor youths in exchange for labor. However, if the Kiowa were like some other acephalous ranked societies in viewing bridewealth as payment for a woman's fertility, then children born to a mother for whom no bridewealth was paid would belong to her family. They would be low-ranking members of an extended polygynous family.

change, whether initiated by arrangement between the families or by elopement of the couple. In this form, men married women of equal or higher rank because both families validated their claims to rank through the amount and quality of gifts exchanged. High-ranking families, by definition, exchanged more gifts than low-ranking ones. In the second form of marriage, high-ranking men gave half sisters or daughters by low-ranking wives to poor young men in return for labor. Only men with the highest rank could give women, and only men without access to valuables accepted them. This kind of marriage constituted the major form of labor appropriation in Kiowa society. The third kind of marriage was not one discussed by Donald Collier: the marriage of already married high-ranking men to lower-ranking secondary wives. These marriages must also have involved gift exchanges, but because the groom's status was already established by his continuing marriage to a high-ranking woman, such exchanges must have served primarily to confirm the dependence of a bride's low-ranking family on her husband's gifts and patronage. These secondary marriages provided high-ranking men and their sons by high-ranking wives with low-status daughters and half sisters to give to poor men in exchange for labor.

It should now be evident how the Kiowa marriage system gave rise to the three "hereditary" ranks and the category of outcasts described by ethnographers and to the male division of labor. The analysis above suggests that the highest rank and the outcast group were mutually determining: first-rank families consisted of polygynous men and their children by high-ranking wives; outcasts were men disowned by their families who accepted the half sisters and daughters given away by first-rank families. First-rank men had outcasts to hunt and herd for them and so were able to spend time warring and raiding for horses they could give away, primarily to high-ranking affines.

The two ranks below the highest consisted of men who married through gift exchanges. Men enjoyed the upper rank if their families could provide enough gifts to enable them to live far from their wives' kin. Men of lower rank lived near their wives' kin and so were subject to their in-laws' requests for labor. The three ranks appeared hereditary because parents' access to horses for gifts determined the residence of newlywed children. The lowest category of outcasts was not hereditary because individual misbehavior and bad luck must have determined which youths lost the support of their kin and so had to accept women as gifts.

Affinal and Marital Relations

Although tension and conflict exist in all family relationships, the form and consequences of these disputes differ according to each society's system of inequality. As feminists argue, the personal is political. This section will explore the ways in which Kiowa family problems were shaped by the inequalities inherent in their marriage system and will suggest why some Kiowa women let their male kinsmen "give" them to poor youths.

Richardson, in writing about quarrels between a Kiowa man and his wife's male kin, begins by positing a socially specific cause for affinal tensions: "This category of dispute situations arose largely from overlapping jurisdictions over a woman" (1940: 65). In Kiowa society, a woman "was always under the protection of her own immediate family, i.e., brother, father, uncle," even as her husband enjoyed "disciplinary prerogatives" if she failed to perform faithfully her duties and obligations toward him: "A certain amount of beating by H[usband] was permitted as legitimate by W[ife]'s kin, but if W were beaten too hard, too much, or without good reason, W's kin stepped in and took her away from H. If W were wantonly killed by H, her kin sought to avenge her death. The coercive threat of taking W away acted as a real restraint to a miscreant H, for it would always cost him and his kin considerable property to get her back, if at all" (Richardson 1940: 65).

But Richardson explains the seriousness of any violation of the "downhill" relation by reference to a universalist assumption about family ties. She suggests that a man's refusal of his wife's brother's request was a serious matter "because of the added emotional ties wrenched when trouble broke out between two affinal groups" (1940: 66). However, the analysis presented above suggests a different interpretation. Although people in all societies may develop emotional ties for their affines, a Kiowa man who did not honor the demands of his wife's kin not only threatened personal ties but also called into question the whole system of unequal rights and obligations based on the "downhill" relation. No won-der Richardson reports that when trouble broke out between affines, political leaders "and people in general were particularly on the alert to restore peace" (1940: 66).

The marriage system of Kiowa society established what may be seen as a triangular relationship between a woman, her husband, and her male kin whereby cooperation between any two parties jeopardized the interests of the third. This description does not suggest that Kiowa women and men actively colluded with spouses, siblings, or affines to harm one another, although some undoubtedly did; rather, the wider system of inequality organized the meaning and consequences of people's actions in such a way that cooperation between two members of the triad prejudiced the interests of the third whether the two willed it or not.

Cooperation between a husband and wife, for example, prejudiced the interests of her male kin. Ethnographers report that a Kiowa man might never refuse a request from his wife's male kin, whose authority was sanctioned by their ability to take back his wife if he balked. A Kiowa informant told Richardson that "a WF [wife's father] always takes W[ife] away when H[usband] refuses a request, even if it is the first time he has refused. But such refusals are rare. In most cases where there is refusal, H thinks he has a strong hold on W and can get away with a refusal without losing her" (1940: 72). As this informant recognized, cooperation between a woman and her husband undermined the ability of her kin to enforce their demands.

Just as cooperation between a woman and her husband allowed him to refuse requests from her kin, so cooperation between a woman and her kin put her husband at a disadvantage. If a woman were willing to return to her kin, then her husband was put in the position of having to comply with his in-laws' requests or lose her. Should she leave, it might "cost him and his kin considerable property to get her back" (Richardson 1940: 65). A husband, of course, could decide to forget an estranged wife and look for another, but, as we will see, men varied in their abilities to attract wives.

Finally, cooperation between a woman's husband and her kin put her at a disadvantage. If a woman's kin were unwilling to take her back or if they readily returned her to her husband when he offered valuables, she lost leverage in her marriage. She would be less able to protect herself from an abusive husband and less able to obtain benefits for herself and her children.

The analysis in the previous section suggests that Kiowa women benefited from keeping their children near them. Not only would a woman enjoy having her children and grandchildren near her as she aged, but married sons who remained in her band would enjoy relative freedom from distant in-laws' requests. It thus seems reasonable to assume that most Kiowa women hoped their husbands would provide enough gifts to attract married children, particularly sons, to their band. It seems reasonable, of course, to imagine that Kiowa men also hoped to keep their married children near them; however, men had competing claims on the property to be used as gifts: obligations to their brothers, an interest in taking secondary wives, the need to divide limited resources among multiple wives and children. It thus seems likely that if a woman's kin did not fully back her demands, she could not ensure that her husband's resources would be expended on her and her children, rather than on his brother or on a co-wife's children.

Just as a Kiowa man whose wife cooperated with her brothers could decide to look for another wife, so a woman whose husband had obtained the cooperation of her brothers could decide to look for another man. Evidence indicates that Kiowa women were not pawns in male-initiated marriage exchanges. Mishkin, for example, writes that "the most common form of marriage among the Kiowa was elopement" (1940: 27), and Richardson observes that "trespass upon a husband's exclusive sexual rights to his wife was by far the most frequent source of grievance" (1940: 80). It is thus clear that Kiowa girls did not wait patiently for their male kin to arrange marriages, nor did Kiowa wives faithfully sit home minding their husbands' hearths. Women took active roles in choosing their sexual and marital partners. But even so, the meaning and consequences of their sexual affairs were structured by the wider system of social inequality.

A Kiowa informant told Mishkin that "women seem to love [high-ranking men] more" (1940: 53), and Richardson reports that "no woman would consort with a man of low rank unless he were most attractive" (1940: 121). It would, of course, require a cultural analysis to understand what Kiowa meant by "love" or what women considered "attractive," but it is easy to grasp why Kiowa interpreted a woman's choice of sexual partner as a statement about his rank. In Kiowa society, the woman who took a lover necessarily chose him over another man—either her present husband or the suitor preferred by her kin. As a result, people interpreting a particular affair or elopement had to explain not why a woman chose a certain man, but why she chose him instead of a particular other. They would naturally tend to assume that she preferred the man who could offer her more—unless she were foolishly attracted by a handsome face.

In all societies, men fight other men who seduce their wives (just as women fight other women who seduce their husbands), but the prevailing social hierarchy determines the form of such confrontations. Among the Kiowa, women's elopements and adulteries often led to property destructions and gift-giving. Since women's sexual affairs were so easily interpreted as statements about men's rank, such affairs tended to provoke confrontations in which conflicting parties exhibited their ability to give things away (see Richardson 1940: 121). Only if the conflicting families were unambiguously at opposite ends of the social scale were status confrontations avoided (Richardson 1940: 119).

Up to this point, I have focused on the effects of this system on the triad of husband, wife, and her male kin, but people's ambitions and possibilities also varied by rank. In theory, every Kiowa man both received requests from his wife's brothers and placed demands on his sisters' husbands who, given the "downhill" relation, could not be the same people. The man who might never refuse a request from his wife's brothers could, by the same token, make unrefusable requests of his sisters' husbands. In fact, it makes sense to imagine that a man's ability to comply with his wife's brothers' requests rested on his ability to obtain compliance from his sisters' husbands. And, if this were true, then it becomes clear that women's possibilities varied according to the ranking (i.e., the needs) of their brothers.

Richardson reports that "the brother-sister bond was actually the warmest, strongest, yet most respectful, in the culture. It was said, 'A woman can always get another husband, but she has only one brother'" (1940: 65). It is easy to understand why brothers loomed so large in women's lives. A woman whose parents were of high rank, and whose full brothers exchanged many high-quality gifts with her husband and his kin, could expect to enjoy considerable power in her husband's household. She could expect, for example, that if her husband failed to provide her and her children with the advantages she felt due a woman of her background, then her brothers would support her complaint. Should she wish to leave her husband, her brothers would welcome her. And should her husband try to get her back, her wealthy brothers—who were supported by the labor of youths to whom they had given half sisters and daughters—could afford to demand considerable gifts from him and his kin before deciding whether or not she would return.

A woman whose brothers were of lower rank, and so did not have others to hunt and herd for them, could not enjoy such security if she left her husband. If her brothers had little free time for horse raiding, and so relied on her husband to supply the gifts they needed for their wives' kin, she could expect that her brothers might send her back in return for her husband's gifts or cooperation. Such a woman could run off with another man, but the amount of influence she would have over him would always be affected by her brothers' need for the goods and services he could provide.

At this point I can suggest an answer to a question that Kiowa ethnographers raise but do not answer: Why did some women let their high-ranking male kin "give" them to poor youths in exchange for help in hunting and herding? Other evidence confirms that women were not simply pawns in male marriage exchanges; both unmarried and married women eloped with lovers and avoided affairs with low-ranking men unless they were most attractive (Richardson 1940: 121). Since it is unrealistic to assume that all poor youths who accepted gifts of women were irresistibly attractive, why would the women agree to live with them? The answer to this question provides the key for understanding how inequality was organized in Kiowa society.

In the previous section, I suggested that co-wives and their children were ranked within polygynous families and that high-ranking men gave away not their daughters by high-ranking wives or their full sisters but rather the daughters of their low-ranking wives and of their mothers' co-wives. In this section, I will examine the relationships among these daughters of low-ranking women, their half brothers, and their full brothers in order to suggest why some women let their male kin "give" them to poor youths.

My analysis of Kiowa marriage suggests that, unlike a daughter of parents who differed little in rank, a daughter of a high-ranking man and a low-ranking secondary wife could not count on her brothers—either half or full—to support her in quarrels with her husband. Most brothers, for example, probably had to shelter unhappily married sisters in order to avoid appearing in need of the gifts the abandoned husbands would offer. High-ranking men, however, who engaged in lavish gift exchanges with their full sisters' in-laws, were in a position to refuse low-ranking half sisters' requests for aid without having others question their wealth; help could therefore be contingent on the sisters' cooperation.

At the same time, the sons of a low-ranking mother and high-ranking father were probably easily coopted into siding with their higher-ranking half brothers against the interests of their full sisters. Evidence suggests, for example, that high-ranking men regularly provided the horses and valuables their lower-ranking half brothers needed to give their in-laws in order to live virilocally.* In contrast to most men of low rank, therefore, sons of high-ranking fathers and low-ranking mothers did not need to obtain their sisters' cooperation in order to ensure access to horses; such men had more to gain from cooperating with their high-ranking half brothers.

It thus seems reasonable to assume that the Kiowa system of inequality created a group of women whose half brothers could refuse to help them without having their high rank questioned and whose full brothers could refuse to help them without losing access to wealth. Such women were presented (whether they realized it or not) with a choice between two less than ideal options: earning their brothers' support by complying with their brothers' wishes or facing the world without supportive male kinsmen. These, I suggest, were the women high-ranking men "gave" to poor youths. Because such women had to earn their brothers' support, these high-ranking men could tell them when to stay with and when to leave their low-ranking consorts. As a result, the poor youths who accepted such women were also presented with a choice between two less than ideal options: working for their patrons or losing their access to wifely services. In summary, the Kiowa system of inequality ultimately rested on two interrelated processes: (1) the continued reproduction of a group of women for whom the best available option was full cooperation with brothers, and (2) the continued reproduction of a group of men who had to accept such women or remain wifeless.

In constructing an ideal typic model of how a ranking system

---

*Richardson, for example, describes the basic Kiowa social unit as a group of brothers and their half, classificatory, and pact brothers (1940: 5), thus suggesting that high-ranking men used their "wealth" to help their "brothers" live virilocally.

based on variable bridewealth might have worked, I have presented a static picture of Kiowa society. Evidence suggests, however, that the Kiowa ranking system was breaking down during the nineteenth century. An adequate historical analysis of this transformation would require more space and more archival and ethnographic research, but my conclusion that the Kiowa ranking system rested on the reproduction of two subordinated groups does suggest one reason why the system might have been in trouble in the nineteenth century.

The Kiowa enter written history as long-distance traders (see Hyde 1959: 139), but once warfare replaced peaceful trading on the Plains, the Kiowa were forced by Cheyenne pressure to ally with egalitarian Comanche bands (see Jablow 1950). Outcast Kiowa men must then have been presented with an alternative means of obtaining wifely services: instead of having to accept "gifts" of women from high-ranking Kiowa families, they could become Comanche, and so marry under a very different system of affinal obligations, described below. There is no direct evidence that Kiowa were losing people to Comanche, but my speculation is supported by reports that the Comanche numbered at least 10,000—despite their low reproductive rate, common to hunter-gatherers (see Wallace and Hoebel 1952: 142)—and that the Kiowa numbered only 1,600 and were constantly seeking to replenish the lower ranks by adopting captives (Mishkin 1940: 42–43; Mayhall 1962: chap. 5).

Conclusion

The model of ranked acephalous societies presented here is based on Richard Emerson's (1962) conception of "power-dependence relations," which he used in analyzing followers' strategies for minimizing power differentials, but which is equally useful in analyzing systems of social inequality. If, as Emerson suggests, the amount of power available to leaders is a function of their followers' needs, then the amount of power generally available in a social system should be related to the efficiency of those mechanisms that recruit people to positions of dependency. This paper, therefore, has focused on processes in Kiowa society that systematically created a group of women who needed brothers' support and a group of men who had to accept such women or remain wifeless.

At the beginning of this article, I suggested that although Kiowa society is less than perfect for illustrating an ideal typic model, its study offers two advantages: available data on social conflict, and the presence of superficially similar, but fundamentally different, neighboring groups. This final section will briefly compare the Kiowa with their nearest neighbors on the Plains in order to suggest that the Comanche, the Cheyenne, and the Kiowa had qualitatively different forms of social hierarchy based on different means of establishing dependency relations. Lack of space and scarce information on the nineteenth-century Comanche, Cheyenne, and Kiowa prevent me from developing this argument in full, but I will build my analysis on Hoebel's report that the three groups valued different behaviors (1954: 131) and on data suggesting differences in band organization, leadership patterns, and the options open to abandoned husbands.

In all three societies, men in insecure marriages had difficulty refusing requests from those who could help them keep their wives, but their marriages were differently validated. In the egalitarian Comanche society, men married with "brideservice" (see Collier and Rosaldo 1981; J. Collier 1984; J. Collier n.d.), and so enjoyed stable marriages once their wives bore children. In Cheyenne society, men needed help from senior kin to acquire and keep wives but, like the men described by P. P. Rey in his analysis of "the lineage mode of production" (1975), they acquired power as their children reached marriageable age. All Cheyenne youths owed respect and obedience to elders who supported them, and all elders, except a few unfortunate ones, had young people to command (see J. Collier 1984; J. Collier n.d.). The Kiowa, as analyzed here, had a marriage system that put some men into a position of lifelong dependency, thus allowing other men to enjoy lifelong freedom from drudgery. The Kiowa appeared to have an hereditary elite because children of high-ranking couples never had to perform menial labor.

The three ways of validating marriage correlated with different social values. The egalitarian Comanche admired the man who "took what he could get and held what he had without much regard for the abstract rights" of others (Wallace and Hoebel 1952: 146). The Cheyenne admired the man who generously supported those needier than himself (Hoebel 1978: 43). And the Kiowa admired the aristocrat who was brave and courteous, above noticing slight insults (Richardson 1940: 120).

The three ways of validating marriages established different kinship dyads as the locus of inequality. Among the Comanche, "daughters' husbands" performed services for their "wives' parents"; among the Cheyenne, "children" obeyed the "parents" who supported them; and among the Kiowa, "sisters' husbands" were obliged to honor all requests from their "wives' brothers." The significance of these dyads is reflected in ethnographers' accounts of group organization. Hoebel (1940) portrays Comanche bands as loosely organized groups of affines. In contrast, Cheyenne living units are described as extended uxorilocal households "consisting of a man and his wife, their married daughters and husbands, their unmarried sons, their daughters' children, and any adopted or dependent relatives" (Eggan 1955: 61). Finally, Richardson writes that Kiowa bands were composed of "brothers" and "sisters" (1940: 5).

Ethnographers also record different patterns of leadership in the three Plains societies. The Comanche had informal "peace chiefs" who could give advice but not orders (Hoebel 1940: 19)—as would be expected in a society where securely married men needed nothing from others. The Cheyenne, in contrast, ritually initiated peace chiefs into office, largely on the basis of the candidates' generosity: "In specific behavior, this [meant] that a tribal chief [gave] constantly to the poor" (Hoebel 1978: 43). Cheyenne leaders, like the Melanesian Big Men described by Sahlins (1963), collected women, children, and strays in their households and then used the products of their many dependents to support others generously and to sponsor tribal rituals. Finally, the Kiowa lacked the distinction between lower-ranking war chiefs and higher-ranking peace chiefs found among the Comanche and the Cheyenne; their leaders were always men drawn from the hereditary elite. The Kiowa were also the only Plains group reported to have recognized named ranks (Hoebel 1954: 170), although ranking occurred among nearby agriculturalists, such as the Ioway (Skinner 1926). In summary, these three different leadership patterns suggest that what men could hope for—and so what women could want for themselves and their sons—varied from group to group.

Finally, the best illustration of the effect of political power-dependency relations on conjugal ties comes from ethnographers' accounts of the different ways abandoned husbands in the three societies retrieved wives who occasionally took refuge with their natal kin. Hoebel does not address this matter in his monograph on

Comanche law (1940)—a striking omission given that he does so in his work on the Cheyenne (Llewellyn and Hoebel 1941: 181) and that Richardson describes the process for the Kiowa (1940: 65). Hoebel's omission suggests that the Comanche lacked culturally recognized ways for a woman's kin to take her away from her husband (and so for her husband to retrieve her).* This inference is supported by Hoebel's report that the kin of a Comanche woman did not seek vengeance if her husband killed her (1940: 73). Hoebel, in fact, portrays Comanche fathers and brothers as tragically unable to protect a woman from her husband's brutality (1940: 73).

In contrast to powerless Comanche parents, Cheyenne parents, particularly mothers, could protect fugitive or errant daughters.† Whatever Cheyenne parents may have felt for daughters, household heads could "maximize property" by collecting "working women" in their production units (Moore 1974: 87). Llewellyn and Hoebel report that a Cheyenne "wife displeased with her husband's conduct 'went home to mother'" (1941: 181). If her husband wanted her back, he had to signal his desire by sending a horse to her brothers. The woman's brothers then "put her through a cross-examination to determine her grounds for divorce. If they were weighty, the disunion was allowed" (Llewellyn and Hoebel 1941: 181).

Among the Kiowa, as already noted, "it would always cost [an abandoned husband] and his kin considerable property to get [his wife] back, if at all" (Richardson 1940: 65). A Kiowa man's ability to keep his wife, therefore, depended on his ability to pay, in contrast to a Cheyenne husband, who had to defend himself against his wife's accusations and probably beg pardon for his faults.

Ethnographers thus reveal that abandoned husbands faced very different situations in the three societies. A Comanche man might kill or maim a disloyal wife without fear of vengeance from her kin. An abandoned Cheyenne husband was expected to defend himself

---

*In brideservice societies like Comanche, men earn their own wives rather than receiving them in exchange for bridewealth provided by their senior kin. Women's kin, therefore, have no "right" to reclaim married daughters. Hoebel, in fact, writes that a woman's only escape from an unwanted husband was to abscond with another man (1940: 73).

†Llewellyn and Hoebel report that a Cheyenne husband had the right to put his wife "on the prairie" to be gang raped by members of his soldier society (1941: 202), but the cases they cite indicate that senior women actively intervened to prevent this from happening.

and beg pardon. And a Kiowa husband was expected to offer goods or services to his wife's kin. In all three societies, some husbands and wives failed to get along, but both their problems and the available solutions were shaped by the wider political systems in which they lived.

These differences in marital problems and solutions illustrate the point I made at the beginning of this article: the women and men who make marriages and other unions are themselves creations of particular societies. Anthropologists cannot regard human social organization as universally a "balance, stable or not, between the political order . . . and the familial or domestic order" (Fortes 1978: 4). There is no familial order apart from a political one. Relations between husbands and wives, parents and children, are shaped by the social system in which they live. Sexual intercourse and childcare may be universal activities, but people perform them with different intentions, expectations, emotions, and outcomes.

If anthropologists studying kinship can no longer assume a universal familial order based on transcultural biological requirements, then we need analytical tools for understanding the social systems that structure people's intentions and expectations. We need systemic models capable of distinguishing among qualitatively different forms of hierarchy. In this paper, I have proposed a model for analyzing ranked acephalous societies, such as the Kiowa and the "Gumsa" Kachin. Beginning with overt cultural values ("war record was the single most important determinant of status in Kiowa life" [Richardson 1940: 14]), I examined the social mechanisms that put some men into the position of working for others and some women into the position of agreeing to live with those men. And I briefly compared the Kiowa to their neighbors on the Plains to illustrate the utility of systemic models for understanding differences in the ways people experience marriage and other cross-sex relationships. Comanche, Cheyenne, and Kiowa people had very different hopes and fears when interacting with kin.

Systemic models of the type proposed here are designed to inform our analyses of historically specific social processes. As anthropologists trying to understand the relationship between concepts of gender and kinship, we must situate both within historically particular social and cultural systems (Tsing and Yanagisako 1983: 516). But because our analyses of historically specific social processes will inevitably be informed by conceptual tools, we need to choose our tools with care. In the past, anthropologists studying kinship have used a conceptual distinction between domestic and politico-jural spheres. I suggest we replace this conceptual distinction—and its variants, such as nature/culture and reproduction/production—with a set of systemic models for analyzing social inequality.

The Mystification of Female Labors

Shirley Lindenbaum

FOLLOWING SISKIND'S seminal essay (1978), it is now almost commonplace to say that relations of kinship are, in certain societies, relations of production. If kinship is understood as a system that organizes the liens we hold on the emotions and labors of others, then it must be studied in relation to gender ideologies that enmesh men and women in diverse relations of productive and reproductive work. The variable constructions of "male" and "female" that emerge in different times and places are central to an understanding of the character of kinship, as the following study of gender in Papua New Guinea will show.*

Ideologies of masculinity and femininity in the highland, coastal, and island communities of Papua New Guinea share many common themes, expressed in the ritual manipulation of body substances and in notions about the generative processes necessary for the creation of a cultural order. Yet the ideologies are not uniform, and a close look at the varied attention given to body parts and substances, and at different notions of procreation and growth, reveals something of the process whereby communities of men and women commit social labor to the transformation of nature.

One set of ideas closely associated with characteristic forms of productive and reproductive relations concerns the importance of semen, a body substance with a particular ritual geography in New

*This is a revised version of a paper delivered in November 1980 at the City University of New York Graduate Anthropology Symposium on Gender Relations and Social Reproduction. I am grateful to Jane Schneider and the other participants in the symposium for helpful comments, and to Rayna Rapp, Joyce Riegelhaupt, and Pam Smith for their close reading of this analysis. The organizers and participants at the Feminism and Kinship conference also provided many instructive suggestions.

Guinea. A contrast between semen-focused societies in which male homosexual behavior occurs during initiation rites and "heterosexual" societies in the central and western highlands that lack semen exchange indicates the interconnections between sexual behavior, gender formation, and productive relations in these cultures. In specific cases, jural claims and structures of commitment recorded in idioms of kinship, marriage, and residence are shown to be closely linked.

Because these interconnections are best illuminated when structures of production or power are undergoing change, the following analysis of "homosexual" and "heterosexual" regions in New Guinea will devote special attention to island and coastal communities whose social forms are undergoing transition.

I should indicate that I do not intend to imply here, or in later parts of this essay, that all societies follow a universal pattern of evolution from one set of sexual, gender, or productive relations to another. My broad comparison of groups is placed in a suggestive framework that I hope points instead to the systematic interconnectedness of these various aspects of cultures. The analysis struggles with what Keesing has recently called "Bateson's problem," the problem of "how partial modes of understanding can be fitted together in a coherent process of explanation" (1982: 17).

The significance of "male" and "female" in New Guinea goes beyond the realm of personal interaction. Papua New Guineans live in a gender-inflected universe in which the polarities of male and female articulate cosmic forces thought to be located in the human body; indigenous theories of human reproduction contain within them an implicit recipe for social reproduction. We should thus be aware that the organization of sexual practices and the formation of gender identities in the small "homosexual" societies of New Guinea are integral to their systems of productive and reproductive work. Use of the term "homosexual" to describe ritualized same-sex relationships in these groups, therefore, differs from our usual sense of the word, in which sexuality is often taken to be much the same at all times and in all cultures and to be a category of existence entirely separate from realms such as the economy or the state (Padgug 1979).

A survey of semen-focused societies (Lindenbaum 1980; Herdt 1984; Whitehead this volume) shows that ritualized homosexual behavior among men is found among a complex of groups along the Papuan Coast: the Marind Anim (Van Baal 1966), the Kimam (Serpenti 1965), the Keraki (Williams 1940), and the Fly River peoples such as the Kiwai and the Mowat (Beardmore 1890; Landtman 1927). A second large and seemingly connected group exists on the Great Papuan Plateau: the Etoro (Kelly 1977), the Kaluli (Schieffelin 1975; Schieffelin 1982), the Onabasulu (Ernst 1978), the Bedamini (Sorum 1980), and the Gebusi (Knauft 1985). Possibly connected also are the eastern highlands fringe groups of the Sambia (Herdt 1981; Herdt 1982; Herdt 1984) and the Baruya (Godelier 1976; Godelier 1982). Evidence of ritual attention to homosexual relationships in the Sepik region comes from the Iatmul (Bateson 1936) and the Wogeo (Hogbin 1970), and there are reports of homosexual joking among the Samo in the Nomad River area (Herdt 1984; Knauft 1985).

In island communities close to the New Guinea mainland, ritualized homosexual behavior has been reported from Fiji, the New Hebrides (Layard 1942; Layard 1959; Deacon 1934; Allen 1967; Guiart 1952; Guiart 1953), New Caledonia (Foley 1879), New Britain (among the Ingiet and Duke of York Islands), and Santa Cruz at East Bay (Davenport 1965). Several authors see signs of an archaic ritual complex (Keesing 1982; Herdt 1984; Van Baal 1966; Williams 1940), which from this vantage point would probably include the northern Australian Arunta (Spencer and Gillen 1927). The male cults of these Pre-Papuan or Australoid-speaking groups are thought to have traveled inland along the great river systems of New Guinea, the Fly and the Sepik, suggesting that the south coast center of cult initiation and a hypothesized Sepik center were perhaps connected in the ancient past (Keesing 1982: 15).

It should be noted that this geographic sketch of same-sex relationships concerns male behavior and thought. Institutionalized "lesbianism" is apparently quite rare. Deacon reports "lesbian" relationships on Malekula, for instance, and Godelier mentions that Baruya women "stroke one another," although "we know little of what actually goes on" (1976: 15). In a later publication, Godelier adds that toward the end of the Baruya female initiation, the initiate rolls in the river mud with her sponsor in what appears to be an imitation of copulation (1982: 82). In a third instance, Du Toit describes a form of homosexual play among the Akana of the eastern highlands, in which two girls caress and pet each other's breasts and genitals as they lie in a position of intercourse (1975: 220). The topic of institutionalized female-female sexual relations has been avoided in the literature, however, and we are not yet in a position to say whether they too may prove to be the focus of ritual attention, ideological elaboration, or social integration.

The male homosexuality discussed here concerns ritually introduced, socially sanctioned behaviors that are kept secret from women and noninitiates: fellatio and oral sex (which occurs among the Sambia, the Etoro, and the Bedamini), sodomy or anal intercourse (among the Kaluli, the Kiwai, and the Keraki), and the application of semen—collected during masturbation (among the Onabasulu) or after the sequential intercourse of many men with one woman (among the Kimam)—into incisions on the initiates' bodies. Since different groups have generally disparaging views about the sexual practices of their neighbors, variations in these practices involve the creation of ethnic identity within a regional complex. As Kelly comments about the peoples of the Great Papuan Plateau: "Inasmuch as the members of each tribe become men in different ways, they are predominantly different kinds of men, culturally distinct beings at the most fundamental level" (1977: 16).

What these behaviors have in common, however, is that they are acknowledged in each society as the sole physical and psychic path to manhood. The cultural gift of semen is said to be the only way older men can ensure the growth, development, and masculinity of members of their own sex, those for whom they are responsible. There is much talk of growth, physical attractiveness, and the formation of the intellect, but no word that translates as "homosexual."

The literature on societies with ritualized homosexuality gives most attention to cultural notions insisting that male reproductive capacity comes not with the endowment of male genitalia, but is induced through the ritual implanting of semen in young men. I suggest that in the cases considered here, there may be also a physical dimension to the matter. Reports from the Simbari Anga, cultural neighbors of the Sambia and Baruya, for example, indicate an unusually high incidence of male pseudohermaphroditism. In a population of 1,800, ambiguity of external genitalia was found among 7, with reports of 2 other cases (Gajdusek 1977).* The individuals

---

*Gajdusek found an additional case of male pseudohermaphroditism among the Baruya-speaking Anga, upstream from Simbari, with no known marriage contacts

were raised to adulthood as males, and several had married and were believed to have fathered children. In one case, villagers attributed offspring to other males in the community, and in another, the individual ascribed his fertility to artificial insemination by hand. This situation contrasts markedly with the customs of the populous Mae Enga (30,000) of the western highlands, whose women abandon "demon children" in the bush (Meggitt 1965), doing away with what they consider to be anomalous births. Unlike the Simabari Anga, the Enga do not have an appropriate gender category, an acceptable social place, or a creation myth explaining the presence of such individuals on earth. The occurrence of persons with ambiguous genitalia may be cause for more serious speculation about the template of sexual identity in small, rather than large populations. Certainly, the cultural universe of these small groups accommodates notions of sexuality less bounded than those of the densely populated highly intensive agricultural systems of the western highlands.

As indicated above, theories of procreation in Melanesia are never simple statements about human reproduction, but contain within them recipes for the reproduction of the known universe. The societies discussed here thus draw upon an ideology of male parthenogenesis and a pattern of male behavior we call "homosexual" to effect production, reproduction, and social continuity. Semen is seen to be the key substance entailed in the regeneration of society. In the central and western highlands, however, where homosexual rituals are absent, a "heterosexual" ethos recognizes women's reproductive labors, and ideas of male productivity becloud instead women's increased contribution to the creation of wealth, a substance of alternate cultural attention. In both regions we find an interdependence among such elements as procreation theory, gender ideology, and the scale and intensity of wealth production. In addition, we find a differential focus on the relations among siblings and affines.

Relations of Production in "Homosexual" Communities

In the "homosexual" societies discussed here, men and women contribute rather evenly to subsistence production and to the gen-

---

between the two groups. Two cases were found also among the nearby Fore groups, although both of these men had rudimentary penises, had married, and had fathered children.

eration of certain trade items, although male labor and male trading activities are accorded somewhat greater social value. Consequently, the Kimam do not think that polygyny increases a man's agricultural production since it is said that "women play only a minor part in agriculture" (Serpenti 1965: 62). Male labor is also a significant element in the construction of the sophisticated mud gardens of both Kimam and Marind Anim, where polygyny is also said to be rare. Moreover, the male endeavors of hunting and fishing provide a large part of the diet in these communities. Landtman, too, speaks of a Kiwai division of gardening labor whereby men do the heavy fencing, and both men and women work together in planting everything except yams, which are considered to be a male crop (1927: 68). In addition, although women make mats, baskets, men's belts, and women's grass skirts—some of which enter into networks of regional trade—and although women paddle the canoes while men steer, men produce the canoes that are an important trade item with the Torres Straits islanders (Landtman 1927: 213).

On the Papuan Plateau, men and women again work together in subsistence activities. The family or hearth group is said to be the single most important and enduring unit of production and consumption among the Onabasulu (Ernst 1978: 189), as is the nuclear family unit among the Bedamini (Sorum 1984: 319). Bedamini adult women also show an independent attitude toward their husbands, perhaps because men and women privately own the products of their separate plots in the communal gardens (Sorum 1984: 327). The tenor of male-female relations in these communities is neither constrained nor hedged with the anxiety characteristic of highland groups—east, center, or west. Etoro men do not fear female pollution, and men and women mingle and interact freely as they perform garden work, sago production, and go about their daily activities in the communal portion of the longhouse (Kelly 1976: 42).

In sum, the division of labor and ownership in the production of most food and goods for subsistence, trade and exchange, though weighted slightly in favor of males, provides rewards for both sexes. The production and exchange of semen, however, creates status differences between older and younger men and especially between men and women. Relations among affinal groups is one of watchful equality, based on the mutual dominance of wife-givers.

The Structures of Marriage and Homosexuality

Beyond similarities in their geography, demography, productive relations and forms of sexual identity, "homosexual" societies in Papua New Guinea have like structures of marriage and homosexual relations, which are mutually supportive. The pattern of marriage in almost all groups is sister exchange, with no payment of brideprice. Although hard to sustain in small groups, sister exchange is said to be the ideal form of marriage among the Etoro (Kelly 1977: 131), the Kaluli (Schieffelin 1975: 60), the Kiwai (Landtman 1927: 244), the Keraki (Williams 1936: 128), the Kimam (Serpenti 1965: 128), and on Malekula (Layard 1942: 104). Other forms of marriage also exist in some groups; for example, the Sambia accept delayed exchange marriage with infant betrothal, a form said to be more characteristic of intra-hamlet marriages (Herdt 1981: 43), and the Baruya allow exchange between two lineages of a sister for a daughter (Godelier 1976: 13). In all cases, a marked effect of structural duality exists between affinal groups (see Hage 1981), a pattern that is reinforced by homosexual ties among men. For, as Kelly notes for the Etoro, the ideal inseminator is a boy's sister's husband. A married sister and her brother thus share the same sexual partner (Kelly 1977: 181–83).

Social relations in "homosexual" societies are characterized by a kind of double affinity, by the return of a woman from an already defined affinal group; men are double brothers-in-law, and the women are double sisters-in-law. Moreover, from the point of view of the cultures in which the custom exists, the gift of a woman is accompanied by a gift of semen, reinforcing the lines of double affinity. In an *ideal* gift cycle, A gives semen to B, and B gives his sister, C, to A. B gives semen to D, a fellow kinsman of A and an affine of B, thereby returning the original semen gift to the lineage of origin. D gives his sister, E (she is also a sister of A), to B, completing the cycle, which is a replication of direct exchange. (See Figure 1.)

Reciprocity is a recurrent motif in the literature on "homosexual" societies (see Schieffelin 1975: 1). The balanced reciprocities of sister exchange, however, are difficult to sustain, and much organizational and psychic energy is expended on keeping the score even. Given that these "homosexual" societies are small and subject to intermittent epidemics and food shortages, problems in ob-

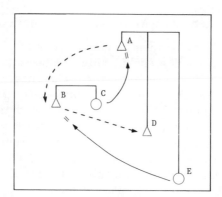

Figure 1.
An Ideal
Gift Cycle.

taining wives are such that some men resort to bride capture, said to be a highly prestigious, if rare, phallic means of acquiring a wife among the Sambia (Herdt 1981: 44). Promised girls may also run away. "Runaway women were received with open arms" among the Kimam, reports Serpenti, "for each local group is always intent on getting as many women as possible . . . at the expense of other local groups" (1965: 128–29). The Kimam and the Keraki sometimes also buy "sisters" from other groups in order to exchange them for wives (Williams 1940: 141).

Since direct exchange, although highly desired, is not often possible, delayed reciprocity is another solution. When delay enters into the system, the structures of power by which affinal groups mutually define themselves becomes apparent. The Kimam have devised one means of keeping the score even: when the first marriage of an expected exchange takes place, the groom's group delivers a payment of goods to the bride's group, which is expected to return it in full when the second part of the exchange contract becomes effective. In such cases, Serpenti notes, this payment has no connection with the ceremonial gift or counter gift of New Guinea highland marriages, but is regarded purely as a "security" (1965: 129).* The boy's group "secures" a future bride and avoids also the indignity of indebtedness to affines.

The logistics of exchange marriage are conveyed in fine detail in McDowell's account of marriage transactions among the Bun, a

*Moreover, this resolution of the problem of broken marriage arrangements is new for the Kimam.

"non-homosexual" society of 218 members in the Angoram Sub-District, East Sepik. Their strict adherence to the sister-exchange rule is ensured by rabbinical definitions of who is to be considered a sister in each marriage transaction and which brothers have a claim upon her. If, for the purpose of one marriage, a woman is said to be the sister of a certain man, her relationships to other individuals are thereby dislodged. Debate about the admissibility of marriages is endemic. Sister exchange is in fact one of the most talked-about matters in the community, and deciphering its complexity consumes more discussion time than any other topic (McDowell 1972: 214).

The logistics of sister exchange, then, are exceedingly problematic.* Although the obligations established by the exchange of women are well considered in the literature on "homosexual" societies, little has been written about the jural and affective connotations of semen exchange. One of the few explicit references to the matter occurs in Spencer and Gillen's account of the prospective Arunta husband: "It frequently happens that the women whose daughter is . . . allotted to him may have a son and no daughter born, and in this case, without waiting on the chance of a girl being born, the man may agree to take the boy. . . . This establishes a relationship between the boy and the man, as a result of which the former has, until he (is circumcised) to give his hair to the man, who on his part has, in a certain way, to look after the boy" (1927: 2:470). The prospective bridegroom looks after the boy by having physical relations with him as though he were a wife and by anointing him with semen, as Layard notes (1959: 106). Here, in the Arunta 8-Section marriage system based on sister exchange, homosexual and heterosexual rights completely overlap. This also occurs among the Etoro, where a man relinquishes access to his sister but acquires access to a brother-in-law when the sister is given or promised in marriage (Kelly 1977: 22, 121–23).

*The pattern of semen exchange would seem to create ideological contradictions, since sisters must also contain some paternal semen substance. Serious ritual attention must be given to separating brothers and sisters so that the brother retains male essence at the time of his initiation or of his sister's marriage. Beardmore (1890) describes one such ceremony for the Mowat peoples (Kiwai). When the brother leaves his father's house to reside with the community of men where he is sodomized, his sister has a "V"-shaped incision cut above her breasts, a scar she is said to carry for life. This could be seen as a castration of the sister, allowing her brother to become a differentiated male being, the sole possessor of their paternal penis substance.

The fusion of brother and sister and their treatment as one person is a theme that echoes throughout the literature on "homosexual" groups, a theme strong enough to lead Layard to speak of the relationship between brothers-in-law as "near incest." Each fulfills for the other the incestuous desire to marry one's own sister, an observance the Baruya might well support. Godelier notes that when a Baruya girl first menstruates, her fiancé ritually declares, "You are no longer your father's, but mine. Look upon me as your elder brother" (1976: 19). Moreover, Baruya men sometimes confess that they would rather marry a sister, whom they know well, than a girl from a different lineage who seems to them a complete stranger (Godelier 1976: 200). Indeed, when Baruya men have no sisters to exchange, they marry a sister from within their own lineage, an arrangement they also describe as marrying "like dogs."*

Semen rights might also be examined from the viewpoint of the potential bride. Serpenti mentions, for example, that a Kimam girl submits to repeated communal intercourse to provide a pool of semen that is rubbed into her future husband's ritually incised wounds. If her fiancé subsequently runs away with another woman, she chastises the husband-stealer by saying that she has worked hard to make her own husband tall and handsome, whereas her delinquent rival's betrothed remains small and puny.

It should be noted, too, that the sexual labor of growing a future husband is only part of the woman's hard work. When her fiancé enters the seclusion of the bachelors' hut to begin an extended period of homosexual education and activity, she moves to his parental house, and from this moment on, her future father-in-law has authority over her and full claim on her domestic labor (Serpenti 1984: 307). In an earlier publication, Serpenti mentions also that Kimam bride-givers have a lien on the labor of the husband: "Wife's brother and father can on practically every occasion claim her husband's help, which the latter may never refuse to give" (1965: 137). Since Kimam marry mother's brother's daughters or a cross-cousin so designated, the reciprocal claims on sexual and manual labor tied to both marriage and homosexual relations are seen to be significant and complex.

Several observers tell us that the bond between the homosexual

---

*This points to a changing ethos in Baruya society. For example, Godelier (1982) notes that the Baruya now no longer observe rituals of homosexuality.

pair is one of deep commitment. Deacon reports that the Big Namba chief becomes angry if his boy lover, without his consent, has intercourse with any other man; if one of the two should die, the survivor mourns him deeply (1934: 216). The relationship between the Malekula chief and his boy lover(s) is a mix of jural rights and affect, for the boy is said to accompany his "husband" everywhere and to work in his gardens. (Chiefs thus acquire many lovers.) The affective bond between wife's brother and sister's husband among the Etoro is also said to be "exceptionally strong" (Kelly 1977: 183).

It might be said that semen is the gift or covenant that keeps the sister-exchange system intact in small communities. Notions concerning the flow of life force between men and between men and women link individuals and groups in complex chains of mutual dependency and obligation. Since semen and sisters pass between affinal groups in both directions, but at different times, each group maintains a balance of services owed and services required. However, contrary to sister exchange, an ideology concerning the exchange of equals, semen exchange is based on a well-defined dominance order. A man cannot give and receive semen at the same time, nor can the donor-recipient relation be reversed. The senior male gives, and the junior receives. An ideal marriage transaction involves two men who exchange sisters; the "atom of semenship," so to speak, requires three male partners linked in descending order.

An unquestioned pattern of hierarchy thereby overlays a design of equality (based on mutual subordination) that causes constant concern and potential conflict. Delayed reciprocity in marriage debts, which occurs with some frequency, creates a troublesome imbalance between exchanging groups. An imbalance of three or more women is said to be sufficient to produce discontent among the Etoro, who express their displeasure in witchcraft accusations against the nonreciprocating kin group (Kelly 1977: 125). The ritually confirmed dominance order of semen exchange thus contains animosities that arise among close kin who are also affines, linking potential opponents in a web of morality and substance characterized by strong affective bonds. The exchange creates jural expectations among semen-connected groups and adds sentiment as a curb on the adversary aspect of affinal exchange. It is at the individual as well as at the group level that the two organizational systems meet.*

That sister exchange and ritualized homosexuality act in tandem may be seen in situations where the two systems begin to break down. For instance, although Beardmore reported sodomy and marriage by sister exchange among the Kiwai in 1890, Landtman found no trace of sodomy by 1927: "I think it quite possible that the customs of the people, changing as they are, may have altered in this respect since Mr. Beardmore's time" (1927: 237). Landtman added that although sister exchange was still the expressed ideal, brideprice marriage had begun to creep in, with an additional return gift from bride's to groom's kin (1927: 245).

In 1965, Serpenti also noted the demise among the Kimam of the bachelor house with its attendant homosexual practices. The young man now stays at home before marriage, and his betrothed no longer moves to his parents' house. It must be assumed that these affines no longer have the same authority over the bride that they once had or a claim on her labors, sexual or domestic; this marks an important shift in social obligations among affinal groups. Significantly, Serpenti also observed the breakdown of sister exchange, supplanted by "the new custom of brideprice marriage." Reflecting upon the factors contributing to this trend, he mentioned the increased interaction among villagers in colonial times under the Pax Australiana, and a larger marriage pool that gives young people an opportunity to find more partners. He speaks too of an increasing dependence on European goods. Many young men now leave the island to work for a year or more in order to acquire these "much coveted items" (1965: 131), which are subsequently circulated at home through brideprice exchange.

The embedding of male labor in brideprice items effects a change in the relations among affines. As Collier and Rosaldo show (1981), young men in brideservice societies (similar to those discussed here) acquire wives by exchanging sisters and by performing continual services for their wives' parents. Bonds of affinity are also a significant component of the relations of production in "homosexual" communities. Kelly notes, for instance, that affinal bonds are

---

*Male initiation ceremonies, centers of semen ideology, also join men who are in potential conflict for the same woman (brothers) and create bonds among wider bodies of men. Sørum suggests that male initiation and healing seances continually create solidary units among the Bedamini (1980: 275).

reinforced at the expense of lineage solidarity among the Etoro and that material gifts from a potential groom to a wife's kin are not reciprocated (1977: 79, 213). That is, affinal structures are an important aspect of productive relations, and a wife's kin hold the upper hand in their lien on her husband's labor. The Kimam express this subordination of wife-receivers by saying, "My wife's kin are the heart, the whole world. If I have anything at all, I share it with them; if I have nothing, I feel ashamed" (Serpenti 1965: 136).

With the introduction of brideprice payments, the social world changes. Relations of production are transformed as different social obligations supplant the former order. New values are accorded to male and female labors, and relationships of dominance and subordination among affines change direction. In the section that follows, we see also that whereas semen was an agent of social reproduction in "homosexual" societies, the place of semen is occupied by brideprice in "non-homosexual" social forms.*

Changing Wealth and Marriage Transactions Among the Iatmul and Marind Anim

It has been argued here that the system of sister exchange and ritualized homosexuality mutually reinforce an egalitarian moral order. As noted earlier, their interdependence is best seen by looking closely at specific cases in which the differential breakdown of sister exchange, homosexuality, and a sense of equality among affines occurs as brideprice and European trade goods intrude into certain communities. For example, the Naven ritual of the Iatmul may be analyzed as a statement of uncertainty about the lines of power in the community following the demise of sister exchange and its attendant rituals of homosexuality.

Sister exchange among the Iatmul is no longer extant. All that remains is a "vague and generally inoperative notion" that children of opposite moieties should marry according to the sister-exchange convention, the "remnant of an aspect that was once functionally salient" (Tuzin 1976: 315). Hints of a prior cultural complex based on homosexuality also appear in the Iatmul myth in which a man rubs his buttocks on the legs of a man marrying his sister (Bateson 1936: 49, 77, 81). The ritual expression of this relationship occurs

*See Godelier (1982) for a discussion of ritual homosexuality, sister exchange, and brideprice.

during the Naven rite when the Wau (mother's brother) offers his buttocks to his Laua (sister's son). This is a curious homosexual relationship, since the male of a senior generation acts as a "wife" to a junior. However, the message is not one of direct dominance, but of switched-circuit dominance, for the Wau offers his buttocks in a burlesque manner. Naven behavior is ironic, and is thus only apparently self-deprecatory. As a meta-communication sustained by inversion (Handelman 1979), the Wau, a male of a senior generation (2 points for dominance) exhibits the "female" behavior of sexual receptivity (2 points for submission), yet the whole is done as raucous play. As a ludic ritual of reversal it is a twisted reassertion of a dominance order of the general homosexual pattern, a communication the Laua recognizes, for he hurries to present the Wau with a gift of compensating valuables.

The matter of dominance and submission is a clue to the changing nature of wealth and marriage transactions in the region. Iatmul now observe brideprice marriage with a return brideprice when the bride shifts to the husband's village. Although the exchange accomplishes a seemingly amicable renegotiation of the affinal contest for dominance, Bateson notes a remaining sense of indebtedness such that the "wife's relatives have always the right to call on the husband for help in any task, like housebuilding, for which a crowd of manual laborers is necessary. When the task is completed, the wife's people will host a small feast for the laborers, or they will at least distribute coconuts to them. This largess is of the nature of a complementary presentation and is usually quite inadequate as a payment for work done" (1936: 79). That is, despite their receipt of a huge marriage payment, wife-givers here retain a sense of superiority. The Naven rite, a kind of theatre of the absurd, calls attention to this phenomenon, perhaps intensifying the sense of anomaly (see Read 1980). The dominance of wife-givers and the subservience of wife-takers is a matter to be returned to shortly. For the moment, it should be noted that the superior position of wife-givers appears to be a contested structural "sediment" in this formerly "homosexual" sister-exchanging Sepik region.

The ambiguous approach to ritualized homosexuality among the Marind Anim also illustrates the connections among gender ideology and productive and reproductive relations. Marind Anim coastal communities are said to have recently abandoned literal sister exchange as well as moiety exogamy. Flamboyant rituals of male initiation, head-hunting, and marriage have also changed since the colonial government banned the great rituals, feasts, and associated sexual practices in 1920 (Van Baal 1966; Van Baal 1984). Van Baal's reconstruction of this cult activity, however, indicates that it entailed not only an ideology of exclusively male fertility and the presence of ritual homosexuality among novices and older men, but also promiscuous heterosexual intercourse. This latter expression of sexuality is said to have occurred on the first night of marriage, and again at the return of a woman's menses following the birth of a child, a ritual acknowledgment of the role of women's reproductive cycles in human fertility. In addition, a mix of semen and female secretion, obtained through promiscuous heterosexual intercourse, was used as a potent curative medicine, a cosmetic, a ceremonial food, a substance required for the fertility of new gardens, and as a lethal component of a sorcerer's concoctions (Van Baal 1984).

Van Baal also suggests that "the Marind Anim were not the devoted homosexuals their praise of sodomy and its honourable place in their value system would suggest" (1984: 161). Of further significance for the discussion that follows, the second initiation of Marind Anim males gives central place to a character called Old Imo Woman, also known as Bad Excrement or Excrement Woman. Novices are introduced to her in violent fashion. Knocked to the ground and dragged by their hair to her house, they have their faces smeared with sperm and excrement, the latter material said to be repugnant to Marind Anim, who participate in homosexual anal intercourse. Novices are forced to lie in the compound of Excrement Woman's house until maggots appear in the fecal-semen matter, whereupon they are bathed and cleaned. The following night's rites introduce the bachelors to heterosexual intercourse.

Although relations between Marind Anim spouses are often said to be cordial and more stable than those in many other Papuan tribes, antagonism between the sexes occurs in ritual life. In one ceremony, for example, men pelt women with piles of excrement (Van Baal 1984). This apparent contradiction between the tenor of daily life and of ritual experience, Van Baal suggests, has to do with the men's realization that their parthenogenetic notions of fertility are failing. Marind Anim marital fecundity is low, and the population has experienced a high incidence of venereal disease with associated female sterility (Van Baal 1966: 25). Thus, Van Baal argues that the Marind Anim are subconsciously aware that their ideology concerning the life-producing male sperm is countered by the demonstrable failure of the fertility process (Van Baal 1984).

Whatever the merits of this argument, it might also be said that changes in the region's political economy have modified notions of gender. The evidence suggests that Marind Anim culture has expanded along the coast from east to west and to the interior as well (Van Baal 1966). The resulting extensive ritual organization of these coastal communities seems incompatible with the maintenance of the narrow ritual and social forms that stem from sister-exchange marriage. The highly visible moiety organizations of ritual life, freed from the isomorphism of marriage exchange, provide instead the basis for broad regional integration in a manner reminiscent of social arrangements in the Sepik region. Here, too, the consolidation and growth of villages is said to militate against the persistence of prescriptive marriage rules, favoring instead a dual organization functionally associated with ceremonialism and social integration on a large scale (Tuzin 1976: 310). As the Marind Anim marriage system thus shifts beyond the boundaries of sister exchange, and as men begin to experience some emotional distance from the notion of semen as the sole agent of regeneration, it might be supposed that Marind Anim males are on the verge of striking their affines with brideprice rather than pelting their women with excrement (see Ferenczi 1914; Fenichel 1938).

The intrusion of brideprice into marriage transactions, along with the demise of semen exchange, is a sign of significant social transformation. Sister-exchange is an egalitarian mechanism sustained by the underlying assumption that wife-givers must also be wife-receivers. As the counter-balancing aspects of sister and semen exchange fade in particular contexts, however, the superior place of wife-givers is questioned, as the Naven rite indicates.

In the highland societies with elaborate brideprice marriage transactions,* the dominance order is reversed; superiority is gained not by giving but by taking more wives from others. More-

*This does not refer to Sambia or Baruya, where sister exchange continues and brideprice, although present, does not constitute the ideal marriage transaction. It should be noted, too, that the Sambia and Baruya, two "homosexual" cultures bordering the eastern highlands, have only recently begun to grow sweet potatoes and to raise pigs. The latter, few in number, are not yet used in wide-scale social exchange (Herdt 1981: 24–29; Godelier 1982: 24).

over, the focus of interest shifts from the women themselves to the objects given in exchange. As Strathern and Strathern note (1969: 158), the center of attention in Melpa marriage transactions in this part of the western highlands is imbalance in bridewealth, not imbalance in women.

Gender Ideology and Social Reproduction in the Eastern Highlands

Although transformations in kinship and productive relations are seen most clearly by comparing "homosexual" regions and "heterosexual" societies of the western highlands, a look at other Papua New Guinea groups clarifies this process of change. Thus, the Iatmul of the Sepik region, and the Papuan Coast Marind Anim have been examined to illustrate the incremental but significant transformation of the connections among gender ideology, sexual expression, marriage rules, and the exchange of labor and pursuit of dominance between affinally related groups. The middle ground between the small, egalitarian "homosexual" communities and the larger less egalitarian, wealth-producing "heterosexual" societies of the central and western highlands is further illustrated by eastern highlands groups. Here, brideprice with cross-cousin marriage replaces sister exchange,* subsistence is based on the moderately intensive production of sweet potatoes and pigs, and a strict ethos of reciprocity gives way to a system whereby some individuals and groups begin to rise above others by virtue of socially valued skills or through the ability to amass wealth, which they press upon others in competitive display. Many features come together to effect this transformation, not the least of which is an increase in women's horticultural labor, the pediment of the system.

Women increasingly perform the garden work that produces root crops for larger human populations and for domesticated pig herds, a form of wealth that is the focus of male and female attention and predominantly male prestige. A shift in the relations of production occurs as women's labor intensifies, brideprice becomes a feature of marriage transactions, and the liens on mutual support are expressed in a patrilineal idiom.

*This marks a shift from direct exchange to generalized exchange. For an illuminating analysis of structural transformations, see Rubel and Rossman (1978).

Eastern highland groups illustrate a further shift in that both semen and maternal blood are acknowledged as procreation substances. Men make "men" by separating boys from their mothers and other females and by committing youths to a community of men and male things. In place of an exchange of semen, the focus in rites of masculinity and male adulthood is on the painful draining and transformation of maternal substances from ambiguously gendered young bodies. In a variety of violent rituals, supposedly held in complete seclusion, the initiates' mothers are severed from the youths, driven back, sometimes ignored, and ideologically disparaged. Ordeals of nose-bleeding, penis-cutting, and forcible cane-swallowing further rid the initiates' bodies of mothers' blood and mothers' food (see Herdt 1982). Moreover, male-female relations take on a sharpness not present in most "homosexual" cultures. Men and women openly express antagonism; ritual protests that begin in an atmosphere of enjoyable obstruction often slip into more unfettered disputes and physical abuse (see Berndt 1966: 171; Newman and Boyd 1982: 255–56). Sexual attack and gruesome punishment for adultery or suspected adultery are the lot of the Fore and of many other eastern highland women (Berndt 1966). In marriage rituals of the eastern highland Gahuku-Gama, men "wound" the bride in her right thigh with a small three-pronged arrow called "anger" (Read 1984: 219), while Ndumba women, neighbors of the Fore, assure each other that "men are the enemy" (Hays and Hays 1982: 244).

Still, the result of this sexual jousting is not a simple male-female polarization. As Meigs notes in a discussion of the eastern highland Hua, "a person's gender does not lie locked in his or her genitals, but can flow and change with contact as substances seep into and out of his or her body" (1976: 406). Post-menopausal Hua women thus acquire male qualities and a kind of ritual purity, whereas older men take on female attributes. Eastern highlanders compose "constellations of gender" (Poole 1981) from the interchange of ideologically impregnated foods, behaviors, and body substances. Young male initiates begin ritual life as quasi-females and, by passing through a series of changing relationships with their male instructors, attain a masculine identity that still combines both male and female elements.

Although the events, ideas, symbols, and sentiments in these initiation rites proceed from a predominantly female beginning, through an ambiguous male-female interlude, to a predominantly male finale, the female remains a ubiquitous presence. Women are conspicuously absent at male initiation. Yet, the rituals are performed behind leafy screens, in the canopied forest, or beside streams near the villages, and the wails, loud stampings, bull-roarers, flutes, chants, and remote songs are meant to carry messages to the women who, as Tuzin notes (1982) are the object of both physical and rhetorical aggression. The suffering initiates are protected by their mothers' brothers, acting as "female" representatives. Since initiation rituals and marriage ceremonies occur simultaneously in these communities, the initiates are reminded of that heterosexual endpoint, marriage to a woman. Male identities are thus created in the context of larger heterosexual events, and the exchange and transformation of wealth, symbol, and personnel in a world inhabited by both "men" and "women" constitutes the whole drama.*

Male initiation rites of the eastern highlands thus convey a complicated set of ideas. As in the "homosexual" communities discussed above, men lay ritual claim to the powers of female reproduction, a mystification of female "reproductive" labor. However, the male claim to the reproduction of society is stated here with less certainty, for blood as well as semen are said to combine to form the fetus. Moreover, maternal nurture is encouraged throughout childhood even if it is later transmuted and voided with the ingestion of male foods and the letting of mother's blood. The exclusive doctrines of male initiation face contradiction also in the timing and enmeshing of the events themselves, as well as in the sexual ambiguity of the key symbols, the erotic male flutes, which the initiates first encounter during their initiation confinement.

The ideology of male parthenogenesis in "homosexual" societies—never a mere claim to biological prowess but an account of the rebirth of all social life—ill fits the social conditions of the eastern highlands. The partially intensive production systems—with new forms of wealth, new labor requirements, and consequently new sets of social relationships—demand other definitions of gender. In these areas, pigs and shells rather than semen are exchanged for

---

*Since many marriages involve the sisters of initiates, the two events combine to orchestrate the necessary differentiation of cross-sex siblings. In "homosexual" societies, sister exchange and ritual attention allows for a similar separation of brothers and sisters without severing their bond.

prestige, and these wealth items become the agents of social re-production, as male ideology glosses over the place of female labor in domestic production. Women are disparagingly equated with the pigs they produce (Hays and Hays 1982: 215), thereby under-mining any claim they might have to these products of their own labor. Women's productive and reproductive labors figure glanc-ingly in ritual and myth, where women are depicted as the original owners of the great creative flutes, subsequently stolen by men, but women do not contribute equally to the current ideology by means of which society is reproduced. Just as "homosexual" societies mute the female role in reproduction, eastern highlanders divert attention from women's productive contribution to things of sta-tus: pigs and adult men. Moreover, affinal relations in these groups are ambiguous. In the 1960's, for instance, Fore men were uncertain whether women or bridewealth had the greater value (Linden-baum 1979), a question answered with assurance by the western highland Melpa who focused without waver upon the marriage wealth itself (Strathern and Strathern 1969).

Appropriation of Female Labor in the Western Highlands

The inquiry into different notions of gender could be extended to the central and western highlands, as Whitehead's chapter in this volume so well illustrates. From the vantage point taken in this es-say, it seems possible to trace change in definitions of gender as well as an ideological shift away from an emphasis on body substances, as men and women objectify their labor and psychic energies in pigs, feathers, shells, and other forms of wealth. In addition to their different symbolic representation and experience of sex and gen-der, forms of economic expansion in the western highlands de-mand different marriage systems, as well as an intensification of women's horticultural labor. In contrast to "homosexual" societies that reproduce and exchange labor among affinally-related groups, in which cross-sex siblings help each other in garden work (Kelly 1977), or in which Malekula chiefs profit from the labor of their lov-ers, western highlands societies derive their labor system from a different ideology and organization of gender and marriage. Broad exogamic marriage rules keep siblings at a distance, corporate groups command the allegiance of patrilineally related men, and the added work of intensified horticulture is provided by an assem-blage of extra wives, bachelors and, in some cases, men of little stature. In the context of the vast ceremonial exchanges of wealth that arise in these high production systems, men draw upon an idiom of reproduction to portray exchange valuables as items obtained without female labor.* The male initiation complex is absent.

Western highlanders abandon the notion that men reproduce adult men and cultivate instead the idea that men reproduce key wealth and key persons—Big Men. If it can be said that the ritual production and exchange of semen in "homosexual" societies ceremonially creates masculinity, the ceremonies of the west pose the notion that men beget a different currency of exchange that is the hallmark of male status in the region. The mystification of female reproductive powers is less the focus of interest here; the appropriation of female labor and the products of female labor command increasing attention. It is in this context, it should be noted, that the givers of bridewealth are said to have social ascendancy over the givers of women.

An illuminating repossession of reproductive idiom by eastern highland women occurs in recent female banking and investment schemes in which women use the ceremonies of birth and marriage as an organizational nexus for reclaiming the products of their own labor. Daughter groups (bride receivers) pay cash (brideprice) to the mothers (bride givers) for the knowledge of "Wok Meri" (Women's Work), women's banking and investment procedures, receiving in return "the girl," a doll or mesh bag of coins decorated as a bride. The brideprice is a loan kept and invested by the mothers for their own purposes, repaid at the end of 9 years when the daughters become an autonomous group, free to sponsor their own "Wok Meri" ceremonies (Sexton 1982).† The impulse to establish all-female associations stems from the women's irritation concerning men's consumption of beer in ceremonial exchange, seen by women as a nonproductive appropriation of female labor.‡ The ceremonies of "Wok Meri" are, in addition, an answer to "Bateson's

---

*Melpa say that Moka shell currency is entirely a male achievement, a statement contradicted at the symbolic level by the red ochre decoration and yellow sheen of the shells, which convey associations with women (Strathern 1979: 534). Ponape men, who are engaged in the exchange of valuables, also speak of "giving birth to" their exchange items (Glen Peterson, personal communication).

†Here, the givers of women appear to be in social ascendancy.

‡Strathern (1979: 545) similarly notes that Melpa women consider beer to be the most naked form of appropriation engaged in by men. Beer enters Moka exchange as the equivalent of a leg of pork, is consumed largely by adult men, thereby adding to contemporary tensions between men and women concerning wealth transactions.

problem," providing a coherent if telescoped account of the interconnections among sex, gender, and productive relations that exist
here as well as in the "homosexual" and "heterosexual" regions of
Papua New Guinea.

Conclusion

This essay has examined the many ways that women and men in
Papua New Guinea articulate their moral, sentimental, and legal
attachments to rights in others and the way they express these
rights in ritual, ideology, and in the daily identifications of kinship.
In order to locate the character of kinship, it was necessary to relinquish a hold on "kinship" itself, and to investigate instead different
gender forms and the associated ideologies of production and reproduction. Certain shared features of "homosexual" communities
gave the groups a common structural profile: stress on affinal
bonds in productive relations underlay men's gifts to affines or future affines, the brother-sister pair emerged as a significant social
unit, and sister exchange was the characteristic marriage form.
Semen exchange between specified males underwrote sister exchange, which was one key to the egalitarian nature of the system
and to its reproduction. And finally, the societies discussed here
drew upon an ideology and a pattern of behavior we would call homosexual to organize production and reproduction in communities of small scale. The Iatmul and Marind Anim gave evidence of
the conflicts in sentiment, service obligations, and gender identity
that accompanied the demise of systems of egalitarian sister and semen exchange during colonial peacetime. The experience of the
eastern highlanders provided a way to explore an analytic transition from a "homosexual" to a "heterosexual" way of life and world
view. With their commitment to the accumulation of wealth, highland societies, especially in the west, were seen to manifest different relations of production and to express a shift in gender ideologies and in the power relations among affines. Different
communications concerning body substances and bodily processes mold and express these arrangements, leading to different
expectations of moral behavior and etiquette in these various locations. Authoritative doctrines about the origin of life encapsulate
the process.

In the small "homosexual" communities that value male labor, men are said to give birth to men, and semen is the prized medium of exchange. In the moderately intensive production systems of the eastern highlands, men create adult men, but attention turns also to the accumulation of a different form of exchange wealth (pigs, shells, and feathers), and female labor receives little ritual or ideological elaboration. In the more populous "heterosexual" regions of the western highlands, men again proclaim themselves to be the genitors of wealth, and women's important contributions to production are concealed. In this latter region, claims on the resources and labors of others are expressed most effectively in a patrilineal idiom that firmly locates community membership in large corporate groups.

The story of "homosexuality" and "heterosexuality" in New Guinea, it seems, is a chapter in the political economy of gender as well as in the history of "money," for women and men are seen to transfer their concern from semen and body substances to more objectified forms of wealth with which to mystify the productive process. Kinship is the idiom through which persons with unique gender identities orchestrate and convey their mutual expectations, emotions, and commitments, all formed in the context of historically changing productive relations.

Fertility and Exchange in New Guinea

Harriet Whitehead

IN A RECENT survey and analysis of fertility cults in New Guinea, I found myself taking issue with Jane Collier and Michelle Rosaldo's 1981 essay "Politics and Gender in Simple Societies" (Whitehead 1986a and 1986b).* Our point of debate was the social and political underpinnings of the notion of fertility as it appears in tribal systems, and the relationship of both fertility concepts and their social base to male dominance. A continuation and clarification of that debate seems highly appropriate here, for these fertility cults appear to be the main centers of articulation for the concepts that figure into New Guinea constructions of both "gender" (as we would call it) and "kinship" (as we would call it).† An inquiry into the social and political base for the fertility cults, and the fertility concept that characterizes them, is thus inevitably an inquiry, although indirect, into New Guinea constructions of gender and kinship.

The direct focus of this article is the question of male dominance in stateless (tribal) societies. More particularly, it is the symbolic apparatus through which the elevation of men over women is accom-

*That survey is "The Varieties of Fertility Cultism in New Guinea," which appeared in two parts in *American Ethnologist*: 13, no. 1 (1986): 80–98; and 13, no. 2 (1986): 271–89. The present paper is a shortened version of the second part. I am grateful to the editors of *American Ethnologist* for permission to include it here.

†Several other factors make it appropriate to present this discussion here. First, the original research for my argument was set in motion by Jane Collier and Sylvia Yanagisako's invitation to me to participate in the Bellagio conference. Second, a volume edited by Collier and dedicated to Michelle Rosaldo seems a fitting place for work that is lineally descended, so to speak, from their own. Thus relationships of intellectual kinship, involving gratitude and obligation, are operative. For helpful commentary on earlier drafts of this work I wish to thank Robert Brumbaugh, Phillip Guddemi, Raymond Kelly, Sherry B. Ortner, and Anna Tsing.

plished and expressed. In New Guinea, as in the cases researched by Collier and Rosaldo, a notion of generalized "fertility" seems to stand at the center of social preeminence. Those categories of social actor culturally endowed with fertilizing powers, those charged with the responsibility for fertility magic and cult, are the same as those whom Western anthropology has singled out as socially dominant. In New Guinea, as in the cases researched by Collier and Rosaldo, official ideology portrays men as more "fertile" than women. The question before us is how to go about understanding this state of affairs. To set the following argument in empirical context, I will sketch in the New Guinea material as briefly as possible (with some inevitable oversimplification), noting regional differences that are germane to the argument. This will be followed by my explication of Collier and Rosaldo's thesis.

New Guinea Tribal Organization and Fertility Cults

Mainland New Guinea is peopled by Melanesians practicing, in varied combinations, horticulture (predominantly of root crops), pig husbandry, and foraging. Nowhere is there any form of centralized political organization. Thus all these peoples are "tribesmen" in Sahlins's terms (Sahlins 1968). Against a background of cultural themes and principles found widely throughout the island, several distinct cultural regions have become apparent. This regional variation has a strongly ecological cast, for the different geographic areas permit different socioeconomic orders. A highly simplified sketch will serve for the moment.

Throughout the high valleys of the central cordillera, called the New Guinea highlands, tribal groups practice intensive sweet potato cultivation and pig husbandry, relying only modestly upon foraged food. (Secondary crops of yams, taro, sugarcane, bananas, and greens are also cultivated.) Population concentrations are high. On the Papua New Guinea side of the island, highlanders are most handily subdivided by their predominant forms of ceremonial exchange (see Rubel and Rosman 1978: chaps. 7–11). Most eastern highlanders—those groups east of the Waghi-Chimbu divide—and groups to the north of the western highlands practice a pig feast ceremonial, in which slaughtered pigs, first dedicated to the ancestors, are distributed by a host group (or a group of joint hosts) to invited allies and affines from different communities.

These communities are expected to reciprocate with invitations to their pig feasts. Western and some southern highland peoples, such as the Enga speakers and the Kakoli, participate in the reversing chain exchange systems called *moka* or *tee* in which solicitory gifts of shells, live pigs, and pork are distributed down a chain of recipients (communities or individuals or both) and a "return with increment" comes back up the chain at some point in the future. There are also occasions in the western and southern highlands in which pigs are sacrificed for ancestors, but often these occasions are partially or totally separate from the more "secular" *moka* or *tee* celebrations.

On the margins of the highlands, and at middle elevations throughout the island, distinctly smaller population clusters practice mixed crop cultivation (bananas, taro, yams, and sweet potatoes), rather extensive foraging, and varying degrees of pig husbandry. These groups, often termed "fringe," are quite varied in regard to ceremonial exchange. Certain groups of the Mountain Ok area—such as the Bimin-Kuskusmin, who apparently stand at the center of a regional trading network—maintain a quite elaborate dualistic exchange process, comparable to a lowland system. The peoples of the Papuan Plateau have ritually unelaborate feasts for surrounding allies, affines, and neighbors; these ceremonies resemble pig feasts in their structure but do not require extensive pig slaughter or the buildup of herds (Poole 1976: 593–613; Kelly 1980: 222–28; Schieffelin 1975: 27, 161–64).

Lowland populations, concentrated along the coasts and large river systems, rely heavily upon wild and humanly propagated sago while cultivating root crops as well. Seafood, game, and the pork of wild and semi-domesticated pigs supply the meat in their diet. Head-hunting, facilitated by canoe transportation, was once common in the lowlands. Denser in population concentrations than the fringe groups, the lowland cultures have greater elaboration of ceremonial exchange as well. Rubel and Rosman divide them into two types, those in which all forms of exchange—women, wealth, ritual services—are concentrated along a moiety axis and those in which marital exchange forms a separate "semicomplex" circuit of women and goods (Rubel and Rosman 1978: chaps. 2–6). In the "separated" systems, nonmarital (dualistic) exchanges take the form of competitive exchanges of male-grown feast crops and/or exchanges of ritual services: burial, initiation, curing. The lowland pattern of pork exchange usually involves fattening designated animals for ceremonial occasions rather than building up herds, as is common in highlands.

In most New Guinea societies, cyclically repeated collective festivals—often spoken of as "cults" in the literature—regulate aspects of exchange and render apparent the current boundaries of political solidarity. The *tambaran* cults of the Sepik and north coastal peoples, the *bans* of the Mountain Ok area, the ancestor-oriented pig slaughters of the eastern highlands, the *moka* or *tee* pig exchanges of the western and southern highlands, the *gisaro* rituals of the Papuan Plateau, and the many-named festivals of southern riverine peoples are all instances. Except in the western and southern highlands and the Papuan Plateau where a separate cycle of bachelor-sponsored initiation cults exist, male initiation is adjunct to, or often a principal focus of, these communal festivals, and the festivals themselves have a ritual character. Both the communal rituals and the bachelor-sponsored initiations, where these exist separately, also exhibit the themes of growth and fertility. The growth of boys into men may be the main interest of the ritual (as in the bachelor cults), but, more commonly, the perceived benefit of regularly celebrating these collective ceremonies is not just male growth but communal well-being: the flourishing of crops and pig herds, the health of individuals in the community, the group's success in warfare, the productivity of wild plants and game. In this regard, these collective ritual systems may be termed fertility cults.

In all areas, men apparently have the ultimate say in the conduct of these ceremonies, which, in more areas than not, are largely closed to women and children. The ritual complex almost always has secrets to which only men may become privy; indeed, the initiation of uninitiated males into the secrets is a common part—and in areas of New Guinea the focus—of the ceremonial complex. The secrets themselves are far from gender neutral. They concern human procreativity, the essential model for all dimensions of regeneration; and they communicate the message that men, or spirit figures responsive to men, control the female as well as the male role in procreativity. It is not hard to see why the term "male cult" is most frequently applied to New Guinea ritual systems. We will later see that the degree of male exclusivity actually varies in an interesting way across the cults of certain regions, and that this variation may help explain what underlies this exclusivity. But let us dwell for the moment on the overwhelmingly masculine character of fertility in New Guinea. In doing so, we focus on the topic that serves as the launching point for Collier and Rosaldo's essay on politics and gender.

Collier and Rosaldo's Analysis of Politics and Gender

Collier and Rosaldo take as their problem the curious observation that in many simple hunter-gatherer and hunter-horticulturalist societies it is men rather than women who are credited with special powers of fertility and regeneration. Anthropological scholarship of the past has always tended toward the opposite prediction: according to Bachofenian reasoning, the closer to the "primitive" and to "nature" a group is, the more likely it is to venerate the mother-goddess. But this turns out not to be so. Rather than Woman the Mother, it is Man the Hunter or Man the Killer who is considered the embodiment of life force in the cultures Collier and Rosaldo examine.

Focusing, for instance, on the hunter-horticulturalist Ilongot of the Philippines, who in the past practiced head-hunting, they write: "'Man the Hunter and Woman' was the title Rosaldo and Atkinson gave their 1975 article on the gender conceptions portrayed in Ilongot hunting and horticultural magic. The title reflects their conclusion that although rice and game are, in many ways, symbolic equivalents, Ilongots equate hunting with headhunting and so with men's valued and life-taking violence, but do not associate women's cultivated produce with life-giving fertility and birth" (Collier and Rosaldo 1981: 308). That life-taking equals life-giving seems to be the implicit formulation here, a formulation that logically privileges forms of interpersonal violence. There are, in other words, two elements to the phenomenon being problematized: the association of fertility with men, and the association of fertility with men's violence. Sets of symbolic associations similar to those of the Ilongot are noted among the !Kung bushmen, societies in lowland South America, and the Australian aborigines. Of the aboriginal Murngin, for instance, Collier and Rosaldo observe: "Murngin rituals display men's unisexual capacities for creation, and their ability to incorporate feminine associations in an all-male ritual context, and so to give life by themselves" (Collier and Rosaldo 1981: 306). The remainder of their essay is devoted to an explanation of this symbolic complex and an argument for explicating gender and sexual notions in light of political-economic dynamics.

To unwind Collier and Rosaldo's argument as succinctly as possible, their fundamental assertion is that what is really being spoken of in the idiom of fertility is the creation of social bonds. In the societies under consideration, the creation of social bonds does indeed derive more from the activity of men than from the activity of women. Why is this? Collier and Rosaldo restrict their attention to societies in which brideservice is the principal means of marriage making and in which this service is fulfilled primarily by a man's continuing obligation to provide parents-in law with hunted game. Such systems are the ones they dub "simple." Marriage ties are the principal social ties in such systems, and men's predominance in social bond making is a function of their greater concern with making and maintaining marriages. The association that men make between male "fertility" (that is, bond making) and male violence derives from their perception—an exaggerated perception in fact—of the usefulness of violence both in hunting (for the game that will be furnished to in-laws and distributed socially), and in establishing the right negotiating posture in encounters with potential brothers-in-law, and in defending their marriages against adulterous rivals (Collier and Rosaldo 1981: 293–94, 309–10, 317–18).

But why is marriage primarily men's concern and not that of both sexes? Collier and Rosaldo answer that at the base of men's greater interest in marriage making is a fundamental political inequality that arises from the sexual division of labor in hunter-gatherer and some hunter-horticultural systems. Whereas women in such societies can rely on the social distribution of meat from the hunt for their share of the male contribution to subsistence (inasmuch as they receive this product at all), men cannot similarly obtain a share of the female contribution. Women do not distribute their gathered and gardened produce beyond their households, and therefore a man without a wife is reduced to dependency upon another man's household for female products and services. There thus arises in men a specifically political impulse toward marriage that is not found among women. Freedom from political dependency is a function of acquiring and keeping a wife.

Men's and women's unequal political interest in marriage, a result of the sexual division of labor, is, in an important sense, the "motor" of Collier and Rosaldo's systemic explanation of the "male fertility" complex that launched their inquiry. In the brideservice system, men, not women, become the chief pursuers of the marital tie, hunting to please in-laws, adopting a readiness for hair-trigger violence in order to discourage rivals for their wives' attentions, and initiating exchanges with potential brothers-in-law to secure their own marriages. It is these marriage-producing and marriage-maintaining actions that, in Collier and Rosaldo's model, create the wider social bonds that constitute tribal society. It follows, in the cultural logic common to such systems in which fertility is associated with social creation, that men much more than women are viewed as a life-giving force in the cosmos. Indeed, their violence—which in their view is the chief guarantor of marital security—appears to the men of these simple societies as the chief ingredient of a generalized fertility: "If, in cultural logic, men achieve their independence through feats of violence, it is also the case that male potency [that is, violent power] (which leads to marriage) is what brings men together in peace and cooperation. . . . Marriage *is* what creates lasting bonds, and insofar as men 'make marriages,' the social order that exists stands as a proof that men, in fact, are endowed with an extraordinary and valuable sort of force" (Collier and Rosaldo 1981: 301).

The fruitful application of this analysis to brideservice cultures leads Collier and Rosaldo to suggest that other cultures' conceptions of gender and reproductivity might be grasped analytically by comparable inquiry into the interplay of marriage and production. They suggest but do not develop the idea that marriage systems in which a bridewealth requirement indebts the groom-to-be to his own kinsmen will produce a greater symbolic emphasis upon women's fertility and motherhood (Collier and Rosaldo 1981: 315, 325).

The idea of treating the complex of marriage and production systems in precapitalist societies as a sort of base with certain inherent inequalities toward which superstructures of ritual belief will be oriented can be traced to Claude Meillassoux (Meillassoux 1975). Although certain New Guineasts have begun to adopt this sort of approach (Godelier 1982a; Godelier 1982b; Modjeska 1982; Lindenbaum 1984; Lindenbaum this volume), no one has yet examined whether or how well the particular Collier and Rosaldo formulation, with its emphasis on the masculine and violent character of fertility, fits the New Guinea case. This is the project to which I now turn.

The Brideservice Model in New Guinea

As noted above, New Guinea abounds with cultural linkages between men and fertility. The most common formulation is the male cultic appropriation of the reproductive attributes of *both* sexes, a formulation virtually identical to that of the Murngin rituals cited by Collier and Rosaldo. As in the lowland South American cultures to which they allude, so too in New Guinea one of the most common mythic justifications for this male domination of ritual is the assertion that women once possessed the rituals but lost them to the men, who thereafter controlled fertility (Oosterwal 1961; Gell 1975; Tuzin 1980; Kaberry 1940–41; Gillison 1980; Robbins 1982; Herdt 1981; Hogbin 1970; Newman and Boyd 1982). In a word, men's dominance of the fertility ritual is not just incidental; it is culturally foregrounded and justified.

The connection between male fertility and male violence also appears in New Guinea cult idiom, most dramatically among the lowland head-hunting cultures, whose cultic symbolism often explicitly makes of the trophy head (which only men can garner) an agent of fertility (Zegwaard 1959; Van Baal 1966: chap. 12; Rubin n.d.; Bateson 1958: 140–41; Forge 1965: 27, 30; see also Bowden 1983; Bowden 1984). The connection is certainly present as well in those highland ancestor cults in which communal fertility can only be assured by militarily avenging the unavenged dead—again a male responsibility (Buchbinder and Rappaport 1976). All in all, the symbolic-ritual complex that Collier and Rosaldo explicate through the dynamics of male political consciousness in brideservice systems is well exemplified in New Guinea. The "superstructure" they describe is there. But what about the marital-productive base?

I have been able to find two New Guinea systems that strikingly fit the pattern Collier and Rosaldo detail for us. One is the Waina-Sowanda group studied by Alfred Gell (Gell 1975). A rather isolated lowland fringe group with few forms of exchange wealth, this society stresses "real" or "close" sister-exchange marriage and the obligation of married men to hunt game for affines. The dependence of bachelors upon the households of married men for supplies of sago—the female contribution to subsistence—is so evidently a source of bachelor subordination that Gell, the ethnographer, comments on it in terms that almost foreshadow Collier and Rosaldo's analysis (Gell 1975: 107–8). Associations exist between sexuality and violence in the culture generally, and, more subtly, a link appears between fertility and warriorhood in the main communal ritual, the *ida*. This ritual also fits my criteria for a New Guinea fertility cult.

The second is the small congeries of tribes along the Tor River drainage in Irian that Oosterwal called "the people of the Tor" (Oosterwal 1961). The Tor are also a sago-dependent lowland population in which women appear to do most of the sago work. Men provide fish and, when possible, scarce game to affines. Direct bride exchange is stressed, and under traditional conditions bachelors are said to have felt their social inferiority and the lack of a wife keenly.* Fertility goals are very explicit in communal male-dominated cult ritual, and the display of enemy skulls and wild boar jawbones in the cult house suggests that fertility is linked to male warfare and hunting (Oosterwal 1961: chaps. 2, 3, 6).

From the viewpoint of a Melanesianist, the Waina-Sowanda and Tor cases lend credence to the idea that Collier and Rosaldo have identified a genuine type of marital-productive system that appears independently in many different culture areas. The posited connections between the elements of this type remain open to question, however.

Another area that initially seems to conform to the suggested model is the Papuan Plateau, also a fringe area. Hunting is an important part of the economy; there is a stress on constantly providing affines with both game and pork from domesticated pigs and on maintaining a balanced exchange of women. Male fertility themes appear in the initiation beliefs, although it is unclear to what extent male violence is tied in with such themes. The expected pattern is jolted out of alignment, however, by the presence of fairly substantial bridewealth in the marriage arrangements of these groups (Kelly 1980: 213ff; Schieffelin 1975).

---

*At the time Oosterwal studied the Tor peoples, the model of politically subordinated juniors set against autonomous senior households was imperfectly realized owing to certain peculiar demographic distortions: an unexplained imbalance in the sex ratio at birth, the early physical decline of both sexes at middle age, and the extremely low fertility rate (see Oosterwal 1961: 36–45, 57–143, 206–10).

This brings us to the first serious problem: the relative scarcity of pure brideservice systems in New Guinea. The great majority of New Guinea societies have a mix of marriage exchange principles. Commonly, there is one level of segmentation in the system—be this clan, subclan, moiety, village, or village part—that is concerned with maintaining a balanced exchange of women over time, a concern that may be phrased as an ideal of sister-exchange, or as an ideal of delayed bride return, or often both; commonly, too, there is a passage of some wealth from wife-taker to wife-giver over and above gifts of game (Reay 1959: 99; Rubel and Rosman 1978; Rappaport 1969: 127–32; Strathern and Strathern 1969: 156; O'Brien 1969: 222–24). Although in certain cultures, such as the Daribi or the Manga, woman-for-woman exchange is viewed as a substitute for a marriage payment and vice versa (Wagner 1969; Cook 1969), the two practices are not in complementary distribution over the island as a whole. In groups such as the Etoro of the Papuan Plateau, the Abelam of the north coastal ranges, or the Telefomin of West Sepik, marriage payments coexist easily enough with an ideal, and often a reality, of direct bride exchange (Kelly 1980: chap. 7; Losche 1982: chap. 2; Poole 1981: 122, 145–51; Craig 1969). Thus the Meillassouxian cleavage, suggested by Collier and Rosaldo, between bridewealth systems wherein a "cadet" is indebted to lineage seniors for his marriages and prebridewealth systems where a young man can take charge of his marital and exchange destiny will encounter insuperable ambiguities in this part of the world.

I should note at this point that Collier and Rosaldo, in a series of (to my mind) ambiguous passages, seem to suggest that direct-exchange marriage is enough to indicate the presence of the political dynamics they are concerned with, even though—admittedly—direct exchange may occur not only in the simple societies they claim as their domain but also in more advanced and more politically complex societies (Collier and Rosaldo 1981: 299–300). Should we then consider the presence of sister-exchange practices, with or without the practice of hunting for affines, with or without the addition of some forms of bridewealth, sufficient evidence of the presence of those political relations that, in the Collier and Rosaldo model, energize the male fertility symbolic complex?

Answering this requires a closer look at the posited origin of the cultural logic that animates male fertility symbolism. Embedded in Collier and Rosaldo's model is a structural actor from whose viewpoint the mystique of male fertility makes sense: the young man in the early stages of his marital career. Driven to seek a wife through the desire for political autonomy, and for the same reason driven to defend his new marriage by cultivating a prickly "don't tread on me" stance, this structural actor is the one most affected by parity consciousness and the one most likely to perceive his violent skills of hunting and fighting as essential to making and maintaining bonds. Whether the cultural logic is spun out by such actors directly or spun out with their viewpoint in mind does not matter; it is most strategically addressed to them. The question thus becomes whether such a structural actor, or viewpoint, is brought into being by New Guinea marital-productive complexes.

In this respect, the New Guinea findings seem to me less promising than the mere presence of parity-oriented bride exchange would suggest. Let me concentrate on lowland practices, for here we find the greatest reliance upon "real" or "near" sister-exchange marriage as well as some of the most flamboyant cultic expressions of the link between fertility and male violence. In the large coastal and riverine village communities where fertility cultism is well developed, the young bachelor—who in Collier and Rosaldo's model should be going out to "make" his own marriage by hunting meat for his future in-laws, demonstrating violent prowess to would-be rivals, and seeking out brothers-in-law with whom to initiate exchange—is largely replaced by the young bachelor who, confined for long periods of time to cultic seclusion, passively awaits the day when adults of the community consider him sufficiently mature to take up residence with a bride designated for him in his childhood. Indeed, in those New Guinea communities where the balanced exchange of women typically consists of the exchange of "real" or "near" sisters, family demographics tend to impel the system toward child betrothal, adoption, and other mechanisms that require a network of negotiating elders and thus remove marriage making from the hands of the younger generation (Serpenti 1965: 124–31, 164ff; Tuzin 1980: 21; Mead 1940–41: 420–21; Van Baal 1966: 122–30, 148–53; McDowell 1972). If anything, the thrust of the system, and certainly the thrust of cultic seclusion, is toward stifling the impulses of young men to take marriage matters into their own hands.

In fact, the virtually pan–New Guinea belief that heterosexual contact threatens male growth would, if taken seriously, act to inhibit young men's impulses toward assertive heterosexual court-ship in the first place. In many areas, there is evidence that the scare lore is taken quite seriously (Herdt 1981; Gell 1975: 111ff; Glasse n.d.; Meggitt 1964; Kelly 1976). Looking back on the Waina-Sowanda case briefly, we find that they too have child betrothals as well as cultural beliefs that cause bachelors to be fearful not of casual sex but of marriage (Gell 1975: 109ff). Thus, even in one of the best examples of the brideservice system, elements suppressive of the bachelor's marriage-making impulses put in their appearance.

The married man's need to defend his marriage from adulterous rivals, by violence if necessary, certainly appears to be present in New Guinea.* The question is, is this alone sufficient to support a symbolic linkage between bond making and violence, absent the other factors?

Finally, there is the crucial matter of the contrast in men's and women's need to marry, an imbalance created by the sexual division of labor. Here we encounter the second substantial difficulty posed by New Guinea systems: this inequality of need between the sexes is hard to establish clearly. Wherever there is vital reliance on either horticulture or sago processing (and this covers virtually all of New Guinea), significant parts of the male contribution to these activities are not organized communally. Male work parties for clearing fields or cutting sago often upon inspection resolve into male pairs (or groups of same) formed through marriage or even wife exchange (Eyde 1967: 215–17; Oosterwal 1967: 136–37; Gell 1975: 109); thus, even men's communal labor would not come into being without women marrying and cannot be viewed independently of this. A woman who relied routinely upon the labor of a father or brothers would certainly not starve; but she, like her bachelor counterpart, would be dependent upon the spouses of others for help that she would normally be expected to receive from a spouse of her own. In light of this state of affairs, the economic impulse toward marriage in New Guinea cannot be thought to arise solely in the hearts of young men. (Indeed, New Guinea has some renown as a culture area in which a young unmarried girl can initiate an engagement by running away to the home of her chosen—who responds to the overture reluctantly, if at all.) In sum, two of

---

*In many cases, the most accomplished adulterers are apparently the older married men who have lost their heterosexual inhibitions (Meggitt 1964; Glasse n.d.); all wives are potential targets, however.

the principal political-economic dimensions of the brideservice model developed by Collier and Rosaldo—men's and women's unequal political interest in marriage, and the ability of young men to forge marriage bonds largely through their own efforts—are for the most part poorly exemplified in New Guinea.

Note that I have not questioned what may appear to be the most mysterious of Collier and Rosaldo's suggestions: that the imagery of fertility, or life-generating potency, is a way of conceptualizing the creation of social bonds and social order. In fact, the symbolism of New Guinea cultism makes this element of their argument very persuasive, just as it supports the notion that there is a link of some sort between fertility and male violence. It is for this reason that their model warrants scrutiny in light of the New Guinea materials. What this scrutiny strongly suggests, however, is that the association of manhood and male violence with fertility is more general than Collier and Rosaldo's focus on brideservice systems would suggest. The symbolic linkage occurs in New Guinea not just in the two cases that nicely fit the brideservice model but in any number of lowland, fringe, and eastern highland cases where the specific political-economic dynamics Collier and Rosaldo describe are not well expressed. One is therefore compelled to look for a more general motivation for this mysterious male fertility complex. In what follows, I will try to spell one out.

Gifts, Blows, and Male Fertility

I suggest that the problem in Collier and Rosaldo's attempts to deal with ritualized male dominance in political-economic terms hinges upon an inadequate exploration of the political economy of tribal exchange processes. It is possible that an eagerness to incorporate relations of production into their models is partly responsible. More likely, these authors are simply following tendencies present in the works of Lévi-Strauss, our prime articulator of exchange theory, whose insights into the dynamics of "gift" economies were prematurely narrowed by a neglect of the hostile side of exchange dynamics and by an overemphasis on marriage. If we retain Collier and Rosaldo's insight that notions of fertility are a means of conceptualizing the creation of social bonds, but expand our analysis of the political economy of exchange processes, we will be able to account for the differing degrees to which fertility is attributed to the sexes in New Guinea cultures generally, as well as the differing degrees to which the cultic control of fertility excludes women in certain regions. By implication, this approach can be extended to the cases covered by Collier and Rosaldo as well.

To bring out those dimensions of exchange theory that are at issue here, it will be sufficient to cite two authors who have most articulately delineated the political dimension of the political economies that arise out of the workings of the principle of reciprocity. The first is Marshall Sahlins (see Sahlins 1968; Sahlins 1972a; Sahlins 1972b), the second D. J. J. Brown (Brown 1979). We begin with Sahlins.

Rather than trying, as has been common in anthropology, to rediscover the functions of the state scattered about in various tribal institutions, Sahlins takes as his theoretical focus the "state of affairs" that exists when the state does not. He boldly compares the stateless situation of tribal societies to Hobbes's state of "Warre," preserving that antique spelling in order to preserve Hobbes's special meaning: that "the nature of Warre, consisteth not in actual fighting [necessarily]; but in the known disposition thereto, during all the time there is no assurance to the contrary." Hobbes's famous conclusions notwithstanding, it is not necessary that the Leviathan of the state rise up to guarantee safety and peace in such a situation. The same can be secured, for intervals at least, through the mechanism of reciprocal gift exchange (Sahlins 1972a: 186–87).

Sahlins works out a continuum of forms of reciprocity that typically appear in tribal systems: at the positive end of the continuum there is the altruistic "helping" among the close in-group. This shades into the carefully balanced giving that obtains between the not-so-close, and this in turn gives way to the "negative reciprocities" of chicanery, theft, sorcery accusations, and vendettas that obtain between those most alien to (or disappointed in) one another (see Sahlins 1972a). Each point along the continuum represents a form of reciprocity, and relations between any two social entities can shift in either direction along the continuum.

It is important to remember this last point—that the "negative" reciprocities are as much a part of a system of reciprocities as are the positive. Some of the best-known articulators of exchange theory—Lévi-Strauss, for instance, and even at points Sahlins himself—tend to confine their theoretical speculations to the peaceful side of the state of "Warre," the exchange of gifts and women, neglecting the violent underpinnings of the tribal political economy. Yet as we shall see, the violent side of exchange is ultimately what will allow exchange theory to encompass the peculiar equation that tribal societies, in New Guinea and elsewhere, tend to make between violence and fertility.

Turning to New Guinea, we find discussions of reciprocity a commonplace in the areal literature. Exchange dominates New Guinea political life and is one of the central dynamics in the formation of the political community. As exchange theory would predict, the politically solidary units and subunits are, in an important sense, constituted in exchange. Those who define themselves as of one kind will be found pooling their resources in opposition to other "kinds," and this opposition takes the form of exchange relations: hostile, friendly, or oscillating between the two (Brown 1979; Schwimmer 1973; Wagner 1969; Rubel and Rosman 1978; Whitehead 1986a; Whitehead 1986b).

What is important in the current context is that throughout most of traditional New Guinea, with the exception of the "secularized" western and southern highlands area, fertility cults are both the instruments through which communal solidarities come to be expressed and the principal regulators of intra- and inter-community exchange. Where fertility cults dominate, cult performances are the occasions for exchange, specific cultic actions are "services" that must themselves be exchanged, cultic initiations and rites of passage situate individuals in exchange partnerships, and cultic magic is considered essential to the production of exchange items. Most saliently, cultic cycles are cycles of production and fighting. The amount of land under cultivation is intimately tied to projected feasting obligations, and cultic taboos abet the accumulation process by forbidding consumption of feast foods. A period of accumulation is often matched by a period of peace, and at the climactic feast of the cycle, traditional enemies may become, in one way or another, participants in the fertility rites. When the feasting interval ceases, warfare promptly resumes. As in the making of gardens, cult instruments are sounded to instigate the making of warriors in distinct phases of male initiation. Indeed, among former practitioners of head-hunting in the lowlands, a head-taking raid seems to have been a necessary step in the next growing cycle of plants and men, since trophy heads constituted a growth agent (see Rappaport 1968; Tuzin 1980: 65–66, 247–48, 319; Gell 1975:

156–68; Read 1952; Bateson 1958:129, 137; Landtman 1927:383; Kuruwaip 1975).

In effect, the fertility cult governs a total political economy, one whose nature must be grasped before political-economic analysis can be accurately applied to it. My own concern is with the question of social dominance. It seems clear that the dimension of dominance that can be glossed as prestige ascendancy is, in these systems, intimately bound up with the way different categories of actors are positioned in exchange processes. In other words, it is intimately bound up with the varying power of different categories of actors to create social bonds. And it seems, too, that the idiom of fertility is a favored vehicle (though not the only vehicle) for conceptualizing exchange processes and exchange power.

Collier and Rosaldo come very close to making this point but are deterred by two factors. The first is their overriding emphasis upon marital exchange, an emphasis that apparently stems from their analysis of men's and women's uneven interest in marriage in hunter-gatherer and hunter-horticultural systems. New Guinea material not only raises questions about men's and women's unequal interests in marriage but also furnishes cases in which the idiom of fertility very clearly attaches to forms of exchange that do not involve marriage. The Yam Cults of the Sepik and north coastal peoples, for instance, provide us with numerous examples of specifically nonmarital, nonkin ceremonial exchanges that are shot through with the imagery of procreation (Tuzin 1972; Forge 1965; Kaberry 1940–41; Bowden 1984). What we are seeing in New Guinea, and I suspect in Collier and Rosaldo's cases too, is simply a general (and common) cultural equation between the capacity for creating social connections through exchange and the power to convey "life" or vitality.

The second limiting aspect of Collier and Rosaldo's analysis is their failure to address fully the exchange relevance of men's violence. Again, an emphasis upon marriage skews their approach. The male of Collier and Rosaldo's simple society is infatuated with his hunting prowess (which enables him to woo potential affines with game offerings) and with his ability to fight off marital rivals. Because both behaviors involve violent skills and both are requisite to making and maintaining the marital bond, the hypothetical hunter, in his cultural logic, inflates violence to the level of a cosmic fertilizing force. This is rather a mystification in Collier and Rosaldo's opinion since—even in these systems—marriage-making requires a good deal less violence than the men seem to think (Collier and Rosaldo 1981: 312–13). Again, New Guinea systems urge a clarification of this situation. The violence glamorized in New Guinea and associated with fertility is very clearly intercommunity violence. In the lowlands it was often head-hunting, violence that garners for the home community the trophy heads that are an ingredient in human and crop fertility; in the highlands it was vengeance against traditional enemies, violence that the clan ancestors require before bestowing growth, prosperity, and well-being upon their descendants. Interpersonal violence attending marriage maintenance is not the wellspring of violence glamorization. True, the two forms of violence may overlap; when adultery and abduction cross the boundaries of political communities, New Guineans—like the Greeks and Trojans—may go to war. But daily bickering over adultery within the political community is apt to be culturally channeled into the unglamorous business of in-group sorcery. In a word, the focal point of violence glamorization in New Guinea is the warfare phase in the feasting and warfare cycle.

What we see in this and what it is necessary to rediscover in exchange theory is that the relation between violence and exchange obtains at a more general level than just the politicization of marriage. In stateless societies, violent responses are themselves a form of exchange inseparably linked to all the others. Recent work by D. J. J. Brown has helped to promote this issue once again, and it is from Brown that I have taken the useful phrase "gifts and blows" (see Brown 1979). In essence, the gift and the blow are opposite ends of an exchange continuum; the positive forms of exchange cannot be conceptually divorced from the negative without obscuring the reasons for the great variety in kinds of reciprocity that exist in tribal systems and the transformability of each kind into another. If we look simply at "balanced reciprocity" (the midpoint in Sahlins's continuum), which is the form of reciprocity that typically obtains between separate New Guinea political communities, we often find empirically that woven together in oscillating patterns are its positive forms (for example, ceremonial feasting), its negative forms (for example, vendettas), and every sort of shading in between (for example, competitive feasting). In the case Brown documents, the Polopa, gift exchanges and violent exchanges alternate cyclically between any two given communities, with the transitions marked by the appearance of giftlike blows or blowlike gifts: "Gifts may be intended to humiliate and pass into blows, and blows may be aimed to miss and pass into gifts" (Brown 1979:712). Eric Schwimmer's work on the Orokaiva is pertinent here as well, for it illustrates how embedded in the Orokaiva cosmology is the notion that feasting and fighting are each other's preconditions (Schwimmer 1973; see also Forge 1972).

The relevance of the inseparability of gifts and blows to understanding the male fertility complex is this: the real masters of social bonding in tribal systems are those in a position to command both. Only the war-makers can agree to the peace. Thus, control of exchange has as one of its preconditions the monopolization of violence. At the same time, peace cannot be made with nothing. Thus another precondition for the control of exchange is regular access to and command of desired items. What is finally required in any system of reciprocity are ways to mobilize and coordinate responses. These ways, differently developed in different systems, are themselves instruments of power, perhaps the most crucial, and it is through them that systems of reciprocity become, always to some degree, systems of domination.

These points allow us to approach from a fresh angle the question of ritualized male domination. Obviously, it is possible for different capacities for reciprocal response, negative or positive, to fall into the hands of different social categories in any system. This differential distribution of power in exchange can be used to account for differential social valuation, including, of course, that which obtains between the sexes. Turning again to New Guinea, I think it can be safely argued that throughout the island men are securely in command of the far negative pole of the exchange continuum. Moreover, this command is not readily undercut, as it can be in some pure hunter-gatherer economies, by the ability of communities to avoid violence by easily separating when conflicts arise. Thus, force becomes a critical instrument in the creation of social bonds. The situational context of this violence serves to legitimize it even before one considers its relevance to the creation of wider social ties. Male violence assumes the face of community "defense." There is no great need for the men of a community to turn their weapons against the women and children in order to establish their dominance. These women and children, like their menfolk, lie under shared peril from the weapons of the enemy outsider.

Men valiantly die in their duty of "protection"; how can one accuse them of selfish interests? The degree to which disputes may be conjured arbitrarily into existence—making "defense" necessary—is probably never clearly perceived by any participants in the system (cf. Modjeska 1982: 92).

Once we move away from "hard" violence, however, and into intermediate and positive forms of reciprocity, there is room for more variability in the distribution of negative exchanges. Although sorcery accusations in the majority of New Guinea societies are traded back and forth between men—in many cases, simply a form of "soft" violence prodromal to armed conflict—women can participate in this sphere. They may be thought capable of certain forms of malevolent magic or, in a more frequent formulation, they are thought capable of soliciting the aid of male sorcerers to prosecute a personal vendetta (Gell 1975: 111–18; Knauft 1984: chaps. 5–8; Robbins 1982: 82).

In the area of positive exchanges, women can participate by providing both valued gift items and certain types of formal (for example, funerary) services. I will confine my attention to two major patterns in their supply of gift items. In one, confined as far as I can tell to parts of the lowlands, the gathered and grown vegetable produce that is central to exchange feasting has not—for some reason—become specialized into the hands of men. The phenomenon of crop gendering so common in New Guinea—and so obviously a way of demarcating an exchange economy that is male from a subsistence economy that is female—is not developed in these particular areas. Thus feast items are the product of an acknowledged joint effort, or even, for certain items, a predominantly female effort (Oosterwal 1961: chap. 2; Van Baal 1966: 18–21, 167–70; Eyde 1967: chap. 1; Lipset 1984).

The second way in which women make a significant contribution to exchange, in both lowlands and highlands but outstandingly in the highlands, is by raising pigs. We may speculate about why it is women who perform this labor. Crop gendering may again play a role, this time with a paradoxical effect. The sweet potato, almost never valued as a feast crop and accordingly left to women to raise (or vice versa), turns out to be the pig's fodder of choice in the heavy pig-raising areas, such as the highlands, where foddering is an essential part of herd management. Another factor contributing to women's involvement may be the compatibility between the demands of tending pigs and the demands of tending families. New Guinea women have achieved a degree of fame for the thoroughness with which they blend pig tending into their domestic routines. The daily close-to-home supervisory activity that pig care entails would hobble a man in most of the activities that ordinarily ensure his prevalence in exchange: traveling, contacting outside groups, trading, fighting. The result is that, although in many areas men perform a great deal of background labor necessary for raising pigs—notably clearing additional gardens and building fences—they are still less visibly and immediately identified with the animals. Often, however, men may counter this disadvantage in visible association with animals by bringing home wild piglets from the bush and farming these out with their wives or by transferring surplus piglets from their wives' herds to the herds of the wives of exchange partners or relatives. The captured or transferred pig tends to be identified with its bringer—a man. In areas where pigs are brought in through "finance" (credit, essentially), they also are identified with their male financier (see Strathern 1979; Josephides 1983). Thus, although pig raising may tend to strengthen women's hands in exchange, there are male moves that can offset this advantage.

It must also be stressed that even when women's contribution to exchange remains relatively unclouded and direct, it does not result in their elevation to social equivalence with men. But it must be remembered that men retain everywhere the monopolization of force as well as some, usually considerable, gift power. Accordingly, it is not illogical that men everywhere operate the means to coordinate feasting and fighting, which, until we reach the western highlands, takes the form of a fertility cult that valorizes to variable degrees male life-giving force.

Yet I think it can be argued from New Guinea cases that women's contribution to exchange does not go unmarked in ideology, including the ideology of fertility. Most importantly, the tendencies (where these are found) in New Guinea culture toward greater ideological articulation of women's "fertilizing" role parallel tendencies toward greater female contributions to exchange, a fact that runs counter to Marxist theories of mystification. I have attempted to show this elsewhere by contrasting two types of New Guinea lowland society (see Whitehead 1986b). One type—which includes "the peoples of the Tor" (Oosterwal 1961; Oosterwal

1967), the Asmat (Kuruwaip 1975; Eyde 1967), the Kiwai (Landtman 1927), and, with qualifications, the Marind Anim (Van Baal
1966; Van Baal 1984)—possesses important rituals or whole ritual
cycles in which mature women participate with men in the ritual
construction of fertility. Female participation takes the form of collective singing, dancing, and sexual intercourse.* The substance
mixtures produced through ritual sexual intercourse, the mingled
sounds produced by men's and women's singing, or both are considered magically generative. The substance mixture may be used
in subsequent gardening magic, and heterosexual contact is often
seen as potentiating various productive enterprises (Landtman
1927: 22, 64–148, 350–55, 390; Oosterwal 1961: 74, 222–24, 143–45;
Oosterwal 1967: 178, 182; Van Baal 1966: 635–45; 949; Eyde 1967:
205–10; Kuruwaip 1975; see also Meeker et al. 1986). This type also
possesses some exclusive male ritual or marks off parts of the male-
female ritual for men only.

The second type of lowland system simply does not include
women in the fertility ritual; rituals of the second type resemble the
male-only parts of the first type's system. The powers of male-
female copulation are represented in artifacts produced and manipulated only by men (for example, the androgynous flutes that
are sounded in high-low pairs); heterosexual contact is cast as antithetical to most productive endeavors. The best examples of the
excluders are the Yam Cult peoples of the north coastal ranges and
foothills: the Arapesh and Abelam groups and the Kwoma (Tuzin
1972; Tuzin 1980; Mead 1940–41; Kaberry 1940–41; Kaberry 1973;
Bowden 1984). The Kimam of Frederik Hendrik Island might also
be included, though elements of female inclusion are also present
in their system (Serpenti 1965; Serpenti 1984).

The contrast in the exchange systems of these two types is noteworthy. In the type with female-inclusive ritual, the gardened or
gathered vegetable produce necessary for intercommunity feasts
represents a contribution from both sexes, or even predominantly
from women; the meat component of the feast comprises both
female-raised pigs and male-hunted game. Furthermore, sexual favors (sometimes homosexual as well as heterosexual) are part of the
currency of exchange, and often "wife-swapping" partnerships are

*The Murik Lakes society may also qualify for inclusion. The female-inclusive
ceremonies and the exchange system in which they are embedded display the attributes singled out here, although I have not been able to find an account of their
ideas regarding fertility (Lipset n.d.; Meeker et al. 1986).

the social axis along which extra-affinal alliances are organized (Eyde 1967: 205–10, 334–58; Oosterwal 1961: 136–37, 202; Meeker et al. 1986; Van Baal 1966). It must be pointed out that these sexual exchanges, like the exchange of women in marriage, aim at bonding men, and there seems at first glance no obvious reason why such exchanges should privilege women in cultic fertility idiom, when marriage (in these and other lowland systems) does not. The difference, I suggest, lies in the fact that in these predominantly endogamous lowland communities, most marriages play no part in intercommunity alliance-making. The sex-exchanges, on the other hand, are a regular feature of intercommunity feasting; thus in the sex-exchanging systems women (and women's food) are participating in a wider sphere of social bond creation, and the outer limits of any exchange system tend to be more ritually marked and valorized. Hence women are more ritually marked and valorized.

By contrast, in the female-exclusive systems, crops are "gendered" so that the prestigious feast crops—typically yams—are grown exclusively by men. Extra-affinal exchanges of these crops, usually but not always competitive, occur in the context of intercommunity alliance making, structurally displacing the exchange of sexual favors and gender-undifferentiated foods. The rhetoric of fertility differs accordingly. Manipulating their "generative" paraphernalia in secret, men procreate and grow two things, male crops and new men (the initiates), which are symbolically equated in ritual (Tuzin 1972: 236–37; Kaberry 1940–41: 356–57). In effect, men are procreating symbolically even as they are reproducing actually the conditions of their rule: gifts (yams) and blows (new warriors). And they are doing so, in these systems, without the assistance of women. We should recall here that the male-only parts of the female-inclusive ritual cycles are similarly concerned with the making of warrior-hunters and with the exchange of the characteristic male gift, hunted game (Oosterwal 1961: 230–47; Oosterwal 1967: 184; Landtman 1927: 357–67, 372–78.* In sum, women dis-

---

*Empirical evidence suggests that the two forms of ritualism—female-inclusive and female-exclusive—may co-exist within the same population, though not necessarily in integration with each other. The south coastal Marind and Kiman both furnish some evidence of dual systems. The predominant system among the Marind appears to have included women, while the predominant system among the Kiman involved female-exclusive rituals and the exchange of male-grown yams. The presence of a good deal of homosexual sexual exchange in both societies suggests another mechanism through which women may be "displaced" in communal fertility ritual (Van Baal 1966; Serpenti 1965).

appear from the ritual construction of fertility in those portions of the ritual system that center on male-monopolized currencies of exchange. In societies in which *all* of the important currencies of exchange are monopolized by men, women disappear from the idiom of fertility entirely.*

Conclusions

This contrast between lowland New Guinea systems that include women in fertility ceremonial and those that radically exclude them reinforces Collier and Rosaldo's interpretation of fertility ideology as a way of making statements about the creation of social bonds and, in my estimation, reasserts the importance of their train of analysis. But the New Guinea data also serve to alter our appreciation of the political-economic underpinnings of social bond making in tribal societies. The problem in applying Collier and Rosaldo's brideservice model to New Guinea is not simply that pure brideservice organization is rare in this area, whereas male fertility imagery is abundant. The problem is a more fundamental one that reveals the limitations of exchange theory as it has come to be deployed. Although they quibble with him, Collier and Rosaldo ultimately inherit from Lévi-Strauss the tendency to overprivilege marriage and underprivilege violent exchanges in the creation of social order in stateless societies. If, as Lévi-Strauss suggests, tribes have chosen to "marry out" rather than be "killed out," it is not the case that they therefore either cease from all killing and threatening to kill or that they rely exclusively upon marriage for their principles of peacemaking. Tracing the significant thread of fertility imagery that Collier and Rosaldo have highlighted for us, we find that the complex web of intergroup exchange in New Guinea retains its violent underpinnings—hence, intercommunity violence is glamorized as fertile—and that a multitude of gift items and services

*Total female exclusion is in fact relatively rare in New Guinea. In highland systems, women's role in pig raising cannot be overlooked, and their ritual contribution in the eastern highlands is reflected in the mixed-sex *gerua* dances that accompany fertility-oriented pig feasts (Salisbury 1965; Newman 1965). The heightened focus upon kin group ancestors as the agents of fertility in the highlands can also be construed as a way of integrating both sexes into the idiom of fertility. Analysis of the highland situation is complicated by the apparent decrease in the importance of fertility cultism in areas of enchained exchanges, the western and southern highlands.

must be weighed in the peacemaking equation. Like the various forms of violence, these gifts each have their particular conditions of production that figure into the role they may play in the construction of a wider social order and into the role that various actors in the system may adopt in relation to them.

Entailed in this reunderstanding of the dynamics of exchange is a reappreciation of the meaning of dominance in tribal systems. Recall that Lévi-Strauss held that male dominance in tribal society is a function of men's right to exchange women. Women do not enjoy a comparable right to exchange men or each other (Lévi-Strauss 1969: 52–68; see also Rubin 1975). This statement left Lévi-Strauss, and subsequent thinkers, with the unanswerable question, How do men obtain this right? Again, the reduction of reciprocity in tribal systems to primarily marital reciprocity is responsible for this impasse. If we see tribal reciprocities as encompassing a range of negative and positive exchanges, each with its particular conditions of production and each amenable to different forms of control, we are able to better understand how certain categories of actor can, by controlling different elements, come to dominate the exchange system as a whole or its highest levels. Monopolizing force and always some areas of the gift economy, New Guinea men predominate as well in the idiom of fertility and in the fertility cults that regulate the political economy as a whole. Women's appearance in fertility idiom and in cultic activity largely depends on the degree to which they can bring to intercommunity exchange, and can claim as their contribution, desired gifts and services.

Part Three

Descent and the Construction of Gendered Persons

Producing Difference: Connections and Disconnections in Two New Guinea Highland Kinship Systems

Marilyn Strathern

IT IS AN intriguing fact that in some Papua New Guinea highlands societies, bridewealth prestations are likened to death compensation, whereas elsewhere they prefigure childgrowth payments.* Different structures of kinship relations are involved. Indeed, in the ways in which women's ties with their natal and affinal kin are conceived, we find greater or lesser weight being put on kinship as such. Through their life-cycle prestations, some highlands societies make room for the generation of what I call non-kinship values.

Where groups such as clans emerge as the units that arrange marriages, the representation of women's clan membership and their passage in marriage is comparable to the idea that men share common substance or claims to land: men and women are equally participant actors and equally subjects of symbolic representation. Obviously, this state of affairs is not restricted to clan-based systems. Harriet Whitehead's article in this collection deals with the extent to which varying constructions of gender are related to propositions about group boundedness itself. I introduce in this article

*This paper was first written in 1982. Much that is germane to its argument has been published since, but I treat these later developments in a forthcoming book, *The Gender of the Gift*. I am in debt to the organizers and participants of the Bellagio Conference for providing such a stimulating forum for these ideas. I am also grateful to Andrew Strathern and Aletta Biersack for their comments on an earlier draft. Richard Fardon and Ladislav Holy were helpful critics of a spoken version given at St. Andrews, as were Ann Whitehead and members of A.F.R.A.S., University of Sussex. Jane Collier and Sylvia Yanagisako have taken considerable editorial pains. I thank Gregory Acciaioli, Paula Rubel, Abe Rosman, Susan Drucker-Brown, Rena Lederman, and Roy Wagner for their comments. Francesca Merlan and Alan Rumsey have since furnished a detailed critique from which I have benefited, as did Meyer Fortes not long before his death. Not for this reason alone, however, do I dedicate this paper to him.

the argument that the sense of boundary that seems to vary so between highlands societies is ideationally generated by concepts that also underline constructions of personhood, for there are significant variations within the highlands in the extent to which "persons" are conceptualized as self-governing agents. Only under certain societal conditions does the "person" seem to emerge as autonomous: where kinship formulations generate entities that cease to be defined by kinship. Autonomy is delineated through idioms of detachment. Only some, and indeed probably only a minority, of highlands kinship systems facilitate such a conceptual disengagement of "persons" from the nexus of kin relations. Gender differences and relations are a powerful symbolic resource to this end.

This argument assumes symbolic intention (that people want to represent ideas about "persons") and reads certain cultural categories (such as male and female) backwards from it. But I proceed backwards with a specific end in mind. We assume too much if we approach the symbols of others as we do our own—if we assume, for example, that "male" and "female" as generalized gender categories are addressed primarily to what men and women do. As I have argued elsewhere, they are already an abstraction from what men and women do.

The reason for repeating this point here is at the center of feminist analysis. Considering bridewealth prestations from the viewpoint of women's attachment to male-defined clans could well look like resurrecting the spectre of men as actors manipulating passive women. I would assert that this can only be read into the data from certain specific preoccupations with agency. I refer to Western ideas that inform much social science analysis. Agency, for instance, is generally recognized in a subject's manipulation of objects, themselves definitively not-agents (at the point of manipulation, the agent is a "person" acting on "things"). Associated notions of power, will, and so forth rest on a Western hierarchism of this kind. When we see men and women in an apparently asymmetrical situation—women moving between clans of men—we are thus apt to take for granted the subject of the symbols involved (women's subordination, their being treated like "objects"). But it is important not to prejudge what is meant in the symbolization of female and male (see Leacock 1981; Sacks 1979). Otherwise, we block out the possibility of crucial insight into social-historical process.

One set of processes demanding explication springs from Paula Rubel and Abraham Rosman's (1978) comparative consideration of highlands societies: the uneven development of ceremonial exchange as a public-political institution with its own ends distinct from the ends of life-cycle and kinship-based payments. Shirley Lindenbaum's article makes the point very clearly. The more we know, the more evident it is (cf. A. Strathern ed. 1982) that the large-scale organizations of the Mendi, Hagen, or Mae Enga types, with their clear conceptualization of prestige and Big-Manship, are in fact extreme in this development, although once taken as typical of the region as a whole. Many more societies are akin to those of the lowlands in their interest in ceremonial prestations based on kinship and the life cycle.

In pointing to one particular ethnographic contrast, I have no doubt conflated others. Shirley Lindenbaum and Harriet Whitehead have surveyed some of the different cultural contexts for kinship-based exchanges. My own interest is in the symbolic mechanisms by which non-kinship values are generated. How is "prestige" perceived as an attribute of political activity? How does "wealth," created by the work of men and women alike (production), come to stand for something that ceases to have reference to that work (transaction)? From where does the notion of a "person" derive? The questions are interrelated: it is in those handful of highlands societies which have highly developed notions of prestige that we also find conceptualizations, first, of wealth as a source of extrinsic value (and not merely something owed to others, or properly belonging to others), and, second, of the person as an autonomous agent.

The notion of agent in these latter societies presupposes a matrix of relationships to which people belong but from which they can also detach themselves. An ideational contrast between connection and disconnection is commonly presented through that between males rooted to clan land and females severed from it. In these particular highlands societies, bridewealth may take the character of death compensation. Also in these societies, we find marked "patrilineal" ideologies (cf. Feil 1984; Shapiro this volume). That is, the concept of a bounded group appears most salient in the presence of the symbolized possibility of detachment from group relations; notions of boundedness are "strongest" where notions of personal autonomy are also pronounced. Whether one takes the boundedness of groups or the autonomy of persons as contextually prior, each is the conceptual precipitate of the other. This could not be the case, however, were there not two kinds of persons—male and female—that could give a concrete representation of the dialectical nature of this structure. (If men are attached to clan land, women are detached; if women are attached to production on the land, men are detached through their exchanges.)

In his article in this collection, Maurice Bloch shows the androgynous Merina deme transcendent over feminine biology—two equally powerful images, drawing on categorizations derived from everyday life. Among the Hageners of the Western Highlands, a strong sense of group collectivity is constantly set off by an equally strong sense of personal autonomy on the part of both sexes. Thus the interests of individual clansmen may appear to resist the interests of their clan; women may appear to resist the interests of men. I present some evidence for the underlying Hagen categorizations. To make the point I juxtapose material from the Wiru in the Southern Highlands, where ceremonial exchange is embedded in a matrix of kin prestations; where prestige, Big-Manship, and personhood are by comparison all relatively undeveloped, and where group boundedness is of little salience. Here bridewealth is assimilated to childgrowth payments. Here symbols of women's and men's attachment to their kin comment on the nature of embeddedness and identity but do little to delineate detachment in anything but an ephemeral way.*

Elsewhere I was concerned with contrasts in the constructions of Hagen and Wiru gender for which a brief sociological analysis of exchange systems was offered in explanation. This article has another starting point. Given the particular constructions entailed in gender formulae, what are the consequences for the conceptualization of other areas of life to which those formulae are applied? I shall argue that Hageners use gender as a vehicle for conceptualizing differences in the qualities of kinship attachments. Auton-

---

*My fieldwork among the Wiru was limited to two months, and I am heavily dependent on Andrew Strathern's ethnographic investigations. A number of the points I make come from joint discussions; I have also drawn freely on his analytical insights.

omy is delineated twice: first, as a characteristic of detached individuals whose interests cannot be aligned with those of their ascribed group; second, as evinced in the product of a relationship between partners, the energy and intent and work that in the case of spouses (like exchange partners) not merely affirms their marital status vis-à-vis each other, but results in joint creations (children, wealth) not exclusively identified with either.

In using the Wiru as a foil to this analysis, I also utilize a contrast between symbolic devices. The discrete categories male and female are brought into a relation of juxtaposition in Hagen society where they can be conflated in Wiru society. But Hagen and Wiru cannot be taken as some sociological or cultural pair. There is a contrast between them according to my axes of analyses, but this is not of a binary kind. I would follow Bloch in arguing that there is no single gender-ordering of values to be found, even within one culture. I demonstrate the point, however, not as he does with reference to differences in kinds of knowledge but to differences in symbolic construction between these two societies (see Colby et al. 1981: 431).

Kinship: Connection and Disconnection

A native speaker of the English language might be forgiven for supposing that kinship was only about "connections." As a "relation" (Schneider 1968), a relative stands for the very idea of relationship. But kinship also produces difference, and qualitative disjunction between certain categories of kin may specifically take the form of disconnections.

Componential analysis of kinship terminologies certainly proceeds on the assumption that particular terminological positions are the product of distinctions (e.g., in terms of age or sex or generation) combining to produce discrete categories. But sequence as well as permutation may be at issue. It is not just that, in Radcliffe-Brown's phrase, a social personality is the product of converging relationships, so that different components of the person's makeup are visible in the different ties he or she has with others (Fortes 1969: 95). Nor even that, in respect of particular kin, "attachment" may be of radically different orders (Leach 1961). If people are seen to shed as well as acquire kinship identity, at crucial developmental junctures what may be stressed becomes not their connection to this set of persons but their disconnection from that set. Social transitions may well focus on non-kinship elements—the acquisition of adulthood, the affirmation of sexual maturity, or the attainment of political office—leaving kinship designations intact. On the other hand, they may deliberately set the person apart from previous kin connections. Rites of passage can be held to effect a change in substance—to replace a boy's maternal body by paternal body, or to endow a girl with sexuality from an outside source. Connections are thus severed, transformed, altered, and persons extracted from a matrix in which they were first embedded.

One notable context is marriage. And the most notable category of persons from the viewpoint of unilineal modeling is the spouse who is not in a position to reproduce himself or herself. Where ideas of flow and transmission of substance provide idioms of relatedness (see Weiner 1978: 176; Weiner 1980: 72; Poole 1981), then such systems also have to provide a symbolic counterpart: ideas of blockage and termination. This is true of certain Papua New Guinea highlands descent constructs with a patrilineal cast, with wives marked out as the non-reproducing spouse. The mother's contribution may have to be obliterated from the children's bodies, or otherwise set against the connections traced through the father. The woman herself may be regarded as severed from the body of her clansmen. As a result, the category "women" connotes detachability. Women are specifically disconnected at particular points in their lives from kinship-based relationships, such as those they enjoy with their parents and siblings.

However, the creation of difference (distinctions in women's and men's makeup) is by no means a uniform process. In the highlands systems to which I have been referring, a woman's detachment from her clan may provide a model of non-kinship values. As less than a full clan member, she, and the matrilateral connections she represents, come to refer not only to extra-clan resources but to resources produced in political contexts no longer classified by the requirements of kin relations. In other highlands (and lowlands) systems, by contrast, disconnection may instead be part of people's efforts to maintain differentiation between categories of kin (cf. Wagner 1977a), to ensure that maternity and paternity make a difference in the constitution of a person. The end result of this second activity is the sustaining of difference itself, and the conceptual entities thus generated must refer back to the underlying kinship connections. Under the conditions of the first case, we find a marked conceptualization of "the person" as distinct from a kinsman. This is less so in the second case. The conditions in question emerge as contrasting modes of symbolization in which gender as a source of difference plays a central role.

Insofar as kinship constructs turn on the perpetuation of similarities and the creation of distinctions, then discriminations between categories of kin are about the difference it makes to a person's status to be the product of various others. Distinctions between the sexes invariably enter into such discriminations. But emphasis on gender alerts us to the fact that differences between the sexes may not, as a technical point, be constructed in the same way—we may not be dealing with a single model of "difference" (cf. Sacks 1979: 6).

What is true of the way differences are modeled will also be true of the way relationships are modeled. Therefore, it becomes analytically significant whether, for example, a shell stands for the whole man, or for part of himself seen as detachable, for this creates distinct structures—the person as an entirety or as partible. Between the sexes, it is significant whether one gender can displace or substitute for the other, or whether the relationship between them always sustains an antithesis. Yet the concept of relationship itself is ambiguous. We use the notion of a "relation" both to subsume identity and to distinguish identity (there is "no difference" between elements) from relational equivalence (elements are linked but remain discrete). Thus D. J. J. Brown (1980: 299) reminds us that descent theory subsumes relation under the principle of definition, whereas exchange theory recognizes the principle of relation as distinct. Issues of this nature led Roy Wagner (1975) to clarify two modes of symbolization—two models of relationship— namely, figurative constructions in which meanings are piled on and images substituted for one another, and literal or relational constructions in which elements are brought together in such a way that the relationship itself becomes a separately cognized entity. The following account draws on these propositions.

Hagen: The Premise of Difference

A Hagen woman is presented as severed from her clan at marriage. Part of the bridewealth that passes from her prospective husband's kin to her clansmen is a category of non-returnable shells called *peng pokla*, "head cutting" (cf. M. Strathern 1972: 104). Indeed, in many respects, bridewealth is comparable to death compensation (paying "for the head") (A. Strathern 1982: 209). In this sense, a woman is detached from her clan. Yet, at the same time, she carries its name with her: Nomane is referred to by her natal clan in the appellation *Membo amb Nomane* (the Membo [clan] woman Nomane [personal name]). Moreover, she becomes an active "road" for the links now established between her own and her husband's clan. The blood she transmits to her children, far from having to be obliterated, symbolizes this channel of communication. I shall show that this is not the paradox it seems.

Hagen bridewealth is a complete transaction; affinal exchanges follow but are overshadowed by the development of full-scale ceremonial exchange (*moka*).* On public occasions, such affinal-maternal kin networks are taken for granted and do not become an overt rationale for staging exchanges (A. Strathern 1978). Yet once daughters and sisters have been symbolically detached, there is no ambiguity about their status as wives; thus it is tolerable for wives to live, as a few do, with their natal kin. However much this compromises ongoing conjugal relations between husband and wife, it does not affect their formal status as spouses—the woman is still married—nor the agnatic affiliation of her children who may well accompany her. For the symbolic detachment through bridewealth makes a wife's standing in relation to her husband unambiguous, such that her movement back and forth between his and her natal home need not compromise their formal marital status, any more than her maternal contribution to their child is a threat to agnatic identity.

Hageners detach the transmission of clan identity from the joint "work" of the sexes in childbirth. Together the sexes make and endow the child. There is a way of referring to the transmission of descent substance as male sexuality (*ndating*) (A. Strathern 1972: 10–11), but it is remarkable that in general parlance, the father's contribution (semen) and the mother's (blood and later milk) are in a

---

*Hagen bridewealth transactions often initiate personal exchange partnerships between a man and his affines. Maternal kin receive child payments and death payments, but the bulk of transactions—even though they are with maternal and affinal kin—are converted into *moka*. From the men's point of view, individual alliance merges into group relations, and women become intermediaries between affinally linked clans.

relationship of equivalence, in that the term "grease" (*kopong*) may refer to all these, as "blood" (*mema*) may also refer to a generalized idea of physiological connection. Mother and father have distinct origins, but their fertility is put to joint use. Making children can thus be regarded as a labor involving "grease" (the contribution of both), as is the planting of crops on the land's surface (A. Strathern 1982: 222).

Indeed, in thinking of the constitution of the fetus, Hageners stress the complementarity in the husband's and wife's contributions, much as the pair works together in all productive activities. Each gives a part of himself or herself while retaining a distinct identity. But clanship produces a skewing. The distinctiveness of the husband's contribution lies in its reference to the fact that food is grown on the immutable underlying "bone" of clan territory: the association between this basis for nurture and the clan body (bone), as well as the name that the father transmits, constitutes the clanship his children acquire.* The wife adds her element to it, as she adds her work to clan endeavors. And it is this aspect of her connections with her own kin from which she was severed when she married. She need undergo no change of internal substance. Her transition from being a daughter/sister to a wife is simply accomplished at the time of the bridewealth transaction. She is first cut off from the clan name. Although she carries it with her and may be treated according to her natal clan membership, its demise with her own death has been foreshadowed;† she cannot represent the clan as its male members can. Second, virilocal residence normally cuts her off from clan nurture: although she may maintain gardens with her own kin, and her children have courtesy rights there, these children of hers are fundamentally nourished by the work she does on her husband's land.

This has consequences for the Hagen construction of person as agent, although I must make it clear that there is no single Hagen

---

*The donations of semen and blood, which belong to a domain of joint parental activity, are conceptually distinguished from the child's acquisition of clan identity as "bone." Men and women both have "bone," of course, as a matter of such identity; however, women are also said to have "no bone" (they lack "strength," insofar as this identity has a different placement in their lives from that of men) (M. Strathern 1972: 159).

†She sometimes transmits her own clan name to matrisegments within her children's clan, but precisely to draw attention to differentiation or to some special relationship in a way men cannot. Men transmit their personal names or personal characteristics such as "short/tall."

term for "person," any more than there is for other analytical constructs such as kinship or political and domestic domains. Later I briefly indicate how their "person" differs from the "person" of certain anthropological theorizing.

Construction involves a significant sequencing, and more than one construction is at issue. When a child is conceptualized as the product of the difference between its parents, it is thus, so to speak, an entity other than those differences themselves. At the same time, it must move in a differentiated world. There is a further sense in which the person is partible, and the relationship between the parts Hageners construct through gender imagery. Consequently, on the one hand, the "child," like the "person," is ungendered. But on the other hand, persons contain within themselves both a male and a female element. There is a salient set of associations between the female part, detachability, and the circulation of wealth objects. Matrilateral connections are part of this configuration (maternal kin are regarded as a source of wealth); yet this component of the person is not simply inherited from the mother. The person in Hagen society is a *reconstitution* of and not a replication of parental input, and this reconstitution is also the source of its status as a non-kinship entity.

I make such an assertion on the grounds of technicalities in symbol construction. It is therefore necessary to be clear about the techniques at issue.* Here I pursue the distinction between a figurative construction, which through substitution builds up or modifies "identity," and a literal one, which detaches a part without compromising identity and thus creates a "relation." A relationship has a product; identity does not.

The former supposes an analogy between the elements brought into conjunction (one element overlaid by another). The latter supposes contiguity, with the part also standing for its source. A part could not stand for the whole in this sense if the two were not of different dimensions. Disjunction is thus set up: the part must be conceptually detachable. Wealth, which comes to men's bodies

---

*The terms "literal" and "figurative" come directly from Wagner's writings (1975; 1977a; 1977b). They address a difference in modes of symbolization that have been treated in other contexts (e.g., Tambiah 1968; Colby, Fernandez, and Kronenfeld 1981), as for instance in Ortner's (1973) deployment of "summarizing" versus "elaborating" symbols. Summarizing symbols lead to a process of substitution (a figurative structure), whereas elaborating symbols spell out relationships (in a literal mode).

("skins") may stand for or refer to the prominence of "men" as transactors; but this wealth is also detachable. Clanship for men, on the other hand, is not. But clans are thereby able to augment their names by something that is not-clanship (such as wealth). For women, the situation is different. It is from clanship that women are regarded as detachable. Ties through Hagen women cannot be regenerative of agnation—not because women are unimportant, but because they importantly stand for something that is not-clanship. Men "add" this (wealth, and the productivity of women) to themselves in such a way as to create for their political transactions values which no longer refer to those of kinship. On the one hand, then, a figurative substitution is created through one attribute standing for another in an encompassing manner (for example, agnation and rootedness in ancestral relations are represented in male attachment to clan land, such that a man disconnecting himself from this land compromises his agnatic status); this creates attributes as intrinsic (men do or do not reside on clan land). On the other hand, an attribute may be regarded as a literal extension or part of the person that persons also have at their disposal; this gives rise to possibilities of disconnection (for example, shells must be got from elsewhere; pigs raised at home can be sent away in exchange). These constructions underlie the circulation of substances and things between persons. In the first instance, objects (such as clan substance) may be metaphorically substituted for persons, and in the transmission of substances actors become "identified"; in the second, objects (such as wealth items) are contiguous with persons, and in the exchange of items actors are "related." These constructions comprise different contexts for the relationship between male and female. It is the literal construction that is particularly of note here, for in creating a "relation" between themselves as differentiated entities, the parties create a product that is different from them.

"Man" (*wuö*) and "woman" (*amb*) are an irreducible lexical pair in the Hagen language, Melpa (Lancy and Strathern 1981; cf. Le Roy 1981). The two terms take on different values, however, depending on the context in question. Where "man" and "woman" each have a figurative status, standing only for themselves, innately differentiated, we may speak of same-sex contexts: men do "male" things; women do "female" things. To take male and female in cross-sex contexts, however, as when the activities of one are compared to the other or the sexes join together in an enterprise, is to enter the domain of literal expression. Here things symbolized as either male or female point up a relational contrast. Gender is used in such comparisons to create distinctions between sets of persons or internal elements within a person. Thus the relationship between work and prestige or between production and transaction can be talked about in terms of relations between women and men or in terms of internal bodily constitution. The point is not just that persons are composed of different elements, but that their constitution models relationships based on antithesis, so that they are what they are not: they are both x and its opposite y. A woman is both attached to a clan ("male") and severed from a clan ("female"), whereas a man is both a household producer ("female") and a transactor ("male").

The Hagen person thus receives both a figurative and a literal structuring. As a product of difference, it is itself internally undifferentiated. The person is analogous in this way to the same-sex construct of the clan (the clan thought of as undifferentiated, male).* However, when the person moves in differentiated relationships, of which cross-sex interaction is a model, it appears partible, with a "part" to dispose of in relation with others. Thus also when a "male" clan no longer simply reflects on itself but comes into relation with others, its wealth and power may be said to be derived from a combination of men's efforts as agnatic kin and women's efforts as disposable daughters and incremental wives. The whole male person has a female part in his makeup; the whole female person a male part. I introduce same-sex/cross-sex contextualization to emphasize the point that the manipulation of gender ideas is crucial to this structuring of the Hagen person. What holds at a formal level in terms of gender (the contrast between male and female refers to differences in the way persons behave, and the person as such is neither male nor female) is replicated developmentally in the production of persons within the household; the human personhood of the child derives neither from one parent nor from the other, but grows as a joint product of their comple-

---

*The comparison between "person" and "clan" was initially made, in formal terms, in respect of their figurative construction. Essentially, however, the person is genderless, whereas the clan sustains same-sex male identity. In literal contexts, a person entering into transactions or engaging in encounters with others becomes, like the clan, partible and assumes a male identity with female disposable attributes.

mentary interaction. Its partibility is created in the context of specific relationships with gendered others. Let me spell out some of the implications of this gender symbolism.

In Hagen there are situations in which, as I have indicated, the figurative identity of male or female is presented as innate or non-negotiable (M. Strathern 1980). Thus, spouses are in a state of non-transformable equivalence; each contributes his or her complementary component to joint activity. By the same token, they are differentiated from the product of the transaction (the pigs they produce or the wealth that comes from affinal exchanges). Whereas a number of entities in Hagen thought exist only in dual relational form (male/female, domestic/wild, prestigious/rubbish), pigs and wealth ("things"), like the person, are not so constructed. These terms do not form one of a pair. As whole entities, they are in turn figurative conceptualizations of the relationship which produced them.

The formal equivalence between men and women as spouses in the context of domestic production, to which each contributes his or her work, is necessarily overridden in contexts in which women are equated with wealth as objects of mediation between clans. Women become a movable, detachable resource that represents outside sources, while men—land-based and clan-tied—provide the identity that is augmented. Hagen clans as same-sex entities can differentiate themselves from like clans only through reinforcing identity. They do so with reference to genealogies and to recent histories that are metaphors of clanship. But they may also compete with others for prestige, test their strength, make claims about their wealth. This is identity augmented. What is augmented is added, symbolically constructed as having an external source, so that wealth, strength, and power metonymically stand for an increment to the clans. The separateness of this increment is marked by reference to gender symbols that make the external source of male clan prestige and strength "female." Thus, although inert wealth is ungendered, when deployed it may be visualized as a female resource at male disposal, and consequently imagined as both or either male/female.

There are consequences for the construction of "women." What is to be added must also be detached. Women who are severed from their clan of origin appropriately stand for detachment. Their relationship to their natal kin and to their affines becomes metonymic in this relational context. They who link clans in alliance are seen as a detachable part of their own, and as contributing this part as an external element to the clans of their husbands. A woman does not, of course, lose her natal identity; on the contrary, it is the essential difference that she carries with her. Neither can she modify the agnatic identity of her husband's clan; she contributes to it her work.

The Hagen "person," then, may emerge as a male entity with additional female attributes. This works for both men and women. There is a sense* in which the wealth and fertility that men acquire through their efforts are female additions to their given identities; there is a sense in which women's identity with their home clans makes them like male persons, although it is an identity they uproot. Hagen women are constructed as at once connected and disconnected. Their loss in marriage is also a wealth gain to their natal clan, and they increase with their work and fertility the husband's clan with whom they are partially integrated. The distinction, then, between male and female is such that if men stand figuratively for clanship, then women stand in a literal relationship to these units. This means that clanship has a dual aspect—both intrinsic (men) and disposable (women). The difference that wives make to a body of male clansmen is emphasized: they simultaneously represent dangerous penetration and profitable routes of expansion. Certain persons—their activities and energies—are thus seen as *added* to other persons, without any compromise of intrinsic identity. Agnation is not modified; the woman is detached, but her agnatic identity is not otherwise altered.

These constructions have repercussions on how men and women live their lives. Detachment presents personal difficulties for Hagen women, who may indeed talk about being uprooted. Certainly, there is a moment of recognized psychological difficulty in their experience at the marriage ceremony. The bride alone carries the burden of transformation. At the outset, she acts as emissary for her own kin; toward the end of the proceedings, she becomes emissary for her husband's kin. Her net bag is filled up with cooked pork, which she bears from her new husband's kin to her own relatives. Willingness to carry the often very heavy load is said

---

*Here, as elsewhere, I am summarizing a number of ethnographic facts. I present them, however, through an analysis of what I take to be the symbolic structures at issue.

to indicate willingness to stay with her husband and bear him many children. Her commitment is as much at issue here as her potential motherhood. Indeed, marriage itself is less a symbol of parenthood than of alliance, and the bride is clearly in this context the object of mediation, the road along which wealth will flow; in belonging to both sides, she also belongs to neither. This is the moment at which she acquires the quality of being "in between" the two sets of men.

At the same time, the construction of gender identity as a prior nonnegotiable given gives women a sense of strength as themselves.* This in turn infuses their contribution to male enterprises with personal vigor; it equally allows room for women to refuse to contribute. Whether or not they help men, in this cross-sex interaction they do not compromise their status as women. Same-sex female contexts for action are not much elaborated; only when a woman contributes excessively to men's enterprises to the point of overshadowing others may she be teased or denigrated by other women for being "too like a man."

We are now in a position to understand why Hagen death compensation for men is likened to bridewealth for women. It is not the loss of life as such or the obliteration of clan connections that seem to be at issue; rather, until the dead man has been (figuratively) reconstituted as an ancestor, he is severed from the clan body. His temporary detachability in symbolic terms puts him into a (literal) relation with it: he is "part" of his clan, but he can no longer represent it as enduring, in the way living male members can; this state is comparable to the permanent detachability of women. In these circumstances, those who have appropriated the "head" must restore equivalence between themselves and the clan body they have decapitated through the medium of compensation. And it is the permanent symbolic detachment of a woman from her natal clan that constitutes her "marriage." That she remains married—whether or not she is living on her husband's clan territory—is guaranteed by the fact that as a woman she can never stand in a figurative relation to her clan. The total collection of shells, pigs, and

*Hagen women do female things but do not have to do "being female." They have few ceremonies of their own; neither first menstruation nor childbirth receives elaborate attention. Significant cultural meaning is not constructed out of these as specifically female (same-sex) matters. It is cross-sex acts that receive attention: when symbols of sexuality and fertility are manipulated to make statements about social regenesis—as in the spirit cults—male *and* female elements are consistently brought together.

money that make up the bridewealth constitute a metaphor for the bride, and its facets all refer to aspects of the bride's position (her work, her sexuality, the nurture she received from her mother). In its transfer, it is metonymically detached from the groom's side and comes as wealth to the bride's side.

The organ *noman* (mind) is similarly constructed. The *noman* is a metaphor for the ungendered person. In Hagen theories of development it derives from exchanges between two gendered others—a child's parents. The father's "work" and the mother's "work" together produce a separate entity (the person/the *noman*). Indeed, the domestic household is the crucial locus for the production of new human beings. Through its parents, it is true, a child receives two distinctive forms of nurture: the father "plants" it in his clan land; the mother feeds it with the products of her labor. But this is not how a child acquires its *noman*. Hageners specifically say the *noman* develops with the child's appreciation of reciprocity (M. Strathern 1968): the productive work of the father and mother, valued as complementary, provides the child with its model of reciprocity. As a definitive attribute of the human person, the *noman* is a self-referential entity, ungendered. At the same time, it can also come into a metonymical relationship with its host. Men's minds are said to be different from women's minds. When a Hagen girl is reluctant to marry, she can be appealed to or can make appeals through reference to her *noman*. But commitment to the interests of others is something she can give or withhold, having control over her mind insofar as it is *both* part of herself and detachable. People can "lose" their *noman*. More importantly, the kind of other-directedness that first characterizes its emergence, in later life is seen to be controlled by will. Thus, the *noman* can refer at the same time to collective orientation and to what in Hagen society is sometimes construed as its conceptual opposite, individual autonomy (A. Strathern 1981).

These symbol constructions allow persons to be conceptualized as added to and subtracted from one another. Hagen clans provide a locus of identity, a unit to and from which the additions and subtractions are made. In this context, men as men are only temporarily detachable, whereas women as women are permanently so. Thus the wife adds work to the endeavors of her husband's clan that is subtracted from her own clan. The two affinal clans, in exchanging "parts" (the woman against bridewealth), each sustain a distinctiveness, the relationship between them being one of equivalence. Persons as such are also potentially partible. In the context of domestic production, spouses act with their distinct parts; they are held in a relationship of equivalence. Each is made distinct by his or her kinship connections. But together they produce an entity, the child as a person, that has a value (as in its definition as autonomous, with a *noman* of its own) not circumscribed by kinship as such.

Wiru: The Premise of Conflation

A Wiru woman is not severed from her kin; Wiru patrilineages are small localized subgroups of dispersed phratries that provide men with names but are not seen as crucial entities in the exchange of brides. Persons are embedded in a set of personal kin ties focused on the transmission of substance that require lifetime payments to maternal kin. Bridewealth marks the start of such payments and anticipates the payments that a husband will make to his wife's natal kin for her child. The association is so close that regular sexual intercourse is supposed to follow immediately after the bridewealth goods have been handed over. The groom makes repeated personal payments, which he and his new wife take to the woman's father until she becomes pregnant (A. Strathern 1980: 61). Proper child payments are made once the child is born. So if Hagen bridewealth is like death compensation in cutting the woman from her kin, Wiru bridewealth is the start of a cycle of child payments that sustain a flow from her kin to herself to her child.

Yet there is a process of substitution. The Wiru husband substitutes his own paternity for his wife's father's paternity, for the father's masculine input must be obliterated. The disjunction set up between husband and father has to be sustained. In this situation, some feel it intolerable for a woman to return home to reside at her father's house. Perhaps a quarter of Wiru marriages in fact take place within or near the village. But a girl whose husband lives elsewhere returns home at her peril; in fact, if she is to remain "married," her only option is to seek another husband. The Wiru mother thus becomes a focus for payments that have to establish her child as the product of her husband's, rather than her father's, paternity.

The necessity of making this distinction is indicated by the threat to identity that a father apparently suffers if his daughter returns to live at home.

Since I introduce Wiru for the sake of comparison, let me point up certain significant points of contrast. Whereas Hagen parents often seek political contacts through a marriage as a way to establish friendly relations with allies, Wiru parents seek a wealthy son-in-law. They virtually discount his political standing in favor of the child payments they hope will follow. A Hagen divorcée can always come home, and indeed is likely to do so before remarrying, whereas a Wiru divorcée is much more likely to go off to another man. It may be added that before marriage, which does not entail betrothal, a Hagen woman is relatively inactive sexually; despite her betrothal as a child, a Wiru woman is likely to have had sexual partners in her own village.

In the one society bridewealth prestations between affines turn into public ceremonial exchange, in the other into personal payments for "skin" or body. If the Hagen adult is an autonomous, self-directed person evincing *noman* (mind, will) in his or her commitment to tasks, including the pursuit of prestige, the Wiru adult is teknonymically known in reference to his or her child, for being a parent reproduces his or her own embeddedness in a personal kinship network (A. Strathern n.d.). Hagen kinsmen regard it as ultimately futile to force a sister or daughter to marry against her will, for a successful marriage depends on the commitment that the partners bring to it. Wiru kinsmen think it crucial that a woman be seen to be married and are prepared to use physical coercion; a father may threaten to kill his daughter if she is reluctant. Whereas Hagen women apparently commit suicide because they are caught between conflicting demands, Wiru women apparently commit suicide in the face of authoritarian domination by either husband or father. A Hagen woman both can be appealed to and can appeal to others, for she has sanctions of her own to bring against her kin or husband; her state of mind must be noted, since if it is upset, her own agnatic ghosts may intervene. Wiru "minds" are not localized; feeling or will (*wene*) is distributed throughout the body, manifested only in *timini* ("nose"), an individuality of disposition. Brides have few sanctions at their disposal (matrilateral ghosts who most frequently send sickness are concerned rather with the bodily substance of their descendants). Finally, we have seen that the

Hagen *noman* is a product of human growth, inherited from neither parent but an undifferentiated manifestation of personhood as such, the combined "product" of the parents' joint activity; Wiru *timini* is paternally derived and thus parentally distinguished from the person's body ("skin," or bodily substance, *tingini*), which is the specific product of mothering.

Wiru phratries provide names for men. Here unilineal descent is not a crucial factor in the status of the nonreproducing spouse, for in relation to this flow the nonreproducing spouse is the husband. I have argued that Hagen wives' efforts add to the achievements of their husband's clan and bring wealth (in the form of bridewealth) to their own. In maintaining their phratry names, however, Wiru men are not in the position of adding to anything: men simply perpetuate their names. It is women who perpetuate substance. In order to do this, their bodies must be seen to undergo transformation. The Wiru wife is thus subject to physical change. She must be the recipient of her husband's paternity, and it was noted that sexual relations are bound up with the completion of the marriage transactions. These culminate in evidence of her transformed state in pregnancy. The husband's contribution here overlays something the wife already possesses, so that the transformation that the Wiru woman undergoes is to have part of herself replaced by another part.* The result is a dual and gendered product, the fetus whose body or "skin" comes from the mother and whose disposition or character comes from the father.

Now, a Hagen woman transmits valued substance to her child, which becomes part of the child without compromising its agnatic identity. Moreover, insofar as the Hagen woman both belongs to her clan and is detached from it, she undergoes no internal modification.† She simply contributes maternal blood that mingles with the paternal contribution of semen; there is no child in her until the mingling takes place. In Wiru, however, the woman's makeup has to be modified. The paternal identity of the material she carries within her must be overlaid by the husband's contribution. In this sense, the Wiru woman is already symbolically with child, whose

*Gillison (1980: 168) describes a similar transformation for Gimi.

†By way of comparison, I would like to draw notice to Bloch's description of Merina motherhood in this volume: maternal vitality can be added to the blessings of the descent group only after the woman representing vital forces has also been cut off from it.

identity must be redefined by the new paternity of her husband (cf. Gillison 1980).*

Equations between persons and wealth in Wiru consequently take a very different form. Wealth is not "on the skin" but is "the skin" itself, and thus bridewealth is seen as in exchange for the bride's bodily substance (*tingini*) (A. Strathern 1980: 60). Moreover, Wiru substance flows from women: fathers impress their names on the child and endow it with individuality. In the manner in which paternal origins must be distinguished from maternal ones, the husband is also being distinguished from his wife's father (cf. A. Strathern n.d.). Making male parenthood different from female parenthood thus resembles the task of keeping separate the terms of a metaphor (Wagner 1977a). Without differentiation, there is context collapse, and one simply becomes the other. In sustaining this differentiation as an activity, the endless flow of goods "produces" kinship. Neither wealth nor women are detachable from this kinship nexus. This has a number of implications.

A single Wiru village comprises sets of people from agnatic phratries dispersed through many. A village conducts wars and pig kills, but its external relations are not mediated through the exchange of women, nor are its internal relations built on unitary (clanlike) kinship between men. Women signify neither exotic resources nor dangerous threats. Rather, relations at the village level are crosscut by the personal networks of individuals, which provide each person with his or her own source of strength and fertility. In the lifelong payments made to their maternal kin in return for their own bodily substance, men and women pay for this substance with goods categorized as male (shells, salt), and receive in return from the source of maternal nurture further gifts that signify the femaleness of this nurture (ribcages of pork). To sustain the initial endowment of health, these gifts must be made perpetually. A person continually gives to his or her maternal kin a masculine version of the feminine substance he or she continually receives from them. It is their internal constitution that is manipulated. In the flow of pork and shells that stand for maternal and paternal elements, the

*These are not observations explicitly made by the actors, but represent an understanding of a range of symbolic equations. I would add that in Gillison's analysis of Gimi initiation and marriage, the constitution of the child occupies a central place. Her insights have obviously been a significant stimulus to this understanding of the Wiru material. I am also grateful for her specific comments on this paper.

transactions themselves create the difference between these elements, and thereby imply their prior conflation.

The transfer of goods sets up a relationship of identity between donor and recipient (cf. Schieffelin 1980). Maternal kin do not alone create a child; thus it is appropriate that a person's substance should be symbolized in male, paternal objects as well. But the more a man gives shells and salt (his individuated, masculinized substance) to his mother's father and brothers, the more these men in turn affirm their own identity *with the mother* who was the vehicle for the transmission of substance; they give back further female substance in the form of ribcages. In receiving payments for the children of their sisters and daughters, then, these men acknowledge themselves as a source of substance conceived by the Wiru in essentially female terms.

Women's own interests undergo change. Initially valuables for the woman herself go to her maternal kin (her mother's parents and siblings); on the birth of her children, her husband is expected to make reparation for their offspring to her parents and siblings. Indeed, women actively promote the flow of goods, to the point of initiating exchanges with men from whom they hope to claim maternal payments. A specific category of women's exchanges is called *langi*, which means "to make a body grow fat." Women give food to their husband's male (especially junior) relatives, for which the men return shells or money; the women are building the men's bodies, a contribution that must be paid for. Although there is a value attached to male individuality—to the energy and generosity with which men fulfill their obligations—there is no marked division between men and women as actors in exchanges. Women are the agents of transformation, turning vegetable produce into shells or money. They transact with men and to a lesser extent with other women. In talking about why she gave food to her husband's brother, one Wiru woman commented that she did not see why a woman should not be like her husband and "work" with his brothers: by giving food to a man, she could expect wealth in return. She thus perceived her behavior on grounds of similarity and identification with men.

Wiru women do not in themselves represent "difference." There is no entity comparable to the Hagen clan to which they are related and from which they can be detached. The subject of skin transactions is the very substance that women share with their children.

Wiru wealth items may be considered part of (examples of) this substance.* Thus, the ribcages contribute female nourishment to the original object of nurture; shells are the male wealth by which a person is individuated. Together, the relationship between the items models the complete person (cf. Battaglia 1983), made of both "body" and "face," and these contributions do not stand for a whole range of other differences; they are reducible only to the difference between the female and male parent whose endowments are so combined. By the same token, Wiru goods are not differentiated as "things" (wealth in the Hagen sense) from donors and recipients in an exchange, but in effect take a male or female form; and a person is not differentiated by the mother's nurture, since the payments he or she makes for it are for himself or herself; the nurture is not convertible into other interests. Consequently the objects used in payments do not come to represent an idea of wealth as a detachable resource.

Wiru women are to some extent thought of as wealth, but here wealth items in turn express the importance of maternal nurture. Thus the husband takes over payments for a woman's skin when he first pays bridewealth and continues to do so until she has children, when these become payments for the children. The children are her skin. The perpetual round of life-cycle payments thereby creates the donor-recipient relationship as itself the subject of the transactions. There is thus little room in the Wiru system for enhancement of prestige of a non-kinship kind through these exchanges. There are no Big Men on the Hagen scale; Wiru men do not have the same hopes of control or influence over the minds of others, and, as we have seen, wealth is not constructed as disposable. Indeed, Andrew Strathern (1978: 78) writes, "The most striking difference between the [Hagen] and Wiru rules of exchange is that in Wiru there is no 'principle of increment.'" Wealth defines identity and cannot therefore be added to it.

---

*The chief component of the payments made to maternal kin is shells; in return, and flowing in the same direction as the woman, come ribcages. If ribcages represent the same substance already embodied in the skin, the action is part of the transfer that constituted the person who is paying for his skin. The food a woman produces, and the vegetable gifts she makes to others, are also part of this constituting substance. The shells in return stand for the child individuated by paternity, giving back part of its paternally constructed self to the maternal kin. Yet neither can stand by itself but depends on the other for completion (there cannot be "face" without "body"). Each requires the other as its encompassing context.

If the differences between men and women in parenthood are not taken as innate but have to be created, then this must occur against a background where male and female stand metaphorically for the same thing (parenthood itself) and thus for one another. What is innate is a conflated entity, and what has to be differentiated are the maternal and paternal contributions. The words "breast" and "penis" in Wiru, as Andrew Strathern has recorded, may be lexically combined to refer to "spouse(s)" (*andonora*). Men and women alike assist in this differentiation by "doing" motherhood and fatherhood. The sequence of exchanges indicates, however, an ultimate encompassment of male by female elements. Consequently, Wiru agnation is not taken as a given. It is, in turn, created by what men do; in individuating sets of men, it does give these men some collective base, as shared names do. Such individuation of personal names and of agnatic association works against the encompassing nature of substance consequently conceived as maternal.

Wiru symbolization does not, therefore, provide the conditions for the construction of what in Hagen society I have called non-kinship values. We might ask, in that case, what the detachment of the Wiru bride is about.

Detachment takes two forms: the first is the sexual submission of a woman to her husband and the substitution of his paternity for what would otherwise be construed as her father's. The second is her change of residence to live with her husband. These acts serve to separate her husband and father, a deliberately sustained differentiation.* The father waits for his daughter's child to be born, especially if she is his eldest, for the payments flowing from this event will establish himself as the recipient. It is this transformation in his role that seems to be the subject of the bridewealth payments, and it is thus that we should understand Wiru bridewealth as the forerunner of birth payments.†

The social persons who must be detached from one another are the bride's father and her intending husband. Obviously, the detachment in question is not from an agnatic body and is not a matter

---

*There is a strong identity between mother and daughter, one that seems to be a conceptual problem for men (both the mother's husband and the daughter's husband) rather than for women.

†In a sociological sense, it does not matter who becomes the actual recipient of these payments, provided there is some self-designated husband to make them.

of being uprooted; it involves men carving a male identity out of a network of kin relations of an ultimately female character. If the Hagen woman has difficulties in bridging contexts (moving from one clan to another), the Wiru man in his relations with the opposite sex has to prevent context collapse (identification with his wife). In fact, the exchanges are so structured that his individuating paternity will be extinguished in his own lifetime, when the gifts he receives for his daughter's children's skins celebrate *maternal* substance. For the Wiru bride, a replacement has taken place, husband substituting for father, her own bearing of children setting up an identity between herself and her mother. Indeed, it seems as though the contrived separation of male and female also leads to same-sex merging between mothers and daughters and between fathers and husbands. Such anxiety and distress as accompany Wiru marriages at their inception turn on these identifications. Father-daughter relations in Wiru society are notable for their incidence of incest and violence. Sexual relations are ambiguous partly because symbolic differentiation focuses not on distinctive genital sexuality but on parenthood: it is maternity and paternity that are created through the skin payments. But these, in turn, are not stable reference points for gender identity precisely because the difference between them is created through the exchanges and is not taken as a given. The result is a celebration of parenthood that equates fathers (the recipients of child payments) with their wives (the cause of them). It appears to be women who reproduce themselves in this system; yet what they reproduce is buried in the bodies of their children and is not a source of autonomy. Autonomy does not emerge as a salient attribute of the person.

As a technicality, Wiru kinship symbols cannot provide the context for the production of autonomous personhood. A Wiru woman is her bodily substance and will reproduce that substance: such individuality as she has resides not in something she is seen to add to her given constitution, but in something inherited from her father. Body itself does not incorporate a notion of complementarity; there is no greatly marked emphasis on a contrast between bone and blood or, as in Hagen, on the combination of blood and semen. What fathers contribute is of a different order: *lene timini* ("eye nose," emotion, aggression, feeling). Fathers are said to contribute their "faces" (also spirit, *yomini*), their character. Gender differentiation is thus self-signifying; the connection between the sexes is not of a relational order, but of a juxtaposition of two in-terdependent entities. If Wiru persons are not detached from kin-ship relations, conceptually speaking, neither are they internally partible. Wealth does not represent the addition and subtraction of parts. Rather, the husband's shells substitute for a substance, which may be thought of as maternal, paternal, or both. He differ-entiates himself from these sources of parenthood only to overlay and thus conflate the one with the other.

Adding and Subtracting Persons

My account has emphasized the makeup of persons in terms of maternal and paternal origins. For the Wiru, this reflects a central preoccupation of public life-cycle exchanges and of similar ex-changes found in a number of highland societies. For Hagen, how-ever, life-cycle prestations are overshadowed by ceremonial ex-change (*moka*) of a different order. Kin ties are treated as a given and consequently are associated less with achievement than political ties between groups and the classification of persons in other terms—as Big Men, as rubbish, and so on. The public domain of *moka* making (transactions) is differentiated from domestic house-hold relations (production) where kin ties bestow an identity taken for granted. Yet it is apt to consider Hagen parenthood—not be-cause the major exchanges in Hagen take this as their focus, but precisely because they do not. The "difference" between male par-ent and female parent holds a different symbolic place in the two societies.

I have tried to follow a significant aspect of folk modeling: that the relationship between maternity and paternity is crucially tied to the relationship between women and men; that mothers are de-fined in the manner in which women are disconnected from or held to be connected to their kin, just as fathers are defined by the qual-ity of men's attachments. In this sense, I have also followed Judith Shapiro's (1981) dictum that we should consider men "as men." The Hagen father has identity as a male clansman; he merely sus-tains that (same-sex) identity by "planting" his child on his clan land. The Wiru father, in constantly paying for his children, has to create his male identity, to sustain a (cross-sex) differentiation be-tween himself and his various female kin and affines, for the dif-ference cannot be assumed as a given.

The Wiru conflation of male and female elements requires that at each generation a new paternal face has to be impressed on the maternally transmitted body. This perhaps accounts for some of the Wiru preoccupation with sexual activity. It is the woman who must feel, as it were, the "difference" that her husband's contribution makes when it overlays what was paternally bestowed. The woman's kin must ensure that what was appropriate male identity for their daughter (her paternal face) should not emerge again in her children. It is an important and emotional matter that another man should be seen to take the father's place and to alter the direction of the skin payments separating the father of her children from her own father. Thus, the significant switch on the man's part comes when he ceases to give (male) shells for his daughter to her maternal kin and gives (female) pork to his son-in-law as a maternal kinsman of her children.

Hagen transformations are of a different order. In some respects "clan" and "person" are homologous, each being at once undifferentiated and a potentially partible entity. Insofar as a clan's members can be severed from it, the internal "whole:part" relationship between it and its members undergoes change. In being severed, the Hagen woman represents not clanship but its disposable assets. The question of conflation does not arise, for she transmits a set of individual connections to her offspring that are in a prior manner thus differentiated from the collective relationship to their clan that the father bestows.* In this situation, it is women's quality as detachable "things" (cf. M. Strathern 1983) that is stressed, and thus they are equated both with disposable wealth† and with its structural equivalent in Hagen society, persons conceived as autonomous entities.

The difference between male and female has a product, although the products in the two societies are not the same. As distinct entities (in same-sex contexts), the Hagen male and female stand for a host of elements. These may be relationally compared (public/domestic, prestigious/rubbish) in cross-sex contexts. Yet there is in ad-

---

*Andrew Strathern points out that child payments in Hagen are not said to be for the child's body, but for its buried feces—for something returned to clan territory.

†The equation between persons and wealth is explicit in A. Strathern 1980 and 1982, which examine Hagen and Wiru bridewealth and mortuary exchanges. M. Strathern 1984 points to the significantly domestic household context in which persons are produced.

dition an outcome of these differences that is neither male nor female but the result of the combined efforts of both: the personal agent. The autonomous adult with a mind to devote to particular tasks, the mark of being "human," is produced from the complementary activities of the husband-wife dyad.

The Wiru product is rather the ongoing effort to sustain distinction, to impress difference upon the person dependent on others around him or her for identity—identities embedded in, rather than detached from, their same-sex links. The person here is a field in which identities are, as it were, merged, and social activity is necessary to perpetually reconstitute their difference. The product of Wiru difference, working through substitution, is what I call dependency or identity.* Whereas Hagen exchanges that begin with kinship (bridewealth) lead to something that is not kinship (political prestige), Wiru exchanges produce more kinship, rendering problematic previous relationships which then have to be affirmed.

This analysis of symbolism allows one to distinguish the meaning of wealth objects from the meaning of the relationships between persons created by the exchange of these objects. Wiru wealth items are part of kinship substance and name; when exchanged against one another, these items imply a conflation between their sources (the different sets of kinsmen) who are thereby constructed as combinations of these elements. By contrast, Hagen wealth items are attached metonymically to differentiated actors whose distinctiveness is simply preserved by the exchange: the items themselves are constructed as standing for something else, and this something else includes the notion of "wealth" detached from kinship and from its sources of production.

I conclude with this statement for a particular reason. Western formulations of "relationship," perceived as an artifact of culture, frequently point to the "person" as an already existing natural entity. In Radcliffe-Brown's and Fortes's usage, the "social person" is an analytical construct that points to assemblages of roles; the various relationships that any individual enters in respect to a multiplicity of others are in this individual overlaid and combined and thus represent his or her total social placement. But the locus of

*Battaglia (1983) has developed the concept as "cover" and demonstrates Sabarl linguistic sensitivity to these differing symbolic operations. I acknowledge a general debt here to her own interest in the construction of personhood, as well as to her observations on the present paper.

convergence is also understood, I think, as an entity prior to the idea of connection or relationship itself. The manner in which people are held to incorporate the substance of others, to share components of the self with others, to be otherwise separated from or attached to others, is assumed to rest on an infrastructure of beings capable of relating. Certainly in Fortes's analyses, the subject that is the meeting place for converging roles is already a moral agent and to this extent enjoys a measure of analytical autonomy.

One intention of this essay is to show how notions of persons as autonomous agents emerge less saliently in certain societies than in others. "Persons" are an artifact of the way in which relationships are handled through the possession and manipulation of things, and especially those things conceptualized as wealth and the subject of exchange transactions. I would describe the Hagen "person" not as a prior condition but as a product of kinship differentiation. Here differentiation between kin, as between the sexes, is taken as a given: exchanges work to produce persons and wealth. Wiru formulations, by contrast, precipitate a notion of substance but not of personhood in the Hagen sense: a flow of substance is a prior given, and exchanges work to differentiate maternal and paternal aspects of it.

I have a second reason for concluding in this way. Michelle Rosaldo and Jane Collier (1981) and Jane Collier (this volume) trace through the consequences of brideservice and bridewealth arrangements at marriage for the conceptualization of political equality and inequality. They show how notions of hierarchy inhere in ideas about gender. Sherry Ortner (1981: 359) specifically argues that "the sex/gender system . . . can be best understood in relation to the workings of the 'prestige system'" (and cf. Ortner and Whitehead 1981: 16). By prestige, she means "the system within which personal status is ascribed, achieved, advanced, and lost" (Ortner 1981: 359). Like "persons," the notion of "prestige" emerges in the highlands under certain special conditions. It is most salient in those systems that conceptualize an increment to identity. The composition of kinship identity is thus itself the springboard for the further structuring of prestige as an element conceptually subtracted from kinship, and gender differences provide a crucial axis for this structure.

The subtracted element assumes two characteristics: it is seen as separate from the sources of its production, and thus has value in itself (the ability to handle wealth as such becomes a measure of prestige); and, as a distinct unit, it can be added to a larger whole. The arithmetical metaphor (cf. Goody 1976: chap. 7) is appropriate for Hagen. Through numerical self-display on the ceremonial ground, clan identity is signaled not only by the (same-sex) unity of ancestral support but also by the fact that each donor of wealth holds separate (cross-sex) assets. The strength of the clan comes from the sum total of numerous wealth-bearing "persons," its prestige a function of this adding together. It follows that donor-recipient relationships in ceremonial exchange are structured on a cross-sex analogue.* Donors give part of themselves (wealth) to recipients. Yet there is no context collapse; they are not merged with the recipients but sustain their distinctiveness. This structure releases objects as a form of wealth separable from the actors. Indeed, Hageners refer to wealth items as "on the skin," and thus disposable between men.

Rubel and Rosman (1978) put Hagen and its Mae Enga neighbor,† with their extensive, politically large-scale, and prestige-oriented exchange institutions, on the end of a continuum of transformations that turn on the types of reciprocity set up by the exchanges of women and wealth. They elucidate the manner in which exchange partners become separate from affines, and ceremonial exchanges from marriage exchanges (1978: 320–23). My own concern has been with the mechanism through which objects themselves, vehicles for conceptualizing relations between persons, are attached to or constitutive of persons (how the symbolic equation is set up). The mechanism is the symbolization processes of gender. Thus we may interpret the whole Hagen ceremonial exchange sphere (transaction) as an act of detachment by Hagen men from the sphere of domesticity and kinship (production). Wiru men's ef-

---

*The aggressiveness of donors and subdued manner of recipients possibly reflect the fact that the donors are giving away only parts of themselves—their strength, their wealth—and thus also are expressing an identity that cannot be compromised by the transaction.

†It is important to note, however, that although there are many similarities between Hagen and Enga and Mendi ceremonial exchange, in the case of Tombema Enga (Feil 1981) and Mendi (Ryan 1969; Lederman 1980), a woman's distinctive participation in exchanges is reflected in the prominent transactional role the bride takes in respect to her bridewealth. Along with this, the Tombema Enga bridewealth is completely returnable by the bride's kin, and the whole series of transactions is more directly bound up with *tee* than Hagen bridewealth is with *moka* (Feil 1980).

forts to detach themselves from maternal kinship find expression in their possession of names that have public currency. Yet whereas Hagen men charge maleness with political meaning, Wiru men tie it back into kinship constructs that oppose paternity to maternal substance. Conversely, women in Hagen may have the character of wealth items—objects with a potential non-kinship referent —whereas Wiru women augment their kinship-based position by stimulating the exchange of goods that celebrate their motherhood.

Instead of asking about the relationship between kinship and politics, gender and prestige, I have tried to demonstrate how an idea of prestige detached from kinship is in fact generated from the kinship placement of the sexes. Wealth items behave differently, so to speak, in the two societies considered here. Where these objects stand for the augmentation of the name that gives identity to men and clans, prestige can be added insofar as people's assets are regarded as detachable. The partition of sisters and daughters from their male kin, in societies such as Hagen, embodies the possibility of detachment itself.

Men in Groups: A Reexamination of Patriliny in Lowland South America

Judith Shapiro

THE anthropological study of kinship has advanced considerably since the time when ideas about matriliny and patriliny were shaped by speculations about the evolution of relationships between the sexes. In the course of the journey, anthropologists became more sophisticated in distinguishing aspects of social organization that had been uncritically merged in earlier writings: descent, residence, kin classification, authority patterns. Concepts of matrilineality and patrilineality became part of an increasingly refined discourse that took descent systems as the key to analyzing social structure. At the same time, social anthropology moved away from what had been a central concern of nineteenth-century evolutionists—the respective positions of men and women in society.[*]

The current feminist movement has, however, brought this issue to the fore once again. Feminist scholars in the field of social anthropology (who have had to contend, to their embarrassment, with a new spate of cultural projections about matriarchy) have turned to the task of building upon and revising kinship studies in light of research about gender's role in social and cultural systems. Feminist concerns are reflected in the recent literature on descent, which includes more explicit consideration of the differential position of women and men in the various societies that have been the

[*]This argument was first developed in a paper entitled "Men in Groups: Descent and Sexual Differentiation in Lowland South America," presented in a symposium on descent in lowland South America at the 1975 American Anthropological Association meetings in San Francisco. I am grateful to Harriet Whitehead, Donald Hunderfund, Irving Goldman, Jane Collier, Sylvia Yanagisako, and Wyatt MacGaffey for their comments on earlier drafts of this paper.

subject of descent-oriented ethnographic analysis over the years (see, for example, Collier 1974; Schneider 1961).

Having made conceptual gains by distinguishing between descent structures and the respective social positions of women and men, anthropologists can now seek a more satisfactory integration of the two concerns. This paper argues that such an integration is particularly useful for understanding descent as it has been described in the ethnographic literature on lowland South America.

Descent Patterns in Lowland South America

Although ethnographers had for some time experienced difficulties in applying the analytic concepts of descent theory to South American societies, attention first focused on this problem in the 1970's (J. Shapiro 1972; J. Shapiro 1974; Taylor and Ramos 1975; Jackson 1975; Goldman 1976; Lizot 1977; Murphy 1979; J. C. Crocker 1979; Seeger 1980). In some respects, the discussion echoed concerns that students of Highland New Guinea societies had expressed about using models derived from research in Africa (Barnes 1962; Langness 1964; Lepervanche 1967–68). The view from South America, however, opened the debate still further, since descent there did not seem to be a basis for forming socially significant corporate groups and since genealogical reckoning extended minimally beyond the community of the living.

Discussions of descent in lowland South America have tended to focus on the absence of certain social structural features among societies of the region. In this article, I will argue for a more positive view of descent patterns in this area by analyzing descent in the context of relationships between the sexes. Taking such an approach will clarify, first of all, why descent in lowland South America is essentially a matter of patriliny.* The particular connections I will be investigating are those that link patriliny to marriage exchange and marital politics, to male solidarity and political factionalism, and to the ritual and cosmological expression of gender opposition.

I will draw my examples from groups whose patrilineal institu-

---

*Certain lowland societies—for example, the Bororo and some of the Northern Gê groups—were described as "matrilineal" in early ethnographic accounts, a label largely rejected in more recent scholarship (Lave 1971; J. C. Crocker 1977; J. C. Crocker 1979). For another view, see W. Crocker (1977, 1979).

tions have been the focus of special ethnographic attention, beginning with the societies of the Northwest Amazon, since the principle of descent is most clearly developed there. Although the applicability of descent concepts has been questioned for other lowland societies, patriliny in the Northwest Amazon presents enough of the classic and familiar features of descent, including a segmentary and hierarchical ordering of descent units, for the use of these concepts to be relatively unproblematic. Next, I will discuss several other lowland societies that have been characterized as patrilineal—the Mundurucú of the Upper Tapajós River; the Akwẽ-Shavante, a Gê-speaking people of central Brazil; and the Yanomamo* of southeastern Venezuela and northwestern Brazil—using the analysis of Northwest Amazon society as a basis for understanding the significance of patriliny in societies where it does not constitute as clear and pervasive a structural principle.

Northwest Amazon Society

Like other peoples of the tropical forest region of lowland South America, groups in the Northwest Amazon area are swidden horticulturalists who also depend for their subsistence on hunting, fishing, and foraging. Their strongly riverine orientation is reflected in the location and layout of their villages, in their travel and communication patterns, and in their cosmological beliefs. Individual communities are largely autonomous politically and economically but are linked to one another through exchange relationships, intermarriage, and ceremonial activities. The groups of the area, in fact, form a network of related peoples that must be viewed as a regional system. In the following account, I will therefore speak generally of "Northwest Amazon" society, drawing on a variety of sources and providing detailed information about groups for whom we have particularly rich ethnographic data on social organization—the Cubeo and Barasana (see Goldman 1963; Goldman 1976; Jackson 1974; Jackson 1976; Jackson 1977; Jackson 1983; Jackson 1984; C. Hugh-Jones 1979; S. Hugh-Jones 1979; Ärhem 1981).

Patrilineal descent operates at a variety of levels in Northwest

*The term "Yanomamo," a generally familiar rendering of the tribal name, here includes the various regional subgroups referred to in the ethnographic literature as Yąnomamö (or Yanõmami, Yanomam, and Sanumá).

Amazon society, from the local community—a longhouse inhabited by a group of male agnates and their families—to phratric units
composed of patrilineal sibs that observe a common rule of exogamy.* Because of the extensive scope of patrilineal descent reckoning, and the pattern of exogamy that results, communities are
linked together over a wide area. Marriage generally unites members of groups that speak different languages, since people who
share a language tend to view themselves as a single exogamous
descent group. There are some exceptions to this general rule, notably the Cubeo, whose marriage system is internally ordered
around three intermarrying subgroups (Goldman 1963: 136). Most
of the groups of the region, however, use language as an idiom for
common descent and marital exchange relations. Individuals are
multilingual, and kin ties are reflected in the sociolinguistic structure of the community (Sorensen 1967; Jackson 1974; Jackson 1983).

Northwest Amazon villages are organized around the principles
of patrilineal descent and sexual opposition. Postmarital residence
is virilocal, and a group of male agnates constitutes the social ar-
mature of the village. Inmarried women are outsiders who come
from various different villages and speak several different languages. In the round of daily events, women and men go separate
ways—men fish, hunt, or socialize together in the village, whereas
women spend most of their time working in their respective man-
ioc gardens.

The village is divided into zones for each sex. The front and back
of the multifamily longhouse on the river are male and female areas
respectively, an opposition that is heightened and formalized during ceremonial activities. Men and women enter and leave the
house through their respective doors. Enclosed compartments for
individual families are located along the side walls of the longhouse
toward the rear. At the back of the house is a women's kitchen area,
at the front, a male ceremonial plaza. Women and men generally
use different parts of the river for their bathing and washing; in the
Barasana village, the women's port is on a small stream reached
from the back of the house, whereas the men's port is on the main
river out front. A longhouse is always oriented toward the river, a
male zone not only because men fish in it but because rivers are as-

---

*I will use the ethnographic present throughout, as do my sources, when speak-
ing of "traditional" institutions. This decision seems appropriate in light of my attempt to explore very general social patterns of long standing in the region.

sociated with the origin of patrilineal descent groups and the mythic travels of patrilineal ancestors. Sacred musical instruments belonging to the descent group are kept hidden at the river's edge (Goldman 1963: 28–33; C. Hugh-Jones 1979: 40–53).

The hierarchical structuring of patrilineal descent units, from the local community to more inclusive agnatic categories, varies some-what within the Northwest Amazon region. The Cubeo have been described as having lineages, sibs, and phratries. Phratries, which are unnamed, are defined as riverine territorial units. Sibs, which are named, are local units that constitute the basic segment of Cu-beo society (Goldman 1963: 26). Lineages are subunits of sibs and are themselves incipient sibs. These different levels of patriliny re-flect a temporal process of segmentation. The Cubeo believe that what is now a phratry was once a single longhouse unit. Ideally, each phratry is supposed to contain five sibs, representing the fin-gers of one hand, which is paired with a matching hand of affinal sibs. Each sib should similarly have five fraternal descent lines, since sib and phratry structure are supposed to parallel one another (Goldman 1976: 289).

Among the Barasana, the major levels of patrilineal organization have been designated by the terms "phratry," "exogamous group," "sib," and "local descent group." An exogamous group is a set of sibs that occupies a continuous territory; phratries are composed of exogamous groups that believe themselves to be related by ties of descent, but do not occupy a continuous area. Phratries represent the widest effective range of patrilineal descent reckoning and, like all other patrilineal groupings in the Northwest Amazon, observe a rule of exogamy. Sibs are the named units of the Barasana descent system. The term "local descent group" is used to designate the unnamed group of close agnates that form the core of a longhouse population (C. Hugh-Jones 1979: 15–22). Christine Hugh-Jones refrains from using the term "lineage" with reference to the Bara-sana, as does Jean Jackson in her general accounts of Northwest Amazon society.

Genealogical reckoning is not of great concern in these societies. Among both the Cubeo and Barasana, there is a gap between the shallow genealogies that indicate relationships among the living and the mythic genealogies of the earliest human groups, which serve as charters for sib identity and may be open to multiple inter-pretations (Goldman 1963: 90, 97; Goldman 1976: 290; C. Hugh-

Jones 1979: 39). A sib's connection to its ancestors does not depend
on establishing, or even fabricating, genealogical links; sib identity
and continuity is reckoned more in terms of geographical location
and the possession of ritual objects. What matters, as far as descent
is concerned, is the general belief that the living members of a sib
are tied to their remote male ancestors by an unbroken line of kinship through men.

Genealogical truncation and an attendant collapsing of past and
present is revealed in naming practices. Each sib possesses a stock
of names that can be used only for its members. Children receive
the names of deceased patrilineal relatives of the grandparental
generation (Goldman 1963: 92; C. Hugh-Jones 1979: 133). This practice inhibits the accumulation of genealogical knowledge (C. Hugh-
Jones 1979: 39). The result is a rapid recycling of sib identities that
foreshortens the historical process.

The lack of genealogical concern among peoples of the Northwest Amazon is tied to their focus on agnatic sibling ties, rather
than father-son ties (C. Hugh-Jones 1979: 39; Goldman 1963: 114;
see also Shapiro and Kensinger 1985). Male sibling groups constitute the core of local communities, form the focus of historical and
mythical accounts, and provide a root metaphor for social solidarity. Sibs within a phratry are believed to be descended from a single
group of brothers, and segmentation at all levels of the system is
similarly conceptualized.

The ranking of the male sibling set by age provides a model for
the hierarchical ranking of all descent units. It is expressed within
the longhouse community in the general belief that the headman
should ideally be the oldest of a group of brothers.* The hierarchical
ordering of sibs reflects the birth order of their respective ancestors
and, hence, the order in which human groups originated. The Cubeo and Barasana, like other Northwest Amazon peoples, trace
their beginnings to proto-ancestral anacondas who traveled along
the rivers these groups presently inhabit and stopped at various
sites to engender human communities. The phratry itself is likened
to an anaconda; its head, associated with the higher-ranking sibs,

---

*An interesting inversion of this structural principle occurs at the local level of
the patrilineal descent organization of the Arawakan-speaking Wakuénai of the
Northwest Amazon. There the youngest member of the sibling set is expected to
achieve the highest status. This theme is also reflected in Wakuénai mythology (Hill
1985).

is pictured at the mouth of the river and its tail at the headwaters, where lower-ranking sibs live (Goldman 1976: 289; C. Hugh-Jones 1979: 33–38).

Sib ranking is thus expressed in both spatial and temporal terms. Among the Barasana, it is also associated with a hierarchy of specialized male roles. The five sibs into which Barasana society is organized, recalling the quinary structure of Cubeo phratries noted above, correspond to a sequence of roles: the chief at the top, followed by chanter/dancer, warrior, shaman, and, finally, servant (C. Hugh-Jones 1979: 27–30, 54–64). The system, which ideally regulates the roles of brothers as well as sibs, does not govern actual social life, and its significance in the past is difficult to determine. It functions primarily as a compelling ideological model of organic solidarity among sib groups. No similarly elaborate complex has been reported for any other Northwest Amazon group, although there is fragmentary evidence for its existence elsewhere (C. Hugh-Jones 1979: 27). Goldman reports that high rank accords with ritual privilege and leadership among the Cubeo and that low-ranking lineages within a sib are viewed as servants (1976: 289). Among both the Cubeo and Barasana, gender serves as a metaphor for these systems of ranking; the servant status implies doing the menial work of women, and the male/female opposition more generally corresponds to the opposition between higher and lower things.

The elaborate system of ranking in Northwest Amazon patrilineal ideology does not place descent groups in any significant hierarchy of power or authority in actual social life, at least during the period in which these groups have been studied. Relationships between local communities, and between the men of individual communities, are essentially egalitarian. This disparity has been commented upon by ethnographers of the region, and there has been some speculation about the possible sociopolitical significance of ranking in the past (Goldman 1963: 98–100; C. Hugh-Jones 1979: 105–6, 275–76; Jackson 1983: 75–76). In contemporary Northwest Amazon societies, rank often figures in the system of marriage preferences, not necessarily in practice, but in the stated ideal that marriage partners should belong to groups of comparable rank within their respective sib systems.

The major significance of the hierarchical descent model, however, seems to be its role in linking social identity to the cosmological order. As is common among South American peoples, the tie between everyday life and the mythic past is a particularly close one; features of the landscape, the physical layout of villages and houses, and the pattern of social ties correspond to cosmological notions of the origins of human society and its relationship to other living beings and to the environment. These relationships are dramatized in the major rituals involving patrilineal descent groups, during which the social space of daily life is transformed into the cosmic space of ancestral beings.

If patrilineal descent in the Northwest Amazon can be said to constitute a political system, the relationships of power and authority it regulates are not those between descent groups, but those between the sexes. Rituals play a central role in this political process, linking the principle of patriliny to the ordering of men's and women's respective roles in society. We can see how this operates by examining briefly some of the major ceremonial activities of the Cubeo and Barasana.

Among both groups, sib membership is ritualized in secret male cult activities that serve to dramatize social boundaries between the sexes and to express symbolically their relationship to one another. In the course of these rituals, ancestral sib spirits are contacted , and boys are initiated into the community of adult men. The ancestral spirits are identified with sacred flutes and trumpets that are kept hidden from women and children. As is common in other South American societies, and elsewhere in the world as well, the male cult is associated with a myth that recounts a time when women owned the sacred instruments. The myth provides a scenario of what social life was (would be) like when (if) gender roles were reversed; it chronicles men's success in seizing control of the instruments, and thereby achieving their culturally appropriate superiority over women (see Bamberger 1974; Murphy 1959; Murphy and Murphy 1974).

The secrecy of the men's cult is protected by sanctions that reinforce gender-appropriate behavior, ensure the reproductive process, and make men the ostensible guardians of the system. Women who violate this secrecy are said to become sexually licentious, overly curious, and talkative—beliefs that reflect male fears of how women would behave if not kept under control. According to the Barasana, women who look upon the sacred flutes and trumpets die in childbirth. Some versions of the cult myth explain the menstrual cycle itself as a consequence of the men's forcing the flutes and trumpets up the women's vaginas after taking the instruments over from them. Corporate phallic aggression also enforces cult secrecy, since the usual punishment for any woman who should happen to see the instruments is gang rape. Some Cubeo men said that such a woman should be put to death by sorcery to keep her from revealing the secrets to other women (Goldman 1963: 193–94; S. Hugh-Jones 1979: 129–32).

A particularly rich account of sib/male cult rites appears in Stephen Hugh-Jones's 1979 study of Barasana ritual and cosmology. The major part of his analysis focuses on an initiation rite called *He wi*, or "*He* House," which involves bringing the sacred flutes and trumpets to the longhouse to be shown to young boys for the first time. The term *He* refers to the sacred instruments and, more generally, to ancestral times and the spirit world. The *He* instruments embody sib ancestors who are at once human and associated with various animal spirits. The *He* House ceremony operates to negate the effects of time on the patrilineal descent system—the continuing process of segmentation that makes relations between men more distant and takes them ever farther from their common origins—by bringing men into direct contact with their original ancestors. Cult initiates are adopted directly by the founding ancestral spirits; this, as the Barasana say, "squashes the pile" of generations (S. Hugh-Jones 1979: 249). As men participate in the cult over the years, they develop deeper relationships with the most remote of their mythic ancestors.

The rites that introduce Barasana boys to the *He* spirits also socialize them into the male role, instilling in them the appropriate qualities of masculinity. Although the *He* are sib spirits, the fact that initiation ceremonies need not be restricted to members of a single sib indicates that the initiates are being accepted into a more broadly defined male community. The activities of the *He* House express the structure of this male social world, invoking the principles of age grading, birth order, and the system of specialized male roles outlined above.

During the period of the *He* House ceremony, special care is taken to ensure separation of the sexes. A screen is set up between the male and female zones of the house, and the women are obligated to flee when the flutes and trumpets are brought inside. In addition to playing the crucial role of outsiders, women also serve

as auxiliaries at various points in the proceedings. They are, moreover, symbolically present even when physically absent: one of the
most important ritual objects, a gourd full of beeswax, is analyzed
by Stephen Hugh-Jones as a female symbol balancing the male
symbols of the flutes and trumpets. Male initiates and the shamans
who lead the *He* House ceremonies are symbolically likened to
menstruating women. In general, the ritual symbolism reveals a
central concern with the respective sexuality and reproductive
powers of men and women. As is the case in many other societies,
the considerable powers attributed to women are invoked and manipulated in ritual activity from which women themselves are
excluded.

The Barasana rituals express both complementarity and hierarchy between the sexes. They reflect a not unfamiliar contrast between the natural advantages of women and the social superiority
of men. Women possess a natural immortality based on their ability
to menstruate, which is thought of as an internal skin-shedding
leading to renewal; they are able to replace themselves by giving
birth to children. The immortality of men is achieved on the social
plane, through sib rituals. In the ritual process of asserting control
over the means of social reproduction, men manipulate symbols
that represent women's sexual functions. As Christine Hugh-Jones
puts it, "The men appropriate the ultimate female powers of sexual
reproduction for themselves and so maintain their control over
women" (1979: 155). This male appropriation of powers believed to
be female is also seen in the figure of the shaman, who officiates at
the *He* House ceremony and who plays a central role in Barasana
life. Although all shamans are men, myth holds that the first one
was a woman (S. Hugh-Jones 1979: 25).

The Cubeo flute and trumpet cult, as described by Irving Goldman, parallels the main features of the Barasana ritual: the vener-
ation of instruments that have ancestral significance and are associated with male potency and fertility; the initiation of boys, who
need not be members of the host village's sib, into a male cult; and
an emphasis on opposition between the sexes (Goldman 1963: 190–
201). Other ceremonial events described by Goldman further illustrate how the ritualized expression of sib relationships is subsumed
within a general dramatization of male/female opposition and
symbolic representations of sexuality. One such event is the drink-
ing party, which brings together different sibs of the same phratry.

Some phases of the proceedings emphasize sib identity; others downplay sib distinctions in favor of the wider solidarity of the male group. Goldman analyzes the difference between men's and women's roles in the ritual's various dances as an opposition between an ordered world of men's social bonds and a disordered, individualistic, and spontaneously emotional world of women. He sees the rhythm and progression of the dances as a metaphor for sexual intercourse (Goldman 1963: 202–18).

Similar features characterize Cubeo mourning ceremonies, which are generally phratric observances in which various sib groups come to offer condolences. In Goldman's view, the single main theme of the mourning ceremony is the sexual interplay between men and women. At one point in the sequence of events, male dancers form groups on the men's side of the house and then alternately penetrate and withdraw from the women's section, passing through a fence constructed to separate them. Throughout the activities of the mourning ceremony, as Goldman describes them, ritually structured and controlled behavior on the part of the men contrasts with spontaneous, reactive, and raucously emotional behavior on the part of the women. The ceremony culminates in an orgiastic free-for-all, in which couples leave the house to engage in sexual activity in the bush, returning to continue dancing and to find new partners (Goldman 1963: 219–52).

In the various Northwest Amazon rituals described above, aggressive interplay between the sexes alternates with all-male activities from which women are excluded. According to Stephen Hugh-Jones, when women are forced to flee the longhouse, "an exclusively male society is brought about, just as in the ancestral times there were no women" (S. Hugh-Jones 1979: 153). Both Christine and Stephen Hugh-Jones argue that Barasana rituals involve the symbolic appropriation by men of women's generative and reproductive powers. Irving Goldman takes a different view, maintaining that male cultism is based on the scrupulous separation between male and female generative powers, this being the explanation for the ritual exclusion of women. In Goldman's analysis, the male community is appropriating the vital powers not of women, but of nature and the nonhuman world in the service of a "collective and asexual [reproductive] process that is regulated by ancestors" (Goldman 1976: 291). These respective interpretations are perhaps best seen as operating on two different levels, Goldman's being closer to explicit Cubeo ideology and the Hugh-Joneses' situated at a critical distance from the participants' own perception of their practice.

Myths of a world without women and myths of gender inversion, which also figure in Northwest Amazon male cults, as we have seen above, recur widely in the gender ideologies of other societies. In this case, they are particularly effective symbolic vehicles for representing and affirming the descent/gender system, as well as for exploring its inherent conflicts.

A set of related themes emerges from the foregoing description of Northwest Amazon patriliny. For one thing, although it is common for exogamy to be a significant defining feature of descent units, it is particularly central in this case. In the Northwest Amazon—and, as we will see, in other lowland societies—patriliny operates within a social system the focus of which is marital exchange. Membership in patrilineal descent units gives men and women their respective places in a regional system of affinally related groups. One might, in fact, say it gives them their opposed places. As we saw, postmarital residence is generally virilocal, and the local community is ideally formed around a group of male agnates. Women's clear and ongoing identification with their natal descent groups, a factor that various ethnographers of the region emphasize, also entails their differentiation from members of the patrilineal groups into which they marry. The general identification of descent groups with language groups, and the attendant rule of language group exogamy, makes the position of women as outsiders even more marked. The solidarity of the descent group tends to merge with the solidarity of the male group, each serving to impart meaning to the other. In cosmological terms, patriliny provides the model of a social universe constructed out of relationships among men.

This general picture of Northwest Amazon patriliny helps bring into focus patterns of patriliny in other lowland societies. To explore these patterns, I will now consider the ethnographic literature on three groups that are relatively well known to the general anthropological community: the Mundurucú, as described by Robert Murphy (1956, 1957, 1959, 1960, 1979) and Yolanda Murphy (Murphy and Murphy 1974); the Akwẽ-Shavante, as described by David Maybury-Lewis (1967, 1971); and the Yanomamo, as described by a number of ethnographers (Chagnon 1968; Chagnon

1974; Chagnon 1979a; Chagnon 1979b; J. Shapiro 1972; J. Shapiro 1974; Taylor 1974; Taylor 1977; Taylor 1981; Ramos 1972; Ramos 1973; Taylor and Ramos 1975; Ramos and Albert 1977; Lizot 1977). The sources I will be using were written at different points in the past three decades and reflect changes in the way ethnographers have approached the description and analysis of social organization in the region. Most relevant to our present purposes is that some of the earlier writings, particularly those on the Akwē-Shavante and Yanomamo, make use of the standard analytic vocabulary of descent theory; later work by the same authors largely abandons that vocabulary as inappropriate. The very difficulties encountered in the more traditional social anthropological accounts, however, are themselves illuminating. By seeing what the problems have been, and by exploring parallels with the Northwest Amazon case outlined above, we can arrive at some general view of the context and meaning of patriliny in lowland South America.

Mundurucú Society

Among the Mundurucú, patriliny is primarily associated with marital exchange patterns and ceremonial life. Named patrilineal moieties regulate marriage and govern other kinds of reciprocal relations as well, particularly those of a ritual nature. Moieties are divided into clans, each having an ancestral spirit that bears the name of an animal, plant, bird, or fish that serves as an eponym for the clan. There seems to be no ideology of descent linking clan members to the "great ancestors" that give them their name (Murphy 1960: 74–75). Clan exogamy is subsumed within the wider division between exogamous moieties, although sexual relations with a fellow clansperson is deemed a more serious infringement than sexual relations with other members of one's own moiety. Important ritual relations between clans, notably the obligation that members of certain clans perform burial services for members of certain other clans, involve clans of opposite moieties and are ordered within a more comprehensive dualistic structure (Murphy 1960: 72).

Mundurucú clans have no corporate identity and no function in organizing social activities. They serve as a mode of social categorization, since clan affiliation is expressed in the Mundurucú naming system (Murphy 1960: 83). The major significance of clanship is as an idiom for social and ceremonial solidarity between men. Since postmarital residence is uxorilocal, bonds of common clanship link men of different local communities. Within the village, clans are associated with a men's cult focused around a set of sacred flutes. These flutes are kept hidden in the men's house, a residence for all the adult males of the village. The flutes are believed to be inhabited by the ancestral clan spirit of the man who made them and hence to belong in some sense to that clan. It is, however, village men, regardless of moiety and clan affiliation, who play the flutes and provide the ritual offerings of food that they require, and it is the village rather than the clan that derives the benefits accruing from these observances (Murphy 1960: 75–76).

From the women's point of view, the secrecy surrounding the men's cult results in a homogenization of the male community that has been aptly described as follows in a general discussion of such cults: "The sanctions against intrusion screen out the men as brothers, husbands, and fathers, and present them as anonymous members of the opposite sex" (Gregor 1979: 268). From the men's point of view, the Mundurucú cult myths appear to involve the cultural fantasy of a world without women (Nadelson 1981), a theme encountered in the Northwest Amazon as well. Once again, the men's cult is associated with a role reversal myth according to which women once possessed the sacred and valued instruments, a myth that expresses the power of women as it justifies the dominance of men. Among the Mundurucú, as in the Northwest Amazon, women who violate the secrecy of the men's cult are subject to gang rape, which is also the punishment for other departures from gender-appropriate behavior, such as sexual promiscuity or failure to recognize the authority of male relatives. The solidarity of the male group in punishing such violations is underlined by the fact that Mundurucú men participate in a gang rape regardless of their clan ties to the victim (Murphy 1960: 109).

In both Mundurucú and Northwest Amazon society, then, a secret men's cult, associated to varying degrees with an ideology of patriliny, serves to express the solidarity of the male community and to emphasize the social boundary between the sexes. In the Northwest Amazon, patriliny, male cultism, and patterns of sexual opposition come together in the role of descent in local group organization; in the Mundurucú case, patrilineal clan relationships are subordinated to the wider local community of males in a village, a process in which the men's cult plays a central role. The major exception to this pattern, and an important source of division within the Mundurucú male community, is the headman's ability to depart from the general norms of uxorilocal postmarital residence. By remaining in his own village, and getting some of his closest kinsmen to do the same, a headman can build up an agnatic faction, which he will commonly seek to perpetuate by passing leadership on to his son.

Akwẽ-Shavante Society

Patrilineal descent in Akwẽ-Shavante society has been described as operating on two levels. At one level, there are three patriclans, whose founders are said to have come out of the ground "in the very beginnning when there was nothing" (Maybury-Lewis 1967: 165). Men symbolize their clan membership through distinctive body paint designs worn on ceremonial occasions. Clans are exogamous, although there is some difference between Eastern and Western Shavante on this point; among the latter, two of the three clans form a single exogamous group, yielding a moiety system of marriage regulation. Dual opposition is, however, a feature of the clan system for all Shavante since the distinction between one's own clan members and all others is expressed in a "we/they" dichotomy that is also fundamental to the semantics of the Shavante kin terminological system (Maybury-Lewis 1967: 167). Although the Shavante, like other Gê groups, have a rule of uxorilocal postmarital residence, there is nonetheless a tendency for clans to be localized within a village since men of the same clan seek to marry into the same house or neighboring houses. Clan locations within the village change over time as men move from natal to affinal households.

The other level of patrilineal descent organization in Shavante life is what Maybury-Lewis calls the "lineage," fellow clansmen who form the core of a political faction within the village. Although Maybury-Lewis refers to lineages as "corporate groups" (1967: 169), this seems to mean only that their members side with one another when disputes arise. Shavante lineages do not show any continuity over time, but rise and fall in accordance with the relatively volatile and factionalized politics of village life. The point of articulation between these two levels of patriliny—the clans, which represent divisions established in mythic times, and the lineages, which are genealogically shallow clusters of patrikin that one analyst has described as "contingent groups of agnates" (W. Shapiro 1971: 65)—is that common clanship seems to serve as a moral idiom for factional solidarity (Maybury-Lewis 1967: 168).

Aside from its role in regulating marriage, patriliny serves essentially to organize male ceremonial and political activity. As Maybury-Lewis points out, women have a tangential relationship to the patrilineal units of Akwē-Shavante society (1967: 104, 303). In his view, Shavante patriliny is one variation on the Gê theme of male communal solidarity; among other Gê peoples, other principles serve to organize men into groups and thereby to oppose the "public" world of men to the domestic world of women (1971: 386).

Yanomamo Society

The Yanomamo have been described by a number of ethnographers who have lived in different areas of Yanomamoland, notably by Napoleon Chagnon, whose accounts are the most extensive and best known. I will first consider information on patriliny among the groups Chagnon studied and then compare material on other Yanomamo groups.

In his early studies, Chagnon speaks of patrilineal descent among the Yanomamo in terms of both lineages and local descent groups (1968: 65–70). Lineages are dispersed patrilineal units of varying scope defined primarily by exogamy and by members' interest in keeping track of their relationships to one another. Local descent groups are groups of agnates residing together in the same village. Yanomamo postmarital residence is generally virilocal, although brideservice may take a man away from his village for some time. Yanomamo villages are usually composed of intermarried kin groups, and affinal relationships play an important role in the organization of community life.

Chagnon describes the local descent group as "corporate" largely because of its role in marital exchange; women members of the descent group constitute its "estate." Chagnon is clearly stretching the concept of an estate in order to apply a traditional corporate descent model to Yanomamo society. He also finds it necessary to modify the definition of a local descent group by noting that Yanomamo local descent groups have a depth of only two, as opposed to three, generations (Chagnon 1968: 68). This change signals the difficulty in borrowing a vocabulary in which group perpetuity and the articulation of minimal lineage units into wider ones are key structural features (J. Shapiro 1972: 100).

In his later writings, Chagnon no longer refers to any Yanomamo patrilineal groups as corporate. His view of the significance of local agnatic groups in Yanomamo marital arrangements has shifted from the collective management of female resources—in fact, marital negotiations do not involve the local group of agnates acting as a unit—to the connection between membership in a powerful agnatic faction and success in acquiring wives. Both Chagnon and Jacques Lizot, another ethnographer who has done research in the same general area, use the term "lineage" for all levels of patrilineal grouping (Chagnon 1979a; Chagnon 1979b; Lizot 1977). According to Lizot, the term "corporate" is not appropriate to any level of Yanomamo patriliny (1977: 62). Lineages are not named. For the sake of convenience, Chagnon commonly labels them according to well-known headmen who serve as points of origin in the tracing of agnatic relations.

The term the Yanomamo use to designate lineages is *mashi*, or "species" (Chagnon 1968: 61; Chagnon 1974: 56; Lizot 1977: 59–60). Lizot provides a valuable discussion of the polysemous nature of this term. He notes that the term is used first and foremost to designate all siblings and parallel cousins of the same sex as ego. This meaning corresponds to the bilateral kin/affine distinction that orders the Yanomamo Dravidian-type kin classification, and at the same time divides the class of relatives along sex lines. The term's usage shows a patrilateral skewing, since it most commonly designates relationships between male agnates. In this first sense of the term, *mashi* refers to kin of the same generation, which raises again the point of the relative salience of sibling relationships.

The term *mashi* is also used to refer to a wider set of patrilineally related kinsmen; this use, according to Lizot, designates a "lineage." Lizot reports that such agnatic reckoning never extends beyond five generations and is generally more restricted than that (1977: 59). The reckoning of patrilineal relationships reflects political strategies and follows the vicissitudes of factional and intervillage alliances (Chagnon 1974: 69–70, 75). Finally, the term *mashi* is used to designate a still wider, and apparently bilateral, sphere of stipulated kin relations.

Yanomamo groups to the southeast do not show the same features of patrilineal organization described by Chagnon and Lizot (J. Shapiro 1972; Ramos and Albert 1977). Although the reckoning of kin ties does reflect some patrilateral skewing, agnation does not yield socially significant categories, nor do political factions crystallize around groups of agnates.

Yet another pattern is found among the Sanumá subgroup in the northernmost part of Yanomamoland, who have been described as having a formal set of named patrilineal units, including both lineages and sibs. Sanumá sibs, which are exogamous, are described as "dispersed patrilineal descent categories, with no recognition of a common ancestor and no clear explanation of their names" (Taylor 1977: 94).* Lineages are groups of agnates with a known common ancestor, a common name, a strict rule of exogamy, a genealogical depth of at least three generations, current or recent localization in a particular village, and a politically important nucleus (Ramos 1977: 75). Since patrilateral male relatives are commonly dispersed—brothers may go their separate ways upon the death of their father, and those who marry outside the village may end up residing uxorilocally for an indefinite period—only about half of the Sanumá population belong to lineages (Ramos 1972: 74). There is no indication that lineages play any significant role in village affairs, although lineage membership has been reported to determine participation in ritualized dueling and the observance of food taboos (Taylor 1977; Taylor 1981).

According to Ramos, whose reseach has focused on Sanumá social structure, neither sibs nor lineages should be characterized as corporate groups (Ramos and Albert 1977: 74–75). In her early work (1972), Ramos had attempted to apply the structural/jural model of descent theory to an analysis of Sanumá society, but later concluded that such a model was inappropriate. Patrilineality should rather be seen as "a native ideology manifested in forms of classification and modes of internal social differentiation" (Ramos 1977: 75).

Patterns of patriliny among Yanomamo subgroups essentially take two forms. In the area of Yanomamoland where villages are large, raiding and feuding more intense, and intervillage political alliances well developed, agnatic ties emerge as a basis for factional alignment. A similar association between agnation and factional

---

*Chagnon (1979b: 385) suggests that what have been reported as sib names may actually be names of old village sites.

politics has been reported for the Sanumá, but this relatively small population living in the shadow of more powerful Carib-speaking neighbors exhibits a different pattern of patriliny. Here, where patrifiliative ties seem to have become more formalized, they serve primarily as a basis for social classification.

Conclusion

This survey of descent patterns from the Northwest Amazon to other lowland South American societies has encompassed social systems so unlike those to which descent theory has been productively applied that the comparative sociologist might simply conclude that there is little point in speaking about descent in these contexts at all. The particular concern with descent's role in the formation and operation of corporate groups with significant economic and political functions—a concern that first restricted descent theory to unilineal systems but later led to its extension to cognatic systems with similar functional characteristics—largely rules out discussion of lowland South America. In speaking of "patriliny" in the societies described above, then, we would be using the term in a minimal sense to indicate the presence of culturally significant, sociocentric, ancestor-focused categories based on patrifiliative ties.

Such a definition of patriliny might encourage very broad cross-cultural use of the term, but it would do little to specify the distinctive features of the sociocultural systems to which the term could be applied. Terms that define minimally are useful and, no doubt, necessary in building up a general analytic language for ethnographic description. Their function in comparative analysis, however, is less to group societies into common "types" than to provide a basis for their comparison. For example, inquiries into lowland South American patriliny can serve as a point of departure for exploring the general ways in which societies in this part of the world differ from societies in other regions.*

The other side of such a contrastive approach is to underline sim-

---

*Scheffler's (1966) attempt to disentangle the various analytic distinctions and theoretical concerns found in the literature on descent continues to be a particularly useful contribution to comparative discussion. For a general discussion of the relationship between comparative definitions and culture-specific categories, using as an example the cross-cultural definition of marriage, see J. Shapiro (1984).

ilarities among lowland societies that show varying degrees of patrilineal organization, relating these, in turn, to societies with a more bilateral ordering of kin relations. The point here is similar to the one made by Goody when he argued against attributing too much importance to the difference among patrilineal, matrilineal, and double descent systems in Africa, choosing instead to emphasize their similarities and to draw more significant contrasts with European and Asian societies (Goody 1973; Goody 1976). In the case at hand, the fundamental similarities among lowland South American societies include certain dominant and recurrent patterns of marital exchange and the centrality of gender as a social structural principle.

Throughout the region, one finds systems of marriage exchange consonant with a generally Dravidian pattern of relationship classification (Rivière 1977; J. Shapiro 1984). Direct, symmetrical exchange, embracing bilateral cross-cousin marriage, is the most common pattern. Many Northwest Amazon societies show a special preference for patrilateral cross-cousin marriage, which links groups in two successive generations through the women that move back and forth between them (Jackson 1977; Jackson 1984). The Akwē-Shavante eschew direct marital exchange between sibling sets in order to preserve a hierarchical relationship between a wife's brother and a sister's husband, the former being superior to the latter (Maybury-Lewis 1967: 223–26).

In the context of marriage rules and marriage exchange, patrilineal constructs appear as one way in which the "elementary structures" of South American kinship are expressed; another revolves around the Dravidian bifurcation of kin relationships within cognatic kindreds. In some cases—for example, the Yanomamo—one can find a merging of the two patterns, as noted above. Patrilineal or patrifiliative ties take on much of their significance in the context of affinity. Among the Mundurucú and Akwē-Shavante, they are part of dualistic structures, in the former case, a system of moiety reciprocity and, in the latter, a "we/they" opposition in which the solidarity of clan ties is ideologically opposed to the tension and distance of affinal relationships (Maybury-Lewis 1967: 237–39). In the Northwest Amazon, the descent/language group defines its own unity and identity with reference to other similar groups to which it is linked through the regional system of marital exchange.

The role of affinity in lowland South American societies, and its implications for how we interpret patterns of patriliny in the region, can also be illuminated by the general model of brideservice societies proposed by Collier and Rosaldo (1981). Their discussion focuses on how male social adulthood is defined through marriage and on how relationships among men depend upon the processes of acquiring and holding on to wives. Their view of the essentially sexual or marital nature of politics in certain societies is particularly appropriate to the Yanomamo. The major theme in Chagnon's various writings on Yanomamo political life is the extent to which alliance formation and raiding patterns revolve around the pursuit of wives and demonstrations of the local male group's effectiveness in defending its claims to women. This, then, is the context for understanding the activities of agnatically based factions in Yanomamo society. We may contrast the importance of women as wives in such a system with their importance as mothers in societies where their value as the source of new descent group members is emphasized.

The association between agnatic ties and political factions also appears in the Akwẽ-Shavante case. Shavante factionalism, however, does not appear to be related to marital politics. The connection between patrilaterally based factionalism and marriage lies rather in how alignments are ideologized in terms of the opposition between kin (or clan) and affine. The basis for factional disputes in Shavante life remains somewhat elusive in Maybury-Lewis's account; he notes that "it is easier to explain who fights among the Shavante than to give a clear idea of what they are fighting about" and ultimately treats factionalism as an irreducible principle of Shavante life (1967: 179, 307). What we may note for the purposes of the present discussion is that an analysis of the role of patriliny in Akwẽ-Shavante life turns largely on an analysis of men's political factions.

As noted above, Maybury-Lewis ultimately came to emphasize the significance of patriliny as one of several modes of men's organization in Gê societies. In the Yanomamo case, it appears as one of two axes of male solidarity, the other being the tie between actual or potential brothers-in-law, which serves as the paradigm for relations of reciprocity and exchange (Chagnon 1968; J. Shapiro 1972; J. Shapiro 1974). We have seen how, in the Northwest Amazon and among the Mundurucú, patrilineal ties become identified with or submerged within the wider male community.

Given the role of gender in structuring the social systems of lowland South America, kinship studies that view differences between female and male activities as a background to sociological analysis or that view kinship and gender as two distinct domains particularly miss the point. To build analysis on the opposition between women and men, as Yolanda and Robert Murphy do in their various studies of the Mundurucú, for example, seems so obvious an approach that we may tend to take it for granted. In the Murphys' analyses, the focus has been on residential segregation, the organization of men's and women's labor, and the extent to which day-to-day socializing occurs among members of the same sex. The ritualization of male/female opposition, particularly in men's cult activities, has been explained in terms of the degree to which women and men form distinct social groups (Murphy 1959).

Another angle on the meaning of men's cults and their relationship to the ordering of male-female relationships is suggested by Collier and Rosaldo's analysis of marital politics cited above. An ideological model of the social universe in which men are seen as the reproducers of the social order seems to emerge from the male ritual activity described here; such a model corresponds to the role of men—men grouped into patrilineal descent units where these figure in the marriage system—as the dominant negotiators of affinal exchanges. As Collier and Rosaldo put it: "Marriage *is* what creates lasting bonds, and insofar as men 'make marriages,' the social order that exists stands as a proof that men, in fact, are endowed with an extraordinary and valuable sort of force" (1981: 301).

In this article, I have explored the articulation between patriliny and the ordering of male-female relationships with particular reference to societies of lowland South America. Let me conclude by noting that ethnographers of another region—Highland New Guinea—have been drawing attention to such an articulation as well. Patriliny in New Guinea presents a different picture from the one described above in that it serves as the ideology, if not the basis for recruitment, of groups that have significant corporate properties. At the same time, the association between patriliny and gender has been emerging clearly in recent ethnographic studies, which have included particularly rich analyses of women's and men's respective positions in society and have explored in considerable symbolic depth the cultural structuring of gender oppositions. Generalizing from this literature, Daryll Feil observes that patrilineal clans are associated with ideologies of maleness and primarily concern relationships among men; he refers to patrilineal descent groups as "androcentric corporations" (Feil 1984: 51).

In moving beyond a focus on patriliny in their analyses of Highland New Guinea social organization, ethnographers of the region are moving beyond, among other things, a focus on the world of men's relationships. The complementary task, one that I have taken up here, is to analyze male-centered social institutions in a way that makes their relationship to gender explicit, rather than to treat them uncritically as structuring principles of society as a whole. In this ethnographic instance, the effect of feminism on kinship theory has been to turn a study of descent into a contribution to what we might, in a reversal of the usual pattern of gender markedness, call "men's studies."

Descent and Sources of Contradiction in Representations of Women and Kinship

Maurice Bloch

THE representation of femininity in many cultures is often elusive and contradictory. Let us consider Sherry Ortner's thesis (1974) that in all cultures women are symbolically associated with nature and men with culture and, further, that this contrast explains the universal cultural devaluation of key aspects of womanhood. Whether an anthropologist decides that any particular case does or does not bear out this thesis almost always seems arbitrary. On the one hand, it is true that nearly all cultures symbolically associate women with uncontrolled biological processes and that this particularly close association is used to rationalize female subordination in one context or another. On the other hand, it is possible to show that, often in the very same cultures, women are also associated with the home, the very heart of "the domestic," which then becomes a feminine symbol of illegitimate power and division opposed to the masculine symbol of clean, unified, undomesticated wilderness (see Strathern 1980; Gillison 1980; Llewellyn-Davies 1981 on the difficulty of applying such notions). This type of contradiction extends to, or perhaps originates in, the field of kinship, where women are often seen as both the source and the destroyer.*

Such contradictions are more than a mere embarrassment to anthropologists. They are so frequent and central that they are more characteristic of the representations of women than a simple association with any particular side of an antithesis. There is therefore something wrong with theoretical approaches that cannot accommodate such contradictions. The problem is rather to suggest a framework that explains the systematically *contradictory* nature of

*I would like to thank J. Carsten, J. Parry and C. Fuller, R. Smith, M. Strathern, and S. Yanagisako for their help in preparing this draft.

representations of women and that associates these contradictions with the most relevant aspects of social constructions.

The Everyday Status of Merina Women and Men

My starting point for such an analysis is the day-to-day status of women and men among the Merina of Madagascar, since the study of their society and culture has forced me, rather belatedly, to recognize the complexity of the representation of women.* If we measure everyday social status by the degree of respect, potential autonomy, and decision-making power that a person enjoys, then the relative status of women in day-to-day domestic, economic, and political life can be considered closer to equality among Merina peasants than among women and men in the majority of ethnographic cases. However, if we want to be more precise, it becomes difficult to summarize the situation briefly, because women's and men's status is so variable. This variation is principally governed by two factors: marriage and residence, and wealth.

Marriage and residence have a particularly strong effect on the status of women and men immediately after they marry, for a new in-marrying spouse has a low status in relation to affinal group members of the same sex. As most first marriages are virilocal, young married women go through a period of systematic humiliation, largely at the hands of their mothers-in-law, which lasts approximately a year. An in-marrying husband is similarly humiliated, but since uxorilocal marriage is considered inappropriate for men, this humiliation does not normally end with time. Because uxorilocal marriage is particularly common when a woman remarries, women who have been married several times frequently have a status higher than their husbands'. Since remarriage is frequent, Merina communities contain a significant number of men lower in status than all women, especially their wives.

The other important factor in terms of the relative status of men and women is wealth, principally land, cattle, and houses. Wealth is related to marital status since one of the most common causes of uxorilocality is that a wife is wealthier than her husband. This is quite a frequent situation since the wealth of women (and to a lesser

*I do not believe that there is much significant difference in the views of women and men on this or other subjects, as most social intercourse among the Merina involves both genders and therefore does not encourage such differentiation.

extent of men) is largely dependent on inheritance, and the Merina system of inheritance, although highly complex (Bloch 1971: 54ff), means that, by and large, men and women inherit equally. (See also Bloch 1974, 1981.)

As a result, Merina women often have relatively high status, and this is manifested in the fact that they are not barred from any political or economic activity, even though political activities are more often than not dominated by men. It is therefore not surprising to find that in many important contexts women are treated with as much respect as men. This equality is indicated in forms of greeting and address, which meticulously differentiate between social ranks but not between genders. Outside the public political sphere, Merina women with sufficient wealth have ultimate control over their place of residence, their marital status, and, to a large extent, their sexual destiny.

The Merina Ideology of Descent

This relatively high everyday social status seems confirmed by the second representation of women that I shall consider here: women as descent group members. The Merina have a clear and continuously emphasized notion of descent, expressed in speeches, moral advice, and proverbs. This is the heart of Merina notions of morality, and it stresses that descendants of particular ancestors should continue to form a unified group, transcending the individual deaths of particular people. This permanence finds its symbolical expression in massive monumental hard-stone tombs, whose impressive proportions make the point nicely. Tombs also illustrate the second aspect of Merina descent: it is not merely a continuous association of people amongst themselves but also a continuous mystical association of a group of people with particular ancestral lands. This is also symbolized by tombs, since tombs "place" people in ancestral lands.

Membership in descent groups is based on recognized filiation with the ancestors in the tomb, irrespective of the gender of the ancestors or of their living descendants. This rule of membership poses a well-known sociological problem of which the Merina themselves are intensely aware. How can such a group remain discrete, and therefore permanent, with such an undifferentiated rule of descent? The Merina answer lies in the continual stress on the notion of *regrouping* the descent group by regrouping corpses in the tomb, regrouping descendants through endogamy, and regrouping land indirectly through endogamy. This is a very clear notion in Merina rhetoric, although precisely to which type of sociological group the idea of descent and regrouping apply is much less clear, both to the Merina and to myself.

What concerns us here is that this general rhetorical notion of Merina descent is based on the irrelevance of gender to membership in and transmission of a descent group and that this leads the Merina to prefer endogamy as a means of holding group members together. The tomb, as is stressed in every speech concerning ancestral matters, contains ancestors "on the father's side and the mother's side" (*lafond'ray lafond'reny*). Similarly, both male and female descendants should be buried in the parental tomb. However, here we may note our first contradiction. Women should also be buried in their husband's tomb if they have borne him three children, and husbands whose wives have lived virilocally should in all cases make a public attempt to have their wives buried with them in their tomb if this tomb is different from the woman's ancestral tomb. This is often done, but in most cases, after a decent interval, the body of the wife is then transferred back to her parental tomb.

Not only are the ancestors in the tomb undifferentiated by gender; this is also true, emphatically if not unambiguously, of the ancestors' living representatives, the elders. The Merina word for elder, *rayamandreny*, means father *and* mother and uses the emphatic 'and' to produce the collocation: "ray-" (father), "aman-" (emphatic 'and'), "-reny" (mother). The emphatic inclusion of both parents in this term is explained by the fundamental character of the representation of Merina descent; it is suprabiological in the sense that it overcomes all the discontinuities created by biology, including sexual differences. Above all, descent abolishes the relevance of the difference between the dead and the living. This is essential to the notion of a descent group, in that the existence of such an enduring entity depends on a succession of substitutive generations. Therefore, the Merina tomb is not a glorification of death but a material manifestation of the descent group's symbolic victory over death, a victory extensively elaborated in Merina funerary rituals (Bloch 1982).

However, descent also involves a negation of the relevance of sexuality and its association with birth and therefore death, which are represented as part and parcel of the same thing. The Merina descent group is represented as reproducing not through biological generation but through superior mystical means. This higher form of reproduction is by blessing (*tsodrano*): the mystical transmission of lifegiving virtue through the generations, from the ancestors, via the elders, to their descendants, who by this means become gradually more ancestral themselves. In fact, this mystical reproduction takes a material form, the blowing on of water by the elders onto their descendants, and this is what the word *tsodrano* means literally. However, as if to stress the nonbiological basis of this process, the complementarity and nondifferentiation of gender is acted out in the practice itself. In order for an important blessing to be transmitted, three elders (fathers *and* mothers) should ideally blow on the water. The first, a man, is "from the father's side"; the second, also a man, is "from the mother's side"; and the third (nonlateral) is a woman. This repeated complementarity expresses well the androgynous character of descent. Descent involves nonbiological reproduction, and therefore the biological differences of men and women are not only irrelevant but antithetical to it.

The Merina representation of descent, therefore, quite emphatically upholds the comparability of women and men—or perhaps the irrelevance of differences between them—and the need for their mutual participation in the flow of blessing, which is the source of group kinship. This negation of the discontinuities of gender is, however, only one aspect of the more general representation of descent as the transcendence of a lower form of life: biological reproduction, which involves the equally discontinuous processes of birth and death.

Gender and Biological Kinship

There is another totally different representation of women and kinship to that of descent. Merina rhetoric continually contrasts the stone tomb, representing indivision and descent, with the house, built of perishable material, which is the locus of households that typically consist of parents and children. As in so many cultures, the house and its focus the hearth are said to be primarily women's territory. For the Merina, the house is also the center of interpersonal kinship, since this is seen as the product of links created by women, and the place where kinship ties are expressed with the strongest emotion. The Merina therefore contrast kinship, an emotional link between individuals, with the morality of the descent group in the same way that they contrast the house with the tomb; this opposition emphasizes the difference between the exclusively feminine sphere and the sphere undifferentiated by gender.

The kinship of descent is the kinship of the blessing that flows from generation to generation without differentiation and without human biology. The kinship of women and houses is visualized as linking individuals biologically one to another and therefore as stressing division within the group; it is therefore antithetical to descent. Not only are the two types of kinship contrasted, but this contrast is one of super/subordination which uses gender to express the superiority of tomb blessing descent over mere divisive *feminine*, house-focused, biological kinship.

Women are linked to biological kinship even more directly than through their association with houses in the antithesis house/tomb. The Merina theory of procreation is that biological birth (not conception) is purely a matter of women and, were it not for blessing, which they receive later, children would be only matrilineally linked to their mothers. This is so for animals and plants who, because they are not linked through blessing, are believed to be "only" genetically related to their mothers, and it is also true of humans, until they are the full recipients of androgynous blessing. This idea explains, among other things, the nature of the Merina incest taboo, which stresses the peculiarly incestuous nature of sexual relations between people related through women, especially the children of two sisters. This "mere" natural-woman kinship is, however, gradually replaced as the child receives, on various occasions through life, the blessing of the nonsexual, non-birth-giving ancestors via the hermaphroditic elders. Natural procreation, interpersonal links, houses, and women alone are therefore pre- and antidescent.

Women in this representation are categorically inferior. For example, the seating and sleeping order of people tends to place men to the northeast, the honored ancestral direction, and women to the southwest. Similarly, it is possible to refer to women, children, and slaves by the same term, *ankizy* (although other terms crosscut this equation).

The devaluation of women in this representation is further emphasized by the merger of negative symbols of death and decomposition with the conjoined notions of interpersonal kinship, houses, sexuality, and women. Death is represented as an inevitable part of biology, sexuality, and, by association, the female world; it stands in direct contrast to the still transcendence and permanence of the tomb (Bloch 1982).

We can, therefore, distinguish three different Merina images of gender. The first, revealed in daily interaction, is a complex picture of men and women who are unequal in many respects that nevertheless seem minor in light of comparative ethnography. The second is linked to the representation of descent as an eternal, life-transcending entity, where the difference between men and women is ignored and indeed denied. The third is associated with the representation of women as the channels of non-descent and biological kinship, and who are therefore considered low, dirty, and divisive. To understand these apparently contradictory representations, we must briefly consider a little more ethnography, which will show how these various views of gender are interrelated in the Merina rituals associated with birth and circumcision.

The Merina Birth and Circumcision Rituals

The Merina birth ritual, a ceremony that takes place in a model house built inside the home, exclusively involves women. As a result, the ritual welds the concepts of kinship emotion, women, motherhood, and the inside of the house in a most dramatic fashion.

By contrast, the circumcision ceremony, carried out for boys of about two years, is a ritual of *coming out* from the house and, therefore, of coming out from the world of women and matrilineal kinship, which the ritual emphatically represents as dirty and polluting. The actual circumcision occurs after a night of dancing and ritual, at dawn, on the *threshold* of the house that the child is "leaving." Immediately after the operation, the child receives the ancestral blessing—which originates from the ancestors (on the father's and the mother's side) and is given by the elders (the father *and* the mother)—and is welcomed into the united descent group, represented outside the house by a group of shouting and rejoicing men.

The clearest message of the circumcision is that the boy leaves the divisive world of women, of the home, of matrilineal kinship, and of biology to be received into the unity of the eternally undivided descent group, where the division between men and women has ceased to exist. There are, however, two crosscurrents in this ritual that challenge the simple opposition between the biological, divisive kinship of women only and the spiritual descent of men and women.

The first such crosscurrent is manifest at the critical moment of the actual circumcision; at that point, people divide simply on gender lines. Inside the house, women crawl about on the floor, humiliating themselves by throwing dirt on their heads, an action that the Merina consider as most polluting and that represents the lowliness of individual kinship and birth; outside, the undivided descent group is represented by men *only*, and not men *and* women, as the ethos of Merina descent blessing would require. This emphasis on gender differences is even more marked in the welcome that the circumcised boy receives from the men as he enters the descent group: "He is a man." Equally surprising is the fact that the symbolism of this entry into the descent group takes on sexual overtones, which go against the central theme of the circumcision, the removal of the child from "biological kinship" of which sexuality is a major aspect (see Bloch 1986: 77–78). In other words, at the central moment of the circumcision ceremony, the main theme of descent by the transferral of ancestral blessing (of both male and female) is seriously skewed by the interference of a simpler gender opposition.

The second contradictory aspect of the ceremony is more pervasive than that noted above. One major element of the circumcision (as of many other Merina rituals) is the freeing of the person from the pre-moral biological world of sexuality, death, and birth, represented by women. Yet the circumcision ceremony also includes a number of symbols associated with this devalued world, symbols that are actually positively valued and are brought in to increase the vitality of the descent group. This is particularly clear for a series of plants and animals which are used and whose great vitality comes from the fact that they are said to be "of living mother." These are "added" to the blessing of descent dispensed by the hermaphroditic ancestors and elders to give it greater "vitality"; thereby implying that, in the end, descent is not enough. This contradiction is, however, modified and to a certain extent lessened by the fact that these matrilineal, natural entities must first be broken, crushed, or chopped by the elders at various stages in the ritual before their vitality can be added and so passed on. The main idea that seems to emerge, then, is that the element driven out with such flourish, female matrilineal nature, must finally be reintroduced if all vitality is not to be lost—but only under the severest and the most brutal control.

The circumcision ceremony seems to reveal two levels of contradiction: its messages about biological kinship are internally inconsistent and its references to gender point to at least two of the conflicting representations of women and men discussed above. On the one hand, the ritual's emphasis on descent and blessing underscores the irrelevance of differences between men and women; on the other, its images emphasize the relevance and hierarchical difference of masculinity and femininity.

However, these two contradictory representations become readily understandable if seen as different stages in the ritual process. The circumcision ritual is, as the Merina always stress, a ritual of blessing. In other words, it is a ritual that creates the epiphenomenal representation of the descent groups. Now it is of the essence of the descent group that it transcends human life; descent groups, as the Merina endlessly repeat, vanquish death, as the tomb remains unchanged from generation to generation. This transcendental image is created in the ritual by a two-act drama, which itself implies an unritualized prologue in everyday experience. The ritual demonstrates the victory of descent, blessing, and nonbiological life by showing the victory of transcendent blessing over a negative element represented by women. In other words, the ritual creation of androgynous descent *requires* the enactment of a horrifying spectacle of a world dominated by women, reproducing by themselves; only in this way can descent emerge through the symbolic destruction of that world.

Yet, if the image of descent depends on the image of "biology," the image of biology itself derives from the representation of everyday Merina social intercourse. In other words, the three images are linked not logically but dramatically, so that the representation of transcendent descent can emerge. First, the everyday has to be reinterpreted to produce a negative ritual representation that involves a horrific image of biology; given to women to act out, this forms the first act of the ritual, but this representation is there all the better to knock it down, in the second act, by the victory of the nonbiological world of descent. As Victor Turner so well points out, ritual is a process of the creation of representation by drama (Turner 1962).

I have argued that the three different views of gender in Merina society are contradictory but interdependent, in that they are part of a process that leads to the representation of the unchanging transcendental descent group. This means that any synthesis of these views as *the* Merina view of gender would be totally misleading. We must recognize that these three representations of gender are not rival concepts but different kinds of knowledge in Merina society. Therefore, the typical notions of "culture" in American anthropology are misleading precisely because they fail to recognize such a difference in kinds of knowledge. This failure inevitably leads to the arbitrary privileging of one representation as *the* Merina view of gender, which can then be refuted by pointing to one of the others.

By contrast, the Marxist concept of ideology is useful precisely because it recognizes that there are different types of knowledge that must be analyzed in different ways. Furthermore, this concept suggests that ideological knowledge is part of the legitimization of authority. In a case such as this, it is possible to say that the representation of descent and the representation of gender it implies conform, in part, to the notion of ideology. They clearly legitimate the authority of elders, the heads of descent groups, and, ultimately, the whole Merina political system as a combination of descent groups (Bloch 1977). Equally important, this legitimizing function explains much about the particular nature of this representation of the descent group. If authority is to be legitimized, it must be represented as part of a transcendental order beyond human action and life. This explains why such an image must be created by denigrating "biology," which it identifies as both evident and low and to which it attributes change and mutability.

There is, however, a problem in using the notion of ideology in this context. Whereas this notion normally implies two levels of knowledge—the ideological and the nonideological—I have distinguished three levels in the Merina ethnography, and I believe it would be possible to construct even more. Which then is the ideological level in this case? And can all these levels, although different in kind, be usefully separated, insofar as they depend on each other as part of one process? The constructions of the level of the biological, for example, is part of the ritual process leading to "descent."

The answer to these questions seems to me to lie in reconceptualizing ideology as a process rather than as a system, that is, as a continual *straining* to reinterpret the everyday in a way that transcends it and establishes authority. This process requires at least three stages, and perhaps more, in order to produce the dramatic dialectic of antithesis by which people attempt in ritual to leave the worldly behind.

Seeing ideology as a continual attempt to create a transcendental order also seems to explain the internal inconsistencies noted in the circumcision ceremony: the use of gender opposition and sexual symbolism to demonstrate the irrelevance of gender differences and sex. The ritual drama achieves its theatrical power precisely by playing with what was already there, to create something which was not. This, after all, is exactly what a theatrical representation involves. In other words, the only tools that can be used are tools that deny the very transcendence of the message—like the cable that makes Peter Pan fly. Hence, gender differences are emphasized as a means of denying their ultimate relevance, and images of gender and sex continually cloud the process, much as images of putrefaction reoccur in medieval representations of the immortality of the soul.

Secondly, there is the problem raised by the apparent need to reintroduce symbols of women and biological kinship after they have been driven out. This, too, seems to be an inevitable part of the ideological process, although for different reasons. As we saw, the Merina notion of descent depends on creating an image of a permanent descent group associated with a valued territory. The timelessness of this notion is principally constructed antithetically by dramatic rituals such as the circumcision ceremony. This is done by first stressing and caricaturing, then devaluing, the biological nature of society and its basis in sexual reproduction. The devaluation is achieved by representing the biological processes of birth, death, and sexuality as polluting, immoral, and needing expulsion; by contrast, the continuity of descent is achieved through the pure moral forces of reproduction by blessing, which so transcend the biological that the divisions of kinship and of male and female are merged into an eternal undifferentiated unity.

Thus here, as I believe everywhere, the construction of the ideological depends on the creation of a nightmarish image of the world, such that exchange, movement, and the irreversible processes of life—birth, conception, and death—can then be devalued and transcended. This construction is in this case achieved through hierarchical gender symbolism. In cases such as this, therefore, the construction of ideology depends first on the emphasis on, and then on the explusion of, the dialectical, biological world represented here by femininity (see Bloch and Parry 1982 for a more detailed version of this argument).

What, then, explains the other contradiction noted earlier, the need to reintroduce the symbols of this world that have been so dramatically driven out in ritual? This need stems from the fact that the constructed image of a still, permanent order that spurns exchange, movement, and, in this case, women, is in the end self-defeating. Ideology legitimates power by reference to a transcendental order, which is defined as an ultimate ideal. By definition, however, the ideal cannot be of this life. The ritual must therefore not only construct the transcendental but also suggest how it can be combined with that which makes the living alive. This is a paradoxical requirement in that the transcendental is constructed by the expulsion of that very element. A compromise can, however, be uncomfortably achieved by reintroducing that purged element after it has been apparently broken and controlled by the transcendental. Vitality, movement, mutability—all represented by women —are represented in the end as acceptable, even desirable, for this life, at least so long as it has been chastened by its initial expulsion, and its disciplined broken reintroduction. The problem is in the end a logical one; rituals simply cannot totally deny this life and be of this world. Again, however good the production, Peter Pan cannot cut his own cable.

We have seen how this process manifests itself in the Merina circumcision ritual, in that the female, natural, matrilineal element is first triumphantly expelled and then *reintroduced*, although under brutal control in the form of natural substances of "living mother." Indeed, at some point, the violence in the ancestral conquest of the negative feminine colors the sexual symbolism discussed above, thereby legitimating sexual aggression directed against women. The necessity for this reintroduction of the feminine and vital seems to lie in the very logic of ideology; because it is ultimately impossible in this world, it must be compromised if the descent group is to survive.

This pattern of internal inconsistency is found again and again in

cultures totally unrelated to the Malagasy and in social and symbolical systems that appear very different. For example, Cantonese
funerals, as described by James Watson (1982), reveal exactly the
same construction. The Cantonese symbolic system, like many
others, makes a sharp distinction between bones, associated with
the male aspect of the person, and flesh, associated with putrefaction, affinity, and women. As a result, bones are kept to fortify the
purely male descent group, whereas the female element is expelled
in order to construct a pure male moral order. This process is acted
out at funerals, which reveal an extreme obsession with the con-
taminating aspect of decomposing (feminine) flesh. Yet this negative representation of the feminine cannot lead to its logical conclusion—a world without women and flesh—and so it is finally
contradicted. Young married women at funerals wear not only
white for mourning, a color thought of as totally nonabsorbent and
therefore impervious to contamination, but also green, a color
thought of as *most* absorbent. The significance of this contradiction
is revealed when women use their green funeral ribbons, which
have absorbed the feared pollution of the decomposing flesh, as
part of the slings that carry male and female newborns, thereby
strengthening their new life by "returning" the lost flesh. The ideology of Chinese descent may require the feminine flesh to be
driven out with a flourish, but, as the green ribbons suggest, human reproduction is not possible without women. Again, the contradiction is an inevitable part of the process of the production of
ideology.

In summary, the contradictory gender representations discussed
above all stem from the Merina's attempt to create an ideology of
ancestral power out of the nonideological. To try to reconcile these
contradictions in one arbitrary cultural or symbolical system—as
Margaret Mead and others have done in similar analyses—would
be misleading; there is not one Merina representation of gender,
but several. To argue that Merina women and men have different
systems would be wrong ethnographically; their actions and statements point to unavoidable inconsistencies. Therefore, allegiance
to the notion of culture, with its implication of a unified cognitive
system, would inevitably have forced this analysis into a fundamental error: unifying gender images of different kinds. The sociological notion of ideology was needed to clarify the different content of these images and the sources for their continual and various

contradictions. If a goal of feminism is to make possible change in gender representations by increasing our understanding of their origin, then we must acknowledge the full complexity of gender construction and realize that the organizing principles of this social process may be a part of a different symbolical process, such as the production of ideology.

References Cited

References Cited

Preface

Rosaldo, Michelle Zimbalist. 1974. "Woman, Culture, and Society: A Theoretical Overview." In Michelle Zimbalist Rosaldo and Louise Lamphere, eds., *Woman, Culture, and Society*. Stanford, Calif.

———. 1980. "The Use and Abuse of Anthropology: Reflections on Feminism and Cross-Cultural Understanding." *Signs: Journal of Women in Culture and Society* 5, no. 3: 389–417.

Introduction

Alexander, Jack. 1978. "The Cultural Domain of Marriage." *American Ethnologist* 5: 5–14.

Appadurai, Arjun. 1986. "Theory in Anthropology: Center and Periphery." *Comparative Studies in Society and History* 28: 356–61.

Ardener, Shirley. 1975. *Perceiving Women*. New York.

Ardener, Shirley, ed. 1978. *Defining Females: The Nature of Women in Society*. New York.

Bohannan, Paul. 1963. *Social Anthropology*. New York.

Boon, James A., and David M. Schneider. 1974. "Kinship Vis-à-Vis Myth: Contrasts in Lévi-Strauss' Approaches to Cross-Cultural Comparison." *American Anthropologist* 76: 799–817.

Bourdieu, Pierre. 1977. *Outline of a Theory of Practice*. London.

Chock, Phyllis P. 1974. "Time, Nature and Spirit: A Symbolic Analysis of Greek-American Spiritual Kinship." *American Ethnologist* 1: 33–46.

Collier, Jane, and Michelle Z. Rosaldo. 1981. "Politics and Gender in Simple Societies." In Sherry B. Ortner and Harriet Whitehead, eds., *Sexual Meanings*. Cambridge, Eng.

Fortes, Meyer. 1949. *The Web of Kinship Among the Tallensi*. London.

———. 1953. "The Structure of Unilineal Descent Groups." *American Anthropologist* 55: 17–41.

———. 1958. "Introduction." In Jack Goody, ed., *The Developmental Cycle in Domestic Groups*. Cambridge, Eng.

———. 1969. *Kinship and the Social Order*. Chicago.

———. 1978. "An Anthropologist's Apprenticeship." *Annual Review of Anthropology* 7: 1–30.

Fox, Robin. 1967. *Kinship and Marriage*. Middlesex, Eng.

Friedl, Ernestine. 1975. *Women and Men: An Anthropologist's View*. New York.

Friedman, Jonathan. 1974. "Marxism, Structuralism, and Vulgar Materialism." *Man* 9: 444–69.

Goodenough, Ward H. 1970. *Description and Comparison in Cultural Anthropology*. Chicago.

Goody, Jack. 1973. "Bridewealth and Dowry in Africa and Eurasia." In Jack Goody and S. J. Tambiah, eds., *Bridewealth and Dowry*. Cambridge, Eng.

———. 1976. *Production and Reproduction: A Comparative Study of the Domestic Domain*. Cambridge, Eng.

Hannerz, Ulf. 1986. "Theory in Anthropology. Small Is Beautiful: The Problem of Complex Cultures." *Comparative Studies in Society and History* 28: 362–67.

Leach, Edmund. 1954. *Political Systems of Highland Burma*. London.

———. 1961. *Rethinking Anthropology*. London.

Lévi-Strauss, Claude. 1966. *The Savage Mind*. Chicago.

———. 1967. *Structural Anthropology*. New York.

———. 1969. *The Elementary Structures of Kinship*. Boston.

———. 1970. *The Raw and the Cooked*. New York.

MacCormack, Carol, and Marilyn Strathern, eds. 1980. *Nature, Culture, and Gender*. Cambridge, Eng.

Maybury-Lewis, David. 1974. *Akwẽ-Shavante Society*. New York.

Meillassoux, Claude. 1981. *Maidens, Meal, and Money: Capitalism and the Domestic Community*. Cambridge, Eng.

Needham, Rodney. 1962. *Structure and Sentiment*. Chicago.

———. 1971. "Remarks on the Analysis of Kinship and Marriage." In Rodney Needham, ed., *Rethinking Kinship and Marriage*. London.

Ortner, Sherry B. 1974. "Is Female to Male as Nature Is to Culture?" In Michelle Z. Rosaldo and Louise Lamphere, eds., *Woman, Culture, and Society*. Stanford, Calif.

———. 1984. "Theory in Anthropology Since the Sixties." *Comparative Studies in Society and History* 26: 126–66.

———, and Harriet Whitehead. 1981. "Introduction: Accounting for Sexual Meanings." In Sherry B. Ortner and Harriet Whitehead, eds., *Sexual Meanings*. Cambridge, Eng.

Parsons, Talcott, and Robert F. Bales. 1955. *Family, Socialization, and Interaction Process*. Glencoe, Ill.

Radcliffe-Brown, A. R. 1952. *Structure and Function in Primitive Societies*. London.

Rosaldo, Michelle Z. 1974. "Woman, Culture, and Society: A Theoretical Overview." In Michelle Z. Rosaldo and Louise Lamphere, eds., *Woman, Culture, and Society*. Stanford, Calif.

Rubel, P., and A. Rossman. 1976. *Your Own Pigs You May Not Eat*. Chicago.

Sahlins, Marshall D. 1972. *Stone Age Economics*. Chicago.

Schlegel, Alice. 1977. "Toward a Theory of Sexual Stratification." In Alice Schlegel, ed., *Sexual Stratification*. New York.

Schneider, David M. 1964. "The Nature of Kinship." *Man* 64: 180–81.
──────. 1968. *American Kinship: A Cultural Account*. Englewood Cliffs, N.J.
──────. 1972. "What Is Kinship All About?" In Priscilla Reining, ed., *Kinship Studies in the Morgan Centennial Year*. Washington, D.C.
──────. 1976. "Notes Toward a Theory of Culture." In Keith H. Basso and Henry A. Selby, eds., *Meaning in Anthropology*. Albuquerque, N.M.
──────. 1984. *A Critique of the Study of Kinship*. Ann Arbor, Mich.
Schneider, David M., and Kathleen Gough, eds., 1961. *Matrilineal Kinship*. Berkeley, Calif.
Schneider, David M., and Raymond T. Smith. 1973. *Class Differences and Sex Roles in American Kinship and Family Structure*. Englewood Cliffs, N.J.
Strathern, Marilyn. 1981. "Self-Interest and the Social Good: Some Implications of Hagen Gender Imagery." In Sherry B. Ortner and Harriet Whitehead, eds., *Sexual Meanings*. Cambridge, Eng.
Terray, Emmanuel. 1972. *Marxism and "Primitive" Societies*. New York.
Yanagisako, Sylvia Junko. 1978. "Variance in American Kinship: Implications for Cultural Analysis." *American Ethnologist* 5: 15–29.
──────. 1979. "Family and Household: The Analysis of Domestic Groups." *Annual Review of Anthropology* 8: 161–205.
──────. 1985. *Transforming the Past: Tradition and Kinship Among Japanese Americans*. Stanford, Calif.
Yengoyan, Aram A. 1986. "Theory in Anthropology: On the Demise of the Concept of Culture." *Comparative Studies in Society and History* 28: 368–74.

Toward a Unified Analysis of Gender and Kinship

Ardener, Edwin. 1972. "Belief and the Problem of Women." In J. La-Fontaine, ed., *The Interpretation of Ritual*. London.
Atkinson, Jane Monnig. 1982. "Review Essay: Anthropology." *Signs: Journal of Women in Culture and Society* 8, no. 2: 236–58.
Benería, Lourdes, and Gita Sen. 1981. "Accumulation, Reproduction, and Women's Role in Economic Development: Boserup Revisited." *Signs: Journal of Women in Culture and Society* 7, no. 2: 279–98.
Bloch, Maurice, and Jean H. Bloch. 1980. "Woman and the Dialectics of Nature in Eighteenth-Century French Thought." In Carol MacCormack and Marilyn Strathern, eds., *Nature, Culture and Gender*. Cambridge, Eng.
Boserup, Ester. 1970. *Woman's Role in Economic Development*. New York.
Bourdieu, Pierre. 1977. *Outline of a Theory of Practice*. Cambridge, Eng.
Caulfield, Mina Davis. 1981. "Equality, Sex, and Mode of Production." In Gerald Berreman, ed., *Social Inequality*. New York.
Chodorow, Nancy. 1974. "Family Structure and Feminine Personality." In Michelle Zimbalist Rosaldo and Louise Lamphere, eds., *Woman, Culture, and Society*. Stanford, Calif.
──────. 1978. *The Reproduction of Mothering: Psychoanalysis and the Sociology of Gender*. Berkeley, Calif.

Collier, Jane F. 1974. "Women in Politics." In Michelle Zimbalist Rosaldo and Louise Lamphere, eds., *Woman, Culture, and Society*. Stanford, Calif.

———. 1984. "Two Models of Social Control in Simple Societies." In Donald Black, ed., *Toward a General Theory of Social Control, Vol. 2: Selected Problems*. New York.

———. 1986. "From Mary to Modern Woman: The Material Basis of Marianismo and Its Transformation in a Spanish Village." *American Ethnologist* 13, no. 1: 100–107.

———. N.d. *Marriage and Inequality in Classless Societies*. Stanford, Calif. In press.

———, and Michelle Z. Rosaldo. 1981. "Politics and Gender in Simple Societies." In Sherry B. Ortner and Harriet Whitehead, eds., *Sexual Meanings: The Cultural Construction of Gender and Sexuality*. Cambridge, Eng.

———, Michelle Z. Rosaldo, and Sylvia Yanagisako. 1982. "Is There a Family? New Anthropological Views." In Barrie Thorne, ed., with Marilyn Yalom, *Rethinking the Family: Some Feminist Questions*. New York.

Dahrendorf, Ralf. 1968. *Essays in the Theory of Society*. Stanford, Calif.

Eisenstein, Zillah. 1979. *Capitalist Patriarchy and the Case for Socialist Feminism*. New York.

Engels, Friedrich. 1972. *The Origin of the Family, Private Property, and the State*. New York.

Etienne, Mona, and Eleanor Leacock, eds. 1980. *Women and Colonization: Anthropological Perspectives*. New York.

Fortes, Meyer. 1949. *The Web of Kinship Among the Tallensi*. London.

———. 1958. "Introduction." In Jack R. Goody, ed., *The Developmental Cycle in Domestic Groups*. Cambridge, Eng.

———. 1969. *Kinship and the Social Order*. Chicago.

Fox, Robin. 1967. *Kinship and Marriage*. Middlesex, Eng.

Fried, Morton. 1967. *The Evolution of Political Society*. New York.

Friedl, Ernestine. 1975. *Women and Men: An Anthropologist's View*. New York.

Friedman, Jonathan. 1976. "Marxist Theory and Systems of Total Reproduction." *Critique of Anthropology* 7: 3–16.

Goodenough, Ward H. 1970. *Description and Comparison in Cultural Anthropology*. Chicago.

Gough, Kathleen. 1975. "The Origin of the Family." In Rayna Rapp Reiter, ed., *Toward an Anthropology of Women*. New York.

Guyer, Jane I. 1980. "Food, Cocoa, and the Division of Labor by Sex in Two West African Societies." *Comparative Studies in Society and History* 22, no. 3: 355–73.

Harris, Olivia. 1981. "Households as Natural Units." In Kate Young et al., eds., *Of Marriage and the Market: Women's Subordination in International Perspective*. London.

———, and Kate Young. 1981. "Engendered Structures: Some Problems in the Analysis of Reproduction." In Joel S. Kahn and Joseph R. Llobera, eds., *The Anthropology of Pre-Capitalist Societies*. Atlantic Highlands, N.J.

Hindness, B., and P. Hirst. 1975. *Pre-Capitalist Modes of Production*. London.

Jaggar, Alison M. 1983. *Feminist Politics and Human Nature*. Totowa, N.J.

Lamphere, Louise L. 1974. "Strategies, Cooperation, and Conflict Among Women in Domestic Groups." In Michelle Zimbalist Rosaldo and Louise Lamphere, eds., *Woman, Culture, and Society*. Stanford, Calif.

Leacock, Eleanor. 1978. "Women's Status in Egalitarian Society: Implications for Social Evolution." *Current Anthropology* 19, no. 2: 247–75.

Lévi-Strauss, Claude. 1949. *The Elementary Structures of Kinship*. Boston.

MacCormack, Carol, and Marilyn Strathern, eds. 1980. *Nature, Culture and Gender*. Cambridge, Eng.

Martin, M. Kay, and Barbara Voorhies. 1975. *Female of the Species*. New York.

Marx, Karl. 1967. *Capital*. Vol. 3. New York.

———, and Friedrich Engels. 1970. *The German Ideology*. Ed. C. J. Arthur. New York.

Meillassoux, Claude. 1981. *Maidens, Meal, and Money: Capitalism and the Domestic Community*. Cambridge, Eng.

O'Laughlin, M. Bridget. 1977. "Production and Reproduction: Meillassoux's *Femmes, Greniers, et Capitaux*." *Critique of Anthropology* 8: 3–32.

Ortner, Sherry B. 1974. "Is Female to Male as Nature Is to Culture?" In Michelle Zimbalist Rosaldo and Louise Lamphere, eds., *Woman, Culture, and Society*. Stanford, Calif.

———. 1984. "Theory in Anthropology Since the Sixties." *Comparative Studies in Society and History* 26: 126–66.

———, and Harriet Whitehead. 1981. "Introduction: Accounting for Sexual Meanings." In Sherry B. Ortner and Harriet Whitehead, eds., *Sexual Meanings: The Cultural Construction of Gender and Sexuality*. Cambridge, Eng.

Parsons, Talcott, and Robert F. Bales. 1955. *Family, Socialization, and the Interaction Process*. Glencoe, Ill.

Rapp, Rayna. 1979. "Review Essay: Anthropology." *Signs: Journal of Women in Culture and Society* 4, no. 3: 497–513.

Reiter, Rayna. 1975. "Men and Women in the South of France: Public and Private Domains." In Rayna Rapp Reiter, ed., *Toward an Anthropology of Women*. New York.

Rohrlich-Leavitt, Ruby, Barbara Sykes, and Elizabeth Weatherford. 1975. "Aboriginal Woman: Male and Female Anthropological Perspectives." In Rayna Rapp Reiter, ed., *Toward an Anthropology of Women*. New York.

Rosaldo, Michelle Zimbalist. 1974. "Woman, Culture, and Society: A Theoretical Overview." In Michelle Zimbalist Rosaldo and Louise Lamphere, eds., *Woman, Culture, and Society*. Stanford, Calif.

———. 1980. "The Use and Abuse of Anthropology: Reflections on Feminism and Cross-Cultural Understanding." *Signs: Journal of Women in Culture and Society* 5, no. 3: 389–417.

———, and Jane M. Atkinson. 1975. "Man the Hunter and Woman." In R. Willis, ed., *The Interpretation of Symbolism*. London.

———, and Louise Lamphere. 1974. "Introduction." In Michelle Zimbalist Rosaldo and Louise Lamphere, eds., *Woman, Culture, and Society*. Stanford, Calif.

Rosaldo, Renato. 1980. *Ilongot Headhunting 1883–1974: A Study in Society and History*. Stanford, Calif.

Sacks, Karen. 1976. "State Bias and Women's Status." *American Anthropologist* 78: 565–69.

———. 1979. *Sisters and Wives*. Westport, Conn.

Sahlins, Marshall. 1981. *Historical Metaphors and Mythical Realities*. Ann Arbor, Mich.

Scheffler, Harold. 1970. "Kinship and Adoption in the Northern New Hebrides." In Vern Carroll, ed., *Adoption in Eastern Oceania*. Honolulu.

———. 1974. "Kinship, Descent, and Alliance." In J. J. Honigman, ed., *Handbook of Social and Cultural Anthropology*. Chicago.

Schlegel, Alice. 1977. "Toward a Theory of Sexual Stratification." In Alice Schlegel, ed., *Sexual Stratification*. New York.

Schneider, David M. 1964. "The Nature of Kinship." *Man* 64: 180–81.

———. 1968. *American Kinship: A Cultural Account*. Englewood Cliffs, N.J.

———. 1972. "What Is Kinship All About?" In Priscilla Reining, ed., *Kinship Studies in the Morgan Centennial Year*. Washington, D.C.

———. 1984. *A Critique of the Study of Kinship*. Ann Arbor, Mich.

Shapiro, Judith. 1981. "Anthropology and the Study of Gender." *Soundings: An Interdisciplinary Journal* 64, no. 4: 446–65.

Strathern, Marilyn. 1978. "Comment on Leacock (1978)." *Current Anthropology* 19, no. 2: 267.

———. 1980. "No Nature, No Culture: The Hagen Case." In Carol MacCormack and Marilyn Strathern, eds., *Nature, Culture, and Gender*. Cambridge, Eng.

———. 1981a. "Culture in a Netbag: The Manufacture of a Subdiscipline in Anthropology." *Man* 16: 665–88.

———. 1981b. "Self-Interest and the Social Good: Some Implications of Hagen Gender Imagery." In Sherry B. Ortner and Harriet Whitehead, eds., *Sexual Meanings: The Cultural Construction of Gender and Sexuality*. Cambridge, Eng.

Tilly, Louise A., and Joan W. Scott. 1980. *Women, Work, and Family*. New York.

Wallman, Sandra. 1978. "Epistemologies of Sex." In L. Tiger and H. Fowler, eds., *Female Hierarchies*. Chicago.

Weiner, Annette. 1976. *Women of Value, Men of Renown: New Perspectives on Trobriand Exchange*. Austin, Tex.

———. 1980. "Reproduction: A Replacement for Reciprocity." *American Ethnologist* 7, no. 1: 71–85.

Wolf, Margery. 1972. *Women and the Family in Rural Taiwan*. Stanford, Calif.

Yanagisako, Sylvia Junko. 1979. "Family and Household: The Analysis of Domestic Groups." *Annual Review of Anthropology* 8: 161–205.

———. 1985. *Transforming the Past: Tradition and Kinship Among Japanese Americans*. Stanford, Calif.

"Sui genderis": Feminism, Kinship Theory, and Structural "Domains"

Barth, Fredrik. 1966. *Models of Social Organization*. Royal Anthropological Institute Occasional Paper, no. 23. London.

Boserup, Ester. 1970. *Women's Role in Economic Development*. New York.
Bourdieu, Pierre. 1977. *Outline of a Theory of Practice*. Trans. Richard Nice. Cambridge, Eng.
Chodorow, Nancy. 1974. "Family Structure and Feminine Personality." In Michelle Zimbalist Rosaldo and Louise Lamphere, eds., *Woman, Culture, and Society*. Stanford, Calif.
Collier, Jane Fishburne. n.d. *Marriage and Inequality in Classless Societies*. Stanford, Calif. In press.
Comaroff, Jean. 1985. *Social Bodies and Natural Ideologies*. Chicago.
Comaroff, John L. 1973. "Competition for Office and Political Processes Among the Barolong boo Ratshidi." Ph.D. thesis, University of London.
———. 1975. "Talking Politics: Oratory and Authority in a Tswana Chiefdom." In Maurice Bloch, ed., *Political Language and Oratory in Traditional Society*. London and New York.
———. 1982. "Dialectical Systems, History, and Anthropology." *Journal of Southern African Studies* 8, no. 2: 143–72.
———. N.d. "Culture, Class, and the Rise of Capitalism in an African Chiefdom." Unpublished manuscript.
———, and Jean Comaroff. n.d. "The Long and the Short of It: An Essay in Historical Anthropology." Forthcoming in Jane Guyer, ed., *Time and Social Structure: An Old Problem Revisited*.
———, and Simon Roberts. 1981. *Rules and Processes: The Cultural Logic of Dispute in an African Context*. Chicago.
Davis, Natalie Zemon. 1977. "Ghosts, Kin, and Progeny: Some Features of Family Life in Early Modern France." *Daedalus* 106: 87–114.
Draper, Patricia. 1975. "!Kung Women: Contrasts in Sexual Egalitarianism in Foraging and Sedentary Contexts." In Rayna Rapp Reiter, ed., *Toward an Anthropology of Women*. New York.
Fortes, Meyer. 1969. *Kinship and the Social Order*. Chicago.
———. 1978. "An Anthropologist's Apprenticeship." *Annual Review of Anthropology* 7: 1–30.
Goody, Jack R. 1973. "Bridewealth and Dowry in Africa and Eurasia." In Jack R. Goody and Stanley J. Tambiah, eds., *Bridewealth and Dowry*. Cambridge, Eng.
———. 1976. *Production and Reproduction: A Comparative Study of the Domestic Domain*. Cambridge, Eng.
———, ed. 1977. *The Domestication of the Savage Mind*. Cambridge, Eng.
Jayawardena, Chandra. 1977. "Women and Kinship in Acheh Besar, Northern Sumatra." *Ethnology* 16, no. 1: 21–38.
Kent, Francis W. 1977. *Household and Lineage in Renaissance Florence*. Princeton, N.J.
Lamphere, Louise. 1974. "Strategies, Cooperation, and Conflict Among Women in Domestic Groups." In Michelle Zimbalist Rosaldo and Louise Lamphere, eds., *Woman, Culture, and Society*. Stanford, Calif.
Leach, Edmund R. 1954. *Political Systems of Highland Burma: A Study of Kachin Social Structure*. London.
Martin, M. Kay, and Barbara Voorhies. 1974. *Female of the Species*. New York.

Meillassoux, Claude. 1972. "From Reproduction to Production." *Economy and Society* 1, no. 1: 93–105.

———. 1975. *Femmes, Greniers, et Capitaux*. Paris.

Nash, June, and Eleanor Leacock. 1977. "Ideologies of Sex: Archetypes and Stereotypes." *Annals of the New York Academy of Science* 285: 618–45.

Nelson, Cynthia. 1974. "Public and Private Politics: Women in the Middle Eastern World." *American Ethnologist* 1, no. 3: 551–63.

Ortner, Sherry. 1974. "Is Female to Male as Nature Is to Culture?" In Michelle Zimbalist Rosaldo and Louise Lamphere, eds., *Woman, Culture, and Society*. Stanford, Calif.

Quinn, Naomi. 1977. "Anthropological Studies on Women's Status." *Annual Review of Anthropology* 6: 181–225.

Rapp, Rayna. 1979. "Review Essay: Anthropology." *Signs: Journal of Women in Culture and Society* 4, no. 3: 497–513.

Reiter, Rayna Rapp. 1975. "Men and Women in the South of France: Public and Private Domains." In Rayna Rapp Reiter, ed., *Toward an Anthropology of Women*. New York.

Rogers, Susan Carol. 1975. "Female Forms of Power and the Myth of Male Dominance: A Model of Female/Male Interaction in Peasant Society." *American Ethnologist* 2, no. 4: 727–56.

———. 1978. "Women's Place: A Critical Review of Anthropological Theory." *Comparative Studies in Society and History* 20, no. 1: 123–73.

Rosaldo, Michelle Zimbalist. 1974. "Woman, Culture, and Society: A Theoretical Overview." In Michelle Zimbalist Rosaldo and Louise Lamphere, eds., *Woman, Culture, and Society*. Stanford, Calif.

———. 1980. "The Use and Abuse of Anthropology: Reflections on Feminism and Cross-Cultural Understanding." *Signs: Journal of Women in Culture and Society* 5, no. 3: 389–417.

Sacks, Karen. 1975. "Engels Revisited: Women, the Organization of Production, and Private Property." In Rayna Rapp Reiter, ed., *Toward an Anthropology of Women*. New York.

Sudarkasa, Niara. 1976. "Female Employment and Family Organization in West Africa." In Dorothy Gies McGuigan, ed., *New Research on Women and Sex Roles*. Ann Arbor, Mich.

Terray, Emmanuel. 1972. *Marxism and "Primitive" Societies*. Trans. Mary Klopper. New York.

Tilly, Louise A. 1978. "The Social Sciences and the Study of Women: A Review Article." *Comparative Studies in Society and History* 20, no. 1: 163–73.

Worsley, Peter M. 1980. "Marxism and Culture." University of Manchester, Department of Sociology Occasional Paper, no. 4. Manchester, Eng.

Yanagisako, Sylvia. 1979. "Family and Household: The Analysis of Domestic Groups." *Annual Review of Anthropology* 8: 161–205.

Mixed Metaphors: Native and Anthropological Models of Gender and Kinship Domains

Ariès, Phillippe. 1962. *Centuries of Childhood: A Social History of Family Life*. London.

Befu, Harumi. 1971. *Japan: An Anthropological Introduction*. San Francisco.

Bender, Donald R. 1967. "A Refinement of the Concept of Household: Families, Co-residence, and Domestic Functions." *American Anthropologist* 69: 493–504.

Bloch, Maurice. 1977. "The Past and the Present in the Present." *Man* 12: 278–92.

———, and Jean H. Bloch. 1980. "Women and the Dialectics of Nature in Eighteenth-Century French Thought." In Carol MacCormack and Marilyn Strathern, eds., *Nature, Culture and Gender*. Cambridge, Eng.

Dore, Ronald P. 1958. *City Life in Japan: A Study of a Tokyo Ward*. Berkeley, Calif.

Evans-Pritchard, E. E. 1940. *The Nuer*. Oxford.

Fortes, Meyer. 1958. "Introduction." In J. R. Goody, ed., *The Developmental Cycle in Domestic Groups*. Cambridge, Eng.

———. 1969. *Kinship and the Social Order*. Chicago.

Fukutake, Tadashi. 1967. *Japanese Rural Society*. Trans. Ronald P. Dore. Ithaca, N.Y.

Meillassoux, Claude. 1981. *Maidens, Meal and Money: Capitalism and the Domestic Community*. Cambridge, Eng.

Miyamoto, Frank Shotaro. 1939. *Social Solidarity Among the Japanese in Seattle*. Seattle, Wash.

———, and R. W. O'Brien. 1947. *A Survey of Some Changes in the Seattle Japanese Community Since Evacuation*. Research Studies of the State of Washington, vol. 15: 147–54. Pullman, Wash.

Ortner, Sherry B. 1974. "Is Female to Male as Nature Is to Culture?" In Michelle Z. Rosaldo and Louise Lamphere, eds., *Woman, Culture, and Society*. Stanford, Calif.

———, and Harriet Whitehead. 1981. "Introduction: Accounting for Sexual Meanings." In Sherry B. Ortner and Harriet Whitehead, eds., *Sexual Meanings*. Cambridge, Eng.

Radcliffe-Brown, A. R. 1952. *Structure and Function in Primitive Societies*. London.

Reischauer, Edwin O. 1974. *Japan: The Story of a Nation*. New York.

Reiter, Rayna Rapp. 1975. "Men and Women in the South of France: Public and Private Domains." In Rayna Rapp Reiter, ed., *Toward an Anthropology of Women*. New York.

Rosaldo, Michelle Z. 1974. "Woman, Culture, and Society: A Theoretical Overview." In Michelle Z. Rosaldo and Louise Lamphere, eds., *Woman, Culture, and Society*. Stanford, Calif.

———. 1980. "The Use and Abuse of Anthropology: Reflections on Feminism and Cross-Cultural Understanding." *Signs: Journal of Women in Culture and Society* 5: 389–417.

Sansom, Sir G. B. 1943. *Japan: A Short Cultural History*. New York.

Scheffler, Harold K. 1970. "Review of *Kinship and the Social Order* by Meyer Fortes." *American Anthropologist* 72: 1464–66.

Smith, Raymond T. 1973. "The Matrifocal Family." In Jack Goody, ed., *The Character of Kinship*. London.

Strathern, Marilyn. 1980. "No Nature, No Culture: The Hagen Case." In Carol MacCormack and Marilyn Strathern, eds., *Nature, Culture and Gender*. Cambridge, Eng.

————. 1981. "Self-Interest and the Social Good: Some Implications of Hagen Gender Imagery." In Sherry B. Ortner and Harriet Whitehead, eds., *Sexual Meanings*. Cambridge, Eng.

Yanagisako, Sylvia J. 1979. "Family and Household: The Analysis of Domestic Groups." *Annual Review of Anthropology* 8: 161–205.

————. 1985. *Transforming the Past: Tradition and Kinship Among Japanese Americans*. Stanford, Calif.

Toward a Nuclear Freeze? The Gender Politics of Euro-American Kinship Analysis

Alexander, Sally. 1976. "Women's Work in Nineteenth Century London." In Juliet Mitchell and Ann Oakley, eds., *The Rights and Wrongs of Women*. Harmondsworth, Eng.

Barrett, Michelle. 1980. *Women's Oppression Today*. London.

Collier, Jane, Michelle Z. Rosaldo, and Sylvia Yanagisako. 1982. "Is There a Family?" In Barrie Thorne, ed., *Rethinking the Family*. New York.

Cott, Nancy. 1977. *The Bonds of Womanhood: Women's Sphere in New England, 1780–1835*. New Haven, Conn.

————, and Elizabeth H. Pleck, eds. 1979. *A Heritage of Her Own*. New York.

Demos, John. 1970. *A Little Commonwealth: Family Life in Plymouth Colony*. London.

Donzelot, Jacques. 1979. *The Policing of Families*. New York.

Flandrin, Jean-Louis. 1979. *Families in Former Times*. Cambridge, Eng.

Fox, Bonnie, ed. 1980. *Hidden in the Household: Women's Domestic Labour Under Capitalism*. Toronto.

Fox-Genovese, Elizabeth. 1977. "Property and Patriarchy in Classical Bourgeois Theory." *Radical History Review*.

Goody, Jack, Joan Thirsk, and E. P. Thompson, eds. 1976. *Family and Inheritance: Rural Society in Western Europe, 1200–1800*. Cambridge, Eng.

Gordon, Michael, ed. 1978. *The American Family in Social-Historical Perspective*. New York.

Goubert, Pierre. 1977. "Family and Province: A Contribution to the Knowledge of Family Structures in Early Modern France." *Journal of Family History* 2, no. 3: 179–95.

Gutman, Herbert. 1976. *The Black Family in Slavery and Freedom, 1750–1925*. New York.

Harding, Sandra. 1981. "What Is the Real Material Base of Patriarchy and Capital?" In Linda Sargent, ed., *Women and Revolution*. Boston.

Harris, Olivia. 1981. "Households as Natural Units." In Kate Young et al., eds., *Of Marriage and the Market*. London.

————. 1982. "Households and Their Boundaries." *History Workshop Journal* 13 (Spring): 143–52.

Jones, Gareth Stedman. 1974. "Working Class Culture and Working Class Politics in London, 1870–1900." *Journal of Social History* 8: 460–508.

Kerber, Linda K., and Jane deHart Mathews, eds. 1982. *Women's America: Refocusing the Past*. New York.

Laslett, Peter. 1965. *The World We Have Lost*. New York.

Laslett, Peter, ed. 1972. *Household and Family in Past Time*. Cambridge, Eng.

Lewin, Ellen. Forthcoming. *The Contours of Single Motherhood*. Ithaca, N.Y.

Liebow, Elliot. 1967. *Tally's Corner*. Boston.

Luxton, Meg. 1980. *More Than A Labour of Love*. Toronto.

Malos, Ellen, ed. 1980. *The Politics of Housework*. London.

Mitterauer, Michael, and Reinhard Sieder. 1982. *The European Family*. Chicago.

Oakley, Ann. 1974. *The Sociology of Housework*. New York.

Petchesky, Rosalind. 1981. "Anti-Abortion, Anti-Feminism, and the Rise of the New Right." *Feminist Studies* 7, no. 2: 206–46.

———. 1984. *Abortion and Woman's Choice*. New York.

Pleck, Elizabeth. 1976. "Two Worlds in One: Work and Family." *Journal of Social History* 10, no. 2: 178–95.

Rapp, Rayna. 1986. "Ritual of Reversion: On Fieldwork and Festivity in Haute Provence." *Critique of Anthropology* 6: 35–48.

———. Forthcoming. "Private Families, Public Problems." In Philippe Schmitter, ed., *Experiments in Scale in Western Europe*. Cambridge, Eng.

Rapp, Rayna, Ellen Ross, and Renate Bridenthal. 1979. "Examining Family History." *Feminist Studies* 5, no. 1: 174–200.

Reiter, Randy B. 1974. *Sexual Domains and Family in Southeastern France*. Ann Arbor, Mich.

Rosaldo, Michelle Z. 1980. "The Use and Abuse of Anthropology: Reflections on Feminism and Cross-Cultural Understanding." *Signs* 5, no. 3: 389–417.

Rosenberg, Charles, ed. 1975. *The Family in History*. Philadelphia.

Sanjek, Roger. 1982. "The Organization of Households in Adabraka: Toward a Wider Comparative Perspective." *Comparative Studies in Society and History* 24, no. 1 (Jan.): 57–103.

Schneider, David. 1968. "Kinship, Nationality, and Religion in American Culture: Toward a Definition of Kinship." In Robert F. Spencer, ed., *Forms of Symbolic Action*. Seattle.

———. 1972. "What Is Kinship All About?" In Priscilla Reining, ed., *Kinship Studies in the Morgan Centennial Year*. Washington, D.C.

Segalen, Martine. 1983. *Love and Power in the Peasant Family*. Chicago.

Stack, Carol. 1974. *All Our Kin*. New York.

Stansell, Christine. 1982. "Women, Children, and the Streets of New York." *Feminist Studies* 8, no. 2: 309–35.

Staples, Robert, ed. 1971. *The Black Family: Essays and Studies*. Belmont, Calif.

Stone, Lawrence. 1977. *The Family, Sex, and Marriage in England, 1500–1800*. New York.

Tilly, Louise, and Joan Scott. 1978. *Women, Work, and Family*. New York.

Weiner, Annette. 1979. "Trobriand Kinship from Another View: The Reproductive Power of Women and Men." *Man* 14: 328–48.

———. 1980. "Reproduction: A Replacement for Reciprocity." *American Ethnologist* 7: 71–85.

Wilk, Richard R., and Robert Netting. 1984. "Households: Changing

Forms and Functions." In Robert Netting et al., eds., *Households*. Chicago.

Yanagisako, Sylvia. 1975. "Two Processes of Change in Japanese-American Kinship." *Journal of Anthropological Research* 31: 196–224.

——. 1977. "Women-Centered Kin Networks in Urban Bilateral Kinship." *American Ethnologist* 3, no. 2: 207–26.

——. 1978. "Variance in American Kinship: Implications for Cultural Analysis." *American Ethnologist* 5: 15–29.

——. 1979. "Family and Household: The Analysis of Domestic Groups." *Annual Review of Anthropology* 8: 161–205.

Zaretsky, Eli. 1982. "The Place of the Family in the Origins of the Welfare State." In Barrie Thorne, ed., *Rethinking the Family*. New York.

Sewing the Seams of Society: Dressmakers and Seamstresses in Turin Between the Wars

Allaria, G. B. 1911. "Le condizioni sanitarie delle operaie delle sartorie di Torino." *Bollettino dell'Ispettorato di Lavoro* 5, nos. 8–9: 555–600.

Barthes, Roland. 1982. "Storia i sociologia del vestiario: osservazioni metodologiche." In Fernand Braudel, ed., *La Storia e le altre scienze sociali*. Bari, Italy. Orig. ed. 1957.

Bloch, Maurice, and Jean Bloch. 1980. "Women and the Dialectics of Nature in Eighteenth-Century French Thought." In Carol MacCormack and Marilyn Strathern, eds., *Nature, Culture and Gender*. Cambridge, Eng.

Cavallo, Sandra. 1981. "Realtà familiari e aspettative di vita: tre biografie femminili 1920–1980." In *Relazioni sociali e strategie individuali in ambiente urbano Torino*. Cuneo, Italy.

Edholm, F., O. Harris, and K. Young. 1977. "Conceptualizing Women." *Critique of Anthropology* 3, nos. 9–10: 101–30.

Galoppini, Anna Maria. 1980. *Il longo viaggio verso la parità*. Bologna.

Gribaudi, M. 1983. "Due generazioni a Borgo San Paolo." Unpublished manuscript.

Harris, Olivia. 1981. "Households as Natural Units." In Kate Young et al., eds., *Of Marriage and the Market*. London.

Levi, G., et al. 1978. *Torino tra le due Guerre: Cultura operaia e vita quotidiana in Borgo San Paolo*. Turin.

Merli, S. 1972. *Proletariato di fabbrica e capitalismo industriale: il caso italiano, 1880–1900*. Florence.

Noce, Teresa. 1977. *Rivoluzionaria professionale*. Milan.

Paci, Massimo. 1982. *La struttura sociale italiana*. Bologna.

Pitt-Rivers, Julian. 1971. *The People of the Sierra*. Chicago. Orig. ed. 1954.

Reiter, Rayna Rapp, ed. 1975. *Toward an Anthropology of Women*. New York.

Rosaldo, Michelle Z. 1980. "The Use and Abuse of Anthropology: Reflections on Feminism and Cross-Cultural Understanding." *Signs* 5, no. 3: 389–417.

Saraceno, C. 1979–80. "La famiglia operaia sotto il fascismo." In *La classe operaia durante il fascismo*. Milan.

Serra, Bianca G., ed. 1977. *Compagne*. Turin.

Società Umanitaria. 1962. *Licenziamenti a causa di matrimonio.* Florence.

Turner, Victor. 1967. "Symbols in Ndembu Ritual." In Victor Turner, *The Forest of Symbols.* Ithaca, N.Y.

Hierarchy and the Dual Marriage System in West Indian Society

Alexander, Jack. 1976. "A Study of the Cultural Domain of 'Relatives.'" *American Ethnologist* 3: 17–38.

————. 1977. "The Culture of Race in Middle-Class Kingston, Jamaica." *American Ethnologist* 4: 413–35.

————. 1978. "The Cultural Domain of Marriage." *American Ethnologist* 5: 5–14.

————. 1984. "Love, Race, Slavery, and Sexuality in Jamaican Images of the Family." In Raymond T. Smith, ed., *Kinship Ideology and Practice in Latin America.* Chapel Hill, N.C.

Anderson, Michael. 1971. *Family Structure in Nineteenth Century Lancashire.* Cambridge, Eng.

Andrews, Evangeline W., and C. M. Andrews, eds. 1923. *Journal of a Lady of Quality: Being the Narrative of a Journey from Scotland to the West Indies, North Carolina, and Portugal in the Years 1774 to 1776.* New Haven, Conn.

Anonymous. 1828. *Marly, or A Planter's Life in Jamaica.* Glasgow.

Ashcroft, Michael. n.d. "Robert Charles Dallas." *Jamaica Journal* 44: 94–101.

Austin, Diane J. 1974. "Symbols and Ideologies of Class in Urban Jamaica: A Cultural Analysis of Classes." Ph.D. diss., University of Chicago.

————. 1979. "History and Symbols in Ideology: A Jamaican Example." *Man* 14: 497–514.

————. 1984. *Urban Life in Kingston, Jamaica: The Culture and Class Ideology of Two Neighborhoods.* New York.

Bolingbroke, Henry. 1809. *A Voyage to the Demerary, Containing a Statistical Account of the Settlements There, and of Those on the Essequebo, the Berbice, and Other Contiguous Rivers of Guyana.* London.

Bourguignon, Erika, et al. 1980. *A World of Women: Anthropological Studies of Women in the Societies of the World.* New York.

Brathwaite, Edward. 1971. *The Development of Creole Society in Jamaica, 1770–1820.* Oxford.

Braudel, Fernand. 1975. *The Mediterranean and the Mediterranean World in the Age of Philip II.* 2 vols. New York.

BRO. Bristol Record Office. Microfilms AC/WO 16[17]e, AC/WO 16[37]. Bristol, Eng.

Brodber, Erna. 1982. *Perception of Caribbean Women: Towards a Documentation of Stereotypes.* Women in the Caribbean Project, vol. 4. Barbados.

Buisseret, David. 1980. *Historic Architecture of the Caribbean.* London.

Campbell, Mavis C. 1976. *The Dynamics of Change in a Slave Society: A Sociopolitical History of the Free Coloreds of Jamaica, 1800–1865.* Rutherford, N.J.

Craton, Michael. 1978. *Searching for the Invisible Man: Slaves and Plantation Life in Jamaica.* Cambridge, Mass.

DeVeer, Henrietta. 1979. "Sex Roles and Social Stratification in a Rapidly

Growing Urban Area—May Pen, Jamaica." Ph.D. diss., University of Chicago.

Dunn, Richard S. 1972. *Sugar and Slaves: The Rise of the Planter Class in the English West Indies, 1624–1713.* Chapel Hill, N.C.

Edwards, Bryan. 1794. *The History, Civil and Commercial, of the British Colonies in the West Indies.* 2 vols. London.

Engels, Friedrich. 1958. *The Condition of the Working Class in England.* Trans. and ed. W. O. Henderson and W. H. Chaloner. Stanford, Calif.

Farber, Bernard. 1972. *Guardians of Virtue: Salem Families in 1800.* New York.

Fischer, Michael. 1974. "Value Assertion and Stratification: Religion and Marriage in Rural Jamaica." *Caribbean Studies* 14, no. 1: 7–37; no. 3: 7–35.

Foner, Nancy. 1973. *Status and Power in Rural Jamaica: A Study of Educational and Political Change.* New York.

Fortes, Meyer. 1949. "Time and Social Structure: An Ashanti Case Study." In Meyer Fortes, ed., *Social Structure: Essays Presented to Radcliffe-Brown.* Oxford.

———. 1953. "Preface." In Fernando Henriques, *Family and Colour in Jamaica.* London.

———. 1956. "Foreword." In Raymond T. Smith, *The Negro Family in British Guiana.* London.

———. 1958. "Introduction." In Jack Goody, ed., *The Development Cycle in Domestic Groups.* London.

———. 1969. *Kinship and the Social Order: The Legacy of Lewis Henry Morgan.* Chicago.

———. 1978. "An Anthropologist's Apprenticeship." *Annual Review of Anthropology* 7: 1–30.

Gonzalez, Virginia Durant. 1982. "The Realm of Female Familial Responsibility." In *Women and the Family.* Women in the Caribbean Project, vol. 2. Barbados.

Goody, Jack. 1972. "The Evolution of the Family." In Peter Laslett, ed., *Household and Family in Past Time.* London.

Graham, Sara, and Derek Gordon. 1977. *The Stratification System and Occupational Mobility in Guyana.* Mona, Jamaica.

GRO 347. Gloucestershire Record Office. Codrington Family Archive. Microfilm 347, C2. Gloucester, Eng.

GRO 351. Gloucestershire Record Office. Codrington Family Archive. Microfilm 351, D1610, C22. Gloucester, Eng.

Hall, Douglas. 1959. *Free Jamaica, 1838–1865: An Economic History.* New Haven, Conn.

Handler, Jerome S. 1974. *The Unappropriated People: Freedmen in the Slave Society of Barbados.* Baltimore.

Heuman, Gad. 1981. *Between Black and White: Race, Politics and the Free Coloreds in Jamaica, 1792–1865.* Westport, Conn.

Higman, Barry W. 1976. *Slave Population and Economy in Jamaica, 1807–1834.* Cambridge, Eng.

IJMC. Institute of Jamaica Manuscript Collection. Nuttall Papers, MST 209. Kingston, Jamaica.

IJMC. Institute of Jamaica Manuscript Collection. MS 1604. Kingston, Jamaica.

Jayawardena, Chandra. 1960. "Marital Stability in Two Guianese Sugar Estate Communities." *Social and Economic Studies* 9: 76–101.

———. 1962. "Family Organisation in Plantations in British Guiana," *International Journal of Comparative Sociology* 3, no. 1.

JIRO. Jamaica Island Record Office. Wills, Lib. 131. Spanish Town, Jamaica.

Lamming, George. 1953. *In the Castle of My Skin*. London.

Lewin, Linda. 1981. "Property as Patrimony: Changing Notions of Family, Kinship, and Wealth in Brazilian Inheritance Law from Empire to Republic." Unpublished manuscript.

London Gazette. No. 19656. Sept. 8, 1838: 2004–5.

Long, Edward. 1774. *The History of Jamaica*. 3 vols. London.

Martinez-Alier, Verena. 1974. *Marriage, Class and Colour in Nineteenth Century Cuba: A Study of Racial Attitudes and Sexual Values in a Slave Society*. London.

McKenzie, Hermione. 1982. "Introduction: Women and the Family in Caribbean Society." In *Women and the Family*. Women in the Caribbean Project, vol. 2. Barbados.

Moreton, J. B. 1790. *Manners and Customs of the West India Islands*. London.

Murdock, George Peter. 1949. *Social Structure*. New York.

Parsons, Talcott. 1955. "The American Family: Its Relations to Personality and to the Social Structure." In Talcott Parsons and Robert F. Bales, *Family, Socialization, and Interaction Process*. Glencoe, Ill.

Patterson, Orlando. 1969. *The Sociology of Slavery*. Rutherford, N.J.

———. 1982. "Persistence, Continuity, and Change in the Jamaican Working-Class Family." *Journal of Family History* 7: 135–61.

Roberts, George W. 1957. *The Population of Jamaica*. Cambridge, Eng.

———, and Sonja Sinclair. 1978. *Women in Jamaica: Patterns of Reproduction and Family*. New York.

Rodman, Hyman. 1963. "The Lower-Class Value Stretch." *Social Forces* 42: 205–15.

Smelser, Neil J. 1959. *Social Change in the Industrial Revolution: An Application of Theory to the Lancashire Cotton Industry, 1770–1840*. London.

Smith, Adam. 1978. *Lectures on Jurisprudence*. Ed. R. L. Meek, D. D. Raphael, and P. G. Stein. Oxford.

Smith, Raymond T. 1956. *The Negro Family in British Guiana: Family Structure and Social Status in the Villages*. London.

———. 1957. "The Family in the Caribbean." In Vera Rubin, ed., *Caribbean Studies: A Symposium*. Kingston, Jamaica.

———. 1963. "Culture and Social Structure in the Caribbean." *Comparative Studies in Society and History* 6: 24–46.

———. 1978a. "The Family and the Modern World System: Some Observations from the Caribbean." *Journal of Family History* 3: 337–60.

———. 1978b. "Class Differences in West Indian Kinship: A Genealogical Exploration." In Arnaud F. Marks and Rene A. Romer, eds., *Family and Kinship in Middle America and the Caribbean*. Leiden.

———. 1982a. "Family, Social Change and Social Policy in the West Indies." *Nieuwe West-Indische Gids* 56, nos. 3–4: 111–42.

———. 1982b. "Race and Class in the Post-Emancipation Caribbean." In Robert Ross, ed., *Racism and Colonialism*. The Hague.

———. 1984. "Introduction." In Raymond T. Smith, ed., *Kinship Ideology and Practice in Latin America*. Chapel Hill, N.C.

———, and Chandra Jayawardena. 1959. "Marriage and the Family Amongst East Indians in British Guiana." *Social and Economic Studies* 8: 321–76.

Stolcke, Verena. 1981. "Women's Labours: The Naturalisation of Social Inequality and Women's Subordination," in Kate Young et al., eds., *Of Marriage and the Market*. London

———. 1984. "The Exploitation of Family Morality: Labor Systems and Family Structure on Sao Paulo Coffee Plantations 1850–1979." In Raymond T. Smith, ed., *Kinship Ideology and Practice in Latin America*. Chapel Hill, N.C.

Stone, Lawrence. 1977. *The Family, Sex and Marriage in England, 1500–1800.* New York.

Turner, Terrence S. 1976. "Family Structure and Socialization." In Jan J. Loubser et al., eds., *Explorations in General Theory in Social Science: Essays in Honor of Talcott Parsons, Vol. 2.* New York.

Walkowitz, Judith R. 1980. *Prostitution and Victorian Society: Women, Class and the State.* Cambridge, Eng.

Wright, Richardson. 1937. *Revels in Jamaica, 1682–1838.* New York.

Rank and Marriage: Or, Why High-Ranking Brides Cost More

Barton, R. F. 1919. *Ifugao Law.* University of California Publications in American Archaeology and Ethnology, vol. 15: 1–186.

Battey, Thomas C. 1875. *The Life and Adventures of a Quaker Among the Indians.* Norman, Okla.; 1968 reprint.

Collier, Donald. 1938. "Kiowa Social Integration." M.A. thesis, University of Chicago.

Collier, Jane F. 1984. "Two Models of Social Control in Simple Societies." In Donald Black, ed., *Toward a General Theory of Social Control, Vol. 2: Selected Problems.* New York.

———. N.d. *Marriage and Inequality in Classless Societies.* In press.

———, and Michelle Z. Rosaldo. 1981. "Politics and Gender in Simple Societies." In Sherry B. Ortner and Harriet Whitehead, eds., *Sexual Meanings.* Cambridge, Eng.

Drucker, Philip. 1965. *Cultures of the North Pacific Coast.* San Francisco.

Eggan, Fred. 1955. "The Cheyenne and Arapaho Kinship System." In Fred Eggan, ed., *Social Anthropology of North American Tribes,* 2d ed. Chicago.

Emerson, Richard. 1962. "Power-Dependence Relations." *American Sociological Review* 27, no. 1: 31–40.

Gibbs, James L. 1965. "The Kpelle of Liberia." In J. L. Gibbs, ed., *Peoples of Africa.* New York.

Gullick, J. M. 1958. *Indigenous Political Systems of Western Malaya.* London School of Economics Monograph, no. 17. London.

Hoebel, E. Adamson. 1940. *The Political Organization and Law-ways of the Comanche Indians.* American Anthropological Association Memoirs, no. 54.

———. 1954. *The Law of Primitive Man: A Study in Comparative Legal Dynamics.* Cambridge, Mass.

———. 1978. *The Cheyennes: Indians of the Great Plains,* 2d ed. New York.

Hyde, George E. 1959. *Indians of the High Plains.* Norman, Okla.

Kroeber, A. L. 1926. "Yurok Law." In *Proceedings of the 22d International Congress of Americanists*: 511–16.

Leach, E. R. 1965. *Political Systems of Highland Burma: A Study of Kachin Social Structure.* Boston; orig. ed. 1954.

Llewellyn, Karl, and E. A. Hoebel. 1941. *The Cheyenne Way.* Norman, Okla.

Mayhall, Mildred. 1962. *The Kiowas.* Norman, Okla.

Mishkin, Bernard. 1940. *Rank and Warfare Among Plains Indians.* Monographs of the American Ethnological Society, no. 3.

Mooney, James. 1898. *Calendar History of the Kiowa Indians.* Seventeenth Annual Report of American Ethnology, pt. 1.

Moore, John H. 1974. "A Study of Religious Symbolism Among the Cheyenne Indians." Ph.D. diss., New York University.

Oliver, Symmes C. 1962. *Ecology and Cultural Continuity as Contributing Factors in the Social Organization of Plains Indians.* University of California Publications in American Archaeology and Ethnology, vol. 48: 1–90.

Rey, Pierre P. 1975. "The Lineage Mode of Production." *Critique of Anthropology* 3: 27–79.

Richardson, Jane. 1940. *Law and Status Among Kiowa Indians.* Monographs of the American Ethnological Society, no. 1.

Rosaldo, Michelle Zimbalist. 1980. "The Use and Abuse of Anthropology: Reflections on Feminism and Cross-Cultural Understanding." *Signs: Journal of Women in Culture and Society* 5, no. 3: 389–417.

Sahlins, Marshall. 1963. "Poor Man, Rich Man, Big-Man, Chief: Political Types in Melanesia and Polynesia." *Comparative Studies in Society and History* 5: 285–303.

Skinner, Alanson. 1926. *Ethnology of the Ioway Indians.* Bulletin of the Public Museum of the City of Milwaukee, vol. 5, no. 4: 181–354.

Tsing, Anna L., and Sylvia Yanagisako. 1983. "Feminism and Kinship Theory." *Current Anthropology* 24, no. 4: 511–16.

Wharton, Clarence. 1935. *Santanta: The Great Chief of the Kiowas and His People.* Dallas, Tex.

The Mystification of Female Labors

Allen, M. R. 1967. *Male Cults and Secret Initiations in Melanesia.* Melbourne.

Bateson, Gregory. 1958. *Naven.* 2d ed. Stanford, Calif.

Beardmore, E. 1890. "The Natives of Mowat." *Journal of the Royal Anthropological Institute* 19: 459–66.

Berndt, R. M. 1966. *Excess and Restraint: Social Control Among a New Guinea Mountain People.* Chicago.

Chalmers, J. 1895. *Pioneer Life and Work in New Guinea*. London.

Collier, Jane F., and Michelle Z. Rosaldo. 1981. "Politics and Gender in Simple Societies." In Sherry B. Ortner and Harriet Whitehead, eds., *Sexual Meanings*. Cambridge, Eng.

Davenport, W. H. 1965. "Sexual Patterns and Their Regulation in a Society of the Southwest Pacific." In F. A. Beach, ed., *Sex and Behavior*. New York.

Deacon, A. B. 1934. *Malekula: A Vanishing People in the New Hebrides*. London.

Du Toit, B. M. 1975. *Akuna: A New Guinea Village Community*. Rotterdam.

Ernst, T. M. 1978. "Aspects of Meaning of Exchanges and Exchange Items Among the Onabasulu of the Great Papuan Plateau." *Mankind* 11, no. 3.

Foley, M. 1879. "Sur les habitations et les moeurs des Néo-Calédoniens." *Bulletin de la Société d'Anthropologie de Paris*, 3d ser., vol. 2: 604–6.

Gajdusek, C. 1977. "Urgent Opportunistic Observations: The Study of Changing, Transient, and Disappearing Phenomena of Medical Interest in Disrupted Primitive Human Communities." In *Health and Disease in Tribal Societies*. SIBA Foundation Symposium, vol. 49. New York.

Godelier, M. 1976. "Sex as the Ultimate Foundation of the Social and Cosmic Order of the New Guinea Baruya." In A. Verdiglione, ed., *Sexualité et Pouvoir*. Paris.

———. 1982. *La production des Grands Hommes*. Paris.

Guiart, J. 1952. "L'Organisation sociale et politique du nord Malekula." *Journal de la Société des Océanistes* 8: 149–259.

———. 1953. "Native Society in the New Hebrides: The Big Nambas of Northern Malekula." *Mankind* 4: 439–46.

Hage, P. 1981. "On Male Initiation and Dual Organization in New Guinea." *Man* 16, no. 2: 268–75.

Handelman, D. 1979. "Is Naven Ludic? Paradox and the Communication of Identity." *Social Analysis* 1: 177–91.

Hays, T. E., and P. H. Hays. 1982. "Opposition and Complementarity of the Sexes in Ndumba Initiation." In Gilbert H. Herdt, ed., *Rituals of Manhood: Male Initiation in Papua New Guinea*. Berkeley, Calif.

Herdt, Gilbert H. 1981. *Guardians of the Flutes: Idioms of Masculinity: A Study of Ritualized Homosexual Behavior*. New York.

———, ed. 1982. *Rituals of Manhood: Male Initiation in Papua New Guinea*. Berkeley, Calif.

———, ed. 1984. *Ritualized Homosexuality in Melanesia*. Berkeley, Calif.

Hogbin, Ian. 1970. *Island of Menstruating Men: Religion in Wogeo, New Guinea*. Scranton, Pa.

Keesing, R. M. 1982. "Introduction." In Gilbert H. Herdt, ed., *Rituals of Manhood: Male Initiation in Papua New Guinea*. Berkeley, Calif.

Kelly, R. 1976. "Witchcraft and Sexual Relations: An Exploration in the Social and Semantic Implications of a Structure of Belief." In P. Brown and G. Buchbinder, eds., *Man and Woman in the New Guinea Highlands*. Washington, D.C.

———. 1977. *Etoro Social Structure*. Ann Arbor, Mich.

Knauft, B. 1985. "Ritual Form and Permutation in New Guinea: Implications of Symbolic Process for Socio-Political Evolution." *American Ethnologist* 12, no. 2: 321–40.

Landtman, G. 1927. *The Kiwai Papuans of British New Guinea.* London.

Layard, J. 1942. *Stone Men of Malekula.* London.

———. 1959. "Homoeroticism in Primitive Society as a Function of the Self." *Journal of Analytical Psychology* 4, no. 2: 101–15.

Lindenbaum, Shirley. 1979. *Kuru Sorcery: Disease and Danger in the New Guinea Highlands.* Palo Alto, Calif.

———. 1980. "Ritualized Homosexuality in Melanesia." Paper presented at the City University of New York Graduate Anthropology Symposium on Gender Relations and Social Reproduction, New York.

McDowell, N. 1972. "Flexibility of Sister Exchange in Bun." *Oceania* 48, no. 3: 207–31.

Meggitt, M. J. 1965. "The Mae Enga of the Western Highlands." In P. Lawrence and M. J. Meggitt, eds., *Gods, Ghosts, and Men in Melanesia.* Melbourne.

Meigs, A. 1976. "Male Pregnancy and the Reduction of Sexual Opposition in a New Guinea Highlands Society." *Ethnology* 25: 393–407.

Newman, P. L., and D. J. Boyd. 1982. "The Making of Men." In Gilbert H. Herdt, ed., *Rituals of Manhood: Male Initiation in Papua New Guinea.* Berkeley, Calif.

Padgug, R. A. 1979. "Sexual Matters: On Conceptualizing Sexuality in History." *Radical History Review* 20: 3–33.

Poole, F. J. P. 1981. "Transforming 'Natural' Woman: Female Ritual Leaders and Gender Ideology Among Bimin-Kuskusmin." In Sherry B. Ortner and Harriet Whitehead, eds., *Sexual Meanings.* Cambridge, Eng.

Read, Kenneth E. 1954. "Cultures of the Central Highlands." *South Pacific* 5: 154–64.

———. 1980. *Other Voices.* Novato, Calif.

———. 1984. "The Nama Cult Recalled." In Gilbert H. Herdt, ed., *Ritualized Homosexuality in Melanesia.* Berkeley, Calif.

Rubel, Paula G., and Abraham Rosman. 1978. *Your Own Pigs You May Not Eat: A Comparative Study of New Guinea Societies.* Chicago.

Schieffelin, Edward L. 1975. *The Sorrow of the Lonely and the Burning of the Dancers.* New York.

———. 1982. "The Bau A Ceremonial Hunting Lodge: An Alternative to Initiation." In Gilbert H. Herdt, ed., *Rituals of Manhood: Male Initiation in Papua New Guinea.* Berkeley, Calif.

Serpenti, L. M. 1965. *Cultivators in the Swamps.* Assen.

———. 1984. "The Ritual Meaning of Homosexuality and Pedophilia Among the Kimam of South Irian Jaya." In Gilbert H. Herdt, ed., *Ritualized Homosexuality in Melanesia.* Berkeley, Calif.

Sexton, L. D. 1982. "'Wok Meri': A Women's Savings and Exchange System in Highland Papua New Guinea." *Oceania* 52, no. 3: 167–98.

Siskind, J. 1978. "Kinship and Mode of Production." *American Anthropologist* 80, no. 4: 860–73.

Sørum, Arve. 1980. "In Search of the Lost Soul: Bedamini Spirit Seances and Curing Rites." *Oceania* 50: 273–97.

———. 1984. "Growth and Decay: Bedamini Notions of Sexuality." In Gilbert H. Herdt, ed., *Ritualized Homosexuality in Melanesia*. Berkeley, Calif.

Spencer, B., and F. J. Gillen. 1927. *The Arunta*. London.

Strathern, A. 1979. "Gender, Ideology, and Money in Mount Hagen." *Man* 14, no. 3: 530–43.

———, and Marilyn Strathern. 1969. "Marriage in Melpa." In Robert M. Glasse and Mervyn Meggitt, eds., *Pigs, Pearlshells, and Women: Marriage in the New Guinea Highlands*. Englewood Cliffs, N.J.

Tuzin, D. F. 1976. *The Ilahita Arapesh: Dimensions of Unity*. Berkeley, Calif.

———. 1982. "Ritual Violence Among Ilahita Arapesh." In Gilbert H. Herdt, ed., *Rituals of Manhood: Male Initiation in Papua New Guinea*. Berkeley, Calif.

Van Baal, J. 1966. *Dema: Description and Analysis of Marind Anim Culture*. The Hague.

———. 1984. "The Dialectics of Sex in Marind Anim Culture." In Gilbert H. Herdt, ed., *Ritualized Homosexuality in Melanesia*. Berkeley, Calif.

Williams, F. E. 1936. *Papuans of the Trans Fly*. Oxford.

———. 1940. *Drama of the Orokolo*. Oxford.

Fertility and Exchange in New Guinea

Bateson, Gregory. 1958. *Naven*, 2d ed. Stanford, Calif.

Bowden, Ross. 1983. *Yena: Art and Ceremony in a Sepik Society*. London.

———. 1984. "Art and Gender Ideology in the Sepik." *Man* (n.s.) 19: 445–58.

Brown, D. J. J. 1979. "The Structuring of Polopa Feasting and Warfare." *Man* (n.s.) 14: 712–32.

Buchbinder, G., and R. Rappaport. 1976. "Fertility and Death Among the Maring." In P. Brown and G. Buchbinder, eds., *Man and Woman in the New Guinea Highlands*. Washington, D.C.

Collier, Jane Fishburne, and Michelle Z. Rosaldo. 1981. "Politics and Gender in Simple Societies." In Sherry B. Ortner and Harriet Whitehead, eds., *Sexual Meanings*. Cambridge, Eng.

Cook, E. A. 1969. "Marriage Among the Manga." In Robert M. Glasse and M. J. Meggitt, eds., *Pigs, Pearlshells, and Women: Marriage in the New Guinea Highlands*. Englewood Cliffs, N.J.

Craig, Ruth. 1969. "Marriage Among the Telefomin." In Robert M. Glasse and M. J. Meggitt, eds., *Pigs, Pearlshells, and Women: Marriage in the New Guinea Highlands*. Englewood Cliffs, N.J.

Eyde, David B. 1967. "Cultural Correlates of Warfare Among the Asmat of South-West New Guinea." Ph.D. diss., Yale University.

Forge, Anthony. 1965. "Art and Environment in the Sepik." *Proceedings of the Royal Anthropological Institute of Great Britain and Ireland*, pp. 23–32.

———. 1972. "The Golden Fleece." *Man* (n.s.) 7, no. 4: 527–40.

Gell, Alfred. 1975. *The Metamorphosis of the Cassowaries: Umeda Society, Language, and Ritual*. Dover, N.H.

Gillison, Gillian S. 1980. "Images of Nature in Gimi Thought." In Carol MacCormack and Marilyn Strathern, eds., *Nature, Culture and Gender.* Cambridge, Eng.

Glasse, Robert M. n.d. "Masks of Venery." Unpublished manuscript.

Godelier, Maurice. 1982a. *La production des Grands Hommes.* Paris.

—————. 1982b. "Social Hierarchies Among the Baruya." In Andrew Strathern, ed., *Inequality in New Guinea Highland Societies.* Cambridge, Eng.

Herdt, Gilbert H. 1981. *Guardians of the Flutes: Idioms of Masculinity: A Study of Ritualized Homosexual Behavior.* New York.

Hogbin, Ian. 1970. *The Island of Menstruating Men: Religion in Wogeo, New Guinea.* Scranton, Pa.

Josephides, Lisette. 1983. "Equal but Different? The Ontology of Gender Among Kewa." *Oceania* 53, no. 3: 291–307.

Kaberry, P. 1940–41. "The Abelam Tribe, Sepik District, New Guinea: A Preliminary Report." *Oceania* 11, no. 21: 233–58, 345–67.

—————. 1973. "Political Organization Among the Northern Abelam." In Ronald M. Berndt and Peter Lawrence, eds., *Politics in New Guinea: Traditional and in the Context of Change, Some Anthropological Perspectives.* Seattle.

Kelly, Raymond C. 1976. "Witchcraft and Sexual Relations: An Exploration in the Social and Semantic Implications of a Structure of Belief." In P. Brown and G. Buchbinder, eds., *Man and Woman in the New Guinea Highlands.* Washington, D.C.

—————. 1980. *Etoro Social Structure.* Ann Arbor, Mich.

Knauft, B. 1984. "Good Company and Violence: The Dialectics of Sorcery Among the Gebusi of Papua New Guinea." Ph.D. diss., University of Michigan.

Kuruwaip, Abraham. 1975. "The Asmat Bis Pole: Its Background and Meaning." *Irian* 3–4: 33–79.

Landtman, G. 1927. *The Kiwai Papuans of British New Guinea.* London.

Lévi-Strauss, Claude. 1969. *The Elementary Structures of Kinship.* Boston.

Lindenbaum, Shirley. 1984. "Variations on a Sociocultural Theme in Melanesia." In Gilbert H. Herdt, ed., *Ritualized Homosexuality in Melanesia.* Berkeley, Calif.

Lipset, David M. 1984. "On Warfare and Male Identity in Murik (1918–82)." Paper presented at the American Anthropological Association meeting, Denver.

Losche, D. B. 1982. "Male and Female in Abelam Society: Opposition and Complementarity." Ph.D. diss., Columbia University.

McDowell, Nancy. 1972. "Flexibility of 'Sister Exchange' in Bun." *Oceania* 48, no. 3: 207–31.

Mead, Margaret. 1940–41. "The Mountain Arapesh II: Supernaturalism." American Museum of Natural History, Anthropological Papers, vol. 37, pt. 3: 317–451.

Meeker, Michael, Katherine Barlow, and David M. Lipset. 1986. "Culture, Exchange, and Gender: Lessons from the Murik." *Cultural Anthropology* 1, no. 1: 6–73.

Meggitt, M. J. 1964. "Male-Female Relationships in the Highlands of Australian New Guinea." *American Anthropologist* 66, no. 4, pt. 4: 204–24.

Meillassoux, Claude. 1975. *Maidens, Meal, and Money: Capitalism and the Domestic Community*. Cambridge, Eng.

Modjeska, Nicolas. 1982. "Production and Inequality: Perspectives from Central New Guinea." In Andrew Strathern, ed., *Inequality in New Guinea Highlands Societies*. Cambridge, Eng.

Newman, Philip L. 1965. *Knowing the Gururumba*. New York.

———, and David J. Boyd. 1982. "The Making of Men: Ritual and Meaning in Awa Male Initiation." In Gilbert H. Herdt, ed., *Rituals of Manhood: Male Initiation in Papua New Guinea*. Berkeley, Calif.

O'Brien, Denise. 1969. "Marriage Among the Konda Valley Dani." In Robert M. Glasse and M. J. Meggitt, eds., *Pigs, Pearlshells, and Women: Marriage in the New Guinea Highlands*. Englewood Cliffs, N.J.

Oosterwal, Gottfried. 1961. *People of the Tor*. Assen.

———. 1967. "Muremarew: A Dual Organized Village on the Mamberamo, West Irian." In Koentjaraningrat, ed., *Villages in Indonesia*. Ithaca, N.Y.

Poole, F. J. P. 1976. "The Ais Am: An Introduction to Male Initiation Ritual Among the Bimin-Kuskusmin of West Sepik District, Papua New Guinea." Ph.D. diss., Cornell University.

———. 1981. "Transforming 'Natural' Woman: Female Ritual Leaders and Gender Ideology Among the Bimin-Kuskusmin." In Sherry B. Ortner and Harriet Whitehead, eds., *Sexual Meanings*. Cambridge, Eng.

Rappaport, Roy A. 1968. *Pigs for the Ancestors: Ritual in the Ecology of a New Guinea People*. New Haven, Conn.

———. 1969. "Marriage Among the Maring." In Robert M. Glasse and M. J. Meggitt, eds., *Pigs, Pearlshells, and Women: Marriage in the New Guinea Highlands*. Englewood Cliffs, N.J.

Read, Kenneth E. 1952. "Nama Cult of the Central Highlands, New Guinea." *Oceania* 23, no. 1: 1–25.

Reay, Marie O. 1959. *The Kuma: Freedom and Conformity in the New Guinea Highlands*. Melbourne.

Robbins, Sterling. 1982. *Auyana: Those Who Held onto Home*. Seattle.

Rubel, Paula G., and Abraham Rosman. 1978. *Your Own Pigs You May Not Eat: A Comparative Study of New Guinea Societies*. Chicago.

Rubin, Gayle. 1975. "The Traffic in Women: Notes on the 'Political Economy' of Sex." In Rayna Rapp Reiter, ed., *Toward an Anthropology of Women*. New York.

———. n.d. "Coconuts." Unpublished manuscript.

Sahlins, Marshall D. 1968. *Tribesmen*. Englewood Cliffs, N.J.

———. 1972a. "On the Sociology of Primitive Exchange." In Marshall Sahlins, *Stone Age Economics*. Chicago.

———. 1972b. "The Spirit of the Gift." In Marshall Sahlins, *Stone Age Economics*. Chicago.

Salisbury, R. F. 1965. "The Siane of the Eastern Highlands." In P. Lawrence and M. J. Meggitt, eds., *Gods, Ghosts, and Men in Melanesia*. Melbourne.

Schieffelin, Edward L. 1975. *The Sorrow of the Lonely and the Burning of the Dancers.* New York.

Schwimmer, Erik. 1973. *Exchange in the Social Structure of the Orokaiva.* New York.

Serpenti, L. M. 1965. *Cultivators in the Swamps.* Assen.

———. 1984. "The Ritual Meaning of Homosexuality and Pedophilia Among the Kimam Papuans of South Irian Jaya." In Gilbert H. Herdt, ed., *Ritualized Homosexuality in Melanesia.* Berkeley, Calif.

Strathern, Andrew J. 1979. "Gender, Ideology, and Money in Mount Hagen." *Man* 14, no. 3: 530–43.

———, and Marilyn Strathern. 1969. "Marriage in Melpa." In Robert M. Glasse and M. J. Meggitt, eds., *Pigs, Pearlshells, and Women: Marriage in the New Guinea Highlands.* Englewood Cliffs, N.J.

Tuzin, Donald F. 1972. "Yam Symbolism in the Sepik: An Interpretive Account." *Southwestern Journal of Anthropology* 28, no. 3: 230–54.

———. 1980. *The Voice of the Tambaran: Truth and Illusion in Ilahita Arapesh Religion.* Berkeley, Calif.

Van Baal, Jan. 1966. *Dema: Description and Analysis of Marind Anim Culture.* The Hague.

———. 1984. "The Dialectics of Sex in Marind Anim Culture." In Gilbert H. Herdt, ed., *Ritualized Homosexuality in Melanesia.* Berkeley, Calif.

Wagner, Roy. 1969. "Marriage Among the Daribi." In Robert M. Glasse and M. J. Meggitt, eds., *Pigs, Pearlshells, and Women: Marriage in the New Guinea Highlands.* Englewood Cliffs, N.J.

Whitehead, Harriet. 1986a. "The Varieties of Fertility Cultism in New Guinea: Part I." *American Ethnologist* 13, no. 1: 80–98.

———. 1986b. "The Varieties of Fertility Cultism in New Guinea: Part II." *American Ethnologist* 13, no. 2: 271–89.

Zegwaard, G. A. 1959. "Head-hunting Practices of the Asmat of West New Guinea." *American Anthropologist* 61: 1020–41.

Producing Difference: Connections and Disconnections in Two New Guinea Highland Kinship Systems

Battaglia, D. 1983. "Projecting Personhood in Melanesia: The Dialectics of Artifact Symbolism on Sabarl Island." *Man* 18, no. 2: 289–304.

Brown, D. J. J. 1980. "The Structuring of Polopa Kinship and Affinity." *Oceania* 50, no. 4: 297–331.

Colby, B. N., J. W. Fernandez, and D. B. Kronenfeld. 1981. "Toward a Convergence of Cognitive and Symbolic Anthropology." *American Ethnologist* 8, no. 3: 422–50.

Collier, Jane F., and Michelle Z. Rosaldo. 1981. "Politics and Gender in Simple Societies." in Sherry B. Ortner and Harriet Whitehead, eds., *Sexual Meanings.* Cambridge, Eng.

Damon, F. H. 1980. "The Kula and Generalized Exchange: Considering Some Unconsidered Aspects of *The Elementary Structures of Kinship.*" *Man* 15, no. 2: 267–92.

Feil, D. K. 1980. "When a Group of Women Takes a Wife: Generalized Exchange and Restricted Marriage in the New Guinea Highlands." *Mankind* 12, no. 4: 286–99.

———. 1981. "The Bride in Bridewealth: A Case from the New Guinea Highlands." *Ethnology* 20, no. 1: 63–75.

———. 1984. "Beyond Patriliny in the New Guinea Highlands." *Man* 19, no. 1: 50–76.

Fortes, Meyer. 1969. *Kinship and the Social Order*. Chicago.

Gillison, Gillian. 1980. "Images of Nature in Gimi Thought." In Carol MacCormack and Marilyn Strathern, eds., *Nature, Culture and Gender*. Cambridge, Eng.

Goody, J. R. 1976. *Production and Reproduction*. Cambridge, Eng.

Lancy, D. F., and Andrew Strathern. 1981. " 'Making Twos': Pairing as an Alternative to the Taxonomic Mode of Representation." *American Anthropologist* 83, no. 4: 773–95.

Leach, E. R. 1961. *Rethinking Anthropology*. London.

Leacock, Eleanor B. 1981. *Myths of Male Dominance*. New York.

Lederman, R. 1980. "Who Speaks Here? Formality and the Politics of Gender in Mendi." *Journal of the Polynesian Society* 89, no. 4: 479–98.

Le Roy, J. 1981. "Siblingship and Descent in Kewa Ancestries." *Mankind* 13, no. 1: 25–36.

Lindenbaum, Shirley. 1976. "A Wife Is the Hand of Man." In P. Brown and G. Buchbinder, eds., *Man and Woman in the New Guinea Highlands*. Washington, D.C.

Munn, N. 1977. "The Spatiotemporal Transformations of Gawa Canoes." *Journal de la Société des Océanistes* 33, nos. 54–55: 39–53.

Ortner, Sherry B. 1973. "On Key Symbols." *American Anthropologist* 75, no. 5: 1338–46.

———. 1981. "Gender and Sexuality in Hierarchical Societies: The Case of Polynesia and Some Comparative Implications." In Sherry B. Ortner and Harriet Whitehead, eds., *Sexual Meanings*. Cambridge, Eng.

———, and Harriet Whitehead. 1981. "Introduction: Accounting for Sexual Meanings." In Sherry B. Ortner and Harriet Whitehead, eds., *Sexual Meanings*. Cambridge, Eng.

Poole, F. J. P. 1981. "Transforming 'Natural' Woman: Female Ritual Leaders and Gender Ideology Among Bimin-Kuskusmin." In Sherry B. Ortner and Harriet Whitehead, eds., *Sexual Meanings*. Cambridge, Eng.

Rubel, Paula G., and Abraham Rosman. 1978. *Your Own Pigs You May Not Eat: A Comparative Study of New Guinea Societies*. Chicago.

Ryan, D'A. 1969. "Marriage in Mendi." In Robert M. Glasse and M. J. Meggitt, eds., *Pigs, Pearlshells, and Women*. Englewood Cliffs, N.J.

Sacks, Karen. 1979. *Sisters and Wives: The Past and Future of Sexual Equality*. London.

Schieffelin, Edward L. 1980. "Reciprocity and the Construction of Reality." *Man* 15, no. 3: 502–17.

Schneider, D. M. 1968. *American Kinship: A Cultural Account*. Englewood Cliffs, N.J.

Shapiro, Judith. 1981. "Anthropology and the Study of Gender." *Soundings* 64, no. 4: 446–65.

―――. 1982. "'Women's Studies': A Note on the Perils of Markedness." *Signs* 7, no. 3: 717–21.

Strathern, Andrew. 1968. "Sickness and Frustration: Variations in Two New Guinea Highlands Societies." *Mankind* 6, no. 11: 545–51.

―――. 1972. *One Father, One Blood*. Canberra.

―――. 1978. "'Finance and Production' Revisited: In Pursuit of a Comparison." In George Dalton, ed., *Research in Economic Anthropology, Vol. 1*. Greenwich, Conn.

―――. 1980. "The Central and the Contingent: Bridewealth Among the Melpa and the Wiru." In John Comaroff, ed., *The Meaning of Marriage Payments*. London.

―――. 1981. "'Noman': Representations of Identity in Mount Hagen." In L. Holy and M. Stuchlik, eds., *The Structure of Folk Models*. London.

―――. 1982. "Death as Exchange: Two Melanesian Cases." In S. C. Humphreys and H. King, *Mortality and Immortality: The Archaeology and Anthropology of Death*. London.

―――. N.d. "Hidden Names." Unpublished manuscript.

Strathern, Andrew, ed. 1982. *Inequality in New Guinea Highlands Societies*. Cambridge, Eng.

Strathern, Marilyn. 1972. *Women in Between: Female Roles in a Male World*. London.

―――. 1980. "No Nature, No Culture: The Hagen Case." In Carol MacCormack and Marilyn Strathern, eds., *Nature, Culture and Gender*. Cambridge, Eng.

―――. 1981. "Culture in a Netbag: The Manufacture of a Subdiscipline in Anthropology." *Man* 16, no. 4: 665–87.

―――. 1983. "Subject or Object? Women and the Circulation of Valuables in Highlands New Guinea." In R. Hirshon, ed., *Women and Property, Women as Property*. London.

―――. 1984. "Domesticity and the Denigration of Women." In Denise O'Brien and Sharon W. Tiffany, ed., *Rethinking Women's Roles: Perspectives from the Pacific*. Berkeley, Calif.

Tambiah, S. J. 1968. "The Magical Power of Words." *Man* 3, no. 2: 175–208.

Wagner, Roy. 1967. *The Curse of Souw: Principles of Daribi Clan Definition and Alliance in New Guinea*. Chicago.

―――. 1975. *The Invention of Culture*. Englewood Cliffs, N.J.

―――. 1977a. "Analogic Kinship: A Daribi Example." *American Ethnologist* 4, no. 4: 623–42.

―――. 1977b. "Scientific and Indigenous Papuan Conceptualizations of the Innate: A Semiotic Critique of the Ecological Perspective." In Timothy Bayliss-Smith and Richard Feachem, eds., *Subsistence and Survival: Rural Ecology in the Pacific*. London.

Weiner, Annette B. 1976. *Women of Value, Men of Renown: New Perspectives in Trobriand Exchange*. Austin, Texas.

―――. 1978. "The Reproductive Model in Trobriand Society." *Mankind* 11, no. 3: 175–86.

―――. 1980. "Reproduction: A Replacement for Reciprocity." *American Ethnologist* 7, no. 1: 71–85.

Men in Groups: A Reexamination of Patriliny in
Lowland South America

Ärhem, Kaj. 1981. "Makuna Social Organization: A Study in Descent, Alliance, and the Formation of Corporate Groups in the North-Western Amazon." Uppsala Studies in Cultural Anthropology, no. 4. Stockholm.

Bamberger, Joan. 1974. "The Myth of Matriarchy: Why Men Rule in Primitive Society." In Michelle Zimbalist Rosaldo and Louise Lamphere, eds., *Woman, Culture, and Society*. Stanford, Calif.

Barnes, J. A. 1962. "African Models in the New Guinea Highlands." *Man* 62, no. 2: 5–9.

Chagnon, Napoleon. 1968. *Yanomamö: The Fierce People*. New York.

———. 1974. *Studying the Yanomamö*. New York.

———. 1979a. "Is Reproductive Success Equal in Egalitarian Societies?" In Napoleon Chagnon and William Irons, eds., *Evolutionary Biology and Human Social Behavior*. North Scituate, Mass.

———. 1979b. "Mate Competition, Favoring Close Kin, and Village Fissioning Among the Yanomamö Indians." In Napoleon Chagnon and William Irons, eds., *Evolutionary Biology and Human Social Behavior*. North Scituate, Mass.

Collier, Jane F. 1974. "Women in Politics." In Michelle Zimbalist Rosaldo and Louise Lamphere, eds., *Woman, Culture, and Society*. Stanford, Calif.

———, and Michelle Zimbalist Rosaldo. 1981. "Politics and Gender in Simple Societies." In Sherry B. Ortner and Harriet Whitehead, eds., *Sexual Meanings*. Cambridge, Eng.

Crocker, J. Christopher. 1977. "Why Are the Bororo Matrilineal?" *Actes du 42ᵉ Congrès des Américanistes* 2: 245–58.

———. 1979. "Selves and Alters Among the Eastern Bororo." In David Maybury-Lewis, ed., *Dialectical Societies: The Gê and Bororo of Central Brazil*. Cambridge, Mass.

Crocker, William. 1977. "Canela 'Group' Recruitment and Perpetuity: Incipient 'Unilineality'?" *Actes du 42ᵉ Congrès des Américanistes* 2: 259–75.

———. 1979. "Canela Kinship and the Question of Matrilineality." In Maxine L. Margolis and William E. Carter, eds., *Brazil: Anthropological Perspectives*. New York.

Feil, Daryl. 1984. "Beyond Patriliny in the New Guinea Highlands." *Man* 19, no. 1: 50–76.

Goldman, Irving. 1963. *The Cubeo*. Urbana, Ill.

———. 1976. "Perceptions of Nature and the Structure of Society: The Question of Cubeo Descent." *Dialectical Anthropology* 1: 287–92.

Goody, Jack R. 1973. "Bridewealth and Dowry in Africa and Eurasia." In Jack R. Goody and S. J. Tambiah, eds., *Bridewealth and Dowry*. Cambridge, Eng.

———. 1976. *Production and Reproduction: A Comparative Study of the Domestic Domain.* Cambridge, Eng.

Gregor, Thomas. 1979. "Secrets, Exclusion, and the Dramatization of Men's Roles." In Maxine L. Margolis and William E. Carter, eds., *Brazil: Anthropological Perspectives.* New York.

Hill, Jonathan D. 1985. "Agnatic Sibling Relations and Rank in Northern Arawakan Myth and Social Life." In Judith Shapiro and Kenneth Kensinger, eds., "The Sibling Relationship in Lowland South America." Bennington College Working Papers in South American Indians, no. 7. Bennington, Vt.

Hugh-Jones, Christine. 1979. *From the Milk River: Spatial and Temporal Processes in Northwest Amazonia.* Cambridge, Eng.

Hugh-Jones, Stephen. 1979. *The Palm and the Pleiades: Initiation and Cosmology in Northwest Amazonia.* Cambridge, Eng.

Jackson, Jean. 1974. "Language Identity of the Colombian Vaupés Indians." In Richard Bauman and Joel Sherzer, eds., *Explorations in the Ethnography of Speaking.* Cambridge, Eng.

———. 1975. "Recent Ethnography of Indigenous Northern Lowland South America." *Annual Review of Anthropology* 4: 307–40.

———. 1976. "Vaupés Marriage: A Network System in an Undifferentiated Region of the Northwest Amazon." In Carol Smith, ed., *Regional Analysis: Social Systems.* New York.

———. 1977. "Bará Zero Generation Terminology and Marriage." *Ethnology* 16: 83–104.

———. 1983. *The Fish People: Linguistic Exogamy and Tukanoan Identity in Northwest Amazonia.* Cambridge, Eng.

———. 1984. "Vaupés Marriage Practices." In Kenneth Kensinger, ed., *Marriage Practices in Lowland South America.* Urbana, Ill.

Langness, L. L. 1964. "Some Problems in the Conceptualization of Highlands Social Structures." *American Anthropologist* 66, no. 4, pt. 2: 162–82.

Lave, J. C. 1971. "Some Suggestions for the Interpretation of Residence, Descent, and Exogamy Among the Eastern Timbira." *Proceedings of the 38th Congress of Americanists* 3: 341–45.

Lepervanche, Marie de. 1967–68. "Descent, Residence, and Leadership in the New Guinea Highlands." *Oceania* 38, nos. 2–3: 134–58, 163–89.

Lizot, Jacques. 1977. "Descendence et Affinité chez les Yanõmami: Antinomie et Complémentarité." *Actes du 42ᵉ Congrès des Américanistes* 2: 55–70.

Maybury-Lewis, David. 1967. *Akwē-Shavante Society.* New York.

———. 1971. "Some Principles of Social Organization Among the Central Gê." *Proceedings of the 38th Congress of Americanists* 3: 381–86.

Murphy, Robert. 1956. "Matrilocality and Patrilineality in Mundurucú Society." *American Anthropologist* 58, no. 3: 414–34.

———. 1957. "Intergroup Hostility and Social Cohesion." *American Anthropologist* 59: 1018–35.

———. 1959. "Social Structure and Sex Antagonism." *Southwestern Journal of Anthropology* 15, no. 1: 89–98.

————. 1960. *Headhunter's Heritage*. Berkeley, Calif.

————. 1979. "Lineage and Lineality in Lowland South America." In Maxine L. Margolis and William E. Carter, eds., *Brazil: Anthropological Perspectives*. New York.

Murphy, Yolanda, and Robert Murphy. 1974. *Women of the Forest*. New York.

Nadelson, Leslee. 1981. "Pigs, Women, and the Men's House in Amazonia: An Analysis of Six Mundurucú Myths." In Sherry B. Ortner and Harriet Whitehead, eds., *Sexual Meanings*. Cambridge, Eng.

Ramos, Alcida. 1972. "The Social System of the Sanumá of Northern Brazil." Ph.D. thesis, University of Wisconsin.

————. 1973. "Personal Names and Social Classification in Sanumá (Yanoama) Society." Paper presented at the Ninth International Congress of Anthropological and Ethnological Sciences, Chicago.

————, and Bruce Albert. 1977. "Yanoama Descent and Affinity: The Sanuam/Yanomam Contrast." *Actes du 42ᵉ Congrès des Américanistes* 2: 71–90.

Rivière, Peter. 1977. "Some Problems in the Comparative Study of Carib Societies." In Ellen Basso, ed., "Carib-Speaking Indians: Culture, Language, and Society." University of Arizona Anthropological Papers, no. 28.

Scheffler, H. W. 1966. "Ancestor Worship in Anthropology: Or, Observations on Descent and Descent Groups." *Current Anthropology* 7, no. 3: 541–51.

Schneider, David. 1961. "Introduction." In David Schneider and Kathleen Gough, eds., *Matrilineal Kinship*. Berkeley, Calif.

Seeger, Anthony. 1980. "Corporação e Corporalidade: Ideologias de Concepção e Descendência." In Anthony Seeger, ed., *Os Indios e Nós: Estudos sobre Sociedades Tribais Brasileiras*. Rio de Janeiro.

Shapiro, Judith. 1972. "Sex Roles and Social Structure Among the Yanomamo Indians of Northern Brazil." Ph.D. thesis, Columbia University.

————. 1974. "Alliance or Descent: Some Amazonian Contrasts." *Man* 9, no. 2: 305–6.

————. 1984. "Marriage Rules, Marriage Exchange, and the Definition of Marriage in Lowland South American Societies." In Kenneth Kensinger, ed., *Marriage Practices in Lowland South America*. Urbana, Ill.

————, and Kenneth Kensinger, eds. N.d. "The Sibling Relationship in Lowland South America." Bennington College Working Papers in South American Indians, no. 7. Bennington, Vt.

Shapiro, Warren. 1971. "Structuralism versus Sociology: A Review of Maybury-Lewis's *Akwẽ-Shavante Society*." *Mankind* 8: 64–66.

Sorenson, Arthur. 1967. "Multilingualism in the Northwest Amazon." *American Anthropologist* 69, no. 6: 670–84.

Taylor, Kenneth. 1974. *Sanumá Fauna: Prohibitions and Classifications*. Caracas.

————. 1977. "Raiding, Dueling, and Descent Group Membership Among the Sanumá." *Actes du 42ᵉ Congrès des Américanistes* 2: 93–104.

————. 1981. "Knowledge and Praxis in Sanumá Food Prohibitions." In Kenneth Kensinger and Waud Kracke, eds., "Food Taboos in Lowland South America." Bennington College Working Papers on South American Indians, no. 3. Bennington, Vt.

————, and Alcida Ramos. 1975. "Alliance or Descent: Some Amazonian Contrasts." *Man* 10, no. 1: 128–30.

Descent and Sources of Contradiction in Representations of Women and Kinship

Bloch, Maurice. 1971. *Placing the Dead: Tombs, Ancestral Villages, and Kinship Organization in Madagascar.* New York.

————. 1974. "Property and the End of Affinity." In Maurice Bloch, ed., *Marxist Analyses and Social Anthropology.* London.

————. 1977. "The Disconnection Between Rank and Power." In J. Freidmann and S. M. J. Rowlands, eds., *The Evolution of Social Systems.* London.

————. 1981. "Hierarchy and Equality in Merina Kinship." *Ethnos* 1–2: 5–18.

————. 1982. "Death, Women, and Power." In Maurice Bloch and Jonathan Parry, eds., *Death and the Regeneration of Life.* Cambridge, Eng.

————. 1986. *From Blessing to Violence: History and Ideology in the Circumcision Ritual of the Merina of Madagascar.* Cambridge, Eng.

————, and Jonathan Parry. 1982. "Death and the Regeneration of Life." In Maurice Bloch and Jonathan Parry, eds., *Death and the Regeneration of Life.* Cambridge, Eng.

Gillison, Gillian. 1980. "Images of Nature in Gimi Thought." In Carol MacCormack and Marilyn Strathern, eds., *Nature, Culture and Gender.* Cambridge, Eng.

Llewelyn-Davies, Melissa. 1981. "Women Warriors and Patriarchs." In Sherry B. Ortner and Harriet Whitehead, eds., *Sexual Meanings.* Cambridge, Eng.

Ortner, Sherry B. 1974. "Is Female to Male as Nature Is to Culture?" In Michelle Z. Rosaldo and Louise Lamphere, eds., *Woman, Culture, and Society.* Stanford, Calif.

————, and Harriet Whitehead, eds. 1981. *Sexual Meanings.* Cambridge, Eng.

Strathern, Marilyn. 1980. "No Nature, No Culture: The Hagen Case." In Carol MacCormack and Marilyn Strathern, eds., *Nature, Culture and Gender.* Cambridge, Eng.

Turner, Victor. 1962. "Chichamba the White Spirit: A Ritual Drama of the Ndembu." Rhodes Livingstone Paper, no. 33.

Watson, James L. 1982. "Of Flesh and Bones: The Management of Death Pollution in Cantonese Society." In Maurice Bloch and Jonathan Parry, eds., *Death and the Regeneration of Life.* Cambridge, Eng.

Library of Congress Cataloging-in-Publication Date

Gender and kinship.
  Bibliography: p.
  1. Sex role. 2. Kinship. 3. Marriage.
I. Collier, Jane Fishburne. II. Yanagisako, Sylvia Junko, 1945.
GN479.65.G46 1987   306.8'3   87-9951
ISBN 0-8047-1366-9 (alk. paper)
ISBN 0-8047-1819-9 (pbk.)